THE
ENTERTAINER

THE
ENTERTAINER

Movies, Magic, and My Father's Twentieth Century

MARGARET TALBOT

RIVERHEAD BOOKS
A member of Penguin Group (USA) Inc.
New York
2012

RIVERHEAD BOOKS
Published by the Penguin Group
Penguin Group (USA) Inc., 375 Hudson Street, New York, New York 10014, USA •
Penguin Group (Canada), 90 Eglinton Avenue East, Suite 700, Toronto, Ontario
M4P 2Y3, Canada (a division of Pearson Penguin Canada Inc.) • Penguin Books Ltd,
80 Strand, London WC2R 0RL, England • Penguin Ireland, 25 St Stephen's Green, Dublin 2,
Ireland (a division of Penguin Books Ltd) • Penguin Group (Australia), 707 Collins Street,
Melbourne, Victoria 3008, Australia (a division of Pearson Australia Group Pty Ltd) •
Penguin Books India Pvt Ltd, 11 Community Centre, Panchsheel Park, New Delhi–110 017,
India • Penguin Group (NZ), 67 Apollo Drive, Rosedale, Auckland 0632, New Zealand
(a division of Pearson New Zealand Ltd) • Penguin Books, Rosebank Office Park,
181 Jan Smuts Avenue, Parktown North 2193, South Africa • Penguin China, B7 Jaiming Center,
27 East Third Ring Road North, Chaoyang District, Beijing 100020, China

Penguin Books Ltd, Registered Offices: 80 Strand, London WC2R 0RL, England

Library of Congress Cataloging-in-Publication Data

Talbot, Margaret, date.
The entertainer : movies, magic, and my father's twentieth century / Margaret Talbot.
p.   cm.
Includes bibliographical references.
ISBN 978-1-59448-706-4
1. Talbot, Lyle—Travel—United States.
2. Actors—United States—Biography. I. Title.
PN2287. T139T35   2012   2012026309
791.4302'8092—dc23
[B]

Printed in the United States of America
1 3 5 7 9 10 8 6 4 2

BOOK DESIGN BY AMANDA DEWEY

While the author has made every effort to provide accurate telephone numbers,
Internet addresses, and other contact information at the time of publication, neither the
publisher nor the author assumes any responsibility for errors, or for changes that occur after
publication. Further, the publisher does not have any control over and does not assume any
responsibility for author or third-party websites or their content.

Penguin is committed to publishing works of quality and integrity.
In that spirit, we are proud to offer this book to our readers;
however, the story, the experiences, and the words
are the author's alone.

In loving memory of Paula Talbot

*And for her grandchildren: Dash, Caitlin, Joe,
Nat, Gabriel, Grace, Eva, Ike, and Lucy,
who would have made her heart sing*

CONTENTS

❧⟳❧

Preface xi

Chapter 1. LEARNING TO CRY 1

Chapter 2. THE HYPNOTIST'S BOY 34

Chapter 3. FOOTLIGHTS ON THE PRAIRIE 82

Chapter 4. HOORAY FOR HOLLYWOOD 121

Chapter 5. GANGSTERS, GRIFTERS,
AND GOLD DIGGERS 149

Chapter 6. MAN ABOUT TOWN 202

Chapter 7. EMPTY BOTTLES 236

Chapter 8. UNIONIZING ACTORS, UNITING FANS 266

Chapter 9. BROADWAY AND B MOVIES 314

Chapter 10. FROM ED WOOD TO
OZZIE AND HARRIET 347

Acknowledgments 405
A Note on Sources 411

THE
ENTERTAINER

PREFACE

—⬡—

A lot of smart women I've known over the years have told me they were Daddy's girls. That was especially true if they had grown up, as I did, in the 1960s or 1970s, when, if one of your parents had a career you wanted to emulate, it was likely to be your father's. I was not a Daddy's girl. Strange to say, I suppose, since you are holding a book I have written about my father. I loved both my parents, but if anything, I was a Mama's girl.

My father was not a listener. He was a talker. A storyteller. While he talked, he was often doing things for me—driving me to school or lessons or friends' houses, cooking tasty meals for us and composing them elegantly on plates. Those stories were artifacts of self-involvement, but they came nestled in the cotton batting of affection, and that made them hard to resist. Besides, they were good stories.

When my father was out of town, traveling with a show, I liked to talk to him on the phone, but mostly what I did when I missed him, what made me feel closer to him, was to go sit on the floor of his meticulously arranged closet and breathe in the autumn-leaf scent of his pipe tobacco. I felt cozy amid the evidence of his tender and particular aesthetics, the rituals of his self-regard. If my mother had ever gone out of town alone when I was growing up, on the other hand, I would have wanted to call her and tell her everything that had happened that day, and how I felt about it, and how my friends felt about it.

Both my parents told stories about our family, the romance that was our origin story, the way my mother had saved my father, and how their children had given them both a new life. But my father told other stories, too, about his own long-running picaresque adventures in entertainment. They were also, I came to realize, stories about the history of show business, and how Americans had responded to it and sometimes remade themselves in its image.

When I was growing up, my father was older than all the other fathers I knew: born in 1902, he had been close to sixty when I was born, nearly eighty when I graduated from high school. His direct connection to the sepia-toned, history-book past—before electricity, before talking pictures—struck me as strange and alienating sometimes. All parents have childless pasts, and most children have difficulty imagining their parents as much younger people, but older parents have many pasts, layer upon layer of remote and peculiar experiences, and their youth is not only implausible but a kind of costume drama, too. As a kid you allow your grandparents their magic-lantern memories, but you want your parents to belong more firmly to the here and now. Yet my father's turn-of-the-century origins also gave me an intimacy with the past that I came to treasure, and a yearning not just to know about history but to feel what it was like.

Luckily, my talkative father was very obliging. He had been an entertainer all his life: a hypnotist's assistant and a magician in traveling tent shows in his, and the century's, teens; a matinee idol in repertory theater in the small towns and cities of the Midwest in the 1920s; a star-in-the-making in 1930s Hollywood; a near has-been who carved out a life as a working actor in B movies and the new medium of television in the '40s and '50s.

S TILL, though I grew up to become a magazine writer—a kind of storyteller myself—I'd never thought of writing about my father till the late '90s, a few years after he died. Then, one October afternoon, on a road trip in rural Pennsylvania with my husband and little son, we got lost. Somehow, we ended up at a roadside attraction that was like a figment of my father's past: a small-time circus show with women in slightly tattered spangles, miniature horses in feathery headdresses, an air of hard-won gaiety. It was a long way from the commercial mass entertainment that I, and even my little boy, were used to, and I was delighted by it. I thought about my father's early years in showbiz, when the relationship between audiences and performers was more of a fleeting secret, when performers shimmered into isolated small towns and entranced the locals and moved on. And I began, not long after, to think that I could tell my father's story as a way of telling the story of American entertainment in the twentieth century. Zelig-like, he'd been present at so many of its transformative moments. I could tell his story, and do what I'd always wanted to do: try to capture the texture of the past.

In the 1920s and 1930s, my father came of age in, and contributed to, a new, more sensual culture of abundance, a new era of mass communication, and eventually mass entertainment. Because the signature media of that era—film—let people experience pictures and voices, and therefore feelings or their facsimiles, from places they had never been and people they would never know, it transformed the sense of self, too. The historian Warren Susman calls this a "shift to the culture of sight and sound," by which he means sight and sound on a new scale, and of a greater variety than Americans could have imagined when most of what they saw and heard were their own families and their own towns.

How to distinguish oneself in a crowd, on the stage of the modern city, and in the eye of a camera was the new challenge. That meant unprecedented attention to personal presentation. The body—its care, its appearance—took on a new importance in a world where some people would make a living displaying themselves on screen, and others would want to emulate them. And it meant the arrival of formal advice and new products that encouraged people to cultivate individual, attention-getting personalities more than character. Personality, writes Susman, was the "quality of being somebody," and the early twentieth century saw the advent of a self-improvement industry that instructed readers in how they could be, or at least look like, somebody.

My father was born in the old order, in which character was predominant. But he grew up, was shaped by, and in turn helped shape the new one, in which personality, charisma, and good looks mattered more and more. As a result he was a little of both—a suave and playful twentieth-century entertainer who found a sense of meaning and mission in the work of entertaining.

This book is not a memoir, though my own memories are woven throughout, and it's not a biography of my father, either, though his memories are the brightest fiber in it. It's an idiosyncratic history of how entertainment evolved in the twentieth century, and how ideas about character and personality—about what made a person interesting, attractive, worthwhile—changed along with it. The way I tell that story is through my father and his life. So it's also a book about being a working actor—what it took, what he gave—to make a life in twentieth-century show business. I'll always be grateful to my father for showing me that you *could* make a life—and even a living—doing what you loved, and that it was almost your duty to try. Even if what you loved was some feckless, creative pursuit that more practical people with better heads for money would try to talk you out of. Even if what you loved was a business that made stars—and you never were one.

Chapter 1

—◦⟨⊙⟩◦—

LEARNING TO CRY

The boy grew up in a hotel for traveling salesmen across the street from the train station in a very small town. The hotel was white clapboard, two stories tall, plain and neat, set about by trees that in the summer grew over the windows and cloaked the downstairs in thick shade. The boy liked to lie on the front-parlor carpet, tracing its wreaths of faded roses and listening for the train whistle, then for the traveling men as they alit, swinging their creaking leather sample cases, then for the smack of their wingtip shoes as they stepped up to the front door. The traveling salesmen wore bowler hats and houndstooth vests and watch fobs. They sat downstairs at the long cherrywood table, packing away the gravy-soaked meals his grandmother and the hired girls cooked for them, holding their sides and laughing. They'd been to Omaha and Kansas City and Chicago. They'd seen skylines ablaze with electric lights and gone to plays—oh, plenty of 'em, and sure, there were pretty girls even in a little burg like this one, they'd tell one another, but, oh brother, how about those gals on the stage? The traveling men never stayed long in Brainard—a night, maybe two. They gave the boy peppermint candies and distracted pats on the head. They hummed little snatches of ragtime while they trimmed their magnificent mustaches.

The boy did not have his own room. His grandmother wanted to keep most of the rooms available for the commercial men, and the few left over for the hired girls, whose fathers sent them to work in the hotel so they could learn how to cook from Mrs. Talbot. The girls were seventeen, eighteen years old, farm girls, from Czech families, though this was before there was a country of Czechoslovakia, so they were called Bohemians or, less kindly, Bohunks. At night, the boy crawled in with whichever of them would have him, snuggling down under their white comforters, listening to their soft snores and the words they muttered in Czech, smelling the faint whiff of onion and caraway on their curled fingers. In the summer, the breeze from the open windows stirred the lace curtains and the tendrils of hair pasted against their necks. In the winter, he pressed as close as he could to their warm backs. He knew only a few words of Czech, but the phrase he remembered all his life was *"Hezká holka, dej mi hubička."* "Pretty girl, give me a kiss."

The hired girls woke in the smudgy light before dawn—Mrs. Talbot was a strict employer—but he scrunched down under the covers, hoping he wouldn't be ejected. At night, the girls laughed, and let him watch as they brushed out their long hair, heavy and glistening as horses' tails, but in the morning they were snappish and yawning, and told him to run along. He did little jigs, sang them a stirring Irish song about a boy and a girl with an ocean between them, told them about how he tried to ride the Jersey cow and how she'd tossed him. At night, the hired girls listened and sometimes clapped their hands with delight, but in the morning, he could try the same routine and they only sighed, stony-eyed, and shoved him out the door. None of them was his mother, after all.

His mother, he knew, was dead. He knew this because his grandmother told him so, and because every so often she called him to her side and took from a small velvet-lined box a lock of his mother's hair. It was pale gold and feathery, like a butterfly's wing. The first time he saw it, he felt nothing in particular, except confusion, because when his grandmother looked at it, she wept, and she was not generally a weeping woman. But the boy, whose name was Lyle, did not remember his mother; he had been just a baby when she died. When he did not cry, his grandmother told him he would get a beating unless he did—"Think," she said, "of your poor mama"—and then she took him over her knees and paddled him. The next time she brought out the velvet-lined box, he thought of the beating and how his bottom had stung, and he managed to squeeze out a tear. It wasn't quite good enough for his grandmother, but it was a start. The time after that, he screwed his eyes shut as tightly as he could and thought not so much of his poor mama as of his poor self, facing another paddling and unable to feel what his grandmother so urgently wanted him to feel. He produced a choking sob, and then, to his surprise, an increasingly persuasive crescendo of them. His grandmother sat back in her chair, exhausted. "That's my boy, Lyle," she said, and then closed her eyes.

The boy grew up to be my father, and when he told me this story, it was without apparent rancor or shock, so matter-of-factly that it was years before I realized what a cruelly perfect apprenticeship it was for acting. He was born in 1902, and grew up in a time and a place— small-town Nebraska—that was in some sense pre-psychological, a time in which people did not yet customarily explain one another's actions and motives with the kinds of concepts—repression and projection, anxieties and drives—that would become so familiar to people a couple of decades later. The language of child development—of children's distinct emotional needs—was not common parlance. A mother could die and a bereaved child be told she had gone away to a better place, without a good-bye, or else be told the truth but also not to speak of her; it was better that way. In his remarkable autobiographical novel *So Long, See You Tomorrow,* the writer William Maxwell describes his mother's death during the influenza epidemic of 1918 when he was ten and growing up in a small Illinois town. His father would walk from room to room and he would follow him, hoping they could talk to each other, but they never did. "When my father was an old man," Maxwell writes, "he surprised me by remarking that he understood what my mother's death meant to me but had no idea what to do about it. I think it would have been something if he had just said this." A child could be adopted and never be told—that was common practice until the 1960s. A son or daughter could be written off as a loss and shame, and that writing-off announced in the local paper, as this father did in the David City, Nebraska, newspaper in 1907: "Owing to the disobedience and incorrigibility of my son, Benjamin Wertz, I hereby notify the public that I have given him his time, and I will not be responsible for any of his acts or deeds and will not assume any of his obligations or liabilities hereafter." And a mother whom a child had never known could die and that child be expected to counterfeit the sentiment thought proper, or else endure a beating.

Much of what was done to children without regard to its lasting impact was irredeemable and indefensible, but sometimes there were surprising comforts to be wrung from a pre-psychological innocence. To our minds, for instance, the idea of sending a boy of six or eight to sleep in the beds of unrelated teenage girls seems deeply peculiar— arousing, perhaps, and therefore confusing. Yet my father remembered the girls fondly; they did not abuse him; they were kind to him; some were lovely to gaze at; his memories of them were the wellspring in him of a lifelong love of women. (His favorite book to read aloud to me when I was a kid was *My Ántonia,* Willa Cather's nostalgic master-piece about a Nebraska boy's chaste love for the older Czech hired girl who was his childhood playmate.) Why his grandmother didn't take him into her own room, I don't know, but bedding down with the hired girls undoubtedly helped him sleep through the raw Nebraska nights as a motherless little boy. As an adult, he saw that his childhood bed-sharing was something one would no longer do—but he was amused and matter-of-fact about it, not ashamed.

And my father would lead a resolutely unexamined life ever after. He did not speculate about what his grandmother could possibly have been thinking when she brandished that lock of hair or how it was that he could call her "a great old gal," which he did, and still vividly remember the tears she blackmailed out of him. The story he told about his growing up was not one of surviving childhood damage—the death of his young mother, the forced separation from his father, the alienating rituals of his grief-stricken grandmother. The story he told, always, was about becoming an actor. It was about the privilege, the thrill, the sensual benediction of holding people, for an hour or two, in thrall. It was about how a handsome face and an ingratiating disposition could propel a boy from Brainard, Nebraska, to Hollywood in the hectic, shimmery heyday of the movie industry. It was about vaulting from a life hunkered down in a cold climate among hardworking Czech and Irish immigrants—farmers, grocers, brakemen—to a life of gin parties in rented villas in Beverly Hills, starlets in creamy satin dresses, weekends at Hearst Castle, days spent impersonating bootleggers and gangsters and society swells, all amid the orange-scented Mediterranean lushness of Hollywood in the 1930s.

He led a life of surfaces, and there is, of course, a great loss in that. There were things he never understood—about himself, his wives, his children. He was a great raconteur with a diamond-sharp memory, but the stories he told were all plot. The psychological *why* of what people had done—left Hollywood in a hurry, abandoned a beautiful wife, drank to excess—was left vague, even the question unasked. When I was a kid, I used to press him for the why, and then eventually I got frustrated and stopped.

The thing about living as a pre-psychological, non-introspective person, though, is that when you make a success of yourself, it tends to confirm a belief in luck and magic. When combined with an innate sweetness of temperament, which my father had, the belief that you have been well served by luck makes you a gracious person. And my father was that. All of his life he felt lucky. Lucky to have been plucked from obscurity, lucky to be an entertainer. The mantra in our family was that our father was a great success—my mother always told us he was, and we believed it, even when he was out of work or acting in B- and C-grade dreck—because unlike so many actors, he had never had to take a job that wasn't in showbiz. He'd been on unemployment. (He always called the government office on Vine Street where he went to pick up the checks "the club" because he ran into so many old friends and picked up so much Hollywood gossip there. For years, I thought it *was* a club, and imagined it as some manly, plaid-wallpapered redoubt.) He'd been in Ed Wood movies, for God's sake. But he'd never sold life insurance or shares in dubious Southern California land schemes, never as a young man had to wait on tables to make ends meet. Sure, he would have liked to have been a star, not just a contract player around whom rumors of incipient stardom swirled like fairy dust for a while. But he was also one of that generation of actors that did not expect to live like royalty, that came here with a sense that talkies might not even last. The actor Wallace Ford used to tell my dad, "Don't buy anything you can't put on the Chief," the train that went between L.A. and Chicago. So he felt lucky when, in fact, he did stay in California for the rest of his life, and fantastically lucky to have found my mother to save him just when he was nearly lost. Lucky to have a whole second life, complete with children he never thought he'd have. Not blessed—he wasn't really a religious man. Not rewarded—he was humble and intelligent enough to know that life didn't really work that way. And while he was a hard worker, proud of never once having turned down an acting job, the truth was that he loved the work. Lucky. And luck made him charming. Why not? He was charmed.

Not that at the very beginning it looked that way. My father always told us that his grandmother had kidnapped him. "My grandmother kidnapped me from my father when I was a baby. She wouldn't let my father see me or even be near me." What this meant, what traumatic emotion the story might contain and conceal I didn't know, but I knew it had to go back to his grandmother Mary's own story. What had driven her to snatch a baby from his own father, a kind and decent man?

Mary Hollywood was an uncommonly tenacious, independent woman—an Irish immigrant as a child, a frontier homesteader as a young woman, and ultimately, a mother and a businesswoman at a time when few women tried to combine those pursuits. When my father wasn't calling her a great old gal, he called her a tough old gal. She was born in 1857 in County Cork, Ireland, on the ultimate Irish birthday, March 17. Her parents, Patrick and Maggie, had the propitious last name of Hollywood. Years later, that fact would make studio PR teams and fan magazine writers giddy—so much so that they would often get carried away and say it was actually my father's real name, not just his grandmother's maiden name. He was really "Mr. Hollywood," only he was too modest or too canny to use the name, sure that no one would ever believe it. That was the one gift of glamour Mary gave my father— that and the remarkable seaglass-blue eyes that shone out of all the Hollywood family's faces.

When Mary was twelve, her parents immigrated to the United States with their thirteen children, of whom she was the eldest. In Ireland, the men of the family had supported themselves by gathering peat, the spongy material formed by decomposing plants on top of bogs and swamps and burned for fuel. "They called themselves miners," my father said, "but what they did was just scrape the peat off top, they didn't go down in the ground for coal or anything. And they thought they could do that here, so they went to Pennsylvania, where they knew there was a lot of mining. Of course, nobody wanted peat for the steel mills in Pittsburgh." Patrick Hollywood and his sons,

Patrick Jr., Barney, Oney, and Jack, managed to find work in the coal mines of Allegheny County, but either because the work was spotty or because they'd had enough of it and gotten restless again, the Hollywoods moved to Iowa, and later to Wyoming.

In Thermopolis, Wyoming, Jack Hollywood opened a saloon, where he developed active sidelines in skirt chasing, cardsharping, and mayhem. Like his sister Mary, Jack Hollywood was blue-eyed, stubborn, and hardy, but unlike her, he seems to have been scantly endowed with loving or dutiful instincts. Any he had would not likely have been nurtured in the lawless atmosphere of Wyoming's Bighorn Basin around the turn of the century. Thermopolis in particular was a hangout for outlaws like Butch Cassidy and the Sundance Kid, and gunfights were nearly as common as jaywalking might be in a more orderly place. Still, Jack Hollywood seems to have stood out for sheer malignancy. "Jack Hollywood first came to the attention of law enforcement authorities in 1893," writes a modern historian of frontier criminality, "but he would reappear time and again, a bad penny turning up well into the 20th century." In 1893, Hollywood was charged with beating a woman, and in 1895 with rape (when he was not convicted, the woman set fire to his saloon). In 1899, he killed a local cattle foreman he had argued with over the man's saloon bill, striking him over the head with a pistol and again getting away with it. In 1909, he was arrested for shooting another man in a dispute over a card game or a woman, or both, and this time he was convicted of manslaughter and ultimately served time in the penitentiary. (First, he appealed his conviction to the state Supreme Court, nervily claiming that the man he did not deny shooting had actually died of pneumonia.)

THOUGH MARY NEVER SEEMS to have cut off ties with Jack or her other brothers who settled in Wyoming, she did choose to make her home far from them. On the trip west, the Hollywood family had stopped in Wahoo, Nebraska, to visit some friends from Ireland. Mary, who was then a handsome young woman of twenty-two, met a man named August Talbot there. They married on Christmas Day, 1878, and the couple homesteaded near Brainard for four years. August does not seem to have been much of a farmer, though. There was drought to contend with, and their crops failed.

In Brainard, a brand-new, raw-looking town on the prairie where they soon moved, August and Mary had a better time of it. The town had been founded in 1878, after the Union Pacific Railroad completed a branch line through Butler County. Soon it was filling up with the newest pioneers to the Midwest, Czech immigrants who'd come to Nebraska to farm the rich, loamy soil. There were plenty of jobs to do in a town that was making itself up as it went along, and August Talbot, whom the local paper described as a "genial, upright man . . . respected and admired by all who knew him," became first the postmaster, then the mayor. But in 1895, August died at the age of forty-five—or, as the headline in the Butler county newspaper put it: "After a lingering illness, Mayor Augustus Talbot breaks the slender thread and crosses the silent river." This was the era when newspaper obituaries still upholstered their news in flowery, Victorian sentiment: "A thick gloom seemed to have settled over Brainard last Sunday which the rest of the Sabbath did not seem able to break but which pervaded the air on Monday morning and every one walked softly, and indeed, it was an hour of sadness, something deeper than that caused by hard times or crop failure."

August's widow, Mary Hollywood Talbot, was then thirty-eight years old, with three young children—two daughters, Pearl and Florence, and a son, Fay. Another son, August, had died in infancy. But Mary was flinty and resourceful. Within a year of her husband's death, she had opened her own business—a two-story hotel with a full dining room and her name etched in gold on one of the downstairs windows. She had never gone to school and could barely read or write. Yet she was the only woman to own a business in town, and one of the few non-Czechs. And she made a success of the Talbot Hotel, running it from 1896 till a few years before she died in 1937, and even after she married her second husband, at the age of sixty-five. Her only real hiatus was the four years from 1915 to 1919 when she and my father lived in Omaha with two bachelor Princeton graduates who after eating at the hotel became so enamored of her cooking that they begged her to come keep house for them. Mary Talbot was celebrated for her cooking. I have my doubts—Ireland meets Nebraska is not exactly a culinary matchup to lick your lips over—but by the standards of the time and place, she must have been pretty artful. Those Princeton men snatched her up, the traveling salesmen kept coming back, and farmers sent their daughters to her in part so they would learn how to make her roast chicken and creamed potatoes, her pot roast and brown gravy, and her apple and cherry pies.

Mary had been smart to set up her hotel across from the train tracks and to cater to commercial men. At the turn of the century, there were thousands of them traveling the newly completed railroads of the Midwest, riding the dusty little lines to the dusty little towns to drum up sales (hence their nickname, "drummers") for everything from toothpaste to farm implements to corsets. By the early 1920s, modern advertising would increasingly replace the face-to-face sales pitch; smoothly crafted ad copy transmitted via radio waves to small-town America was more reliable for most companies than the armies of blustery drummers they once dispatched. But for now, the commercial men were the fast-talking purveyors of the latest thing, fanning the whiff of the city that clung to them—and there were plenty of them. As the Brainard newspaper proudly asked in 1909, "Who says Brainard isn't a busy burg when the Talbot Hotel Register shows 22 traveling salesmen in town at one time?" The locals gave Mary Talbot all due credit for knowing a market when she saw one. "To the popularity of this estimable landlady," noted an item in *The Brainard*

Clipper in 1902, "and the excellent manner in which the Brainard hotel is conducted is due the high and extensive reputation this hotel bears among the traveling public, and especially with commercial travelers, who are the most critical and perhaps the best judges of houses of this character. Mrs. Talbot spares no pains nor effort to please her customers and meet all the requirements of a first-class and up-to-date hotel. The rooms are clean, comfortable and inviting, and this pleases those who have occasion to stop at public houses. The tables are always supplied with the best the market affords in the way of substantials and delicacies. This is a $2.00 a day hotel and well worth the rate." By 1910 or so, Mary Hollywood was prospering sufficiently to have Talbot Hotel stationery printed up boasting of her establishment's "Steam Heat" and "Electric Lights." Never mind that for most of Lyle's youth, Brainard's electricity was available only in the evenings, from sunset till ten p.m.

The Talbot Hotel in Brainard, Nebraska, where Lyle was raised.

But if Mary devoted most of her time and formidable energy to pleasing the traveling public, there were still the children to think about. Pearl, the eldest, was outwardly dutiful but yearned to get away from Brainard. The youngest, happy-go-lucky Fay, had a passel of friends among the Czech boys and was off playing baseball with them every chance he got, his Boston terriers, Dinty and Jigs, yapping alongside him. And then there was Florence, the middle child. There is a photograph of the five of them taken when August was still alive. They all wear the grave expressions that nineteenth-century photographic portraiture seemed to elicit. Even energetic little Fay, with his long luxurious mane of curls, like a mini George Custer's, looks somber. Florence, who is maybe eight or nine in the picture, has her arms around her mother and sister, her fingers curled protectively around her mother's shoulder, and though she, too, is unsmiling, her gaze is bright and intent beneath a crescent of bangs. She has an aquiline nose, a delicate, elfin little face with the promise of a strong chin, and her mother's clear blue eyes. I see her somehow not as the child her mother loved the best—for in Mary's fierce way I imagine she loved them all— but as the one who brought her the most pleasure. Florence was the one she watched skipping home down main street and allowed herself to feel vain about, the one whose pale, thoughtful face suddenly flushed with happiness actually made Mary look up from her work for a moment or two to drink the girl in.

Florence got older, and prettier. Unlike other girls born blond, she seemed to grow fairer as she got older, her hair more wheaten, her skin more alabaster. She had a light step, a dreamy air, and a pretty tremolo when she sang. She attracted attention without even noticing it or seeming, at first, to care. One day in town she met a young man named Ed Henderson, a farmer's son who didn't care much for farming. He'd gotten a job in Brainard as a barber, or as the local paper called it, a "tonsorial artist," a job for which his twinkly sociability suited him. "If you need a Hair-cut, singe, shampoo, Dye, tonic, or

Mary Talbot, née Hollywood (right), with her husband, August Talbot, and children Fay (foreground), Pearl, and Florence (behind her mother).

anything else in the tonsorial line," his ads promised genially, "just drop into my shop and see if I can't please you. Yours, to please, J. E. Henderson." Ed was funny, but unlike some of the salesmen at the hotel, he didn't laugh at his own jokes. He was skinny and jug-eared with deep brown eyes and a sweetly mischievous way about him. (He kept that temperament till he died. When my brother was a little boy and visited him in Omaha, they used to ride around town in Ed's old car, which he'd christened "Goldie." My brother would say, "This is a Chevrolet, right, Grandpa?" And Ed would say, "Oh, yes, but you have to whisper when you say so. Goldie thinks she's a Cadillac.")

Florence and Ed fell in love, and on November 11, 1901, they got married. He was twenty-two and she was a year younger. The wedding had taken place not in or near Brainard, which was odd for two Brainard kids, but in Pittsburgh. The notice in *The Brainard Clipper* was cheerful enough, though it included a coy note that the news had come by "grapevine telegram" from Pennsylvania, not from Mary Talbot. "Both young people are well-known here, having grown up from childhood in our midst, and their host of friends all join with the Clipper in extending congratulations and wishing the young couple abundant success and happiness." Still, when I followed the little trail of local newspaper items about them in the months leading up to that announcement, I could see that the Talbots and the Hendersons had been in some sort of disarray. Florence had been abruptly packed off to Allegheny City, now part of Pittsburgh, by herself to visit an aunt for "a few months." Ed Henderson seemed to be on the verge of leaving town for good but kept changing his mind about where and when he was going. He and his brother were planning to sell their barbershop and then they didn't and then they did; Ed was going to move to Keokuk, Iowa, or maybe it was David City, Nebraska.

As I spun through the microfilms of the old Brainard newspapers, searching for keys to my father's childhood, I think I found why Mary Talbot so resented Ed Henderson. He and Florence had married in November, and my father was born in early February. Florence, then, would have been well into her second trimester of pregnancy when she and Ed married. Perhaps Ed hadn't known his girl was pregnant, and her mother had sent Florence to her aunt in Pennsylvania with the idea that she would have the baby there and give it up for adoption. Perhaps Ed, thinking she had left him willingly, was unhappy enough that he'd been making halfhearted attempts to start over somewhere else. That seems more likely, given his character, than another scenario: that he planned to abandon her. Perhaps Ed and Florence, frantic upon realizing she was pregnant, had snuck off together without telling her mother she was pregnant—though they could hardly have kept it from Mary Talbot forever. In any case, Florence's pregnancy would have been a crisis for them all.

It wasn't that premarital sex was quite as rare in late-nineteenth-

Ed Henderson (left, with guitar) and a friend,
probably around the time he met Florence.

and early-twentieth-century America as we might imagine. Historians have pointed to the turn of the century as an important pivot for sexual behavior, especially among women. A study conducted by the social scientist Lewis M. Terman found that 90 percent of women born before 1890 were virgins when they married, but only 74 percent of those born between 1890 and 1899 were, and 51 percent of those born in the first decade of the new century. The sex researcher Alfred Kinsey observed a similar trend: women born around 1900, who came of sexual age around 1916, were two to three times more likely to have had intercourse before marriage (and were more likely to have experienced orgasm). As for men, the historians Steven Mintz and Susan Kellogg point out, the chances of their having premarital sexual experiences did not increase, but the chances of their having them with women who were not prostitutes did. For the first time, large numbers of young women were moving alone to cities like Chicago and New York, taking jobs as stenographers or factory girls, leading the kind of unchaperoned lives that social reformers worried about. They gathered in amusement parks and dance halls and nickelodeons and, like Sister Carrie, sometimes took up with seductive, unsuitable men whom their families would never meet.

If sexual affairs before marriage were more likely in the city than in the country, they were hardly unknown in conservative, rural areas, either. The clues are few and scattered, but you can find them. Saddest of all are the criminal records testifying to the deaths of young, unmarried women who sought abortions. One such woman was Rosa Petrusky, whose story was discovered in the archives of the Wisconsin Historical Society in the early 1990s. Rosa died in 1896 after an affair with a farmer's son left her pregnant and the young man took her "along the road," as she told it, to a doctor who had "done something to her, had probed her womb." There are characters in fiction, like Willa Cather's Ántonia, who has a baby out of wedlock when the feckless train conductor she's supposed to marry reneges on his promise. ("Another girl," the narrator observes, "would have kept her baby out of sight," but Ántonia insists that her daughter's portrait hang in a "great gilt frame" on the wall of the local photographer's shop.) There is a remarkable diary kept from 1876 to 1880 by a young man named Rolf Johnson, whose family settled on the plains of Nebraska. In one town he frequented, he ran with a "sporting" crowd who shared with him pictures of the "fast women of the town stark naked." Rolf writes often about his visits with a young woman named Thilda, whose parents disapproved of him, probably with good reason. "Weather foggy and misty," reads one diary entry. "Received a note from Thilda inviting me to call this afternoon as she would be alone. Called and found her all alone, her folks having gone visiting. Spent the afternoon very pleasantly and staid until about ten o'clock this evening, and we played 'love in the dark' as we lighted no lamp not wishing to be watched from without through the windows."

But Florence was on the other side of that early-twentieth-century Rubicon. She had been born in 1880. For a young woman like her, from a small town, sex before marriage would have been a very daring matter, something that might have made her feel as though she were standing on the edge of a windswept cliff, exhilarated and frightened. Where would a couple like Florence and Ed, I couldn't help wondering, even have had sex? Cars hadn't yet exerted their revolutionary effect on American courting habits, freeing young couples from the porch swing and the watchful eyes of their parents. No one in Brainard even owned an automobile till 1908. There was the hotel, but it was a bustling place, and Mary Talbot was an intimidating presence, up and down the stairs in her black taffeta, calling out orders to the hired girls and clipped greetings to the traveling men. In the late spring, when Florence must have gotten pregnant, it was warm enough, perhaps, to lie down in a field of green wheat. And nighttime at the turn of the century was even more of a friend to a rural couple hungering for each other's bodies than it would be later. There were no electric lights at all on the streets of Brainard till 1907, and most of the residences glowed only with kerosene lamps in 1901. Love in the dark was always a possibility.

Of course, women were supposed to be virgins when they married; they were supposed to guard what one medical text of the day called "the largest diamond in the crown of youthful virtue." A publicized extramarital pregnancy meant ruinous scandal chiefly, it need hardly be said, for the woman. Still, if the couples who succumbed to temptation remained couples and married soon enough, secrets could be kept, reputations preserved, mores undisturbed. Florence and Ed's trouble was that their marriage did not come soon enough. By November, Florence would have been showing. It may have broken Mary Talbot's heart to send her dear girl away, but it must have been a comfort to know that people in town wouldn't be whispering about the belly under Florence's wedding dress. Or maybe there was another concern at work: Mary was a widowed mother running a hotel frequented by single men, and she didn't want them getting any ideas about the kind of girl Florence was. Maybe she even worried that a pregnant young woman on the premises would give the hotel she'd worked so hard to build up a bad name. And if that was true, then given what happened afterward, the knowledge that she had made a business-minded calculation about her daughter's life might have haunted Mary for the rest of hers.

Just after the wedding, Ed and Florence settled in Pittsburgh. For Ed, who loved meeting new people, and who had dreamed of a wider ambit, the city offered a welcome jolt of freedom and energy. He quickly secured a job as a streetcar conductor, work that suited his amiable extroversion. For Florence, a delicate mama's girl who was warmly attached to the people she loved but shy with strangers, it must have been harder to feel at ease. Ed had always been restless on the farm where he grew up, and he knew he didn't want to be a farmer, but Florence had liked her little prairie town. Even its scouring winds brought a bloom to her pale cheeks. Perhaps she felt the relief of not being gossiped about in a place where few knew them, and where she and Ed could represent themselves as having been married longer than they had been. But she must have been lonely and homesick, too, especially in a city so manifestly uncongenial to a country girl.

With a population of 320,000, Pittsburgh in 1902 hadn't yet made it into the top ten biggest American cities, but it would certainly have made it into the top ten most polluted. Smoke from the open-hearth steel mills and coke plants covered the city in a perpetual mantle of darkness. A walk through downtown streets meant brushing away cinders and soot that sifted down from the sky onto shoulders and hair, and streetlights often had to be turned on during the day to

Ed and Florence, just after they were married.

cut through the speckled gloom. The nineteenth-century writer James Parton described the city as "hell with the lid taken off."

The young couple lived in a boardinghouse that may have reminded Florence of the hotel she grew up in, but without her mother. On February 8, 1902, she gave birth to a baby boy at the Homeopathic Medical and Surgical Hospital in downtown Pittsburgh. The setting itself was a reminder of how far Florence was from home. City hospitals were dismal, disreputable places, and it was predominantly unwed mothers and the poor who gave birth in them. Most better-off married women had their babies at home, attended by a midwife or a family doctor, and usually with female relatives on hand. Over the course of the century, as standards of cleanliness improved and infection rates fell, hospital delivery emerged as the safer, more modern way to go. In 1900, less than 5 percent of births nationwide took place in hospitals, but by 1939 half of all births and 75 percent of urban births did.

Florence evidently had no one in Pittsburgh to whom she was close enough to ask for help; Ed would have felt ill-equipped to assist at his baby's delivery, even if men were willing to do such a thing at that time.

The handwritten birth registration for my father has a line for what it calls "color" and records that this male baby was white, and that his parents' birthplaces were Plattsmouth and Brainard, Nebraska. But the spot for the baby's first name was left blank, as though his young parents were too overwhelmed to give it a thought. Somewhere along the way they chose Lyle, an unusual and romantic sort of name that belonged to no one they knew. In fact, they weren't quite sure how to spell it, with the result that Lyle would go through the first twenty or so years of his life as Lyel, or Lysle, or more common, Lisle, with the *s* silent.

When Boy Henderson, a hearty, healthy, full-term baby, was about three months old, his mother fell seriously ill with what turned out to be typhoid fever. This was one of the quintessential infectious diseases of the nineteenth-century city, a disease that spread through contaminated food and water in places where the sewage disposal consisted of dumping human waste into rivers that doubled as municipal drinking water supplies. Pittsburgh had one of the worst typhoid problems in the country until the city started filtering its water supply in 1907; typhoid began a retreat that led to its virtual elimination there by the 1920s. Other big cities that adopted modern filtration systems experienced similar declines, though in the early twentieth century, people who carried the germ without exhibiting symptoms continued to spread typhoid. (The most famous of these "healthy carriers" was Mary Mallon, aka "Typhoid Mary," the Irish immigrant cook who was forcibly quarantined for twenty-six years on an island in New York's East River after she'd infected more than fifty people.)

Typhoid typically lasted for about a month—whether it killed you in that time period or you survived it—and signaled its arrival with a high fever, headache, and malaise. Diarrhea and cramps followed. Sometimes patients were affected by delirium, which could make them agitated; for this reason, typhoid was also called "nervous fever." Even before the disease struck her, Florence surely spoke of going home. And once she was ill, it was heartbreakingly clear to Ed what his young wife wanted: she wanted her mother. Her mother, who could snap a sheet like a sail in a stiff wind and tuck it in as smooth as a skipping stone; her mother, whom Florence could remember standing by her bed when she'd been feverish as a child, holding a glass of lemonade gleaming with tiny pearls of condensation; her mother, with her big, chapped hands, cool and heavy on Florence's forehead, pressing away the hot, pulsating lights behind her closed eyes; her mother, who would pull back the curtains in her room to reveal a bright blue square of prairie sky. Her mother, who would know what to do.

In the middle of May 1902, *The Brainard Clipper* was reporting that the young Henderson couple, Ed and Florence, had returned to town. "Mrs. Ed Henderson is at present confined to her bed at the home of her mother, Mrs. Mary Talbot, with typhoid fever." Ed was taking care of their baby. If Mary had hoped to conceal the fact that her daughter had given birth so soon after marrying, she must have quickly given up the idea. Social shame was the least of it now. Mary hired a doctor and a trained nurse from Omaha, at what must have been significant expense, to help her tend to her daughter. Then, on May 28, the paper reported that Florence had "been called from earthly life quite suddenly," four days after she had arrived home. Her condition had continually deteriorated, until "Wednesday evening, about 9 o'clock, when the pain seemed to leave her and her spirit passed peacefully away. Her death was a shock to her many friends here."

In her crippling grief, Mary Talbot might have done a number of things. She might have brought both Ed and the baby to live with her; she might have visited him frequently wherever they settled (she was an intrepid-enough traveler). What she did, instead, was brisk and extreme: she snatched baby Lyle from his father, took him to the courthouse in David City, and officially changed his last name to Talbot. She banished Ed Henderson from her life and from his son's. She was done with him, this man who had made her daughter pregnant out of wedlock, then taken her away to the city that killed her. Never mind that Mary herself might have banished Florence to Pittsburgh; she would never have had to if Ed hadn't done what he did.

LYLE'S KIDNAPPING by his grandmother was unusual, even in a time and place when custody matters were often handled in rough-and-ready fashion. But in other ways, his upbringing was probably typical of the early-twentieth-century Midwest. He grew up under the kind of child-rearing regime that combined sentimental display, physical punishment, serious regular chores, and a great deal of unsupervised roaming. When he was a baby, Mary dressed him in the long, white, lacy gowns that were just beginning to go out of style for boys, wheeled him around in a grandly filigreed wicker carriage, and had him pose for formal portraits neatly clasping his chubby little hands.

When he was two, he went to his first Fourth of July picnic—the kind that towns like Brainard took very big. There were long orations by red-faced state senators in straw boaters. There was a greased-pig race—catch the pig, and that was your prize—a slow mule race, a fast mule race, a fat man's race, and a baby's race. When Lyle was six, he and all the kids in town participated in an uplifting program about their American heritage. Bohumila Kabourek and Bessie Kavalec sang "Washington and Liberty," Vladimir Hlavac performed "Revolutionary Tea," and Lyle was sandwiched between Minnie Bongers and Elmo Dockstader doing an unidentified patriotic song.

From the time he was small, Lyle was expected to sweep up around the hotel, to deliver messages and newspapers to guests, to light the kerosene lamps at night, and to take his grandmother's

Jersey cow, Babe, out to graze. But he was free, especially on the long, hot summer days when he wasn't in school, to wander down the unpaved streets and wooden sidewalks, out into the tall grass, and down to the gulches, where a boy could gorge himself on gooseberries and blackberries and wild plums. The prairie was nearly treeless, but when you found a tree, a cottonwood leaning over a creek bed, say, you could lie under it and gaze up at the twitchy shimmer of its leaves and above them the towering banks of clouds that throbbed with light in the vast blue sky. You could doze off to the metallic whir of the cicadas amid the larkspur and chicory and Queen Anne's lace. You could feel what Willa Cather's Jim Burden felt when he first came to Nebraska: "motion in the landscape; in the fresh, easy-blowing morning wind, and in the earth itself, as if the shaggy grass were a sort of loose hide, and underneath it herds of wild buffalo were galloping, galloping."

It was a funny thing, maybe, for a little motherless boy, but Lyle was a seeker after beauty, wherever it might be found in a spare, rough-edged country town. After he died, my siblings and I found a small box of papers he'd managed to keep from the one-room schoolhouse he attended in Brainard. Among them was a letter he'd written but never sent, from late April 1912, when he was ten years old.

> *Dear Emil, Come over to my house Sunday. We are going to go violet hunting. Joe Peharek and I are going. We invite you to come with us. We are going down by the old bridge and catch minoes.*
>
> *We will get violets and Dutchmans' breeches. There is a tree in the creek which has a swing on it. We will swing on it. The violets are out, Your friend, Lyel Talbot*

Violet hunting! What a delectable pursuit!

In general, though, Lyle preferred the attractions of town: Smersh's drugstore, where they sold penny candy; Rudy Stanke's meat shop, where he could stand outside with the Czech kids and breathe in the scent of smoked sausages; Hausner's cigar factory and the Suchy soft-drink factory, where the root beer and sarsaparilla came in glass bottles with rubber stoppers that made a satisfying pop when you yanked them out. Because Bohemian immigrants came from a culture that placed a high value on musicianship, Brainard was, for a town of its size, unusually well stocked with musical groups—several small dance orchestras, a brass band or two—and Lyle liked to go to all the dances where they played. In town, Lyle got up to stuff and always found kids to get up to it with. He put on plays in tents that he made with clotheslines and sheets—one of the advantages of growing up in a hotel was that there were always plenty of linens—casting the Horacek and Smersh kids, the Hvlacs, the Dvoraks, and the Janeks, even when they stammered out half their lines in Czech and he could just barely understand them. He'd charge a penny for tickets to the shows, or if the kids didn't have a penny, a pin.

One time, a traveling man who sold chewing gum asked Mary Talbot if he could leave some of his supplies in her cellar till he came back to town. Lyle and his friend Emil discovered the treasure, and started removing gum cartons, one by one, and stashing them around town in secret hiding places. Soon they found they could use the gum like money, offering packages to kids who would do their chores for them. Their barter system proceeded smoothly until the night of the town dance, when Lyle was delighted to find that his gum connection was a magnet for girls. As the evening wore on, and more and more wrappers littered the floor, Mary Talbot figured out where they'd come from, grabbed Lyle by the ear, and steered him all the way home without letting go.

On another occasion, he became entranced with the labels on the canned goods his grandmother kept in the cellar—painterly renditions of luscious peaches and tomatoes, mighty mountain ranges, noble

Indian chiefs. In a fever, he peeled them all off and hid them away in a corner of the barn where he knew he could pull them out to admire in private. When his grandmother sent him down to the cellar for a can of cherries, and he came back with a can of green beans, she was furious, and when she marched down there herself and saw row after row of blank cans, she knew that for months she would have no idea what she was opening up to cook for the hotel guests each day. She gave him a whipping as rough as the ones she used to give him when he first saw his mother's hair and didn't cry.

Mary Talbot was a stark disciplinarian and a commanding, determined character. But she loved Lyle, and she had her ways of showing it. She'd make him his favorite treat, applesauce and sugar on brown bread. When he turned seven, Mary threw him a party at the hotel in Brainard, with pink cake and ice cream and little paper cups filled with nuts. For his tenth birthday, he had ten boys and ten girls over to play games, tell one another's fortunes, and watch him open his grandmother's present, a George Washington costume, with a toy gun and hatchet to go with it.

She also took Lyle with her on occasional trips to visit her mother and brothers in Wyoming, vividly rugged excursions into the Wild West that Lyle never forgot. To get to Thermopolis from Brainard, he and his grandmother took a train and then a stagecoach. His great-grandmother, with whom they stayed in a house with no indoor plumbing, was a frontier version of his grandmother. Formidable old Maggie Hollywood had gone native in Wyoming—she smoked a corncob pipe and had a cloak made of weasel pelts. Lyle heard whispering about his great-uncle Jack's having killed a man—in fact, it was worse than that—but Jack must have been capable of enough bonhomie that he did not scare a little boy. In fact, my father knew the saloon-keeping uncle with the beautifully waxed mustache as "Happy Jack" Hollywood, a man who was often in high spirits. Fortunately, my father seems never to have been there when the high spirits, fueled by too many hard spirits, turned to rage.

On these trips, Mary Talbot accompanied Lyle to the mineral hot springs for which Thermopolis was named, and showed him how to dip coins and spoons that tarnished instantly and came out black. When Lyle was a young teenager, she took him out to California two or three times to visit other far-flung relatives. Mary and her grandson were among the tourists to California who were becoming a stereotype, who'd head back to the cold Midwest with wilting poppies in their lapels and their suitcases stuffed with lemons and figs.

WHEN LYLE DELIVERED THE NEWSPAPER to hotel guests in Brainard, he'd often dawdle on the stairs, reading. Even to scan the headlines was to know that worse things than his grandmother's whippings happened to children all the time right in his own little corner of Nebraska—and perhaps to resent those whippings less than another, less informed, less constitutionally hopeful boy, might have. Infectious diseases had not yet been subdued by vaccines and antibiotics, and children died of scarlet fever, typhoid, measles, tetanus, and minor wounds gone septic. Flash floods swept families from the gullies where they'd set up tents getting ready to homestead. Accidents were frequent and ghastly at a time when horses and buggies were now suddenly sharing the countryside with trains and motorized vehicles, when kerosene was the basic fuel lighting homes, and when the idea of systematically protecting workers from harm on the job was still decades away from becoming the norm. The newspapers described the accidents they reported on with a distinctive mixture of grisly detail and incuriosity about why such things might happen so often, or how they might be prevented from happening in the future. In February 1902, the Brainard paper reported on a young married woman who was badly burned when a kerosene lamp spilled its contents over her while she sat up late at night working at her sewing machine. "The lamp was sitting on the machine, when it tipped and broke. She ran to an outside door and threw herself down the stairs, a blazing mass. She screamed, 'The baby is in there!'" The sleeping infant was rescued; the young woman died.

Rural papers of the day often carried reports of suicides. There were immigrants and pioneers who, like Ántonia's gentle, cultured, town-loving father in Willa Cather's novel, must have realized they were fundamentally unsuited to a harsh, lonely life on the plains. There were farmers who couldn't make a go of it and despaired; young wives who couldn't face lives yoked to taciturn or cruel husbands; people who suffered from mental illnesses that would not have been diagnosed as such, let alone treated, and for whom the leaden gray of a prairie winter was one order of desolation too much.

The word "incorrigible" comes up a lot to describe young people who were—what, exactly? Difficult in ways we would call difficult now—hyperactive, aggressive, prone to criminal behavior? Maybe, but it was also applied to boys who ran away from home, girls who slept with boys, adolescents of both sexes who bridled at the lives laid out for them: farmer, farm wife. Accounts of such behavior emphasized its paroxysmal suddenness, as though people were machines that could wind down or spin out of control without warning. In 1902, for instance, the Brainard paper reported that "Miss Katie Bluechel, a popular young woman of West Point, has become mentally unbalanced and was taken before the insanity commission for inspection. She was judged insane and taken to the hospital at Lincoln." When newspaper accounts ventured theories for aberrant behavior, they kept them brief and telegraphic, and favored physical rather than emotional explanations, as the Brainard paper did in 1897, with an item about a seventeen-year-old Bohemian boy named Frank. He had been "overcome by heat while threshing, since which time he has been a raving maniac."

Contemporary newspapers did not seek to fill out a story of personal tragedy with psychological commentary from experts or interviews with friends. The horrible thing had happened; it was graphically described and it was over. In September 1904, when a Mrs. Cole committed suicide at her home, *The Brainard Clipper* ran the item under the blunt headline "Woman Blows Her Head Off," and described what happened this way: "She loaded and cocked both barrels of a shotgun, put the muzzle under her chin, and discharged one barrel. It is thought she was deranged. The corpse was discovered lying on the kitchen floor by two little girls, who notified the men in the field. Mrs. Cole was the mother of a daughter, 3 years old, and of a baby, 2 months old."

THE LOCAL NEBRASKA NEWSPAPERS GAVE an airing to the wider anxieties in turn-of-the-century America, too. Writers fretted about the surplus of unmarried men because of immigration, the rise in divorce rates, the threat of "race suicide" when white native-born Americans had fewer children, the sissification of modern boys and the neurasthenia of overeducated, underexercised modern men, and the fact that "women today had invaded at least 30 percent of the employments" and were busily exchanging "the birthright of womanhood, wifehood, and motherhood for the mess of pottage known as a business career."

But small-town newspapers like *The Brainard Clipper* could also excite wanderlust and a sense of adventure, especially for a boy like Lyle, who loved his little town all the more the farther he got away from it. The paper was always reprinting thrilling yarns of blackguards on the loose and rugged men in extremis (Jack London was a favorite author), intermixed with articles about the peculiar ways of foreigners. When Lyle was growing up, the Brainard paper ran long articles about the high life in Paris, the adventures of Captain Scott in Antarctica, the quest for El Dorado, and the lives of pearl divers in Japan. The new century carried a sense of possibility both reckless and exhilarating, and the Brainard paper reported breathlessly on bold inventions of the future—a spineless cactus, a car that would carry its own track to lay down where roads were impassable, a means of sending photographs by wireless. It noted, too, the "craze to do something new," and cited "some of the latest and most extraordinary ways of performing strange feats," including a couple who got married in a hot-air balloon.

Closer to home, there were more realistic glimpses of the world to come. In 1902, Carrie Nation turned up in Beatrice, Nebraska, where she visited "three of the leading saloons of the city, under escort of Sheriff Washington," the *Clipper* reported. At each of them, the six-foot-tall hatchet-wielding temperance crusader "informed the bartenders of their probable destination in the other world, and remarked that she had smashed finer places than these." When even a small-town Nebraska paper could strike such a sarcastic note about Nation, who would have thought that in less than two decades her radical approach to the alcohol problem would be enshrined in the Constitution as the Eighteenth Amendment? In 1908, Brainard got its first automobile. It was owned by one Anton Sobota, who, the *Clipper* noted, "has not yet become experienced in its management, or else it is an unusually unruly machine, as it seems to prefer to run anywhere else rather than in the middle of the road, and on at least one occasion, it even attempted to climb a tree." And in 1912, a gang of bank robbers shot its way out of the penitentiary in Lincoln during a late-winter blizzard. The convicts had to hijack a milk wagon driven by a young farm boy to get out of Lincoln. But, like the tommy gun–equipped gangsters who would dominate crime and its depiction in the 1920s and 1930s, they were "well-armed with modern weapons," and ruthless enough to kill not only the warden and two guards but also the farmer who fed them breakfast.

Sometimes, when Lyle brought the papers, one or two of the traveling men would invite him to stay awhile, and he'd sit on the floor,

knees drawn up to his chest, and listen while they puffed on their
cigars and read headlines aloud. They were a loud, teasing lot, big
and bluff as circus bears in his grandmother's doily-draped rooms.
The traveling man, Henry James wrote in 1907, held "completely
unchallenged possession" of dining cars and hotels with his "primal
rawness of speech" and "air of commercial truculence." For Arthur
Miller, such men "lived like artists, like actors whose product is first of
all themselves."

Lyle learned from them to show off a little, to put himself forward. He wasn't an athlete, not one of the many boys around Brainard
who would play baseball from dawn till dusk, if they could. He wasn't
much of a student, either. But his memory for names and faces was
impressive, and he could recite sentimental poetry by heart. At ten, he
was also a flirt, with a keen longing to be admired—a playboy, one of
his friends at the time would later call him. I think he must have had,
even then, the makings of the man who would be my father—a man
who was vain and even narcissistic, but who had the grace, as some
vain people do, to use his self-regard for love's sake; who could make
you feel that his love for you was a more wonderful thing for the very
reason that it came from such a handsome and charming man. At
twelve, he wrote a letter to President Wilson, whose daughter Nellie
had been married that year in a much-publicized ceremony at the
White House and who had been preoccupied by the revolution in
Mexico, where he had just sent troops for a brief skirmish. Lyle had
evidently been told about both of these developments, but he couldn't
have been paying terribly close attention.

"Dear Mr. President," he wrote, first apologizing for not having
come to his daughter's wedding. He would have, only he had to stay in
Brainard and watch the office while the hotel clerk "went to K.C. to
have a time of his life." (You can hear the young clerk crowing to Lyle,
"Hey, little buddy, I'm going to have the time of my life in K.C.!")

"How are you getting along with those Mexicans down in Mexico," Lyle inquired without benefit of punctuation. "If I was you I'd shoot the whole bunch. Appoint me Captain and I'll do it for you." There was a lot worth noticing about Lyle, Lyle strongly, if rather confusedly, felt.

The Post Office was on fire down here in Brainard and if it wasn't for me it would burn down the whole town I've got a little hatchet and I chopped one of your cherry trees down. I would tell you what Ma done to me then I guess you now I never told a lie so don't you think I'll be a president when I get big. Say do you need a messenger boy or a broom sweeper if you do I'll take the job . . . Say do you smoke if you do I found a cigar and I'll give it to you. My teacher's name is Mabel Bentley. I married Emma Sypal yesterday. I caught some fish yesterday they were minoes. I'll send you a few of them. You had better come to Brainard and stay for a vacation you wouldn't want to go back to D.C. You would see such pretty girls. Your Friend, Lyel Talbot, Hotel Manager.

In all this time, Lyle scarcely knew he had a father. He would have liked one, no doubt, and maybe thought someone along the lines of President Wilson could step into the job. His grandmother didn't have much time for him. In addition to the responsibilities of running the hotel, she had charge not only of Lyle but also of two nieces, girls she had taken in after their mother, one of Mary's much younger sisters, was killed in an automobile accident. Yet if Mary felt overwhelmed, that didn't mean she wanted Lyle's father around to help. She still blamed Ed for her daughter's death, and found it easier to love Lyle if she thought of him as Florence's alone, the product of some sort of virgin birth. It helped that with his blue eyes and strong profile he looked more like his mother than his father.

Ed, however, had not relinquished the hope that he might have a

Lyle, at age eleven.

relationship with the son he had known only as an infant, when he himself had been newly widowed and sunk in grief. He had stayed in Brainard, but when Mrs. Talbot saw him, she crossed the street to avoid him. Sometimes Ed would stand across from the hotel till Mrs. Talbot sent one of the hired girls over to chase him off or, worse, did so herself. In 1904, when Ed was twenty-four, and Florence had been dead two years, he remarried. Ed's new, Danish-born wife, Anna Nielsen, was only nineteen, but she was already a gentle, forbearing woman who had a motherly way about her, though she was never to have children of her own. Ed and Anna were married in Grand Island, where her parents lived. The newlyweds hosted a dance and party at a hall in Brainard, inviting everyone in town, and hoping perhaps that the intransigent Mrs. Talbot would come and bring Lyle. She did not. Lyle was fifteen when he finally persuaded his grandmother to tell him who and where his father was, and to let him meet Ed. "She wouldn't let me, as a child, see my father—of course I didn't know what she was doing," Lyle told an interviewer in 1989. "It was when we moved to Omaha and my dad was living there that I actually knew I had a father I could see and talk with." Maybe she was worn down with trying to keep Ed at bay, or maybe she thought that Lyle, at fifteen, had a right, finally, to know his father.

Ed and Lyle's reunion was an affectionate one from the start. Ed was not one to hold grudges, and neither he nor his teenage son was the sort of ruminative, introspective type who might have dwelt darkly on the time he had lost. Anna, Ed's new wife, did everything she could to promote their relationship. Still, it might not have been the success it turned out to be if it hadn't been for the unlikely bond these two men from rural Nebraska shared: an itch to entertain, a jones for the spotlight.

Chapter 2

—∘⟨⟩∘—

THE HYPNOTIST'S BOY

On the grassy midway of a carnival in Valentine, Nebraska, Lyle leaned against the Kewpie doll stand. He was nervous and couldn't quite get the stance right. He had dressed carefully for his first day on the job at the Walter Savidge Amusement Co.—a straw boater, a wide tie with bold circus stripes, a crisp white shirt—and he thought he looked pretty good. But what was he supposed to be doing, exactly? It was noon, and the day was hot; the air gave off a scorched, dusty smell. Families filed by—mothers who looked like his grandmother, tired and dignified in their ankle-length best dresses; fathers intently surveying the sideshow signs ("Baby May, America's Fat Girl," "Man-ho, Man-Ape Alive"); crying kids already sticky with lemonade and taffy; pretty teenage girls with cloche hats and bare arms tinged pink. The girls looked at him curiously but not unkindly. He was seventeen, lean and handsome, even if he seemed somewhat at a loss. He cleared his throat. "Kewpie dolls," he tried experimentally, barely audible. Then louder: "Win your girl a Kewpie doll!" Kewpies were new and wildly popular. They had been designed by a beautiful artist named Rose O'Neill, who was known as the "Queen of Bohemian Society," and who became so wealthy from the marketing of the little dolls that she could afford to maintain both a handsome brownstone on New York's Washington Square and a villa on the island of Capri. Valentine, Nebraska, was a long way from either Washington Square or Capri, and Lyle had never heard of the beautiful Rose O'Neill, but he did think the Kewpies were cute, with their saucer eyes and naked tummies like mounds of marzipan, and he knew girls liked them, so after a while, the shouting got kind of fun. Especially when the girls loitered and laughed encouragingly. "They're flirts, these Kewpies," Lyle called out. "You can't resist 'em!"

By early afternoon, though he was sweating under the brim of his hat and could hear his voice going hoarse, he had found himself as a barker. It was okay; he could do this. But the truth was that Lyle would have done anything to work at the carnival—swept up stale popcorn and filthy sawdust, brought Baby May all her meals, hammered tent stakes into hard-baked soil. This was where he wanted to be—the world where dressing to look sharp counted as work, where it took no deep thinking to figure out how to make people happy. A couple of years earlier, his grandmother and he had moved to Omaha, where she had gone to work for the two Princeton men who loved her simple, starchy cooking. Lyle and his grandmother each had a room on the first floor of a rambling frame house, and the bachelors each had a room upstairs, with matching black-and-orange pennants hanging in both rooms. Mary Talbot had enrolled Lyle at the Omaha High School of Commerce, which offered classes like stenography, telegraphy, and salesmanship, along with the standard academic subjects.

At some level the instruction must have taken hold, because all his life my father had admirable penmanship, a fondness for stationery, and excellent record-keeping habits. While he was on the road with a play, as he often was for months at a time when I was a little girl, there were two places I went to feel nearer to him, two places that seemed especially redolent of him. One was the closet where he stored his shoes, each with its own polished wooden shoe form, and his pipes, wrapped in their own soft swatches of fabric. The other was the desk in my parents' bedroom, one of those French provincial replicas made of shiny mahogany, where the accoutrements included a blotter, a chunky glass pen stand, and a filigreed letter opener that I admired greatly and was occasionally permitted to use. He was the sort of person who used a label maker to fix names and dates to mementos and owned personalized bookplates (his were adorned with the masks of comedy and tragedy). And he kept elaborate scrapbooks, with the names of every town he ever played in, along with clippings, reviews, studio publicity stills, and snapshots of him and his friends, from the time he was seventeen and working for the Walter Savidge Amusement Co. to his last TV appearances when he was in his eighties. Some of that self-chronicling impulse stemmed from the fact that he was an actor, and in his own understated midwestern way, kind of thrilled with himself, and some of it stemmed from the fact that he loved print and paper. He was a haunter of L.A.'s outdoor newsstands, a subscriber to every new, hot-sounding magazine of the moment, from *Life* and *Look* in the 1930s to Tina Brown's revived *Vanity Fair* of the 1980s, a collector of cartoons, a clipper of coupons, an assiduous worker of crossword puzzles. He was the parent who took me to buy my school supplies every year at the Sav-On drugstore, and I'm not sure which of us enjoyed that errand more.

But even if the habits Omaha Commerce taught him stuck, Lyle did not make a great success of his tenure there. His report cards, which, naturally, he saved, show mostly B's, with a smattering of C's and D's. And though the school did put on plays, Lyle didn't manage to win a single part. The teachers favored a kind of oratory that was not his forte. They liked commanding elocution in the style of Nebraska's own William Jennings Bryan, or the mighty brayers of the

Chautauqua circuit. Interviewed in his seventies, Lyle remembered a plum role that had gone, instead of to him, to a boy who had auditioned by reciting from *Horatius at the Bridge*. I looked it up—it's a very long poem by the nineteenth-century Briton Thomas Babington Macaulay, and it has lines like "Shame on the false Etruscan / Who lingers in his home / When Porsena of Clusium / Is on the march for Rome." My father was not a big poetry reader, but there was one poem he liked to say, and it was short and sweet: "If of thy mortal goods thou art bereft, / And from thy slender store two loaves alone to thee are left, / Sell one, and with the dole / Buy hyacinths to feed thy soul." The poem is attributed to the medieval Persian poet Saadi, but Lyle had learned it for a play and didn't know where it came from. He just liked the sentiment. He was one of life's hyacinth buyers—not especially good with money, respectful of fleeting joys, tenderly susceptible to beauty. And though his grandmother disapproved, his father, it turned out, shared the hyacinth principle.

It was his father, the man he'd been allowed to discover when he was a teenager, who had gotten him the job with the Walter Savidge Amusement Co. Ed Henderson and his second wife, Anna, had just joined the Savidge company as performers and were paid $50 a week to appear in the plays that accompanied the carnival amusements. Ed was a "general business" actor, meaning he played assorted character roles; and Anna was "second business," meaning that she played the maids and the old maids and the mothers. Because traveling tent shows valued actors who could flaunt at least one other vaudeville-style talent—this was known as "doubling in brass," since often the second talent was playing a brass instrument—Ed honed the extras. In between acts, he'd tell jokes, juggle, manipulate marionettes he made himself, and sometimes mug with Anna in a plywood mock-up of an automobile labeled "Safety First" (they were meant to be country bumpkins trying and failing to control their first car).

How they had gotten themselves launched in show business was a bit of a tale, and Lyle loved to hear his father and stepmother tell it. Ed had been working as a barber again in Omaha, and as Anna would say, decades later, "We were just two, ordinary, small-town people." Ed, she recalled, "thought there was nothing in this world like barbering." Ed and Anna had taken rooms on the top floor of an apartment building, whose landlady was a garrulous older woman named Lucy Hayes, with a daughter also named Lucy. At night, the four of them would play charades and sing at an upright piano in the parlor. As Ed put it, "The two Lucys sort of adopted us, and we adopted them." In years past, the older Lucy had been the wardrobe mistress at a downtown theater called the Boyd, and those, for her, had been glory years. The greatest actors and actresses of the American and European stage had performed at the Boyd—Madame Modjeska, Lillie Langtry, Edwin Booth, even Sarah Bernhardt on her American tours. Young Lucy, who had grown up in the wings, had been as stagestruck as her mother, and she begged and pleaded with the management till they cast her in some bit parts. Now she was a grown woman and wanted to start her own stock company, of which she, naturally, would be the leading lady. And she wanted to recruit Anna and Ed as her first players.

It wasn't only her fondness for her mother's tenants that made Lucy Hayes think she could suddenly transform them into professional entertainers. Ed may have been a farm boy turned barber, but everyone who met him remarked on his flair for storytelling. One of his customers at the barbershop was the mayor of Omaha, Jim Dahlman, and he had a long-standing bet with Ed that the young man would end up on the stage someday. Ed's own father had been an upright Presbyterian farmer who "didn't think acting was exactly respectable for any decent man," as Ed recalled. But his maternal grandfather had been a circus tumbler whose specialty was a somersault performed atop an elephant. At eighty-four, he'd tried to replicate the feat for a rapt audience of family members at the Hendersons' farmhouse, though presumably there was no elephant on hand, and maybe that was a problem, for the old man sustained injuries of which he would die a few days later. Still, Ed figured that dying in your eighties from an excess of high-spirited show-offiness wasn't such a bad way to go, and he fervently admired his grandfather.

And Anna, well, Anna was a surprise. Though she was modest and mild-looking, a quietly devoted follower of Christian Science, she had spent her adolescence in Grand Island, Nebraska, turning up for every show that ever came to town and always "going home imagining I was that girl on the stage." She loved Ed, and if he'd woken up one day and announced he wanted to be a sea captain, she would have been as doughty a companion shipboard as she was on the road. But the fact was, show people pleased her, and if she was mostly along for the ride, she was game. She could play a dignified straight woman to Ed's goggle-eyed rubes (I always picture Margaret Dumont in the Marx Brothers movies). She could talk with equal ease to porters, bellmen, puritanical landladies, attitudinous artistes, dangerously sentimental drunks, and fretful parents in search of their stage-bent daughters. And when need be—the locals had taken offense to a show or one of its performers; a blizzard, tornado, or flu outbreak threatened—she could pack in a hurry.

The night Ed and Anna made their debut, they opened at an opera house in Council Bluffs, Iowa. A lot of small midwestern cities and towns had "opera houses," though nobody was planning to stage *Carmen* or *Rigoletto* in them. It was just that the term "theater" still had a disreputable taint when small towns started erecting permanent entertainment venues in the late nineteenth century. Some of the opera houses were fairly grand-looking edifices, with facades trimmed like wedding cakes and heavy velvet curtains for the stage. But in many cases, "playing the opera house" just meant performing on the second floor of a stolid clapboard building with a dry goods or grocery store on the first floor. For Anna, whose personal ambitions were modest, opening night at the Council Bluffs opera house went off quite well. "I had never played a part in my life," Anna recalled. "But in that first play, I had three parts, a young girl, an unhappy old maid, and an old sot."

For Ed, it was a different story. Mayor Dahlman had come from Omaha, and brought a contingent of his friends, all of whom were seated in the front rows. "As soon as I came out of the wings, they started hollering up at me, things like 'Gimme a haircut,' or 'Gimme a shave,' or 'Who's next, Ed?'" Poor Ed was so rattled that his brain instantly purged itself of all the lines he had memorized. Then the good-time Charlies in the front row began hollering, "Ed, it's your turn, now! Why don't you say something?" Ed's role called for him to stand by the fireplace a lot, so the next time he came out onstage, he put the script on the mantel as a prompt, but he kept forgetting to turn the pages and was soon lost again.

By the early twentieth century, audiences were beginning to settle down into the respectful comportment we're used to in the theater today. But there were still holdouts, audiences as unruly and participatory as they had been in the early nineteenth century and indeed in Shakespeare's time. Sure, small-town audiences loved it when a traveling show came around, but that didn't prevent them from getting rowdy. Whole families turned out, and if the mood struck them, kids in the front row blew raspberries, while their older brothers whistled and catcalled. For some unfortunate performers, audiences prepared special hazings. Perhaps the most notorious of these targets were the Cherry Sisters, who were known as the worst act in vaudeville. Addie, Jessie, Lizzie, and Effie Cherry grew up on a farm near Marion, Iowa, and took to the stage to support themselves when their parents died. (They had a fifth sister, Ella, who stayed home on the farm.) Since their recognizable talents were few, they mostly pranced around the stage in black tights and bloomers, recited essays and poems, and banged on a drum. The signature poem one of the sisters recited— "Cherries red and cherries ripe, / The cherries they are out of sight, /

Cherries ripe and cherries red, / Cherry Sisters still ahead"—might actually have played as titillation, except that, alas, the sisters' looks did not seem to have met with much male approval. Rumor had it that theater managers spread nets across the stage when they performed, to catch all the rotten fruit and other homemade missiles lobbed from the audience (though the sisters always insisted that this was an exaggeration). Still, three of them—Addie, Effie, and Jessie—had the gumption, or the desperation, to keep performing well into their forties. In 1896, Oscar Hammerstein, the theater impresario and grandfather of the librettist, brought them to New York, where their performances drew so many (undoubtedly jeering) spectators that they were credited with saving his organization from bankruptcy. It's not at all clear that the Cherry Sisters were in on the joke.

Indeed, two years later, they lent their name to an influential libel case when they sued *The Des Moines Leader* over an especially nasty review the paper had run of one of their performances. In 1901, the Iowa Supreme Court—after asking for a description of the performance—ruled in favor of the newspaper, and the decision became a precedent for protecting a critic's license to sneer. "Surely," the court opined, "if one makes himself ridiculous in his public performances, he may be ridiculed by those whose duty or right it is to inform the public regarding the character of the performance."

After that first night of heckling, Ed suffered nothing as ignominious as the poor Cherry Sisters did. For the next twenty years, he and Anna would tour throughout the Midwest with a half-dozen theater companies. They did short stints, too, as vaudeville-style entertainers on showboats that plied the Mississippi River. Ed never forgot his lines again, or if he did, he learned to cover for it without looking like an idiot. And every once in a while, just for the reassuring pleasure of messing up in a controlled way, he'd ad-lib some rascally bit of business onstage. In one role, playing a villain opposite an arrogant actor he didn't much like, he was supposed to be decked by the guy. But one night, Ed refused to fall down. "My attacker kept going through the motions of flooring me," he recalled many years later. "Finally, the guy exploded, 'Lay down, you damn fool!'"

Along the way, Ed also developed a line of skits based on the idea of a country bumpkin confounded by city ways and modern inventions. Since his audiences were predominantly rural, and living in an era that saw the introduction of an astonishing array of new technologies, they seemed to enjoy the spectacle of characters who were like them but more clueless, and they were comforted by the simultaneous suspicion that however clueless those rubes onstage might be, they were essentially good people, which was more than you could say about a lot of city folk. Ed's characters were flummoxed by automobiles, phonographs, and especially electricity. His audiences were busy mastering those things but not always with ease. One of his most popular skits involved a country lad who goes to stay in a hotel where he sees an electric light for the first time. To him, the object looks like a milk bottle hanging from the ceiling with red wires mysteriously sprouting from it. "When it came time to go to sleep," he confides to the audience, "I took my knife and cut it down. You never saw such hell come out of two wires in your life." Some humor translates across the decades, and some doesn't. But Ed knew his audiences, and you can see how a joke like that might have been cathartic for them.

Ed wanted to take his son along with him on the road as soon as school let out for the summer, and Lyle was beyond eager. He wanted to be near his father and stepmother, whom he could see right away were more jovial, playful people than his grandmother had ever been. Their obvious devotion to each other was something else Lyle had not encountered up close before and was drawn to, particularly since they had a way of warming other people with the glow of it. When Ed and Anna bought a small apartment building in Omaha a few years later, for instance, a local reporter dubbed it a "haven for newlyweds." It seemed that the Hendersons, wanting to encourage young married

Ed and Anna Henderson doing their
country-bumpkins-with-their-first-automobile act.

couples to live as happily as they did together, charged them below the going rate for starter apartments. Anna baked Danish pastries for Lyle when he came to visit, and encouraged him to call her "Mother." Ed was a joker who started a tradition of giving his son the same hideous tie on Christmas and getting it back from Lyle the next; it went back and forth between father and son year after year, elaborately wrapped each time.

Joshing aside, Lyle took his new filial duties seriously. In his scrapbook is an undated newspaper clipping, probably from 1919, that offers some advice to modern sons: "Of course, you are much older now, than when you learned to call him father. . . . Your clothes fit better, your hat has a more modern shape and your hair is combed in a different style. In short, you are more 'fly' than you were then. Your father has a last year's coat and a two year old hat, and a vest of still older pattern. He can't write such an elegant note as you can (but how

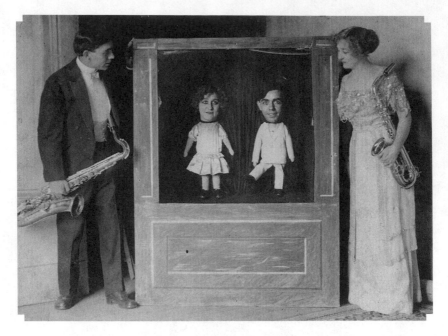

Ed and Anna with two of the puppets he made himself.

about his checks?) and all that—but don't call him the 'old man.' Call him 'father.'"

In those first two decades of the twentieth century, small-town America was not the entertainment desert we might imagine. But neither was entertainment in constant supply, available at the flick of a switch. Much of it was homemade—town hall dances with polkas and waltzes provided by Bohemian or Polish orchestras, sing-alongs, wedding celebrations. And what was not—the circuses, carnivals, itinerant theater troupes, Wild West shows, Chautauquas—enjoyed a relationship with its audiences that was at once more enchanted and more familiar. More enchanted because this was razzle-dazzle that came to town, visited upon you at intervals over which you had no control, like freak weather. More familiar because the performers stayed at a boardinghouse in your town for a week at a time; you saw their laundry hanging out to dry, heard the bareback rider grousing at

Ed Henderson with two fresh-faced fans clutching glamour shots of him and Anna.

the clown as they dragged their trunks to the train station. Disapproval of performers required a close policing of the boundaries between them and their audiences, and that in itself was a kind of intimacy. A landlady would have to tell a person to his face that she wouldn't take actors in her respectable establishment, as landladies would tell my father in Portland, Maine, and in Boston. And on the day a troupe came to town, its leading man and lady would sometimes promenade down main street in their finery—derby hats and diamond stickpins for the men, whispering taffeta and glinting ear bobs for the women—nodding coolly to passersby, advertising their glamorous separateness but so close up that you could smell their perfume and their sweat.

Of all the visiting entertainments of the late nineteenth and early twentieth centuries, the splashiest and most redolent of freedom was the circus. Circuses were then experiencing their golden age, testing out ever greater feats of derring-do: the first human projectile fired from a cannon (1880, Rosa M. Richter, aka Mademoiselle Zazel); the first three-ring circus (1881, Barnum & Bailey); the first successful triple somersault on a flying trapeze (1897, Lena Jordan); the first record set for the number of times a rider could leap on and off a running horse (1915, Poodles Hanneford). High-wire stunts and other aerial acts exerted a powerful hold on the imagination in those last decades before the airplane permanently extended our reach into the skies. And they were not the only feats of ascension that transfixed audiences. Like the Wizard of Oz in Emerald City, hot-air balloonists were mythic sensations at the turn of the century and just before, especially in the flat and windy Midwest. One of the most remarkable was Thomas Scott Baldwin, an orphaned young aerialist—his parents were murdered by ruffians in front of him when he was twelve—who went to work as a brakeman on the railroad. His talents were discovered by a circus manager who saw him performing acrobatics atop the train cars. Baldwin became a star ascensionist, working the county fair circuit with his brothers in the 1880s. With them he also invented a primitive parachute but never bothered to patent it, because as he said, "We never thought anyone else would care to try it." (Given that it consisted of a balloon from which Baldwin would rip a panel, allowing hot air to escape as he fell from heights of up to two thousand feet, he probably had a point.)

The day the circus came to town. Running away to join the circus. Those were the classic tropes of early-twentieth-century rebellion. As expressions, they're still with us. But when my father was growing up, there was more of a reality behind them. It actually happened, not infrequently, that the circus came to town and scooped up an errant boy or (less often) girl, and it meant more then because there were fewer means of escape from small-town life. Circuses were about daring and pleasure for their own sake. Their feats were entirely innocent of practical purpose and produced nothing of value, only oohs and aahs. For most rural audiences, nothing one did in spangles and face paint could be considered labor. It had no worldly relation to the hard lives most of them led. It belonged instead to some loopy land of

Cockaigne, to the rock-candy mountain where people preened and played instead of toiling and praying. That circus training in fact involved a prodigious amount of work was not the point. The object of the circus performance was to annihilate, in one adrenalized burst of admiration after another, the labor behind the feat. To make what was strenuously effortful look effortless, to soar through the air with insouciant grace, was to offer audiences a glimpse of liberation. In his memoir, an early-twentieth-century circus manager named Bert Chipman has a passage that captures the fizzy sense of freedom circus people sometimes felt, and sometimes transmitted to their audiences: "Four walls get awfully small when the circus comes to town. What's that? Flag's up, come and get it! Boy, smell the java! Spuds with the jackets on! Give 'em all they want! Where do we go from here? Who knows? Who cares? Only the ever-changing panorama each day and each night, the *chug-chug* and rumble underneath, with the shrill midnight shriek of the engine. Then you nestle back in sweet contentment. It's a hard life. So they say. Undoubtedly so, but don't it kind of tug at your heartstrings—lure you, so to speak?"

Carnivals, which combined rides (the new Ferris wheel, for instance, still in the category of a thrill ride) with games of chance and the peculiar tradition of sideshows, were less glamorous. They had a reputation for being "cheap and sleazy" in comparison with the "splendor and prominence" of some of the other branches of the amusement industry, as the sociologist Robert Bogdan writes. Circuses, too, traveled with sideshows displaying human oddities, but carnivals had more hootchy-kootchy performers along with the freaks and geeks. Grift—the various means of parting customers from their money that included rigged games of chance, shortchanging customers, and sometimes out-and-out stealing from their pockets—ran rampant in carnivals. Still, since few towns could afford to maintain a year-round amusement park, the popularity of traveling carnivals steadily grew in the early twentieth century. In 1902, there were seventeen carnivals touring the country, while by 1915, there were forty-six, and by 1937, three hundred.

Mary Talbot may finally have been reconciled to Lyle's having a relationship with his father. She harbored a grudging respect for Anna, she could see that Lyle was delighted to have a father in his life, and in her own fierce way she loved Lyle. But to allow him to join *a traveling carnival* with the Hendersons, even just for the summers? That took some energetic talking on Lyle's part. What helped was that Walter Savidge boasted of running a cleaner carnival than others. He hired mostly married couples, figuring they'd be a stabilizing influence and less likely to fool around with the townsfolk, told his performers to refrain from smoking or drinking on pain of fines or dismissal, and most of all, cracked down on grift.

Other carnies sneeringly called it "the Sunday School carnival," but Savidge embraced the term. "Pure entertainment and clean amusement is our motto," one flyer promised. "Roughs and toughs will not be tolerated." Every once in a while there'd be reports of carnivals and even whole circuses run out of town by angry citizens, and Savidge didn't want to be in that sheepish club. The upstanding rep was good for business. As a headline in the Bonesteel, South Dakota, *Enterprise* put it, "Walter Savidge Amusement Company, Clean and Worthy, Drawing Large Crowds." Omaha's *World-Herald* noted that "the crew is not made up of crude fellows who flop in strange places. No, indeed. Savidge and his co. are welcomed with open arms each year in towns that he has played before." Maybe it was this kind of publicity that persuaded the occasional parent to entrust her children to him, as this mother did in a painstaking letter to Savidge: "At my Son request to writh to you and give my consent for him to go with your show wich Mr and Mrs Fred Hugart as our Friends wanted him and said it would be all right for him to go. I am willing if you think that he is not to young (as he is 15 years) and it would be all right if not he can Come home from Wayne be for you leave. I hope it will be all right. Alex is well thought of here and will be missed by many. From Alex Mother, Mrs Julius Quintal."

Savidge was the sort of impresario who thrived in the era before radio, movies, and television nationalized entertainment. He and his company were known really only in Nebraska, but there they were well known, for they traveled to innumerable small towns, and their arrival each year was an event. The company was, in its way, remarkably successful. It lasted from 1915 to 1941, and at its height employed 125 performers. It had a Ferris wheel "brilliantly lighted" by the company's "own electric light plant" and it had its own brass band. It had a snake charmer, a trick horse, a family of midgets, a man who ate with his feet, and an act billed as "Darwin's Original Monkey Man," perhaps someone with a condition like hypertrichosis, which causes excessive hair growth all over the body, but quite possibly just a black man who was willing to act like an ape, which, distressingly, was a way to make a living in early-twentieth-century America. ("Missing link" acts were also, for many Americans, their first exposure to the language and concepts, however freely interpreted, of Darwinian evolution.) There's a story that Bert Chipman, the circus manager, tells about an African-American man who did a Beast of Borneo routine to the thrill and repulsion of white audiences, until one day while he was shaking the supposedly impregnable steel bars of his cage, they popped out, and the men and women who'd been watching and jeering a moment before ran screaming. Maybe for somebody like that, roaring at his audience was a way to show the contempt he must have felt for people all too willing to believe him a beast, even when he wasn't wearing the matted wig and shackles of his disguise.

The Savidge show went for a touch of class, sort of, with Baby May, of whom the ballyhoo bragged both that she weighed 480 pounds and that she spoke seven languages. What was the fascination of that, exactly? Maybe it was the idea that a superior intelligence could be housed in a body regarded as grotesque, a brand of irony or poignancy

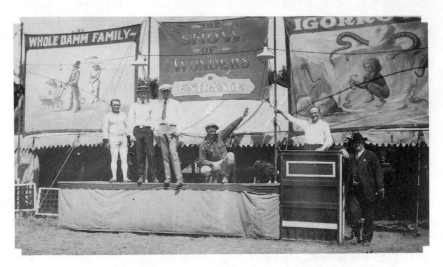

Lyle (third from left) with some of his pals from the Walter Savidge
Amusement Co., in front of posters for the sideshows.
I'm not sure what the Whole Damm Family did.

that sideshows often engaged in. You could see it at work, for instance, when they presented families of midgets as European royalty, or "missing links" as gifted painters or soulful poets—people whose talents and distinctions were belied by the physical packages they walked around in. Perhaps here the sideshow offered us a distorted mirror image of ourselves, for many people have the sense at one time or another of being trapped in a body that does not do justice to their scintillating inner selves.

But if that mode of presenting a performer like Baby May helped forge an empathetic connection with the audience, it's hard to imagine how the other aspects of her act could. Its central conceit—fat people appearing, for humorous effect, as though they were babies or children—was a mode of entertainment that, like the whole sideshow enterprise itself, strikes most people today as weird and cruel. It was certainly popular in its time, though, a time that lasted at least into the

1920s. (What probably killed it was the sexual scandal that forced the silent-era comedian Roscoe "Fatty" Arbuckle off the public stage.) Dainty Dolly, Baby May—what a riot to call obese performers by such diminutives and to compel them to dress up in rompers and knee socks. Gluttony, I suppose, seems to us a childish sin, and it suited some people to think of fat adults as children who'd never grown up. Poor May. I hope she really did speak seven languages and could mutter curses in Dutch or Portuguese or mentally transport herself to distant lands when all the carnival-goers, scrawny people mostly, filed in to gawk at her.

The Savidge sideshow also traveled with "Koo-Koo, the Bird Boy," a billing that makes me shudder even now, imagining a child who made birdlike squawks—an autistic child, perhaps—and "Clara-Leroy," the sister and brother Siamese twins. It had, in short, "thrilling and unbelievably strange people. An amazing congress of human paradoxes." At the same time it had no less astonishing wonders of natural science and new technology—an octopus, for instance, and an "electric bulb burning." It had a waterproof tent that seated one thousand people. And the Savidge company performers traveled on their own twenty-car train painted red and yellow on the outside and equipped on the inside with mahogany seats, beveled glass mirrors surrounding the berths, and sinks with hot and cold running water.

Savidge himself had been one of those restless boys who could not resist the lure of the circus. He was born in Deloit, Nebraska, in 1886, into an Irish coal mining family that, like my father's, had moved from Ireland to Pennsylvania, then westward to Nebraska, where they homesteaded. As a kid he had seen a couple of acrobatic acts he never forgot. Most boys were content to watch and whistle under their breath and go home for a hot supper, but Walter had to try some of that wild stuff himself. He hung a rope between the shed and the barn of his father's farm, and with the phlegmatic cows and somewhat more excitable chickens for an audience, taught himself to inch across it. He climbed to the top of the windmill and jumped, using an umbrella as a parachute, which actually sort of worked if you didn't mind a lot of bruises. Pretty soon, local fair organizers started hearing about the tricks Walter had taught himself to do and were inviting him to perform.

In Wayne, Nebraska, he particularly impressed a young woman in the audience named Mabel Griffith, whose father, the president of the county fair, had hired Walter for $5 that day. Years later, after Walter had started a theatrical company with his brother, and Mabel was teaching piano and living on her own, Walter went to visit her in Wayne, found her clever and levelheaded, and persuaded her to marry him.

In the winter, when the Savidge carnival was headquartered in Wayne, many of the performers fanned out to find work with theater companies in little towns throughout the Midwest. Sometimes the Savidges would go with them. To Mabel's chagrin, most of the hotels they stayed in were cold and shabby, with heat only in the hallways. After the shows, Mabel would stay late to play the piano for dances that brought in extra money for the company. In the spring, they'd start touring on the train, which was more comfortable. A reporter from the Wayne newspaper who caught up with her when she was an old woman, long after Walter had died, summed up Mabel's attitude toward life on the road this way: "It was hectic and they were always on the go, and it was really her husband's life. She didn't despise it, but would never do it again."

The trouper's life could be hazardous, no doubt about it, and the hazards began with what nature meted out. The region of the country known as Tornado Alley would not seem the best place to put a lot of big tents out in open fields every summer and then pack them with men, women, and children. But Tornado Alley was favored territory for many tent shows, because in the Midwest they had the best setup for reeling in sizable audiences. Nebraska and the surrounding states had plenty of farmers who lived in small, isolated, dull-as-dust settlements, but who were affluent enough to own automobiles, which

Walter Savidge (seated) and some of the roustabouts
after a tornado at Neligh, Nebraska, July 1920.

they could drive into the nearest good-sized town to see some entertainment—a visiting troupe of actors, a circus, or even an itinerant moving picture show. The Midwest had the highest rate of automobile ownership of any region in the country in the 1910s, and according to a 1919 report from Paramount Pictures, Iowa was the state with the highest percentage of cinema patrons who got to the movies by car. Women drove, too, and farm women in the Midwest were more likely to make frequent trips to town by car than their counterparts in the South. Compared with the West, which had fewer small towns than anywhere else in the country (the population tended to cluster in big cities on the Pacific coast or else to scatter, like dropped beads, on far-flung ranches), the Midwest held a robust network of small towns, connected by railroad lines, which made it feasible for entertainers to work a regular circuit.

But it wasn't just a matter of geography or patterns of settlement. Attitudes were different, too. In New England, blue laws restricting entertainment on Sundays still cast a puritanical pall on entertainment in general. In the South, evangelical disapproval did much the same, and segregation compounded the effect, reducing the potential audience by more than half in some places. The Midwest, by contrast, was home to many Central and Northern European immigrants, people like the Czechs my father grew up with, who did not, with some exceptions, harbor a religious antipathy to music, dance, and other such worldly pleasures. All that was the good part of touring the Midwest. The bad part was the tornados.

THE TROUPERS AND THE CARNY PEOPLE called them "blow-downs." An audience could be sitting there waiting for the show to start and a cyclone could come along and blast the tent clean away. There the people would be left, befuddled, bareheaded, in the sallow light and whirling wind, their scared and delighted kids screaming, their hats cartwheeling away amid brightly colored programs that whirled around them like confetti. Or, more gravely, a tent could collapse on top of the people inside, as happened once in Perham, Minnesota, where a fire then broke out and badly burned many of the trapped spectators. In my father's first scrapbook, a series of photographs shows the aftermath of a twister in Neligh, Nebraska. In one, the Savidge company's Ferris wheel lies on the ground like a crushed Tinkertoy. That storm came in the morning of July 19, 1920, so fortunately there were no carnival-goers present when the tent blew down and the Ferris wheel collapsed, but under one photo Lyle wrote, "A $10,000 loss was estimated." Fires were a menace, too, because show tents were coated with a highly flammable waterproofing compound made of gasoline and paraffin wax. (That practice came to an end only after a horrific fire in 1944 at an afternoon performance by the Ringling Bros. and Barnum & Bailey Circus in Hartford, Connecticut, killed 167 people, mostly women and children, and injured hundreds of others.) But it was winds that often started the fires, by knocking over lights.

Lyle lasted only two seasons at the carnival. It wasn't that he disliked that brand of entertainment. He loved circuses all his life, thought clowns were genuinely funny and poignant (long after a lot of people started thinking they were a little creepy), and maintained a childlike delight in the antics of clever pigs, hardworking showbiz dogs, dancing horses, and all other trained animals. Working at Savidge's carnival, he developed an abiding fondness for salted peanuts in the shell, ice cream cones, and cotton candy (which had just been developed by, among others, a dentist in New Orleans; a dastardly plot to drum up business, perhaps?).

I don't think my father objected to sideshows, either. Not many people in those days did. Hundreds of freak shows crisscrossed America in the late nineteenth and early twentieth centuries, and from the point of view of most contemporaries, they were actually more acceptable than other theatrical entertainments, since they offered an edifying experience: a chance to study the human curiosities that cropped up with some regularity in God's great plan. This marked a turn from the eighteenth century, when people with various abnormalities were shunned as evil omens, living manifestations of the sins or witchcraft of their parents. The forces that had just begun, in the 1910s and 1920s, to make sideshows seem uncivilized, were not always so benign themselves. The eugenics movement, for example, which upheld the notion that disabilities should be stamped out by encouraging procreation only among the genetically "fit," implicitly suggested that anomalous human beings should be hurried off the public stage. Genetic discoveries and the medicalization of difference meant that such people were now to be considered, in Robert Bogdan's words, "'humble and unfortunate' pathological rarities, a far cry from the interesting curiosities or 'lusus naturae' they had been in the past." The freak's new role was to be not a public exhibit but "a patient of physicians, to be viewed on hospital rounds and in private offices, by appointment only." This was a mixed blessing. There's mercy in being far away from jeering crowds, but the asylums where disabled people often ended up were no sanctuaries. (And in a way, we have our own version of human-aberrance-as-entertainment today: reality TV shows where people violate their own privacy for fun and profit.) "They weren't fakes," said Mabel Savidge of the sideshow freaks; they "were pleasant people, and weren't bothered by being on display as they felt it was their living and they made good money."

What must have been difficult for Lyle was the chronic outsider status of the carny people and the way they cultivated it. Some of the means by which they marked their separateness were fun for him—the lingo, for instance, because he liked words. There were the vivid bits of carny argot that would make it into general usage—shill, hokum, mumbo jumbo. And there were the more arcane terms that stayed on the inside: an "aginner" was somebody who disapproved of entertainments, "heavy sugar" was a lot of money, a "bender" was a contortionist, a "monkey" was an easy mark, an "apple knocker" was a rural dweller.

But carny people, even the cleaner ones like the Savidge employees, also tended to feel a solidarity that was compounded in part by their hostility toward the regular folk—the rubes, the yokels—who came to see them. And the hostility was often returned—by disapproving churchmen, by local defense committees set up during World War I to promote the idea that all stray men should be drafted and sent overseas immediately, and sometimes by bored local boys who wanted an excuse to clock somebody and found one in the chicanery of showmen. "It was no infrequent occurrence to be set upon by a party of roughs, who were determined to show their prowess and skill as marksmen with fists and clubs if required," the circus impresario W. C. Coup wrote in 1901. "As a consequence, showmen went armed, prepared to hold their own against any odds. Not once a month, or even once a week, but almost daily, would these fights occur, and so desperately were they entered into that they resembled pitched battles more than anything else." A lot of carny people took pride in their slipperiness, their ability to put one over on the proper, stay-at-home folk.

The Savidge Amusement Co. may have been a Sunday-school carnival, but it probably wasn't free of grift altogether. Lyle wasn't a hoodwinking type, though, and didn't hold the locals in contempt or get a cynical kick out of their disapproval. Part orphan that he was, he warmed to a sense of belonging and hungered for a little more class, for the shiny armor of acknowledged glamour. What would, in later years, give him the mojo he needed to perform was the belief that people needed him and respected his talents; if they did, then he would step up, and by Jiminy, he'd entertain them. It was his job, and he took it seriously. But the idea of scraping up business by faintly unsavory means, or cheating the people like those he'd grown up with in Brainard, made him shrink inside when he wanted to be elegant and expansive.

WHAT HE LONGED FOR, longed for so much that it made his throat go dry and his fingertips tingle sometimes when he thought about it, was to be up onstage himself. And how would he get there? Well, maybe that didn't matter so much. In the spring of 1919, Lyle was back in Omaha with his grandmother, back at Commerce High, restless as a kitten. One afternoon, as he thumbed idly through the *World-Herald*, an ad caught his eye. Maybe it wasn't exactly what he'd had in mind, but he grabbed his jacket and headed out the door anyway. If he got it, it'd be a job onstage, all right, and he would have gotten it all on his own, with no help even from his pop.

"Wanted: hypnotist's subject. Steady employment for the right sort of boy. Travel required. Apply to MacKnight, the Hypnotic Fun Maker," the ad read. It gave the address of a boardinghouse in town.

MacKnight, when he answered the door, proved to be a tall man with a florid complexion, a long face, and waves of Brilliantined hair. His gaze was unnerving, appropriate for a hypnotist, Lyle thought, except that it looked less like he was peering into the depths of your soul and more like he was straining to see who might have snuck up on his coattails—a bill collector, perhaps, or an irate husband. MacKnight had shed his first name somewhere along the way, and for all Lyle knew, even the last name had been filched. Lyle got the impression that until recently a man who looked an awful lot like MacKnight had been running a haberdashery in Omaha. Maybe it was while fitting men's hats, running his fingers authoritatively over each distinctive skull, that he had first conceived the idea of reinventing himself as "the man who knew." Or perhaps he had become aware of an uncanny ability to make people buy hats they didn't want. In any case, hypnotism was a way for a certain kind of man to get ahead in those days, and MacKnight must have recognized in himself the sort of qualities—a reliably unblinking gaze, an air of moonstruck gravitas, romantic hair, scruples as bendable as cheap spoons—that would be useful in that line of work. At that moment, he was the man who knew that this earnest, good-looking kid on his doorstep would be a good sleeper for his act. Audiences would like the boy's wide blue eyes, his wet-behind-the-ears look. MacKnight gave him a soda pop and hired him.

Many years later—my father was in his seventies by then—he remembered MacKnight this way when some college students in Texas asked him about his early days in showbiz. MacKnight, he said, "had sort of landed in Omaha and was living in this rooming house. He couldn't get a job, and you know a hypnotist out of work is a pretty sad thing. And he couldn't pay his rent, but he courted the landlady and she had fallen in love with him and that took care of his rent. So now he tells her, 'Oh, I'm a hypnotist and I think we can take out a show.'" And either she was pretty well besotted with MacKnight or pretty bored with her life as it was, or it was an intoxicating combination of the two, but she decided to sell the rooming house to finance MacKnight's show, and away they went, with Lyle in tow. Lyle and his girlfriend, Peggy, whose father was a banker in Norfolk, Nebraska. Peggy was seventeen, chestnut-haired, and musical. "Her family were rather influential people," my father would recall, "and they didn't want their daughter going off into show business, but she was determined to go, so she just kind of left home." Peggy played the piano, and MacKnight had said, why yes, he surely could use a little mood music for his show.

When I was a kid, I didn't take much interest in the stories my father sometimes told about these early years. They seemed so far away and small, like images glimpsed through the wrong side of the binoculars. If you have a father who is much older than other fathers—mine was nearly sixty when I was born—the idea of the distance he has come and the decades he has lived through before he even thought of you can make you feel a bit peculiar. It's a little like when you learn how short a time human beings have lived on this planet compared with the age of the planet itself. As compelling as your reality is to you, you're just a sliver on the timeline, a hiccup, a shrug. My father never made me feel that way, but sometimes his past did sound dauntingly crowded with people and events that had little to do with the benign and very domestic figure I knew. It seemed, when you went back far enough, to have more to do with what Greil Marcus calls "the old, weird America" than I could get my head around sometimes. I was a teenager before I started asking my dad to tell me those stories, and then I couldn't get enough of them—their very weirdness, his role as an emissary from a past that really was like a foreign country, fascinated and delighted me.

When we flipped the magic lantern of memory back to his stint with the hypnotist, the scenes it lit up were strange indeed. From the 1890s through the early 1920s, the country underwent a hypnotism craze, and in his way my father was part of it. This was the era of the unconscious mind, or rather of its scientific and popular discovery, of the trickling in of Freudian ideas, of the fascination with lie detection, autosuggestion, and other manifestations of hidden desires and motivations. As Alice Hamlin Hinman, a psychologist at the University of Nebraska, wrote in an early-twentieth-century essay on hypnosis, scientists realized that "no consciousness is single," and our old ideas of personal identity could no longer hold. More and more, we "perceive within ourselves the double and multiple selves, potential in the wider scope of mental life," of which actors, children, and hypnotic subjects were already aware. At Harvard, William James undertook experiments with hypnosis, and Gertrude Stein participated in research on automatic writing, letting her subconscious dictate what her hand would write and trying to pay as little conscious attention as possible. ("Strange fancies began to crowd upon her," Stein later wrote of the experience in third person, "she feels that the silent pen is writing on and on forever.") In Boston, James and his colleagues at the American Society for Psychical Research, including Alexander Graham Bell, investigated mediums, thought transference, and other occult phenomena in a spirit that was skeptical but not really debunking. Meanwhile, the sensational popularity of George du Maurier's 1894 novel *Trilby*, the story of a timid young woman who could sing like a diva when controlled by a hypnotist named Svengali, lent even practitioners like MacKnight a certain frisson. (*Svengali*, meanwhile, entered the language as a synonym for a manipulative mentor, though the character in the book had been an anti-Semitic stereotype.) And oddly, electricity gave hypnotism a boost. Hypnotists often compared the mesmeric force to electricity and incorporated electrical devices into their shows, and early explicators of electricity often compared it to magic (both Thomas Edison and Nikola Tesla had the nickname "Wizard").

Hypnotists had been around since the eighteenth century, practicing their soporific art with varying degrees of efficacy and legitimacy. But in the early twentieth century, even the ones who were in it purely to entertain often called themselves "Professor" and draped themselves in the mantle of science, of modernity as well as mysticism. Not that most people were thinking about, say, William James as they watched some so-called Professor in evening dress put his entranced subjects through their ridiculous paces—making a stout and dignified man of business crawl around on all fours and bray like a donkey, or a couple of joshing, muscle-bound lads mince around like winsome girls in trailing dresses—until he'd snap them out of it, and they'd stand there befuddled, claiming to have no memory of the spectacle they'd just made of themselves.

But the spectacle was not limited to the theater. This was the period when hypnotists who came to town drummed up business for the evening show by means of extreme measures in the heart of town. One such stratagem was to place a supposedly hypnotized subject in a shop window for twenty-four hours. Sometimes he'd be lying in an open casket, rosy lips sewn shut. Townspeople would gather around to stare at the sleeping subject—his fluttering eyelids, the soft exhalations of breath lifting his chest—and the hypnotist would swirl his cape and doff his top hat, and announce that "tomorrow, this sleeping boy, now in a deep slumber which I, Professor So-and-So, have induced, will be revived, again by me, on the stage of your own fair Opera House!" Other times, the mesmerized boy in the window might be, for example, pedaling a bike that had been suspended from the ceiling by wires for hours and hours on end. That was the window display offered by a hypnotist called The Great Griffith in Gary, Indiana, in 1914. It didn't go well, though. The "sallow, slender youth" who was Griffith's paid subject pedaled himself into exhaustion, the *Chicago Tribune* said. A mob threatened Griffith when the boy fell off the bike, "his hair hanging in his eyes," perspiration "soak[ing] his natty bicycle suit," but his legs still milling madly. MacKnight, the hypnotist my father went to work for, would later gin up a more wholesome version of the boy-in-the-window: he'd supposedly put one of the guys in his act under his telepathic control, set him up at a table in a store window all day, and have him play checkers with any challengers.

If he was even more daring, a hypnotist would bury an entranced subject alive for a few days. The sleeper would be placed in a coffin fitted with ventilation shafts, which visitors could also peer through. Though subjects were supposed to be in such a deep reverie that they would not need to eat or drink, the truth was the shafts were also used as conduits to slip food and drink underground when no one was there to see. The effect was a slumber that looked a lot like death, the fascination of which owed a great deal to that resemblance, as well as to the echo of fairy tales.

Sometimes the subjects rebelled. Wives who traveled with their hypnotist husbands and had to undergo repeated burials tended to get irritated after a while. Thrilling as it might be for spectators, the stunt must have been damp, dull, and more than a little creepy for the subjects, even those who saw it as a good chance to catch up on their sleep. And sometimes, if the money wasn't coming in, they went on strike. A reporter from *The Atlanta Constitution* described this scene, a kind of Lazarus moment as interpreted by the Three Stooges: "'I say on deck there,' yelled Wilcox from the grave. 'What are the receipts so far?' 'Seventy cents,' came the answer from the ticket puncher. Then again from the cheerless grave: 'Well, I guess we'll call it off, there's nothing doing,'" whereupon the pragmatic Wilcox insisted on having himself disinterred immediately. Still, though the trick clearly had its hazards ("Buried Hypnotist Nearly Drowns During a Rain," read one headline), concerned locals who tried to put a halt to it rarely got anywhere. "Hypnotist Has Right to Bury Wife Alive," declared a headline from Emporia, Kansas, where somebody had tried in vain to find a city ordinance forbidding such a thing.

The lure of a hypnotist became in these years an accepted explanation for why spouses strayed, teenagers ran away, nice young salesgirls went off with strange men they met on trains. "Was Hypnotized and Then Wedded," read a headline in *The Atlanta Constitution* in 1896. "Man Used Occultic Power to Win Himself a Bride." Hypnotism was the explanation the *Los Angeles Times* offered in 1919 for why a young woman named Thelma Steinbrenner, whose husband was a soldier in France, found herself in thrall, and in a hotel room, with an older, married hypnotist. It was the reason that a family of seven lay virtually comatose in an Illinois farmhouse for four days while a mob gathered outside calling for their reawakening ("Rudolph Bartag and His Entire Family Put Under Hypnotic Influence Last Tuesday at Ticona, Ill., by Leo Lenzer, Who Tries Vainly Day and Night to Arouse Them"). It was the excuse offered in 1910 by a Wall Street employee accused of stealing stocks and bonds from the strongbox at his office. "Says Broker Is Hypnotist," the headline read.

Particularly when sons and daughters left home in a hurry, their parents sometimes latched onto the halfway comforting idea that they must have been hypnotized. A fourteen-year-old boy from Azusa, California, who wandered off with a footloose ranch hand must have been hypnotized by the older man, his mother told the papers. A toolmaker in his early twenties who left a fiancée in Detroit to travel with a hypnotist for a year, and who was finally brought home by his family "in a very nervous condition," must have been under some sort of powerful mental enchantment. Of course, children and young people were occasionally taken by brutes and pedophiles—and maybe, given how familiar the notion of hypnotism was in those days, some of these abductors tried or pretended to hypnotize their captives. But many of the teenagers and young men and women in their twenties who crop up in these stories were probably willing accomplices, tugged along on the rope of their own desire for a fascinating stranger or by a dream of what it would be like to wander from town to town, strangers themselves. If they were caught and brought home, or sheepishly returned on their own, they and the people who loved them could always invoke the irresistible power of hypnotism. At the turn of the century, when more young men and women had the possibility of living anonymously in big and disorderly cities than ever before in American history, there was just more decamping and disaffection, more seduction and disappearance, for families left behind to try to make sense of.

In 1906, *The New York Times* reported the tale of Eleanor Balliet and Grace Hemstreet, both fourteen, who had the misfortune, the *Times* implied, to live on Staten Island, and worse than that, in Tottenville, which the paper portrayed with condescending sympathy as a slough of tedium set among mosquitoey marshes. Eleanor believed herself to be an elocutionist with an attractive voice; Grace had taken piano lessons; and both girls dreamed of careers onstage. But "not even the faintest reflection of the glamour of the Great White Way can be caught on the Tottenville horizon," the *Times* noted sadly, "and in the scenes they light Tottenville has no share at all." One Fourth of July weekend, the two girls tried to leave Tottenville behind. Eleanor and Grace had taken in two performances by a visiting hypnotist named Professor Santinelli, who employed as subjects a couple of young men of some charm, both named William. While hypnotized onstage, the Williams sang and played the piano and violin "at the 'Professor's' pleasure." The two girls, "their hearts . . . sick with yearning for brighter things," as the *Times* put it, responded warmly to a letter from one of the Williams imploring them not to waste their talents in the marshes of Staten Island. A couple of days after they ran away to meet Santinelli and the two Williams at the train station, Grace and Eleanor were found by detectives sent by their parents. The detectives had to break down the door of the hotel rooms where the starstruck Tottenville girls were staying with the young men.

I suppose my father was more like Grace and Eleanor than he was like some of the other teenagers in these tales. There were no William equivalents in his story, but like the Tottenville girls, he saw hypnotism as a way to get onstage. He was not under MacKnight's spell, not even when he conscientiously tried to be. But he was, as it turned out, a pretty convincing pretender. During the first half of the show, Lyle would do a few magic tricks. He wasn't much good at them, but Mac-Knight kept trying out different personae for him—"The Singing Magician," "The Nutty Magician," "The Magical Chatterbox," and in a moment of desperation, "The Silent Worker"—with the hope that the singing or talking or conspicuous muteness would make up for Lyle's disappointing sleight of hand. "Then in the second half of the show," my father recalled, "MacKnight would hypnotize subjects who came up from the audience, and he'd get them to do all kinds of things, and some of them I think he really did hypnotize but others would sort of fake it. He had people who traveled along with him, and I was one of them. I was supposed to sit in the audience and then come up onstage. And the audience must have known very well that I was a phony, because I had just done my magic act in the first part of the evening! But then I went out and sat in the audience, and he said, Will any volunteers come up, and up I would jump along with someone else. Of course, I was supposed to be hypnotized, but I never was. I wanted to be. I thought, Gee, I mustn't fake this, because it was supposed to be for real, but he could never get me to be really hypnotized, so I always did have to fake it." (Or, as he told a fan magazine in the 1930s, "The only person who had ever hypnotized me was some extraordinarily good-looking girl.") MacKnight instructed Lyle to wear simple clothes, to look nervous on the way onstage, to twist his cap in his hand, maybe trip on the ramp with an abashed glance back at the audience. And at all that, Lyle excelled. The audience couldn't wait to see what MacKnight, the Hypnotic Fun Maker, would make this poor country boy do.

The advertisements for MacKnight's show promised a farce comedy between acts—something called "Fooling Father" was a frequent offering—and an evening that combined "Mystery, Fun, and Science." MacKnight served up a little of everything, starting with telepathy. As "The Man Who Knows," he invited audience members to write down their questions about business affairs or the whereabouts of missing

The hypnotist and his subjects, rendered ridiculous.

relatives, and to hand them in at the door. MacKnight had perfected the generic answers—you will be reunited with the one you are missing; your investments will pay off—but he delivered them with enough brio to nourish hope, however false.

The centerpiece of the act, Lyle's big moment and MacKnight's, was when Lyle had a rock broken on his chest. MacKnight would grip one of Lyle's hands and stare fixedly into his eyes, commanding him, limb by limb, to go rigid, and to sleep, SLEEP, sleep. With an assistant's help, he would lay Lyle down with his feet on one chair and his head and shoulders on another. All Lyle had to do was hold his body taut (he was supposed to be in a state of paralysis) and keep his eyes shut, while his girlfriend, Peggy, played spooky music on the piano and MacKnight set the rock on his chest. The hypnotist would call up the town blacksmith, or somebody else who looked strong, and have him swing a mallet and break it.

My father always claimed there was nothing to it, really. He wasn't worried; he never got hurt. MacKnight had explained the principle of the thing: His body would give with the force of the blow; if he was flat on a table, sure he might get injured, but suspended as he was, his resilience would protect him. That made sense to Lyle—he was a fundamentally trusting sort, and besides, this was his chance to command the stage, vulnerable and unseeing though he was in those moments with the mallet poised above him. As he lay there, trying to sink into semi-consciousness and never succeeding, keeping his eyes shut anyway, Lyle realized that what he was doing was acting. His first show was in Sidney, Iowa, in November 1919, and he refined the routine in a string of small towns in Iowa—Blockton, Diagonal, Macedonia, Silver City—that November and December.

In the afternoons when they arrived in a new town for a show that night, it was Lyle's job to go search around for a suitable rock. (I've since read, in a book called *Secrets of Stage Hypnotism*, that stones of about two hundred pounds are best, since "a heavy stone will break with practically no jar to the sleeping subject, while a smaller one would shake him severely.") It was winter when he started. The mud of the unpaved streets was frozen and as hard as iron under the thin soles of the fancy shoes he'd bought with his first paycheck. The wind was like a solid object he had to lean into sometimes, and it hurled snow at him with what seemed like a malevolent force. He felt lonely, sometimes, but a little electric current of excitement about the night ahead lit him up inside. And then the next day, he'd be less lonely when he wandered around town. Kids ran up to him and called him "Atlas," and even if they punched him in the chest to see how hard it was, well, they had a laugh together.

It turns out, though, when you look it up, that people occasionally got injured or even killed doing the human plank, as it was known. It's a famous trick—often with the variation that the hypnotist will stand on the human plank's chest—but one of the original don't-try-this-at-homes. Or maybe at all. In Woonsocket, Rhode Island, in 1901, a human plank named Thomas Bolton was crushed to death by a stone that was described in the papers, perhaps with some exaggeration, as weighing six hundred pounds. The chairs gave way, he fell, and the stone rolled onto his head. One evening in 1909, Professor Arthur Everton of Newark, New Jersey, suspended his hired subject in the human plank position and stood nimbly on his chest for a few moments, as he had done so many times before. But this time, when he propped him up and set about reanimating him, the fellow slumped to the floor, senseless. In jail and charged with manslaughter, the hypnotist insisted that the young man was not dead but still in a deep trance. The hypnotist's wife wept and pleaded with the authorities to let her husband's mentor, a man named Davenport, try to revive the young man. When they relented and called Davenport in, a reporter from one of the wire services was permitted to watch: "The little room was in absolute silence as Davenport applied first his ear, then the tips of his fingers over the motionless heart. Next he bent his head down low over the head above the black cloth, placed his lips close to the ear of the body he sought to raise and said sharply and eagerly, 'Bob!' It was a trained voice, the voice of a man drilled to shock or command the senses, and it startled without moving the intent group of watchers. 'Bob! Your heart! Your heart is beating!'" There was no response, nor would there be, and though Everton, in a state of nervous collapse, kept telling anyone who would listen that Bob was surely alive, an autopsy showed he had died of a crushed aorta.

In 1913, the wife of Louis Jacobson turned up in domestic court in Chicago to complain that her hypnotist husband regularly "put her in a trance, stretched her across two chairs, and then invited heavy footed men in the audience to walk over her face and body," reported the *Chicago Tribune* under the headline "'Human Bridge' Turns on Husband." Mrs. Jacobson had the bruises to prove it, she told the court. Moreover, when she had become too ill to work, the hypnotist had deserted her and their six-year-old son, Buster. "Jacobson admitted all of his wife's recital was true, excepting the part related to his hypnotic powers. 'That,' he said, 'was plain bunk. My advertisements were faked. My wife was a willing faker, too.'"

There was, clearly, a sadistic impulse at work in hypnotic exhibitions, though I doubt my father saw it quite that way. It wasn't his habit to look for the darker psychological strands in things, and he forgave a lot in the service of a good show. But part of the fun lay in making people do embarrassing, even humiliating things. That was all well and good if you were part of the act, getting paid for it, and moving on to the next town, but for the people left behind, it was another matter. In a how-to pamphlet on hypnotic exhibitions, for example, Professor L. A. Harraden suggested the following cruel setup: "Take a dignified young lady" from the audience, hypnotize her, then "tell her that she is growing old and wrinkled and has a good deal of superfluous hair on her face." This, Harraden noted, "will naturally put her in very low spirits." Then, tell her a doctor can remove all these blemishes with an electric needle, and give a hypnotized young man a "lead pencil—not too sharp—with which to operate." The whole scene "never fails to delight a family party, and produces roars of laughter while the poor girl never afterward hears the rest of her mustache and wrinkles." The same incessant teasing might be in store for the two unattractive older people made to act out Romeo and Juliet, or the woman with a voice like a screech owl made to deliver an aria, or the dazed young men who'd danced with each other cheek to cheek.

Of course, maybe some part of them wanted to do it. Maybe it was sometimes liberating. Social roles could be constraining in small towns, and here was license to behave utterly outside them and blame it on a trance. (The cross-dressing theme, for instance, was rampant in these shows.) Maybe some of the people who went up onstage and did something wildly out of character were enacting their own version of running away with the hypnotist, but just for the evening. Even if you have been successfully lulled into a deeply relaxed and suggestible state, it won't force you to do something to which you are truly averse. A lot of what was happening with the true volunteers onstage was a kind of hysteria, a placebo effect. That was the whole idea of using hired subjects like Lyle; not only would they "warm up a frigid audience," as Harraden put it, but "by force of example and that epidemic peculiarity of nervous conditions," they could make other people think they were hypnotized and act accordingly. So it felt real, not like something they had faked, and maybe that helped when they thought about it later—sure, they'd done something crazy, but they just couldn't help themselves, no one could have.

There was something rather cavalier about the way hypnotists regarded their hired subjects, whom they called—and this tells you something—horses. Everton seems to have been genuinely distraught at the death of poor Bob. MacKnight was kind enough, though my father never felt close to him. But a lot of hypnotists seem to have regarded their horses as cheap stage fodder, and more or less expendable. "They are comparatively easy to find, and can be purchased for a small price," Professor Leonidas wrote in his 1901 *Secrets of Stage Hypnotism*. "Offer any somnambulistic youth $5 a week and expenses and an opportunity to travel, tell him that you will always tell others that he is getting $50 a week, and he is yours for as many seasons as you desire his company. In fact, $5 a week is good pay for a subject. There are lots of boys who would go for room and board and cigarette money."

Reliable hypnotic subjects were worth getting a hold of, but not necessarily paying or treating properly. "Yes, these good sleep artists want some vice, some glaring sin, and they are happy. Get a good subject; one who can be put into catalepsy or made to eat the delusive strawberry that is supposed to grow on the fertile stage and he is the boy to purchase, hire or kidnap!" Boys could more easily be "procured," as Leonidas rather unfortunately puts it, in the country than in the city. "If the town is a small country village or a prosperous country town of a few thousand, there are always enough boys doing nothing in particular that can be engaged for the season." The city was different—there you'd run into professional somnambulists who valued their services as highly as the greatest thespians. Some boys who would come to try out expected they'd be faking it, but Leonidas claimed to be looking for people he could really put under. To prove his seriousness, he'd stick a hat pin into one of his hypnotized subjects—they were supposed to be impervious to pain in that state—while the would-be new ones looked on.

The hypnotism craze ran its course eventually. Not that hypnotism itself ever disappeared; people still see hypnotists to help them quit smoking or relax, and you occasionally even hear about stage hypnotists. But it was no longer a phenomenon to which errant behavior was widely attributed. It had not turned out to be the sensational magnetic force, the magical science it looked to be to many people. It was not the psychological equivalent of electricity, a way of controlling and illuminating neural circuitry invisible to the eye. Research psychology and psychoanalysis would take over those hopes of illuminating the emotional underneath, and hypnosis would be relegated to the more gimmicky margins. The movies would take over much of the wowing of audiences with visual trickery: special effects on screen stirred the places in people's imaginations that stage magic—levitations and disappearances and somnambulism—once had. By the 1920s, and certainly by the 1930s, you no longer saw headlines like the one that ran in the *Chicago Tribune* in 1905: "Hypnotism Peril to Entire Nation: Army of Itinerant Svengalis Spreading Dangerous Teaching Through

Country." Discontent with hypnotists had been growing for years. Though the shows fascinated audiences, they repelled many reformers, who found they smacked of exploitation, of the sexualized display of vulnerable bodies. These itinerant Svengalis were "sweeping the country, subjecting victims to all sorts of cruelties for the morbidly curious or for advertising purposes," as the *Tribune* article put it, picking up on fears that Americans were an enervated race already. "They are leaving behind them a trail of maimed bodies and weakened intellects." A *New York Times* editorial called hypnotic exhibitions "degrading," and added that "the exhibitor might as well be allowed to chloroform people in public in order to amuse a mixed audience with the phenomenon of their narcotization." Starved of venues and audiences by the decline of the road-show circuit, starved of goodwill by an evolution in attitudes—the same sort of evolution that led to the growing distaste for freak shows—stage hypnotism lost its magnetic appeal.

By then, my father had long since given up the hypnotism business. One frigid January afternoon in Worth, Missouri, MacKnight told him that the show was canceled that night for lack of business, and that he didn't have the money to pay him. The landlady had perhaps grown tired of the adventure by then, or was disappointed in Mac-Knight's hypnotic abilities offstage. In any case, she was no longer emptying her pocketbook for him. Maybe that was when my father first developed his freelancer's optimism, his belief, which his children share, that Something Will Turn Up. Of course, we get antsy between gigs; so did he. Somewhere in the back of my mind is the tiny flicker of fear that I will never get another writing assignment, and he must have felt the same about acting, a still more unpredictable business. You can always write alone, even if there's no prospect of publication; but acting, unless you do soliloquies all your life, pretty much requires other people. When I was growing up in the 1960s and 1970s, before answering machines, the ringing telephone was promise incarnate, a clunky red talisman of hope, and for one single reason: It might be the agent calling. I was trained in phone politesse from a very early age—to chirp "Talbot residence" when I answered, and if the caller asked for my dad, to say, "May I tell him who's calling, please?" And, oh, when it *was* my father's agent, offering him some chance to return to the stage or the cameras, how lucky I felt to be the one tearing through the house to tell him who was on the phone. Generally, we could use the money, and always, my dad was thrilled to be working again. Our job was to be ready, and to be ready was to be hopeful—no matter how long the hiatus between jobs, even if the part was small, for a small part could be a cameo, and a cameo could be classy.

The thing that turned up that January evening in Worth, Missouri, was a telegram. It came from a magician who called himself Mock Sad Alli. The clerk at the rooming house where Peggy and Lyle had been staying, and where they had enough cash to stay for exactly one more night, had scrawled the message in pencil on a piece of butcher paper. Mox, as his friends knew him, was an old friend of Ed Henderson's who was touring with an outfit called the Wertz and Whetten tent show. He told Lyle there was a place for him and Peggy in the show. For $50 a week each, plus transportation and minus board, Lyle could do a little singing and a little patter between Mox's magic acts, and Peggy could play the piano.

Peggy and Lyle were on the train the next morning headed for Stratton, Colorado, Wertz and Whetten's next stop. They didn't get all the way there by train because Wertz and Whetten played what was known as the inland circuit—the towns they went to weren't on the railroad lines. "There were twenty-five people in the company, and in most of those towns, they had no hotels," my father would recall. "We'd live at people's homes. Maybe a farmer had a spare room. You'd pay sixty cents a night and that included breakfast."

The company trundled from town to town in a caravan of boxy, black automobiles, with slogans advertising the show painted on the sides. The players would lean out the windows to call back to one another, flirting, cracking wise, each shout unfurling white scarves of steam in the cold air. The towns were so spare and small they made Brainard look like the big time. Lyle took a lot of snapshots. His father had given him a Brownie camera to bring with him on the road. Brownies were still new at the time—the first basic cardboard model had come out in 1900. Like a lot of young people especially, Lyle was delighted with the idea that you could take photos on the fly and that they didn't have to be serious or dignified. You could show your friends looking the way they wanted to instead of the way their parents wanted them to. You didn't have to sit stiffly and patiently as you did in a professional photographer's studio, with its long time exposures and daunting expense and earnest aura of commemoration. You could take pictures just so your friends would have the fun of mugging for the camera or to pump your own memory about a place you'd been. In his scrapbook from those years, there is a snapshot from the Wertz and Whetten tour that shows a wide grassy expanse in Kirk, Colorado, empty except for one distant figure standing stock-still and a plain, one-story wooden building. Under it, my father has written drolly, "A Busy Day."

A show like Wertz and Whetten's operated on the smorgasbord principle: Put it all out there, and the people would not only find something to like but, with any luck, come back for more. And as in vaudeville and variety shows, the acts ran the gamut. When Lyle and Peggy joined the company, for instance, it included, in addition to the supposed "Hindoo" magician Mock Sad Alli, a dancer and actress named Tootsie Galvin, who had lately been entertaining doughboys before they shipped off for France ("Cheer up, Tootsie is coming," read the flyer, "direct from 18 months engagement at Camp Pike, Little Rock, Arkansas"), a comedic juggler known as "The Wizard of Motion," a jazz orchestra, and a play that poked fun at Swedish people. These Swedish dialect yuk-fests were actually quite popular then in the Midwest, when Scandinavian immigrants, who had begun arriving in the

1850s, with a peak wave in 1910, were both plentiful and still something of a novelty. "Ole Olson" and "Yon Yonson" were stock characters in the tent show repertory: good-hearted, slow-witted, blond-haired lads squeezed into too-small clothes. (It was a variation on the American country-bumpkin character known as Toby.) Though their English was fractured, though they were pigeon-toed and clumsy (if strong), the joke was not entirely on them. In the plays that featured them—plays like "Ole, the Swede Detective," "Ole on His Honeymoon," "One Year Over," "A Yenuine Yentleman"—the Ole and Yon characters acted out stories of adaptation, of immigrants learning, quicker than you might expect from outward appearances, what it took to get by in America.

As for the alluring Tootsie, her photo shows a chubby-cheeked girl of perhaps seventeen or eighteen in a short, poofy dress and white ankle boots. You could imagine her determinedly twirling a baton in some suburban high school homecoming parade today, but she was hot stuff in an era when showing your knees really meant something. A clip from one of the Colorado papers, written in the voice of a smitten young rube, gave a sense of her charms: "If that young leadin' man gets any wages, it's an outrage because he does nothing but make love to Tootsie from start to finish, and if I could do that, I would pay the people what runs the show."

Lyle and Peggy did a little of everything, too. Peggy was soon being billed as "Miss Peggy Schaefer, the saxophone wonder." (Her conservative family must have been aghast—if they knew, that is. The piano was one thing; refined young ladies did play the piano and the harp, even if they didn't usually do so for hypnotists. But the sax was associated with jazz, with nightlife, with walks on the wild side. Peggy must have had gumption.) Lyle, meanwhile, had a line in "unique and witty songs and sayings," some of them sentimental and Irish, such as "A Fire Laddie, Just Like My Daddy." He even did a blackface routine, in which he performed a song about Little Eva going to heaven, from the perennially popular play adaptation of *Uncle Tom's Cabin*. Sometimes he stepped in as Ole or one of his Swedish sidekicks. He did magic tricks, but as he told an interviewer years later, he wasn't much good at them: "I had been around enough to know that if your tricks weren't playing (and they rarely did), you had to talk to the crowd. So I would get up there and do this long, nervous monologue. I didn't even know what I was saying half the time."

Oh, and he was in charge of the guinea pigs that Mock Sad Alli was conjuring up in his act at the time. Mainly he was in charge of making them disappear—offstage, that is. They multiplied rapidly, and Mox never needed that many in his act. But Lyle, being soft-hearted and fond of animals, didn't want to just dump the guinea pigs by the side of the road or drown them. It took most of the day sometimes, going door-to-door and stopping kids on the street, to find homes for the scads of baby guinea pigs. Thanks to him, my father would say, there were guinea pigs all over Colorado.

In some ways, the best part of the tour was Mox himself, for he turned out to be a kind and generous man, as well as a magician of considerable talent. His real name was Charles Mathas, and he had been born in Germany. He knew, however, that a magician needed a touch of exoticism—a German accent hardly counted when Germans were the largest group of immigrants in the United States. Hence the stage name Mock Sad Alli, a nod to the mystic East, and to an earlier magician who'd used the same pseudonym. Mox had a broad, domed forehead, melancholy deep-set eyes, and straight, black hair that he parted neatly on the side. His wife, Dorothy, who was also his assistant, known, depending on the act that night, as either "Muhamatra" or "Lady Jane," had a homely, intelligent face and dark, wavy hair that she tied back loosely with a ribbon. In some of her pictures, she looks a bit like her contemporary the anarchist Emma Goldman. The costumes Dorothy wore were fetching and bohemian, with Peter Pan collars, artistic stripes and polka dots, black tights and bloomers. Mox

The magician Mock Sad Alli and his wife. The inscription reads:
"To my Student and Pal Lyle, Mox and Lady Jane, 1919."

and Dorothy saw themselves as au courant, part of the "modern magic" movement that embraced the theatricality of illusion. They did not claim to derive their powers from the realm of the supernatural; they were performers, and well-trained ones, who drew on a codified repertoire of tricks. My father remembered that the two of them always seemed quite close, as husbands and wives who work together and outside the mainstream often are. They reminded him of his father and stepmother. If you walked in on Mox and Dorothy backstage, they always looked like one of them had just said something amusing to the other, something they would obligingly repeat if you asked them to but that wouldn't quite translate. On the streets of the little towns they'd tour, you'd see them strolling together, Mox's hand fitted gently into the small of Dorothy's back.

A few years ago, I came across a tribute to Mock Sad Alli written by a fellow magician in a magazine called *The Sphinx*. The magician, E. G. Ervin, was writing in the 1930s, looking back fondly on Mox's heyday. "He was a master of misdirection"—the magician's strategic art of diverting an audience's attention—"but mechanism of any nature was tabooed. He would never rely on it. A match, and 'to hell with it,' was the doleful end to a newly acquired coin ladder that failed to function at a Saturday matinee." His repertoire was "varied, but not extensive," Ervin recalled, "so he'd become quite adept at varying the mood in which he presented the tricks"—sometimes pouring on comic patter throughout, occasionally proceeding in "somber silence." And Mox could milk an audience. "His favorite method of getting 'response' was by explaining that his next effect was entirely new, something that had never been seen before. His pathetic appeal, 'please do not fool me. If you don't like it, don't applaud' inevitably brought results." If an audience seemed unimpressed by a trick, he would repeat it "by request." When he had to take a role in the Wertz and Whetten company plays—most often as a butler or a villain—he could never memorize the lines as written and stumbled through with ad-libs. But his performance of magic was another story—in that he was graceful and sinuous. "Among his pet tricks," Ervin wrote, "was the appearance of a silk in a tumbler held between the hands, the sleeves rolled up to the elbows. A beautiful piece of misdirection—perhaps, but how it got there was incomprehensible."

Mox liked to help out fellow performers who were down on their luck, but he had supreme tact and a magician's skill when it came to saving a friend's pride and concealing where the help had come from. In a scrapbook kept by a Princeton graduate and magic buff that is in the holdings of the Princeton University Library, I found stories about Mox's footing the bill for a fellow magician who was languishing in a TB sanatorium, and arranging a carnival job for another sickly colleague, whose salary he secretly paid. The poor man earned enough money in this way to fund a trip back to Chicago, where he had friends and where he died soon after.

But while Mox was always gracious and avuncular, the tour Lyle went on with him hit its share of snags. In Vernon, Colorado, in February 1920, the Wertz and Whetten show was canceled because of a flu epidemic. After a hiatus, the troupe went on to Kansas in March and from there back to Colorado. In April, a late and heavy snowfall shut down business in Florence, Colorado. Peggy left the show and went home to her family. Lyle, too, went back to Nebraska, and at his father's suggestion, took a job with the Walter Savidge company again while he waited for brighter opportunities to materialize. Mox went to Los Angeles, where he and Dorothy took an apartment downtown on Alvarado Street and where he died some time later, "practically helpless," the recollection in *The Sphinx* maintains, "through a long ailment" and a "prolonged confinement in a Los Angeles sanitarium."

In one of my father's scrapbooks, there is a snapshot that shows Mox and Dorothy, Peggy and Lyle, and a raw-boned, black-clad Fred Whetten, the troupe's co-owner, who is standing a little apart from them. Mox looks formal, dignified, and slightly anxious, squinting professorially into the sunshine. Dorothy has her arm looped through his and a shy smile on her face. Lyle is leaning back, one arm draped casually over Peggy's shoulder, jacket thrown open, newsboy cap tilted rakishly above his smiling face. He seems cocky and full of life. And Peggy, in a black beret, her heart-shaped face exceptionally pretty, looks radiant.

I don't know what became of Peggy, but I like to think of her and

Wertz and Whetten tent show, 1920. Note the elaborately painted backdrop.
Tootsie Galvin is in the front row, center, wearing white stockings. Lyle's girlfriend
Peggy is second from right in the front row. Lyle is in the back row behind
the woman in the light-colored coat, Mrs. Whetten.

to imagine her memories of that adventure. My father said she never went back to showbiz and that he never saw her again. But I wonder if, having given up the raffish life of the traveling show, she found herself yearning for it now and then. I picture her leading the more respectable life that she had, deep down, always expected she would. Maybe she had married a doctor or a young man who worked in her father's bank, and had become the lively mother of several children. Her husband would love it when she played the piano for him—so soothing to the nerves after a long day at work—but the children were always begging her to play the saxophone. *Why, she didn't even own a saxophone anymore, wouldn't hardly know where to find one, you silly ducks.* Maybe when she told her husband about those days, she played it light, made him chuckle about the vanities and eccentricities of the hypnotists and the jugglers and the Tootsies. Maybe when she was alone with her children, though, she made it all seem more magical, like scenes in a snow globe that she took out and gently tapped, making it glitter for them, and for her.

I imagine that maybe the sweetest memory—one that lived only in her mind, because she never even told the children about it—was of a particular night when in some farmhouse's creaky-floored spare room she had brushed her hair until it shone, put on her charming little beret, and headed out. On the way to the hall that night, the snow had crunched underfoot and the stars winked like tinsel in the big, black sky. Lyle had surprised her, running up to her all out of breath, catching her in his arms and kissing her full on the mouth. Afterward, she could feel the warm ghost of his kiss, a tingly pressure on her chapped lips.

And that night Mox would have done her favorite trick, the one where he made paper flowers pop out of what seemed to be an empty cardboard tube. She could easily have figured out how he did it, but she had willed herself not to. She loved the moment when the flowers burst forth like a flame in the darkness, like spring when you were sure it would never come. Mox would bow to his wife, presenting the bouquet to her with a flourish. That night, maybe Peggy kept glancing backstage and she could see Lyle there. She felt especially beautiful, as brilliant as the paper flowers, as powerful as electricity, and even in the pooled shadows behind the curtain, Lyle could have sensed the light she was making. He ran his fingers over his lips to remind her of the kiss. Her cheeks flushed. The paper flowers bloomed. It was magic.

Chapter 3

❦

FOOTLIGHTS
ON THE PRAIRIE

Lyle sat on one of the blue folding chairs under the tent, his throat taut, his eyes burning. The actors were rehearsing but without him. The night before—his first night playing an actual role in a full-length play—had been a disaster. Every time he thought about it, he squeezed his eyes shut, trying to erase the demoralizing picture. It was July 1920, Jefferson, Iowa. Lyle was eighteen, full of pep, a bit of a hayseed still, but with aspirations to savoir faire and with a pilot light of ambition that would have been hard to extinguish. Today, though, it was nearly out.

A few weeks before, Lyle had borrowed a suit from his father, gotten some photos taken, and managed to land a job filling in at the Chase-Lister theater company for a more experienced older actor whose drinking had gotten out of hand. The play he was to debut in was *Her Other Husband*, a melodrama with a small-town setting. Lyle was supposed to be a drunkard who has run off and whose wife assumes he has died. (It was evidently a case of typecasting for the original

82

Lyle, the young actor.

actor.) Then one night, long after his virtuous wife has remarried, this time to the local minister, the lush turns up. Of course, there's a fight, but the lush, being a lush, is meant to lose, ignominiously. The minister was played by Raymond Ketchum, the company's leading man and co-owner, and a man Lyle greatly admired, as he did most people who'd give him a job.

Waiting backstage, Lyle was nervous, but it was more than that, and better. If nerves made you feel like you were one guitar string being plucked over and over again, this felt like being strummed. Everything around him seemed louder, sharper, more vivid. There were lots of kids in the audience, and he thought he could hear them wriggling around on their squeaking chairs, pick out the patent-leather protest of their new Buster Browns. He could smell the sweet, sharp scent of the trampled grass on the tent floor. He could hear the summer night sounds outside the tent—crescendos of cicadas, a lazy wind plucking at the tent flaps. He could see the shine of stage makeup and perspiration on the leading lady's face as she rustled past him.

And then, suddenly, somebody was clamping his arm and propelling him onstage, and there he was, with the audience gasping and hooting because here—surprise!—was the prodigal husband. Adrenaline made his fingertips tingle and his face feel hot. He made as if to slug Ray Ketchum, just as he was supposed to do, only instead of swinging past Ray's face, his fist made contact with it, and Ray slumped heavily to the floor. For a moment, Ray was out cold. He lay back, scarcely moving. Then he inched up on his elbows, looking shocked and furious. Blood was pooling on his split lower lip, trickling steadily over his chin. Chase-Lister advertised itself, with peculiar understatement, as "The Show Without a Headache." The slogan popped into Lyle's mind as he stood over the felled leading man, for Ray would surely have a headache soon if he didn't have one now. As somebody hastily brought the curtain down, Lyle could hear Ray whisper, "You're fired."

So it was over, Lyle thought—the whole cockeyed dream he'd had of acting on the stage. He sleepwalked through the rest of *Her Other Husband*, assuming, correctly, that his dismissal was meant to take effect after the play was over. If everything had been brighter and louder before, now it was muffled, the other actors' voices sounding in his ears like watery murmurs through the wall of a neighboring hotel room. What could they mean to him now except as prompts to steer him numbly through his paces, and eventually off the stage forever?

Lyle couldn't know it then, but there would be other moments like this; there are in every veteran stage actor's life. There was the time, a few years later, when he was supposed to be shot onstage and the gun jammed. From the wings, somebody whispered, "Well, kick him, then!" So his fellow actor did. Which might have been fine, except that Lyle's next line was "I die by the hand of the assassin!" The audience howled, but what should he have said—"I die by the foot of the assassin"? There was the time, many years later, when he was acting in a play in San Diego, and some befuddled guy wandered in from the alley, through the stage door, and right into the middle of a scene. Lyle quickly ad-libbed. "Oh, hello there, Barney! We weren't expecting you! But since you're here, could you go out and get us a bottle of wine?"—a piece of direction the intruder, who was clearly three sheets to the wind, was only too happy to take. Or the time when he played the role of an aged knight who went everywhere in the company of his faithful sheepdog. One evening, without warning, the faithful sheepdog bit him squarely on the ass. He was in the middle of a speech, a speech he continued until it was done. (The fake chain mail helped.) But by then he was a pro, and if not exactly used to such things, at least confident they wouldn't be the ruin of him, and well aware there was a lot you could put over on your audiences in a pinch. They'd be grateful for it; they didn't want the spell broken any more than you wanted to break it.

Raymond Ketchum met him at the tent the next morning. There was a bruise the size of a carnation blossoming near Ketchum's mouth, but he looked calmer. "Mr. Talbot, how old did you say you were?" "I know I said I was twenty-one. But I'm really only eighteen." "And how much experience do you have?" "Well, I was on the stage for a year as the assistant to the hypnotist MacKnight. Oh, and I'm a member of the Amateur Magicians Correspondence Club of America." Ketchum sighed. "I'll tell you what," he said, "You go away to some smaller company and work for a year and get some experience. Then if you still feel you'd like to be with us, write me and I'll find a place for you." Lyle was humiliated, though perhaps not so totally that he did not stop to wonder if there *was* a smaller company.

He had a dim notion that he would wait—wait for what he didn't know—so he sat himself down under the tent. After a while, Raymond's wife, Sally, came in and sat down beside him. Sally was the leading lady. She had a stalky neck and grave, bulging eyes; in truth, she looked a bit like a pensive box turtle. But she was kind and she was soft on Lyle. She laid her hand on his forearm. And to Lyle's embarrassment and relief, he began to cry. "Do you really want it that badly?" she asked. When he choked out a yes, she said, "We'll fix it up, then. I'll talk to him." The release of being understood by a sympathetic woman was immediate, warm and almost illicit. Dear Sally, wonderful Sally.

The upshot was that Chase-Lister cut his salary from $25 a week to $15. Lyle could stay—if he agreed to do a bit of everything except act. He'd help put up and take down the tent, he'd sell candy and popcorn between acts. He'd go around town posting the "Tonighters," small posters on brightly colored paper that announced the play that was on "Tonight at the Big Tent." ("Near the end of the season, they'd have a lot left over," my father would recall years later, "and maybe we weren't going to do that one show enough to use up the Tonighters for it, so Mr. Chase would just change the name of the play that night" to match whatever extra posters they had around.)

Lyle figured that eventually the management would throw him a few parts, and he was right about that. In the meantime, he watched and he learned, and he read what he could about acting. He was a sincere young man, the sort who clipped newspaper articles that seemed wise to him and pasted them in his scrapbook or carried them around in his wallet. One of his prized clippings excerpted an essay by the celebrated Broadway actress Laurette Taylor. He found its elevation of youth and imagination over experience and tradition in acting both reassuring and exhilarating. "The only thing experience can teach the youngster is the necessity of hiding his experience. The more experience he gets the harder he should dissemble before his audience. The thing is to preserve your imagination. Always think of preserving it, deliberately," Taylor wrote. And, she counseled, "Don't ever travel with people who haven't enthusiasm. They have no imagination and may make you work yours overtime to no purpose. Avoid rabid realists. They are slowly starving their imaginations by giving them the obvious."

Lyle knew enough about acting to appreciate that this was a new era in which personality, passion, and good looks mattered more than perfect elocution or grandiosity, those hallmarks of a fine performance in the nineteenth-century theater. By today's standards, performers at the start of the twentieth century would still have sounded artificial, guided by what one contemporary commentator called the "sucking dove" school of speech. But compared with earlier styles of acting, theatrical gestures were less extravagant, speech less declamatory in the first decades of the twentieth century. "Sincerity, innocence, urbanity, wit, intelligence: these and other qualities did more to attract playgoers than the stentorian manner of an earlier day," as Benjamin McArthur, a historian of American theater, has written. "Combined with good looks and an attractive figure or physique, they became an unbeatable combination." The early-nineteenth-century American theater had placed no particular premium on looks; actors and actresses alike were sometimes mammoth, often homely. But expectations changed over the course of the century, particularly as photography multiplied the images of performers—in theater windows, on cigarette packages and postcards. And looks would become paramount with the dawn of movies and the close-up.

"It is a plain fact," the actor William Gillette observed in 1914, "that personality is the most important thing in really great acting." The *New York Times* theater critic Adolph Klauber made a similar point, with greater ambivalence: "The person, not the artist, is wor-shipped in our playhouses," he observed in 1905. A fine actor infused his role with life, real life, even as he supercharged it. The new style of acting had something to do with the advent of realism in other fields, like literature, and something to do with the new prominence of psy-chology. And it drew on and in turn fed a larger transition that the historian Warren Susman, among others, has outlined: the movement from a culture of character in the nineteenth century to a culture of personality in the twentieth. It's a generalization, but the personal challenges for twentieth-century Americans had less to do with mak-ing themselves worthy in God's eyes than with making themselves appealing and alluring in the eyes of their fellow human beings—even those whom they didn't know and who didn't know them. The word *personality*, which had made occasional appearances in the late nine-teenth century, became common in the first decade of the twentieth. To distinguish oneself in a crowd, on the stage of the modern city, and in the eye of a camera was the new goal. It meant, as the contemporary self-help books posed the challenging task, highlighting one's indi-viduality without verging into eccentricity, being distinctive but still a recognizable type. It meant taking advantage of new counsel and new industries to refine one's self-presentation. For men, there were self-improvement books and courses that showed how to cultivate commanding personalities bolstered by forceful speaking voices and physiques. For women, there was the booming new mass market in beauty aids—face creams, lipsticks, rejuvenating hair products. (A 1922 magazine ad for Woodbury's soap made the point neatly: "Strang-ers' eyes keen and critical—can you meet them proudly, confidently—without fear?")

"From the beginning," Susman writes, "the adjectives most fre-quently associated with personality suggest a very different concept from that of character: *fascinating, stunning, attractive, magnetic, glow-ing, masterful, creative, dominant, forceful*. These words would seldom if

ever be used to modify the word *character*." Actors were cultural pioneers in this regard—living to be looked at—just as they were in more
unconventional living arrangements—divorce, female independence.
(Actresses at the turn of the century worked for longer spans of their
lives than did women in any other field.)

Lyle knew as he sat rereading Miss Taylor's essay night after
night that he was a long way from the London stage or the New York
stage or even the Cincinnati stage. His ambit was tent theater performed in little windblown towns on the plains, and his hope was that
eventually, if Ray Ketchum ever let him act again, he might someday
move up to a regular resident stock company, maybe in Sioux Falls or
Oklahoma City. When after a few months Ray relented and Lyle did
get back onstage, and when newspaper reviews started describing him
in certain terms, terms that suggested sex appeal and personality as
much as if not more than "histrionic ability," he knew he was getting
somewhere. He was, the papers said, a young man "whose good looks
are not wasted on the feminine portion of the audience." He was a
"handsome," "pleasant" fellow in possession of a "virile and buoyant
personality." He seemed "youthful," "impulsive," and "innocent" with
a "silly" sense of humor and, at the same time, an "alert," "collegiate" air.

The world that Lyle inhabited in his twenties and the country's is
a lost world—the world of traveling theater troupes and local repertory
companies that, before the definitive arrival of mass entertainment,
could still command people's desires and imaginations. Soon it would
be overwhelmed, first by radio and movies, then by television. But
from the 1880s till the late 1920s, touring companies were what
brought America its most reliable entertainment, what sparked, season
after season and however creaky the machinations onstage, its sense of
make-believe. Riverboats on the Mississippi and elsewhere had offered
the first touring venues for American theater in the early 1800s, but
with the rise of the railroad, companies could make it to small towns
all over the country. In the last thirty years of the nineteenth century,

notes Don Wilmeth, a historian of theater, "nearly every village and hamlet began to construct a local 'opera house' to accommodate traveling entertainments, creating a vast theatrical network known as 'the road.'" In 1900, there were 350 companies touring continuously—many of them in tents, or "under canvas," as the slogan went, during the summer, and in the opera houses when the weather turned cold—and millions of people saw them. "While it lasted . . ." Wilmeth writes, "tent rep was energetic, vital, immensely entertaining, and successful and truly belonged to the people. Indeed, the combined yearly attendance at tent shows during its heyday exceeded that of the New York stage, despite the frequently makeshift, shabby quality of the performances."

Bessie Robbins, the high-spirited leading lady of a company both Lyle and his parents toured with, once complained to a friend about a crying baby in the audience at one of her performances. The friend's answer was like a little love song to these makeshift shows. "Bess Robbins," the friend chided her, "the mothers of those babies have saved egg money for months to get to see you tonight. Some of them came forty miles by horse and buggy because you are the brightest spot in a very dreary existence. Any time your audience boasts a baby, it means the mother is a devoted fan—and you be grateful." Bess never forgot her friend's gentle chastisement: it reminded her, she said, "not to seek applause but to give happiness."

Giving happiness in this way could be an arduous business, though. True, traveling actors of the 1910s and 1920s didn't have it as hard as their predecessors in the nineteenth century. Traveling players in the early nineteenth century had been men and women of Bunyanesque stamina: they almost had to be, just to cover as much ground as they did in the years before the railroad. They trekked ahead on foot to post their one-sheet advertisements on rocks and trees; performed in barns, mills, stables, attics, and hotel lobbies, for audiences perched on rough-hewn benches and logs, before footlights that might consist of tallow candles stuck into potatoes or beer kegs that had been nailed to the floor. The actor John Langrishe and his troupe once had to abandon their wagons after the roads became impassable, and hike six miles, toting wardrobe and scenery, into the town of Bear Gulch, in the Montana Territory, where they performed in a butcher shop for the next two weeks. The actor Solomon Smith recalled an occasion when, while floating down a river in Maine, he spotted a white handkerchief flying from a pole stuck in the riverbank—the usual signal indicating a town was there to receive him and his players. But this time when they disembarked, they stared around in surprise, for there was no town anywhere to be seen. "Oh, you are looking for the houses!" the man who'd clambered down to meet them exclaimed. "Bless ye, they are not built yet." Indomitable spirits that they were, Smith and his fellow actors performed that night anyway.

The great nineteenth-century actor Joseph Jefferson's autobiography is full of stories about his pioneer-like adventures on the road. "We traveled from Galena to Dubuque on the frozen river in sleighs," he writes at one point, describing a tour with his actor parents in the 1830s; "smoother work than the roughly rutted roads of the prairie, but it was a perilous journey, for a warm spell had set in and made the ice sloppy and unsafe. We would sometimes hear it crack and see it bend under our horses' feet: now a long drawn breath of relief as we passed some dangerous spot, then a convulsive gasping of our nearest companion as the ice groaned and shook beneath us. Well, the passengers arrived safe, but horror to relate! The sleigh containing the baggage, private and public, with the scenery and properties, green curtain and drop, broke through the ice and tumbled into the Mississippi."

Troupers of the nineteenth century dodged outbreaks of cholera, diphtheria, and yellow fever—Jefferson's father succumbed to the latter on the road. They coped with their own and other actors' addictions to alcohol, laudanum, morphine, and opium, and with the degeneration of syphilis, which imposed a particularly cruel fate for an actor: memory loss that audiences sometimes laughed and hissed about. At other moments, life for a player was dreamlike, fantastical. Having discovered that hoisting one of the richly painted backdrops as a sail would increase his boat's speed on the Ohio River, the young Jefferson delighted in his power to lure "wonder-stricken" farmers and their children down to the riverbank. "For a bit of sport, the captain and I would vary the picture, and as a boat teamed past we would show them first the wood scene, and then suddenly swing the sail around, exhibiting the gorgeous palace. Adding to this sport, our leading man and the low comedian would sometimes get a couple of old-fashioned broadswords and fight a melodramatic combat on the deck. There is no doubt that at times our barge was taken for a floating lunatic asylum."

But even in my father's day, the trouper's life had its hardships, starting with constant travel through raw and lonesome towns scattered like corn feed over the Midwest. His scrapbook records that as he toured with the Chase-Lister company between September 23, 1920, and January 23, 1921, he played a total of twenty-five different towns throughout Nebraska, Colorado, and Wyoming, working every day but Christmas. The engagements would last anywhere from two days to a week, with a different play performed every night. Often the actors were riding "milk-and-vegetable trains" that made frequent stops, and switching trains in the middle of the night on frigid little open platforms, where the wind came scouring off the plains and nearly stopped your heart. If you arrived in the morning, you might get lucky and find a place open that would sell you a cup of coffee and a doughnut, and if you were young and often hungry like Lyle, you'd stuff your pockets with any of the warm, sugary sinkers that had been left behind by one of your fellow actors before you ran for the train. It meant carrying your own trunks, the trunks made so sturdily by the Taylor company that it eventually stopped making them because they lasted too long—big, wooden steel-cornered wardrobes that inspired some troupers to say they'd been born in one. (My father's stood in our garage for years, a thing of almost monumental heft and mystery whose burnished wood still shone like butterscotch candy.)

Hotel keepers sometimes banned actors, or hung curtains in the dining room to partition them off from the decent folk eating there. Merchants sometimes complained that the show people drained business from the local stores when they came to town, since while they were there, the locals would be spending all their pin money on playgoing. Chase-Lister once issued a wry rejoinder to such accusations that tells you something about actors: "Every Tuesday morning the management pays out to the people of the company, something over $600.00. If you are at all familiar with the habits of theatrical people, you will know that most of this money is spent in your town before the following Sunday."

When actors did find accommodations at a hotel or private house, the rooms were often stark or shabby, and in the winter, drafty and cold. My father recorded the names of all the hotels and houses he stayed in, along with their prices, which averaged a dollar a night. "Stopped at Elkhorn Hotel, and it's punk," he noted laconically of a place in Ewing, Nebraska. Philip C. Lewis, a former trouper who wrote a history of the theatrical circuit, recalled that players frequently opted for the hotel nearest the station "because it was so vital to make the trains (the usual weariness of the actor involved the risk of oversleeping)," and also out of the hopeful feeling that for a night or two, how bad could it be? "This meant, in aggregate, that they were spending their lives in faded, frequently filthy ('Don't look under the bed') rooms, with temperatures at extremes, where the electric light was small improvement on the candle; places noisy with drunks, singing chambermaids in the halls, doors crashing; beds with sags, lumps or thinly covered springs, broken window shades, broken windows, no closets, no bath—and despite prayers, sometimes bugs that made acquaintance in the middle of the night." Bessie Robbins remembered one small-town landlord who put the whole company of twenty or so men and women together in one big bedroom. "You know each other, dontcha?" she recalled him saying. "Thought you'd like to be together."

The troupers would find crazy places to rehearse during the day—the local undertaker's cooling room for corpses on a hot summer afternoon, or in a patch of yard behind somebody's shed with an audience of goats and pigs. Backstage, conditions weren't much better. "The actor who secures a looking glass that is not cracked or a wash stand that is not in eminent danger of toppling over," wrote one trouper, "is indeed considered fortunate, and as for a carpet on the floor, that is a luxury seldom found." Lewis observed that in the dank basements of opera houses where the actors dressed, "the lighting was often installed by someone who never thought actors might want to see themselves in a mirror as they make up." There were good reasons why "trouper" became a synonym for someone who persevered. "There were no understudies," Bessie Robbins recalled. "You played your part whether you felt like it or not. Of course, when you were sick someone would give you a friendly push from the wings. Once on the stage you forgot about not feeling well."

And that was all if the show didn't run out of funds, leaving its actors stranded in unfamiliar towns with barely a dime. "Layed off 1 week, acc't no bookings," my father writes from Sterling, Colorado, in mid-December 1920. He had to hold off till early February in Fairbury, Nebraska, just before his nineteenth birthday, to buy the new overcoat he needed for the prairie winter. Naturally, actors were good at putting on a front. "We broke actors sometimes do our span of poverty in the grandest style," my father told a magazine interviewer in the early 1930s. "Because we must keep up the old front, we have starved to death in high-powered cars with elaborate wardrobes and excellent hotel addresses. It's fun, of course, to look back on it all, but it's the devil to go through."

As he got older, it was mostly the lark of it all that he remembered. The touring companies Lyle acted with in the 1920s—Chase-Lister,

Clint and Bessie Robbins, the John Winninger Players—were like big, rumbustious families headed by husband-and-wife teams whom he looked to as surrogate parents, parents more fun-loving than most people's in those days. The troupes were communities unto themselves—self-contained, close-knit, yet capable of conferring certain freedoms that the rest of society did not enjoy. Older women continued to work onstage as long as they wanted to, or as the joke went, as long as the corset industry held out, and they continued to act, in many cases, opposite young and handsome men like Lyle. (One such actress, Flora DeVoss, performed ingenue roles for so long that after a while she felt compelled to issue a sort of explanation, however misleading: "Perhaps you knew Miss DeVoss, perhaps you knew her mother, perhaps you knew her grandmother.") Because husbands and wives often worked as acting teams and ran the companies together, their relationships could be uncommonly egalitarian. As Lyle's stepmother, Anna, said of her partnership with Ed Henderson, "There's no 'lord and master' in our household. Each one has a say and that makes for real harmony." Women worked well along into their pregnancies—deft costuming could hide a lot—and couples raised children on the road. Bessie Robbins, who herself had been born to theatrical parents—she was their middle child, "the ham in the sandwich," as she put it—recalled rehearsing with her baby "on my hip for a year. Directors put up with anything in those days."

Fellow actors played pranks on one another, teased and needled and annoyed one another, broke one another's hearts, loved and comforted one another. My father, as he went from juvenile to leading man in tent-rep and then stock companies, was forever falling in and out of love. There was a pretty musician who played in the orchestra, several actresses, and a seventeen-year-old Omaha flapper named Mary Bell, who was written up in the paper for having "appeared on the streets with a portrait of Clarence Darrow painted on her right knee and another one of Bill Bryan on her left." Mary's insouciant Scopes-trial reference didn't last long, alas. Her "plans for tripping the light fantastic with her new knees at a fashionable dance last night went a glimmering when her father saw the gleaming countenance of Clarence and Bill on Mary's shapely patellas," and demanded she scrub them off.

Far from their families—families who might have shunned them anyway—troupers were free to make up their own traditions. At Christmas, they'd gather in the lobby of their hotel to sing carols, then repair to a private dining room, if there was one, to eat Christmas dinner together. On their birthdays, they'd write and recite poems for one another. One year, a fellow actor presented Lyle with this charming tribute, in honor of his affection for loud ties:

> *Some may long for the soothing touch*
> *of lavender, cream, and mauve.*
> *But the ties you wear must possess the glare*
> *of a red-hot kitchen stove.*
> *The books you read and the life you lead*
> *are sensible, sane, and mild.*
> *You like calm hats and you don't wear spats,*
> *but you wear your neckties wild.*
> *So I give you a wild tie, brother,*
> *one with a lot of sins,*
> *a tie that will blaze in a hectic haze*
> *down where the vest begins.*

They maintained a store of backstage dos and don'ts, some of which persist to this day, for actors, like baseball players, are often superstitious. Never play or sing "Home, Sweet Home" in the theater; that meant your show would close soon. Never use a Bible onstage—it was bad luck—substitute a dictionary instead. Never say "Macbeth" in the theater; that, too, brought bad luck, for the story had come down over the centuries that the play had real black magic incantations in it. Never say the last line of an act during rehearsals; say "tag" instead.

There is a charming silent movie from 1926 called *Exit Smiling*, and when I watched it recently, I thought that it probably captured what it was like to be in one of those traveling rep companies as well as anything you could see today. Movies about small-time theater enjoyed a bit of a vogue in the 1920s. The director Frank Capra made a silent film called *The Matinee Idol*, about a Broadway star who falls in love with the lead actress in a troupe so lousy that he has brought them to New York to perform as a joke, just as Oscar Hammerstein did with the hapless Cherry Sisters. The recently rediscovered silent film *Upstream*, directed by John Ford, is a backstage tale about a Shakespearean actor and a woman from a knife thrower's act. It was as though Hollywood's moviemakers were already nostalgic for what seemed a simpler, more amateurish form of entertainment. Not that they didn't make plenty of fun of it in these movies. The troupe in *Exit Smiling* is touring with a play called *Flaming Women*, in which the actor starring as the swashbuckling lover is really a prissy, seemingly gay, fussbudget, and the actress playing the sweet and innocent girl he must rescue is a sly, gum-snapping sexpot. "Among the very few places fortunate enough to have escaped 'Flaming Women,'" one of the wry intertitles reads, "was the town of East Farnham."

But there is affection in the portrait, too. Beatrice Lillie, a wonderful comic actress with a face like a crescent moon and luminous, intelligent eyes, stars as Violet, who plays the maid roles and acts as the company's maid offstage. Violet is gawky, a lovable goof. She wears a beret that looks like a small flying saucer or a giant pancake. Trying for vampish sophistication, she tosses a marabou boa around her shoulders but it lands on her tush, where it hangs like a fluffy tail as she glides off, unawares. Still, Violet also has an irrepressible sense of her own fundamental worth; she can never resist applause, sashaying onstage for a curtain call when she hasn't even been in the play that night. And she is touchingly convinced that her loyalty to the young runaway who has just been hired—with her finagling—as the juvenile actor will eventually earn her his love. (He's played, with boyish eagerness and moodiness, by the ill-fated, drug-addled Jack Pickford, the younger brother of Mary.) The theater is full of kids and babies and grandparents, even when the play is the risqué-sounding *Flaming Women*. The backstage is a grubby jumble of backdrops and discarded costumes, with writing scrawled on the walls: "No check cashing at the box office," "This show ruined me," and below that, "Is that so?" One of the actresses steals a lightbulb from backstage and tucks it in her purse; one of the actors nicks a cloth napkin from a lunch counter and sticks it in his pocket like a handkerchief. On the train, the actors play cards together, looking up to stare at the desolate prairie outside the window. They set out chairs and use the platform outside the caboose as a front porch to read the newspaper or romance one another. And they eat together in their own train car, at a long, narrow table, complaining genially about the food. "Beans again—what is this troupe, the Boston opera company?" says the slatternly, gum-chewing actress. Every time the lantern-jawed old actor starts a story with "When I played with Edwin Booth . . ." his fellow actors get up, one by one, and leave the table.

I think that in those years as a traveling player my father cultivated his own collection of habits, and that they stayed with him, helped carry him, really, through life. He never had the steadiest of moral compasses, nor much in the way of self-knowledge, and at times, he might have been completely undone by his love of a good time and the wrong woman. But he always maintained the habits of professionalism and of small attentions to himself that can hold a person together when little else does. I think there are probably many people like that, people who manage to live good and productive lives less for any deep reasons of character than for the fact that they've acquired, somewhere along the way, certain rituals of reliability and self-respect. Lyle always showed up at the theater; he always knew his lines. He did not leave the house unless he was well turned out; he believed that was part of the social contract we implicitly make with our fellow human beings.

One of those clippings in his scrapbook from the 1920s is an article in which the writer observes how important it is for a stage artist to be beautifully attired and irreproachably prepared at all times. This writer had once asked an acrobat he knew, a man "who never slighted a trick no matter how unresponsive the audience," how it was that he had come by this attitude. The acrobat says that he had been apprenticed to a troupe when he was a little boy and that every morning he would go practice for the boss, who would invariably be lying in bed reading the paper. Standing beside his boss's bed, the young acrobat would perform forty backflips. And although the boss never took his eyes off the paper, he knew when the boy was cheating on a trick, and would strike him with a horsewhip. "He nearly killed me once for going onstage in soiled tights." It was hard, the acrobat admitted, but it was good for him: "The audience has a right to see your best work done in the best way." I think that was the sort of message my father took to heart all his life (though he would have had no sympathy for the use of the horsewhip), a message about a performer's debt to his audience, and in fact, about all of our debt to our friends and acquaintances—the debt of charming them, of going to a party, a restaurant, or even the grocery store, animated by the sense that we are *on*, or should be, that yes, the world *is* a stage and we have a duty to bring a little sparkle to even the most mundane scenes in the play.

In those years as a bachelor on the road, Lyle became a man who could take care of himself, a man with a fine little set of domestic accomplishments. The father I knew could whip up an omelette as neat as an envelope, a tasty chow mein with water chestnuts and crunchy bean sprouts, a corned beef hash and poached egg breakfast that was like something from the diner of your dreams. He could darn a sock using a little wooden egg. He could fold handkerchiefs and shirts with the crispest of creases. His dresser drawers, which I some-times sneaked into my parents' room to admire, were models of bento box–like precision and symmetry; the memory of them sometimes shames me when I yank open the overstuffed nests of tangled clothes in my own house. He could pack, as he did for me when I was a girl, tasty, old-fashioned lunches—date-nut-loaf-and-cream-cheese sand-wiches, cold fried chicken, celery and radishes and hard-boiled eggs accompanied by tiny foil packets into which he'd folded a sprinkling of salt, cans of apple juice he'd freeze overnight so they'd be ice-cold and slushy when I opened them at school.

His morning shower and its accompanying toilet were elaborate routines, more time-consuming than my mother's or mine. After step-ping out of the shower and wrapping a towel around his waist—the moment I might be allowed to come in if I needed to grab something from the bathroom—there was a careful side-to-side buffing of the shoulders and back with a second, coiled towel, followed by a generous sprinkling of talcum powder and an application of Sea Breeze astrin-gent or Lilac Vegetal to the face and neck. The Sea Breeze smelled sharp and bright and then quickly dissipated, but the Lilac Vegetal was weird: it was an old-fashioned barbershop aftershave that smelled horrible—like rotting lettuce—straight from the bottle but then magi-cally faded into an intoxicating, powdery lilac scent. He'd perfected the art of the short nap—a half-hour at about four, lying down fully clothed but shoeless in bed—that renewed him for the evening (definitely a useful habit in the theater). He knew from life on the road how to take care of himself with little treats, and truth be told, he hoarded some of them later in life, even when he wasn't on the road. Maybe his broke fellow actors used to nip into his supplies and he'd never forgotten. (My mom and I occasionally pilfered from the drawers where he tucked them, though some of the treats—canned Vienna sausages—were treats only to him. The supplies of cocktail peanuts and Hershey's bars, on the other hand, we'd happily skim from.)

His time with the traveling shows in the 1920s coincided with the crossword puzzle craze, and he got hooked. The puzzles had been appearing in papers since 1913, but the first crossword puzzle book came out in 1924 (it launched the publishing enterprise of young Richard Simon and Max Schuster) and became an instant hit. Thesaurus sales shot up. The Baltimore and Ohio Railroad outfitted all of its passenger trains with dictionaries. A man in New York was arrested for refusing to leave a restaurant until he'd finished his crossword puzzle. And Lyle started working them, scrunched in the passenger seat of the troupe's automobiles with his knees tucked under his chin. His pals in the Chase-Lister company called him "the great crossword pizzler of Omaha." This was to be a lifelong love. *The New York Times Magazine* was his and his alone in our household until he'd finished the Sunday puzzle, in ink.

ONE BIG CHALLENGE for any touring or stock company in those days was getting enough material. A touring rep company might do a different play every night for four or five nights; a stock company put on a different play each week. At the turn of the century, a lot of the companies had become dependent on play piracy. There was nothing new about the practice of secretively copying down plays, then selling them cheaply, in defiance of copyright. Some version of it had been going on since Shakespeare's time (when a less meticulous copyist transcribed the most famous line from *Hamlet* as "To be or not to be, / Aye, there's the point"). But at the end of the nineteenth century, the business had become organized and highly profitable.

The most "unblushing and enterprising" play pirate of the era, in the words of *The New York Dramatic Mirror*, was Alexander Byers, a businessman who operated out of a cramped office on LaSalle Street in Chicago, from which he dispatched stenographers to theaters all over the country to take verbatim notes on the dialogue and stage business in popular plays like *The Rose of the Ranch* and *The Girl of the Golden West*. In his office, he employed about twenty female typists who rendered the notes into scripts. Byers then sold the scripts, six for twenty-five dollars, to unscrupulous impresarios determined to avoid paying authors' royalties, and to small-town operators who may not have known they were breaking the law. It was evidently an efficient operation: in 1911, after federal marshals raided Byers's Chicago Manuscript Company, confiscating seven thousand manuscripts, *The New York Times* described the office as "not more than 20 feet square, and in this space were crowded the desks of the women employees as well as those of the officers of the company and the files of the plays."

As the raid showed, though, play pirates and the repertoire they peddled were on the defensive in the early twentieth century. In 1909, Congress passed a stricter amendment to the copyright law, which made both stenographers who copied plays without permission and dealers who sold them liable to fines and imprisonment. (Previously, only actors and managers who put on pirated plays had been punishable.) Byers and others like him changed their spots and became legitimate script brokers.

By the late 1910s and the 1920s, small-town audiences wanted something different anyway. For years they had been satisfied with the hoary chestnuts of repertory, or what was known as the "the blood-and-thunder circuit": endless iterations of *Uncle Tom's Cabin*, the temperance melodrama *Ten Nights in a Bar-Room*, or the British weepie about thwarted mother love, *East Lynne*. Plays like *The Old Homestead* that trafficked in nostalgia for the frontier or encouraged their audiences to congratulate themselves on not being city folk were popular, too. Increasingly, though, small-town audiences wanted plays that showcased the new manners and morals of the 1920s—the lives of women who smoked and drank and necked and wore their skirts short; the challenges of companionate marriage between two independent-minded young people—shows that brought big-city sizzle and spark to the local stage. If a play could be advertised as straight from New York, all the better. It was no longer good business to hide a show's Broadway imprimatur by rechristening it with a new title, as the play pirates did. *The Old Homestead* was out; *Flaming Women* was in.

In a way this was no surprise, for the social and sexual landscape of the 1920s was rapidly changing. Marriage rates were up, and people were marrying at younger ages. In 1890, the median age for men to marry was twenty-six, and for women, twenty-two; in 1920, the ages had fallen to twenty-four and twenty-one, respectively. The wider availability of effective contraception—condoms and diaphragms—was the key. Contraception permitted couples to postpone childbearing by means other than postponing marriage, and it encouraged them to expect mutual sexual satisfaction. For the first time, marriage manuals openly preached the importance of a happy sex life to a happy marriage. On the other hand, while the advice industry upheld the notion of companionate, sexually healthy marriage, it did not advocate economic independence or professional ambition for women. Feminism was a movement on the wane in the 1920s, and most men did not want their wives working outside the home. As the historian Paula Fass writes in her study of the decade's young people, they "seemed to believe in complete equality for women in the home but not outside it."

The 1920s gave rise to the first youth culture in the United States, to a succession of fads, and to the very notion of a fad. Peers exerted a new level of influence at a time when more and more young people were attending high school and college. Mass communications and national advertising meant that when a youth-driven fashion—raccoon coats or bobbed hair or mah-jongg—arrived on a campus somewhere, it was almost guaranteed to spread. The movies showed a world where lovemaking, ardent and artful, was at the center of life, and portrayed new techniques of seduction and arousal that young people, especially, learned to imitate. Manners and mores shifted in this way, too, and one result, writes Fass, "was a sexual revolution"—one that wasn't predicated on a sudden increase in sexual intercourse but on "new patterns of sexual play. The young evolved a code of sexual behavior that was, in effect, a middle ground between the no-sex-at-all taboo officially prescribed by the adult world and inculcated by their families, and their own burgeoning sexual interests and marital aspirations. To this dual purpose, youths elaborated two basic rituals of sexual interaction—dating and petting" (both nicely facilitated by the automobile and the movie theater). Dating was an innovation in that it meant pairing off rather than socializing with groups, and unlike courtship, was not necessarily supposed to end in marriage. Petting could be anything from a kiss to making out to fondling the breasts and genitals, any of which, as Fass writes, "would have automatically defined a woman as loose and disreputable in the nineteenth century. . . . In the twenties, to maintain one's position with peers, petting was permitted," and even encouraged for unmarried young people (petting parties were a real phenomenon), but intercourse was not.

It was, of course, the era of the flapper. Flapper style meant cutting your hair in a chin-length bob instead of maintaining the long, heavy tresses that had to be elaborately pinned atop your head in public. It meant wearing loose, short, drop-waisted dresses that allowed for freedom of movement and a hint of androgyny, and silk stockings that revealed the skin beneath, instead of wool or cotton. Flapper behavior meant feeling free to apply lipstick and smoke in public and to drink alcohol. One of the ironic effects of Prohibition, in fact, was to encourage women to drink alongside men, now that alcohol consumption had been moved from rough bars and other masculine enclaves to fashionable speakeasies and private cocktail parties, where women were freely invited. It meant pretending to be, or really being, flippantly hedonistic and insouciantly frank. It meant taking rebellious, sometimes childish pleasure in scandalizing the many authority figures who disapproved of you.

And scandalize they did. In Kansas City, a woman's six children were taken from her and placed in a Mennonite orphanage because her bobbed hair and flapperish attire had offended fellow citizens. School boards and hiring agencies banned teachers with short hair and skirts, or as the Eastern Teachers' Agency put it, teachers who were "giddily attired." Newspaper articles blamed suicides, divorces, and spikes in crime on bobbed hair and the looser morals that seemed to go with it. In 1922, when *The Literary Digest* asked college deans and high school principals, along with editors of religious weeklies and college papers, to offer their verdict on flappers and their fellows, the result was an article titled "The Case Against the Younger Generation." The editor of *The Lutheran* declared that "a spirit of libertinism is abroad among our youth. . . . Women paint and powder and drink and smoke, and become an easy prey to a certain class of well-groomed and well-fed high-livers." The dean of women at Gooding College in Idaho at least allowed that young people weren't entirely to blame. How could they be expected to rise above the conditions modern society had surrounded them with, "in the way of jazz music, modern dance-halls, public swimming pools, auto joy riding, luxury and freedom, the sensual and suggestive movies, where they learnt to see nakedness and where immorality does not seem so bad?"

It makes sense, of course, that the movies would be a vector for these new attitudes. Movies fetishized beauty, they seduced by close-up, they partook of the kind of castaway morality that characterized the Hollywood colony's early years. They invited spectators to swoon in the dark and to fit themselves, in their stirred up imaginations, into the arms of the lovers on screen. Even allowing for the exaggerated fretting about the effect of movies on youthful morals, there seems to be good evidence that people in general, and the young in particular, did indeed get ideas from them. The interviews with and essays by (mostly) University of Chicago students that were produced for the Payne Fund Studies, the first-ever investigation of the impact of the flickers on adolescents, are full of lively accounts of how the movies moved them. "No wonder girls of older days before the movies were so modest and bash-ful," one female student writes. "They never saw Clara Bow and Wil-liam Haines. They didn't know anything else but being modest and sweet. I think the movies have a great deal to do with present day so-called 'wildness.' If we didn't see such examples in the movies where would we get the idea of being 'hot'? We wouldn't. I know a fellow that (every time I'm with him) wants to neck. He wants to practice, I guess, but I have a sneaking suspicion that he got his method from the screen. It's so absolutely absurd. I get a kick out of watching him work up a passion—just like John Gilbert, but it doesn't mean a thing."

A male college junior offers this frank and charming assessment: "As this is a confidential paper I can say that the movies have done much to influence my behavior toward the opposite sex at the present. The hot love scenes in the pictures now get under my skin and I have the urge to re-enact them. Clara Bow is extremely attractive. Express-ing my sentiments in Anglo-Saxon 'She could put her shoes under my bed any time and be welcome.' Her pep and life seem to overwhelm me and I have a desire to be with her even though I know that is impossi-ble." Young people had learned through the movies, they said, how to feel disappointed by their own looks, gazing in the mirror with dissat-isfaction after an evening spent staring at the magical faces of Garbo or Valentino. They had learned how to behave in restaurants and nightclubs, how to deploy their sex appeal, how to pet. "The technique of making love to a girl received considerable of my attention," writes one earnest young man. "It was directly through the movies that I learned to kiss a girl on her ears, neck and cheeks, as well as on her mouth, in a close cuddle."

In the 1920s, plays of the sort my father was doing in the small towns and cities of the Midwest made an impression, too. They brought news of the modern. Sometimes the titles—*Up in Mabel's Room*, *Why Wives Go Wrong*, *Compromising Sally*—made the plays sound racier than they were. Tent show managers might put a play

One of the plays about modern marriage that Lyle starred in was
showing at this theater in St. Louis in 1930. Note that a movie
called Free Love *was playing next door. Just as on Broadway,*
which acquired the nickname the Great White Way because its
theater marquees were lit with so many electric bulbs, theaters
in smaller cities bejeweled themselves with thousands of lights.

with such a title on for just one night—the last night of the run—
allowing them to promote it all week and, as the theater historian
William Slout notes, giving "the audience a year to get over the
disappointment of finding nothing in the play to equal the shocking
title." Still, even that was something new: the idea that small-town

theatergoers of both sexes would pride themselves on seeing a show with a risqué title. And though the plays may not have been great—comparatively few survive in published form to judge—contemporary reviews make it clear that some did give a brisk airing to questions of love, sex, and the new morality.

A number of them, for instance, dealt forthrightly with the challenges of marriage for young couples—a subject of considerable interest, given the rash of young marriages. Jazz babies, many commentators worried, and with some reason, made difficult transitions to married life. They had been accustomed to a level of fun and freedom in their lives before marriage that previous generations, particularly of young women, had not. Wives often expected a higher standard of living than their husbands, and like the flapper wife in the popular novel of that name, longed for expensive face creams and beaded bags and speedy little roadsters when their husbands wanted them saving their pennies for a rump roast on Sundays. Moreover, expectations of marriage itself were higher. Marriage was alluring in theory, but in reality it could also be trying, especially for the young. Sex was now supposed to be a rewarding part of marriage for both partners; and movies had raised the stakes on erotic bliss. At the same time, husbands and wives were supposed to be friends, sharing an idealized intimacy as equals.

So a play like *New Toys*, which Lyle acted in with Bessie Robbins, struck a chord. *New Toys* was about "marriageitis," according to the Sheridan, Wyoming, *Post-Enterprise*. And "despite its domesticity, its aroma of cooking meals and crumbs on the carpet," it was "swift-moving and vivid," because it was "a cross-section of the turbulent second year of any young couple's married life. Will and Ruth have reached the stage where the rose of their romance is showing pale gray edges, where she sighs for a career, and he for adventure. His untidiness has begun to annoy her while he has a husbandly intolerance of cosmetics and ambition." The idea of newlyweds whose love is put to the test by money woes and the wife's ambition for the finer, funner things was a recurrent theme in these marriage plays, with the frequent motif of the wife "vamping" her husband or deploying baby talk to exact more cash or shimmy out of housework duties.

Some of the most popular touring plays punctured religious sanctimony and double standards. They both reflected and promoted the distaste for moral righteousness that characterized the liberal politics of the era, especially among the otherwise fairly apolitical young. Take a play like *Saintly Hypocrites and Honest Sinners*, which Lyle performed in several times with different companies, for it was widely and frequently produced. The play tells the story of a young minister newly ensconced at a church that is dominated by a man named Deacon Stromberg, who bullies the congregation with his supposed righteousness but turns out to be a double-crossing mortgage lender and a lecher. *Saintly Hypocrites and Honest Sinners* played, wrote one newspaper reviewer, like "an illustrated sermon against narrow-mindedness and bigotry. You sit in the audience and place the characters portrayed in your own church or your own neighborhood. You'll say to yourself, that's the way so-and-so acts." Reviewers and audiences loved this particular sermon. It was bracing to see the young minister's happy-go-lucky brother, "who carried his religion in his heart rather than on the lapel of his coat," treated as the hero of the piece, and to see young people portrayed as more humane and authentic in their misbehavior than their elders were in their sanctimony. A decade or two earlier, that would have been an unacceptable message for small-town American audiences, but by the early 1920s, they were lapping it up.

Then there were plays like *Flaming Youth* and *Our Dancing Mothers* that specifically offered audiences a glimpse of life among the gin-splashed fast set, "up-to-the-minute" stories about "the jazzy proclivities of the so-called best people," as an ad for a play Lyle did in Oklahoma City promised. There was *Charm*, which introduced the audiences to the vogue of learning charisma by means of a self-help book. There were crime stories that schooled audiences in the slang they'd need to know for all the gangster movies to come. (Reviewers of these plays would carefully set words like "inside job" and "moll" in quotation marks or italics.) There was a big crop of plays, many of which Lyle acted in, centered on women who gave birth outside marriage or, almost as naughty, toyed with the idea. *It's a Wise Child* was about a young woman who feigns pregnancy by an unknown lover to get out of her engagement to a respectable elderly man. (According to a paper in Buffalo, where Lyle starred in the play, "It made no concessions whatever to the stork myth.") *Cradle Call* was a Hollywood satire cum eugenic comedy about a well-brought-up young woman who decides to help advance the race by arranging to have a baby with a handsome movie actor she has picked out for the purpose: her intelligence plus his looks equal the perfect offspring. The dialogue, claimed the Philadelphia *Evening Bulletin*, was "saturated with suggestiveness, spice, and sexy innuendo." *Little Accident*, written by the Greenwich Village bohemian Floyd Dell, ended with the marriage of its erstwhile young lovers and new parents, but got its laughs along the way from knowing references to what one reviewer referred to as "the human gestation period."

In some ways, stage actors were more effective ambassadors for the new sophistication than screen actors because they were so much more accessible—glamorous but close at hand. This was particularly true when they were performing with stock companies as Lyle did in the late 1920s in Sioux Falls, Oklahoma City, Oakland, Columbus, Buffalo, Portland (Maine), Memphis, Lincoln, and Dallas—staying anywhere from a few weeks to a few months at a time. Under those circumstances you got to know the locals a bit—at least the matinee girls and stage-door Johnnies who came to all your performances. Lyle would model clothes for local department stores, turn up for charity events, accept invitations to join local lodges. "There's something homey and neighborly about a stock company," a writer for *The Buffalo News* observed. "The actors' dressing rooms are stampeded after a performance by admiring friends who 'knew them when' or come to welcome favorites of a former season. Here to stay several weeks, the players are as eager to make friends as is the audience to peer into the mysteries of the world backstage."

But stock actors were also like local representatives for modern, urban values and styles. Lyle's leading ladies, for instance, were mostly pert flapper types. There was Marion Sterley, who had short dark hair, a formidable nose, and a magnetic gaze. She excelled in roles like Patsy in *Patsy Steps Out*—"the go-and-get-him flapper in this joyous story of a girl who insists that 'no' is not an answer," as one reviewer enthused. Then there was Mary Kay Bell, a dainty ingenue with a madcap way about her that local papers played up. (She was probably the same Mary Bell who'd adorned her knees with references to the Scopes trial.) They loved it when she was seen "dashing about town in a recently acquired automobile she has christened Sappho." There was a Kentucky-born actress with the unlikely name Alney Alba who wowed audiences with her leopard coat, her brand-new bob, and her "slender, boyish figure." (Apparently she wowed Lyle, too, because he asked her to marry him. "I had a marrying complex" back then, he would tell a fan magazine a few years later. "I think I invited more women to marry me than any unattached male in the United States.") And there was Ione Hutaine, whom the newspapers portrayed as a carefree, bohemian type, a girl who was making up her own identity as she went along, in a way that seemed delightfully strange and new at the time. She'd been born Ione Hull, but she "just couldn't vibrate to it," as a reporter for a Buffalo paper put it. Then she took up the study of numerology. "She'd go about through the streets in the trolleys, trying to pick a name that would suit her personality. She went to bed exhausted one night, and in the morning Hutaine frolicked through her mind. Hutaine. It was perfect. Then she took her numerological chart and sure enough it clicked."

Lyle, too, promoted some cutting-edge tastes. His favorite reading matter, he told interviewers, was *The American Mercury*, the satirical magazine edited by H. L. Mencken. His favorite expression was

"Hi, kid." His "favorite pet" was "an animal cracker." When he was asked to choose the winner of a beauty contest in Oklahoma City, he said, he went with the one whose photograph showed her to be of what he called "the modern type of beauty," a young woman with a simple, boyish coiffure and a small frame. "All the girls are queens, however," he added gallantly.

He frequently pronounced himself a great fan of long-distance motoring and of aviation. In the summer of 1927, he was invited by a high school French teacher he'd been seeing to accompany her and her class on a trip to Europe, where he hoped to find work on the London stage. The London stage had no use for an actor from the American Midwest at that moment; it had plenty of actors of its own. But Lyle wasn't due to sail home on the *Leviathan* till August, so he found a room in London (at a hotel that charged extra for "dogs, electric lights and electric iron"), and went to plays at the Palladium, the London Hippodrome, and the Haymarket. One afternoon he made the trip from London to Paris on Imperial Airways, the first commercial aviation company in Britain, then only three years old. Regularly scheduled commercial flights for passengers were still a novelty in the late 1920s and would remain so until after World War II. The Imperial Airways brochure promised that "air stewards"—short young men or teenagers, since the confines were tight on these biplanes—would "point out places of interest en route, attend to the comfort of passengers and serve light refreshments from the buffet." Lyle kept the buffet menu, which offered a choice of "whiskey, brandy, soda, lager, ginger ale, lemonade or lemon squash," along with "plain or cheese biscuits." The cloud cover had been thick over the Channel and the pilot had flown below it, so low that Lyle could see people walking about on the decks of ships. Though he stayed in Paris long enough to sample the delights of the Folies Bergère, the Moulin Rouge, and the Opéra, the flight thrilled him more than any of them. "Despite Lindbergh," a newspaper interviewer quoted Lyle a few years later, "he believes Europe is outstripping us in passenger planes and safety flying." He is "an ardent believer in aviation." In Memphis, he told one of the local papers, he and his leading lady Marion Sterley liked to "sneak away to an airport and enjoy a spin in the clouds," courtesy of a local pilot. Lyle was photographed in a white suit with goggles and leather aviator cap atop his head, Marion standing nearby in a sporty knee-length skirt and high-heeled T-strap shoes. "Nothing beats an airplane ride for thrills, for an outing to take one's mind off his or her cares and to freshen the body and mind," was the composite answer of the two.

But Lyle was not quite as sophisticated as he sometimes sounded. In 1929, he had a chance to try out in New York for the unsubtly named play *Sex*, which had landed its author, producer, and star, Mae West, in jail for ten days on an obscenity charge two years earlier. *Sex* was the story of a madam in Montreal's red-light district, and its raunchy, burlesque-style humor and working-class slang, combined with its star's decidedly unflapperesque surfeit of curves, had created a furor among critics, who generally despised it. As one reviewer chided, "West cavorts her own sex about the stage in one of the most reviling exhibits allowed public display." Still, West biographer Marybeth Hamilton writes, the play was a success with a certain kind of audience. It "became what we would term a 'cult' hit, drawing young, self-conscious patrons—*Variety* called them 'jaded weisenheimers'—who were bemused by the novelty of real 'dirt' on Broadway." West had made the most of the publicity that came with her jailing—boasting to reporters, for instance, that she had worn silk underpants each day of her incarceration—and two years later, she had enough financial backing to take the show on a road tour, opening in Chicago. That was what Lyle was auditioning for.

"There was still a lot of corn in me, even though I'd been in the business in little midwestern plays for years," Lyle would recall many years later. "My agent sent me over to audition. Mae was sitting out in the audience watching us; there were about ten of us up for it—all young guys auditioning for the role of a sailor." West was sitting with

Jim Timony, the Irish Catholic lawyer who had been her lover, became her business manager, and would be her friend all her life—a beefy, big-hearted guy with a cane, as my father remembered him. "She also had a stage manager whom she picked up in England. He had a cockney accent and he knew all Mae's lines. I was very serious, I needed a job, and there was this guy playing Mae West's part with a cockney accent! And it's a seduction scene! I was holding the script, reading the lines, and he had his arm around me because that's the way it was in the scene. Finally it was down to four or five guys and I was one of them, and I had to play the scene with the great Mae West. Well, it was too much for a guy from Nebraska. I could hardly wait to get the hell out of there!" West was overwhelming, in a way that none of his younger, less powerful, more lithesome leading ladies had been. She ran the show, and she radiated sexual aggression. "My agent wanted to know what happened and I lied to him. I said, 'Oh, I don't think she liked me, Mr. Brown. Besides, I gotta go back home to Nebraska; my mother is very sick.' So I hid out for about a week or so and then I called and said, 'Well, I'm back in town, Mr. Brown.' And he said, 'Oh, gee, you're too late. Miss West wanted you for the play, but they're already headed for Chicago.'" Some years later, Lyle would be playing what he called a "seductee" of West's again, but by then he'd shed enough corn to handle it.

Hollywood in the 1920s, though, seemed too distant and capricious a prospect for him to take much interest in. Movies were all well and good, but he loved a live audience. When Lyle was twenty, the distinguished silent film actor Henry B. Walthall, who had played big roles in a number of D. W. Griffith movies, including *The Birth of a Nation*, had come to Omaha to do a show. Ed Henderson and Lyle went to meet him backstage, and they played a round of golf together. Walthall took a shine to Lyle, and insisted on writing him a letter of introduction to the producer Louis B. Mayer. "I have a keen interest in his trying the motion picture field of acting," Walthall wrote of Lyle.

"He has had considerable stage experience with stock companies throughout the middle west, is wholesome, and unspoiled by ego." Lyle did meet with Mayer on a trip to Los Angeles that he took with his grandmother, but nothing came of it.

In 1928, though, when Lyle was visiting New York, he and the actor Pat O'Brien were hired to do an early sound movie shot on a Warner Brothers soundstage in Brooklyn. Warner Brothers, the pioneering studio when it came to sound, had started producing short movies using a system called Vitaphone, in which records were made to accompany the films, then played on phonographs hooked up to movie projectors in the theaters. There were plenty of skeptics, including the father of motion pictures himself, Thomas Edison: "No, I don't think the talking moving picture will ever be successful in the United States," he declared in 1927. "Americans prefer silent drama. They are accustomed to the moving picture as it is and they will never get enthusiastic over any voices being mingled in. Yes, there will be a novelty to it for a little while, but the glitter will soon wear off and the movie fans will cry for silence or a little orchestra music." The Warner brothers, especially Sam, disagreed. The studio actually made hundreds of Vitaphone shorts between 1926 and 1930, most of them depicting vaudeville acts and jazz and classical concerts.

The sound movie Lyle made in Brooklyn was actually a narrative, though it did highlight the singing of the chanteuse at its center. It was a gangster-loves-nightclub-singer two-reeler called *The Nightingale*, which Pat O'Brien remembered as "a two-day stint in a rapid celluloid adventure, shot with the speed of an Indian arrow." They were paid $25 a day. The microphones were hidden in vases and behind curtains. Mikes suspended on long arms, or booms, were not in use till about 1930. So the actors on *The Nightingale*, as on other early sound films, had to project their voices toward the hidden microphones, getting near enough to them without seeming to be talking into a vase.

In any case, Lyle was still feeling so committed to a future onstage that in 1929 he started his own theater company, The Talbot Players, in Memphis, a city where he had enjoyed previous success in stock. The local press was enthusiastic about the venture—Lyle's youth, his ambition to bring the latest Broadway fare to Memphis, his astuteness in picking his actresses "with an eye towards masculine appeal"—all boded well. The Memphis *Commercial Appeal* boasted that Lyle had toured 6,200 miles, looking at twelve companies and thirty-two plays before hiring his players. He may indeed have cast his net that far and wide, but several of the players he ended up with were people he knew well—his former leading lady and fellow aviation enthusiast Marion Sterley and his own parents, Ed and Anna Henderson. (Anna was delighted to be working with Ed and Lyle again: "They're as alike as two peas—both overgrown boys with a penchant for teasing," she told a reporter, "but I don't mind a bit.") There would be a ten-piece orchestra, Homer Guenette and his Syncopators, playing between acts. Audiences in those days still expected full scenery changes, complete with rotations of heavy furniture (minimalist sets that merely suggested a locale were a long way off) that took a while, so you needed something to entertain people while they waited. And Lyle put out an earnest, folksy-sounding pledge in his programs: "I'm mighty happy to be back with you again. Really, it's just like being home. . . . Please remember we are here for one purpose: to please and entertain you. Will appreciate helpful suggestions and constructive criticism."

His timing, though, was lousy. The Talbot Players opened Labor Day weekend with a zippy romantic comedy, *This Thing Called Love*. But it was an especially hot late summer in Memphis, and the theater was sticky and airless. Then the company had to move venues in the middle of the run after some of the financial backing fell through; my father's business sense was never too keen. The stagehands went on strike for three days, during which time the actors shifted scenery, and when the stagehands returned, they demanded and got the full salary for the days they'd missed. *Laff That Off* was the next play on the

The company poses in front of the Lyceum Theatre in Memphis.
Lyle is at the center. His stepmother, Anna, is in the checked coat,
and his father, Ed, looking dapper, is second from right.

schedule, and "that title surely does strike home," Lyle told a reporter. The actors stayed loyal—and Lyle and his parents split a single salary—but it wasn't enough.

By then, live theater was facing unprecedented competition from the new talking pictures. *The Jazz Singer*, the first feature film with synchronized dialogue, had debuted in New York in 1927 and was still playing two years later. Sound was rough, it was true. When a movie called *Glorious Betsy* opened in New York and L.A. in 1928, a director who saw it noted that "poor Dolores Costello's excellent voice came out at times as a deep rich baritone, while Conrad Nagel thundered in a sub-human bass, like immortal love declaiming through the Holland Tunnel. When they whispered together confidentially, the resulting sounds took me back to the old woodshed of my boyhood where the hired man wielded a mean saw." But audiences were crazy for talkies; it was clear, by then, that Thomas Edison had been wrong and that early sound-booster Sam Warner had been right. And in Memphis, Lyle was feeling the aftershock.

The Commercial Appeal was sympathetic to The Talbot Players and sniffy about the talkies: "It happens that at this time Memphis is disposed to give its attention to the new vogue, the talking picture. The public's enthusiasm for the talking picture is not to be construed as evidence that the art of the stage is dead here, however. The talkie must go far in its development to win a name for art. The only conclusion to be drawn is that Mr. Talbot and his company came to Memphis at an unfortunate time." But this was the very problem: the more theater was seen as art and film as entertainment, the smaller the audience for theater would be. The kinds of plays that Lyle had been doing were not art, and until the talkies, people seemed to know that. The theater they saw in their hometowns seemed to them like glitzy, racy, less than serious stuff. Now, though, it was gaining the good-for-you label of high art—surely the kiss of death. When another Memphis paper opined that people should be more interested in art such as the Players purveyed and less interested in "epicurean pleasures," you knew the Players were doomed. The movies did not kill theater, of course, but they did with a few exceptions kill the touring tent theater and local stock companies where my father had learned to act. Regional theater never recovered its former kudzu-like vigor, and from the 1920s on, the undisputed capital of the stage was New York.

The theater in Memphis went dark October 24 and The Talbot Players disbanded. The stock market crashed one week later, which surely would have dealt the final blow anyway. The players themselves had been loyal to the end. "I've never seen such splendid spirit by any manager or any company," one of the actors wrote in an article for the Actors' Equity magazine, "and all Memphis agrees it's a disgrace to permit such a company to disband, but the truth is we can't offer the amount of entertainment that talkie houses do at their price and still exist." He went on: "The entire run has been hectic but we'd all go through it again for Lysle," for "no manager could have treated his players better," and with such a "perfect spirit of Equity."

Lyle got himself hired as a leading man for brief runs in Greenwich, Connecticut, and Boston, and then in 1930 for a full season in Dallas. Somewhere along the way he married a young actress he'd met in New York; her name was Elaine Melchior, and she had played a

Lyle in Dallas, but ready for Hollywood.

small part in *The Nightingale*. They drove around together and had a lot of laughs—that was how Lyle described the courtship later—and were married two months after they met. "We somehow just drifted into it," he told a fan magazine in the early 1930s—and evidently out of it more or less the same way. "There was nothing dramatic about it. We never quarreled and are excellent friends even today. Maybe if we'd had more money or our respective stage jobs had not continually separated us, we might have made a go of it. I'm quite sure ours was one of the politest marriages on record." They were married in August 1930, divorced less than two years later, and scarcely lived together in between.

In Dallas, the theater company went belly-up and the owner absconded, leaving Lyle with $5. But as he would say later, "In my life, just when I have been on the verge of giving up, a telegram arrived," and this time it was from an agent named Arthur Landau, asking if he could come to Hollywood for a screen test. A talent scout had seen Lyle on the Dallas stage and sent back a very intriguing report. To his keen embarrassment, Lyle had to tell Landau that he was too broke even to pay the price of a train ticket; Landau wired him the money. The Depression loomed, the theater outside New York was fading from the picture, but Lyle had been saved by a telegram, shoved genially along to the next era of entertainment history and the one place in the country that was making it.

Chapter 4

─◦⊶◦─

HOORAY FOR
HOLLYWOOD

The trip from Dallas took two days, and on the afternoon of the second day, as the train wound down through the San Gabriel Mountains, Hollywood was still a winking gem too far away to get the measure of. From the train window, Lyle gazed out at miles of sagebrush and yucca. In the distance, pine trees clung to serried ranks of brown mountains stippled with snow. Then, as the train descended toward Los Angeles, and shaggy date palms replaced pine trees, he began to notice what people always noticed about the fringes of L.A. in those days: its raffish, cockeyed air, its sinuous neon signs and motley collection of billboards. "On the main highways leading into Los Angeles," Carey McWilliams would write of the 1930s, "the roadside signs tell the story of the city's improvised economy: canary farms, artificial pools for trout fishing, rabbit fryers, dogs at stud, grass-shack eating huts, psychic mediums, real-estate offices, filling stations, vacant-lot circuses, more rabbit farms, roadside peddlers, hobby shops, hemstitching storefront evangelists, bicycles to rent, and frogs for sale." And Lyle noticed—how could anybody from Nebraska not—that the sky in early February was a bright enameled blue, that the streets, even the dingy ones down near the La Grande train station, were festooned with pepper trees and acacias, that the empty lots were vibrant with poppies and wild mustard, birds-of-paradise and red bottlebrush.

When Lyle arrived in L.A. at seven-thirty in the evening, his new agent, Arthur Landau, met him at the station. To Lyle's chagrin, he had to confess that he didn't have the money for a hotel, just as he was thanking the older man for the price of the train ticket. But Landau was ready for that. He told Lyle he'd stake him a place to stay, and sent him over to the Ravenswood Apartments on North Rossmore, an Art Deco monolith where you could rent by the week. In a day or so, the agency would send him to Warner Brothers Studios for a screen test. In the meantime, he could have a look around.

In some ways, Hollywood in the early 1930s was still a small town. It had first been settled in the 1880s by a wealthy couple from Topeka, Kansas, Harvey and Daeida Wilcox. The Wilcoxes had purchased 160 acres of land, where they tended fig and apricot orchards and attracted a community of God-fearing teetotalers like themselves. In 1903, when Hollywood officially became a city, it was a sleepy, dusty, pious little burg that prohibited both alcohol and factories. One industry its city fathers could not keep out—could hardly have anticipated, in fact—was the movies. In 1907, the Selig Polyscope Company of Chicago had started producing movies in nearby Edendale (now Silver Lake). In 1909, D. W. Griffith began coming to Los Angeles from New York every winter with his company. The new arrivals built open-air wooden platforms to film on; and when interiors were needed— a parlor, or a police precinct, or an artists' garret—they draped canvas over the tops to block the telltale natural light. In 1911, the first studio opened in Hollywood itself, and three years later, Cecil B. DeMille, who had set up shop in an old livery stable on Vine Street, filmed *The Squaw Man*, the first feature-length movie made in Hollywood.

Southern California's attractions for the moviemakers were obvious: year-round sunshine, without the tropical cloudbursts of a climate such as Florida's, and a rich variety of outdoor settings from mountains and deserts to trolley-filled downtown streets and empty beaches. But these were not the only advantages. Unions had made no headway in Los Angeles and labor was cheap. Moreover, the independent studios, including those of DeMille, Griffith, and Samuel Goldwyn, were eager to put a country's length between themselves and Thomas Edison's Motion Picture Patents Company. In New York and New Jersey, in the very early days of the film industry, private detectives and process servers rendered moviemaking a risky business for anyone who didn't use cameras under Edison's license. Hired toughs were known to shoot holes in cameras, break equipment, and hijack cars from filmmakers who resisted the Edison Trust's monopoly.

To its new transplants, Los Angeles felt remote—from the patent's trust enforcers, from their own and the country's past, from the towns and cities they'd grown up in that would take them days, maybe weeks, in that era before passenger airplanes to get back to. The locals began calling the picture people a "colony," and that was fitting. Like colonists, they stuck together, and impressed the native population as peculiar and threatening. If the locals were sometimes amused by how the picture people took over a street for a Keystone Kops chase or a romantic rescue on horseback, that didn't mean they wanted anything to do with the wastrels. Signs for rooms to rent in Hollywood often specified: "No actors or dogs."

By the time my father arrived there in 1932, the movies had effectively taken over Hollywood, turned it into a company town, spun it into a word that stood simultaneously for a place (perhaps its least significant meaning), an industry, and a state of mind. Yet its small-town soul had not entirely disappeared. Coyote and deer no longer wandered down from the mountains into the streets, nor did goats and pigs occupy the muddy streets as they had in the 1910s. But there were no buildings more than four stories high, and the streets that surrounded Hollywood Boulevard were packed with modest frame houses and little stucco bungalows painted in the pastel shades of candy hearts. Hollywood Boulevard was a kind of main street with regular stops, where movie people ran into one another—the tailor where my father once had to wait outside while Greta Garbo was being fitted for a man's suit; the Pickwick Bookshop, whose Russian immigrant owner had named it in honor of the Dickens character; the ice cream parlor C.C. Brown's, which served, in chilled tin bowls, the hot fudge sundaes invented there; the restaurant Musso & Frank, where actors and writers ate flannel cakes for breakfast, Welsh rarebit or smelts or a simple chop, the kind Philip Marlowe liked, for dinner; the wide front porch of the old Hollywood Hotel, where once upon a time in the silent era nearly all the actors had lived.

The business of the movies and the people it attracted made Hollywood a uniquely fanciful and sensual place. Even on a first, quick visit, the feeling was hard to miss. The seductive weather lured people outside, and so did the impulse for self-display that had impelled many of them to Hollywood in the first place. One visiting writer noted that if you drove on Sunset Boulevard near Gower, where the so-called Poverty Row studios turned out B movies, you'd often spot "cowboys in chaps and sombreros and extra girls in the traditional slacks and dark glasses, bright kerchiefs protecting their freshly waved hair, lunch[ing] at corner hot dog stands or gossip[ing] and talk[ing] shop." The young hero of Aldous Huxley's Hollywood novel from the late 1930s, *After Many a Summer Dies the Swan*, is transfixed on his first car ride through Los Angeles by the "enormous" "dark-green and gold" citrus groves, by the mountains "trac[ing] their uninterpretable graph of boom and slump," by the welter of billboards ("CLASSY EATS. MILE

HIGH CONES / JESUS SAVES / HAMBURGERS"), but also by the fleeting glimpse of a young woman "doing her shopping in a hydrangea-blue strapless bathing suit, platinum curls, and a black fur jacket."

Visitors were struck by the abundance of good-looking people and the casual display of bare shoulders, arms, legs. Lillian Symes, a writer for *Harper's Monthly*, tartly analyzed the anthropology of beauty in a 1931 dispatch from Los Angeles. "For nearly twenty years," Symes wrote, "the motion picture industry has been attracting to the section a goodly portion of the world's most beautiful human specimens. A symmetrical, wide-planed face and a perfect figure, or a clean-cut arrow-collar chin were for many years the prime requisites of the industry. Their possessors flocked to the Southwest by the thousands. Many achieved places for themselves in the films. Many more failed to do so, but stayed anyway; for there are few places in the world more comfortable to live in. Natural selection did the rest. The sunbronzed, half-nude babies playing upon the steps of stucco bungalows or on wide green lawns, the bare-headed, bare-limbed children dashing about the streets—a trifle too permanently waved, too briefly French-frocked perhaps—all tell the tale. And to keep up the adult quota of perfection, a fresh supply of pulchritude arriving on every train."

The movies left a mark on architecture as well as bodies. There were the palace-like movie theaters—magnificent fantasias on exotic themes like Sid Grauman's Chinese and Egyptian theaters, both built in the 1920s. But, after all, movie palaces could be found in other big cities as well. What Los Angeles had that other cities did not was, first, a fantastical mélange of houses built for its stars—imitation French châteaus, sprawling Spanish-style haciendas, columned replicas of stately plantation homes, Moorish castles with pointed arches, stone courtyards made musical by splashing fountains, and terraced gardens punctuated by topiary. In its commercial buildings, Los Angeles had a penchant for stores and restaurants in the shape of coffeepots, puppies, ice cream freezers, zeppelins, windmills, and owls, as though the city were one big rebus poem. The original Brown Derby restaurant, that much beloved Hollywood institution, was, of course, a very large brown derby. "EAT IN THE HAT," read the modest afterthought of a neon sign that sat atop it. A chain of cafeterias called Clifton's designed its restaurants to look like South Seas paradises or redwood groves; one had a re-creation of the Garden of Gethsemane in the basement, where patrons could go to pray and where they might see the owner's standard poodle kneeling as though praying, as he'd been trained to do. "Imagination," noted the California writer Frank Fenton, "had run around this city like an artistic child. Somewhere it showed a pure and lovely talent. Somewhere it was crude and humorously grotesque." Actually, the city's examples of playfully literal architecture, its giant doughnuts and derbies and dragons, probably served a purpose. In a new city full of new arrivals, they helped people navigate, establish places to meet. Come to Los Angeles and it would quickly offer you a treasure map. Thanks to the pioneering work of a Danish immigrant, Otto K. Olesen, who called himself the "King of Illumination," it became a city crisscrossed at night by klieg lights—brilliant arrows to toyland. Their silvery beams swept the skies over Hollywood to announce movie premieres, yes, but also just regular stuff: the opening of hamburger joints, Spanish dance schools, Maytag appliance shops, or a revival rally led by the evangelist Aimee Semple McPherson. By day, a city that was essentially a desert kept its lawns green with the novel *swish-swish* of sprinklers.

Even in the 1930s, there were people complaining about the fakery, the superficiality, the disorienting sense of impermanence, the preening, the juvenile—as the critics saw it—enthusiasm for throwing together disparate architectural styles. The writer James M. Cain, a transplant from the Mid-Atlantic, complained of Los Angeles in 1933: "The thing simply won't add up. . . . To me, life takes on a dreadful vacuity here, and I am going to have a hard time indicting it. Frankly,

The Sphinx realty office: L.A.'s commercial architecture was often fanciful.
The Bruce Torrence Hollywood Photograph Collection

don't know exactly what it is that I miss." For the literary critic Edmund Wilson, life there was imbued with the "hollow feeling" of a "troll-nest where everything is out in the open instead of being underground." Lillian Symes titled her Los Angeles dispatch "The Beautiful and the Dumb."

My father loved Los Angeles instantly. The sunshine, the bougainvillea, the banana trees, the ersatz castles, the girls in their strapless bathing suits, all of it. He was thirty years old, and he had been on the road since he was seventeen, a love-the-town-you're-in (what

A premiere at Grauman's Chinese Theatre, 1930.
The Bruce Torrence Hollywood Photograph Collection

was it called again?), pack-your-trunk-in-ten-minutes, sleep-sitting-up-on-the-train, give-the-folks-what-they-came-for Middle American trouper. But here? Here he could stay.

If only they'd let him. If only he could snag a job in motion pictures. But it was 1932, three years into the Depression, and a job was no easy thing to get ahold of, in the picture industry or any other. (A reputable agent inviting you out to Hollywood meant you would almost certainly get a screen test, but it was no guarantee that a studio would sign you.) In 1930, four million people had been out of work; by 1931 that number had doubled; in 1933, the worst year of the Depression, it would climb to almost 13 million—or 25 percent of the nation's workforce. Coming on the heels of the prosperous 1920s, this was a crushing, emotionally dislocating new reality. Nearly everyone, including my father, knew somebody who'd been rendered destitute. Millions of savings accounts had been blotted out, tens of thousands of businesses had gone belly-up. And though people tend to think of the movie industry as the Depression's singular island of good fortune, in the early 1930s, at least, it hardly looked like that. Radio was the only part of the entertainment industry that flourished throughout the Depression. The price of radios had fallen—from about $90 in 1930 to about half that two years later—and once you had one, it served up basically free entertainment; you didn't need to fill your car with gas or pay a subway fare or have a decent dress to put on.

In 1929, the movie industry had been enjoying unprecedented success. The novelty of talkies had attracted record numbers of moviegoers: some 80 million per week in 1930. But within a year, ticket sales began to fall. By 1932, they had tumbled to 55 million a week. Virtually all the studios suffered millions of dollars in lost profits. Warner Brothers alone went from posting profits of $14.5 million in 1929 to reporting losses of $8 million in 1931. In a frantic bid to win back customers, the movie theaters, most of which were owned by the studios, began innovating new enticements. They offered double features, cut ticket prices from thirty cents to twenty, gave away china, stockings, turkeys, and cash prizes, eliminated the ushers who had been de rigueur at the movie palaces in the 1920s, and began selling popcorn and candy, a practice they had never before allowed because it was associated with carnivals and burlesque while the movie palaces strove for elegance. (Thanks to the Depression—and the motion picture exhibitors' response to it—the popcorn harvest in the United States grew from 5 million pounds in 1934 to 100 million in 1940.) In March 1933, when FDR declared a four-day bank holiday, the studios administered a 50 percent pay cut, to last eight weeks, for everyone earning more than $50 a week. *Variety* asked plaintively whether "the moving picture will ever again know the popularity of those peaks it reached in the silent era and then again with sound." A *Los Angeles Times* headline from September 1934 was gloomier still: "Hollywood's 'Boom Days' Gone Forever."

In fact, by 1935 the industry would right itself. Movies would become the beloved escape from Depression dreariness we've often heard they were. The schemes for luring ticket buyers into the theaters paid off, the advent of screwball comedies along with a spate of better, or at least more family-friendly movies—costume dramas, swashbucklers, classy biopics—proved irresistible to audiences. And as *Variety* pointed out, the repeal of Prohibition in 1933 helped, too: "In many cities there had been no downtown life to speak of for the 13 years of the Great Mistake, whereas repeal had the effect of immediately bringing life to hotels, restaurants and other places in such downtown zones where the larger theaters are located." The picture industry had taken a beating, but it got back on its feet much quicker than just about any other.

Even without the Depression, the odds of making it in the picture business—especially as a performer—were always long. That warning had been coming out of Hollywood for at least a decade before my father arrived. Books that ostensibly offered practical advice on how to make it in the movies were often laden with cautionary tales. A 1924 example called *What Chance Have I in Hollywood?* mixed stringent practical advice (Don't come to Hollywood without $2,000 to live on and be prepared for a hundred turndowns from casting directors before you got your first job) with tidbits about the attractions of Southern California (Strawberries year-round! A system called the cafeteria!) and the dire, titillating stories of girls who lost their way there. Consider the fate of one "Mamie Swamp," who left "Cottage Grove, Kansas," seeking stardom in L.A. but ended up as a prostitute in Baja. (It was always worse, in these tales, to suffer such a fate in Mexico.) In the 1920s, mail leaving Hollywood came with a sticker that read: "TELL YOUR FRIENDS. Don't try to break into the Movies in Hollywood

until you have obtained FULL, FRANK, AND DEPENDABLE INFORMA-
TION from the Hollywood CHAMBER OF COMMERCE . . . IT MAY SAVE
DISAPPOINTMENTS."

The Los Angeles papers regularly ran stories about the dashed
dreams of aspirants to stardom. It was almost a journalistic genre unto
itself: the flip side of the overnight discovery story, and in its way, just
as much of a testament to the power of Hollywood. The dashed dream
stories made the successes look all the gleamier and dreamier against
the murk of their sadness. In the early 1930s, the ultimate such story
was that of Peg Entwistle, a New York stage actress who had relocated
to California in 1929 in the hope of making it big in the pictures. Now
that talkies had arrived, a theatrical career was a more prestigious calling card in Hollywood than it had been in the silent era, and Entwistle, who was blond, blue-eyed, and pretty, as well as stage-trained and
British-born, was at first hopeful. In Los Angeles, she acted in a play
with Humphrey Bogart and Billie Burke, the future good witch
Glinda, for which she received respectful notices. But by 1932, Entwistle had landed only one bit role in a movie, a lurid female ensemble piece
called *Thirteen Women*, about a vengeful murderess on a mission to kill
her former sorority sisters. RKO, the studio she had signed with,
dropped her contract. She was deeply discouraged about her career—
and who knows what else; it's always the shattered Hollywood dreams
we hear about in such cases—so much so that she decided to take her
own life.

She chose a singularly dramatic method. One September morning in 1932, Entwistle climbed into the steep, scrub-covered Hollywood Hills, to the base of the sign that then read "HOLLYWOODLAND."
The fifty-foot-high letters, outlined at night in a blaze of lightbulbs,
had been erected to advertise a housing development in the hills, but in
the eight years they'd stood there, they had already become a widely
recognized symbol of moviedom. Entwistle climbed a ladder that had
been left behind by workmen, and leapt from the top of the H. A hiker

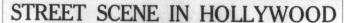

STREET SCENE IN HOLLYWOOD

Thousands buck the line on every call issued for a few movie picture extras. This is a sample of the customary massed assault on the employment bureaus resulting from an ad for a very few men and women to work in an insignificant scene. The wage is meagre for a day or night of hard work.

Don't Try To Break Into The Movies
IN HOLLYWOOD

Until You Have Obtained <u>Full, Frank and Dependable</u> Information

FROM THE

HOLLYWOOD CHAMBER OF COMMERCE
(Hollywood's Great Community Organization)

It May Save Disappointments

Out of 100,000 Persons Who Started at the Bottom of the Screen's Ladder of Fame
ONLY FIVE REACHED THE TOP

A warning for dreamers.
The Bruce Torrence Hollywood Photograph Collection

found her body later that day. Entwistle, the *Los Angeles Times* surmised, could no longer "endure what she apparently had regarded as the ignominy of defeat in her encounter with fickle filmland."

Usually the cautionary articles were less tragic, but in their matter-of-fact way, no less discouraging. The movies themselves—with their silver-nitrate shimmer, their slithering satin evening gowns, their Art Deco splendor, their ardent lovers, their luminous close-ups—kept fueling the desires that were so often thwarted. The story lines—take, say, the shy girl plucked from the chorus and launched into the stratosphere when the show's star breaks a leg—did their part, too. A person could get ideas.

Still, the warnings kept coming, and they probably exerted a dual influence: they piqued the fascination of regular filmgoers with no intention of trying their luck in Hollywood—imagine a town so freakishly overrun with beautiful people, a town buzzing with the exotic phenomenon of female ambition!—and at the same time discouraged a few aspirants to film fame. "Beauty-Filled Movie Village Has but Few Chances for Unknowns," read a 1933 headline in the Los Angeles *Herald-Express*. "Casting directors are rather frantic about it. They feel that if they don't send out warnings that Hollywood is tough pickings, that theirs is a sin of omission and the world will presume them to be double-eyed, deceiving pied-pipers and hundreds more stranded girls will miss regular meals." With fewer jobs available at drugstores and diners for the displaced "belles from back home," the situation in the early years of the Depression was even more discouraging. "Only one girl out of every 400 has a slight chance of being a motion-picture chorus girl!" declared the lede of a *Los Angeles Times* article from 1934, which was based on an interview with a Hollywood dance director named Dave Gould. "According to Gould, between 4500 and 5000 girls invade Hollywood annually seeking fame in films. A scant 2 percent of this number become bit or featured players. The remainder usually try the chorus, with small chance for success." But the pedantic Gould didn't stop throwing cold water. "In fact," he stressed, "their chances are even less than the cold figures indicate because already there are approximately 500 beautiful girls in filmland of proven dancing talent and beauty." Some of the articles must have been the products of studio publicity machines that detected a nice angle in playing up the hunger for stardom—but there was some truth to them, too: it really was a colossal gamble.

Actors had it a little easier. Perhaps there were marginally fewer of them. But there were enough. Talent scouts working for Paramount in New York in the mid-1930s claimed that they took a look at 1,500 performers a week, male and female, of whom ultimately about twenty-five a year were brought to Hollywood. MGM reportedly auditioned 5,000 people a year, of whom 1 percent were given screen tests, and only a few of those were signed. Even the men and women working as extras, who since the mid-1920s had been reporting to Central Casting, where they registered by age and type, had a struggle securing jobs. Only thirty of Central Casting's 17,000 extras worked more than three days in 1930.

Lyle knew most of this—if not the numbers, then the anecdotes. Even with his something-will-turn-up optimism to buoy him, like a Ping-Pong ball bouncing around on a column of air, his pennilessness at the moment made him nervous. Maybe that's why on the train from Dallas, he'd lost his voice, and had to greet his agent at the station in tones barely above a whisper. "Here I was on my way to talking pictures on borrowed money from a man I'd never seen," my father recalled, "and I lost my voice." Landau, the agent, was a kind man, but this was ridiculous. *An actor who couldn't talk? In the talkies? Please.* Still, Landau's instinctive courtliness—and the sincere hope that he wasn't wasting his money—kicked in as he dropped Lyle off, and he offered some words of encouragement that the younger man clung to. It was just "a train cold," or "nerves," but in either case, Lyle wasn't to think about it; his voice would come back.

Lyle wandered through the streets near the Ravenswood the next day, subsisting on black coffee and liverwurst sandwiches from the lunch counter down the street. He smiled and pointed when he wanted something so as not to strain the precious vocal cords. He hummed experimentally to himself. The air was clear and dry. Sprinklers tossed their rainbow-beaded garlands of water over the lawns of stucco apartment courts. The grass was springy beneath his feet. Gradually, his voice, that burnished baritone instrument he so relied on, returned to him. He sang the song he'd been humming: "If I never had a cent, / I'd be rich as Rockefeller, / gold dust at my feet / on the sunny side of the street." The next afternoon, forty-eight hours after he'd arrived in L.A., he found himself on a Warner Brothers soundstage about to make a screen test.

One thing Lyle felt certain of: The material he had chosen for his test was perfect. It was a scene from a play he'd done in Dallas, *Louder, Please.* His role was that of Herbert White, a brash and charming young publicity man for a movie studio who runs afoul of the studio's deeply unpleasant head of production. Both men are crazy about the same actress, and she is keen on the publicity man and forever having to fend off the production head. The dialogue was quippy, and the pace was modern and frenetic, with a lot of ringing phones and shouting. And Lyle had the part wired. In Dallas, he'd gotten great reviews for his portrayal, with one of the papers calling his performance "a striking individual triumph for this deft young player who wooed, lied, ranted, raved, cajoled, implored, threatened and almost never left the stage during the evening." The same review noted that the play's author, Norman Krasna, who had himself toiled in Hollywood, "must have been fired, for nothing short of a dischargee's grudge could have inspired the healthy, boisterous, infectious malice of his composition. He writes directly for your anti-cinema bloodlust, tearing limb from limb the entire system of screen publicity and exposing to your sadistic delight the incredibly genuine processes of synthetic fame." Did it cross Lyle's mind that somebody *in* Hollywood might take offense at such an acid portrait *of* Hollywood? No, it did not. The studio in the play was called Criterion Pictures, after all, and heck, there was no such studio! Lyle didn't really know much about Hollywood in those days.

When the test was done, the director walked over and said, "Talbot, that scene you did, was that from a play called *Louder, Please*?" "Yes, yes," said Lyle, pleased and surprised that the man recognized the scene. The director spoke slowly, as though Lyle himself might be slow: "You don't know the story of that play?" "No," said Lyle, beginning to feel a faint tom-tom of alarm in his chest, "I don't know anything about it at all." "Well," said the director, "that play is kind of taboo on the lot here. The man you referred to as 'King' in there, the one you're having a conflict with, is the head of this studio—Darryl Zanuck."

Louder, Please was indeed a play à clef. Krasna had worked in the publicity department at Warner Brothers before turning to playwriting and then screenwriting. Herbert White was a thinly veiled version of Hubert Voight, a legendary movie PR man. And Kendall King, who is described in the dramatis personae as "No good. Our heavy. A pretty big man. Foppish. Rattish," was a thinly veiled version of Darryl Zanuck, the head of production at Warner Brothers. Zanuck, as it happened, was a small-town Nebraska boy like Lyle. He had been born in Wahoo, Nebraska, in 1902, which made him the exact same age as my father, and like my father, he'd had scant formal education. He'd started in the movie industry in the 1920s, writing stories for Rin Tin Tin. Now he was on his way to becoming one of the most powerful men in Hollywood. He would leave Warner Brothers the next year to found his own studio, Twentieth Century Films. Though brilliant at what he did, he was also domineering, crude, and womanizing. "I don't think," said the director, "uh, this test is something you'd want Mr. Zanuck to see."

Lyle swallowed. "Can't we do it over?" But the director was already looking down at his clipboard, scanning the names of the other hopefuls he was to film that day. He had made up his mind: as sorry as he kind of felt for him, he was done with this yokel. "No," he told Lyle. "I have no authority to do it over. We have other tests to make. I can't do anything for you."

"My God, I was then in the depths," my father would tell a journalist years later. He got on the phone to the assistant in his agent's office, an ambitious young guy named Lew Schreiber. Schreiber was the type who hitches his wagon to a big macher's star and rides it for all it's worth. He had been Al Jolson's gofer, and when Jolson didn't need him anymore, he'd set his sights on making himself indispensable to Darryl Zanuck. His bid for the big man's favor was very much a work in progress. For now, Schreiber was working in the office of Arthur Landau, Lyle's agent, and was Lyle's handler that day. "How was the test?" Schreiber asked, rat-a-tat-tat, as soon as he heard Lyle's voice. "Well, gee, Mr. Schreiber. I don't know. I may have made a big boo-boo here." That was the way Lyle talked. Schreiber was a young guy, but he was still "Mister." And other than an occasional "hell" or "damn," Lyle was not given to profanity or even to coarse language. A couple was "having a love affair," even if the reference was clearly to a one-time sex act, as in "he opened the door, and there they were having a love affair right there on the floor." People were "sons-of-guns," or they "loused things up." Sometimes, more childishly, they "made a boo-boo."

On the other end of the line, Schreiber's voice took on a little metal. He said, "Oh yeah? What happened?" Lyle told him, "Well, the scene I did was from that play, Norman Krasna's play."

"Louder, Please?"

"Yes."

"What did you do that for?"

"I don't know. You said to take a scene from a comedy and—"

"Well, you didn't say you were going to do *that* comedy!"

Lyle stammered something about how he wasn't thinking about the content of the play so much as he was about the rhythm of the scene, how fast-paced and funny it was.

Schreiber said "What the hell!" He was sputtering now, ready to wash his hands of Lyle right then and there. Then his voice grew calmer, but it was an ominous calm, and he told Lyle he'd really done it, screwed them both. And he hung up.

"I was terribly upset," my father recalled, "so I went to the office on the corner of Vine and Sunset. Mr. Landau was in and I went to him and I was really low. I told him the story.

"He was such a sweet man. He said, 'Lyle, don't worry. Tomorrow, I'll take you to Paramount, to other studios.'" Landau must have figured Warner Brothers was a lost cause now, but with any luck, word of Lyle's accidental chutzpah wouldn't get around to the other studios.

What happened next back at Warners, Lyle heard about only after the fact. Zanuck had gone in to see the screen tests. He was in a good mood, striding in wearing riding britches, swinging the polo mallet he sometimes carried around the lot since he'd taken up the sport. When the test came on, Zanuck watched it all the way through—and, as my father heard it told later, he laughed. He didn't say a thing about the play the scene was from; he just laughed. "Maybe," my father used to speculate, "he thought, here was this actor who was naive enough or stupid enough or *something* enough to do that kind of scene for his screen test, for gosh sakes, and for whatever reason that particular day that struck him as funny."

Lyle had another lucky charm that day: the presence in the screening room of the director William Wellman. Directors and producers would often stop by when screen tests were being shown to check out the new prospects, and that day the visitor happened to be Wellman, a gifted director who in 1927 had made *Wings*, the first film to win an Academy Award for best picture, and who would go on to make the original version of *A Star Is Born*, *Nothing Sacred*, *Beau Geste*, and *The Story of G.I. Joe*, among many other films in a long career. At Warner Brothers, in the early 1930s, he was one of the masters of the taut, socially conscious little dramas for which the studio was famous. He was also notoriously tough, allergic to authority, a man whose bluster and cussedness had earned him the nickname "Wild Bill." When World War I broke out, Wellman had volunteered for the Lafayette

Flying Corps, a squadron of American pilots who flew missions for France before the United States entered the war. They were, to use the kind of language he would have, brave sons of bitches flying rickety-ass biplanes. Wellman earned the Croix de Guerre, was shot down by antiaircraft fire, and ended up more or less patched together, with a serious limp and a metal plate in his head. While working as a flight instructor in San Diego after the war, he'd made up his mind that he wanted to get into the film business. His plan, according to his biographer, Frank Thompson, was to don his uniform and medals, fly his plane up to Los Angeles, and land on the polo field at the Pickfair estate. He'd heard that the actor Douglas Fairbanks, Sr., whom he'd met by chance some years before, was hosting a party with this wife, Mary Pickford, that day. The stunt worked; Fairbanks was so impressed with Wellman's nerve that he got him a job in pictures, first acting, which Wellman hated, then directing.

Though he was a handsome man, Wellman reminded one young actor who worked with him of Popeye the Sailor—scowling, pipe-smoking, with a wild shock of hair. Yet for all his gruffness, he had a soft side: he doted on his wife and seven children and spoke with warm emotion of the men he'd flown with in World War I. As scrappy as he was in his attitude toward studio bosses and toward actors he thought of as prima donnas, he was also intensely loyal, especially to people lower down in the pecking order. Once, when the studio installed a coffee machine on the set of one of his movies, obliging the crew to pay for coffee that had formerly been free, Wellman went on a mad tear and rolled the offending machine off the soundstage and into the men's room. He told a studio official who came down to investigate that he'd throw his ass in there, too, and Jack Warner's next. The crew got their free coffee back the next day.

That day in the screening room, as he watched my father charge through the lines from *Louder, Please*, Wild Bill turned to Zanuck and said, "Hey if you sign this guy, I want him for my next picture." "Yeah,"

Zanuck replied. "We're gonna sign him. If you want him, you got him." The film Wellman had in mind was called *Love Is a Racket*. It was Lyle's first Hollywood picture, and in it he played a suave gangster—the kind of role he would go on to do often—opposite Douglas Fairbanks, Jr. Directing a languorous, appraising gaze at a young woman he's just met, Lyle delivers the best line in the picture: "If I felt half as good as you looked, I'd go out and kill myself while it lasted." About a week into the shooting, Wellman ambled over to Lyle and clapped him on the back. "You know, Talbot. You're really something. You're terrific." Lyle was flattered, thinking Wild Bill was referring to his work in the film. "Thanks, Mr. Wellman," he said eagerly. "I'm enjoying working with you, too."

"Oh," said Wellman, with another bearish swat. "You're okay in the part. But you're really *something*. You guys from the theater. You know what I mean." He went on in this vein, as Lyle nodded politely, ever more puzzled. "That test of yours." Oh, thought Lyle, *that*. "You really gave it to Zanuck. Good for you." Wellman, the indefatigable tweaker of authority, loved the idea that Lyle was the same breed. The fact that Lyle was not was no discouragement.

My father would go on to work with Wild Bill on two other films. They got along, though Wellman couldn't resist setting him up, as he often did with actors, in the interest of filming a good manly brawl. On a football movie called *College Coach*, shot at the Rose Bowl in the middle of a hot summer, Wellman had brought in football players from USC, UCLA, and Stanford. In one scene, the opposing team was meant to tackle Lyle, playing a cocky college football star who was supposed to emerge out of the pileup triumphant, holding the football. Wellman, my father said, took the football players aside and told them, "Don't worry about tackling Talbot, because he used to play football in Nebraska"—not true, of course. "He was a helluva player there, so he can take care of himself." The trouble was, said my father, "these real football players can't pull punches anyway. How are you going to get a big tackle to pull his punch? He's in there showing off, getting paid to play football for a picture. So when this scene comes, they tackle me, and I don't come up. I'm out cold. Wellman's yelling, 'Hey Talbot, Talbot, goddamn it, Talbot, get up.'" Talbot did, but only after being carried off the field in a stretcher and having his ribs taped.

For a fight scene between my father and the actor George Brent, rivals for Barbara Stanwyck's favor in a movie called *The Purchase Price*, Wellman took each man aside and conspiratorially told him to give it all he had. Lyle was a new guy on the lot, he reminded Brent, and might not even be around that long. Brent was a big star, he told Lyle, but that was precisely why Lyle had to clock him, show what he was made of. Brent and Lyle compared stories and decided there'd be no unnecessary roughness that day. Maybe Wellman's psychological manhandling paid off anyway: it's a good fight scene, with both men reeling in convincingly punch-drunk fashion, and Lyle ended up with a bleeding scalp when he slumped against the set's plywood wall where a nail head was sticking out. "Wellman, of course, loved it," recalled my father. "Real blood."

Through it all, Wellman continued to insist that Lyle had done the *Louder, Please* screen test on purpose to stick it to Zanuck. One day, after Lyle felt a bit more comfortable with Wellman, he tried to level with him: "Bill, look, you don't think I would be stupid enough to do that, do you? I was broke, I didn't have a sou. I could have been blackballed in Hollywood the rest of my life."

"Sure, Lyle, have it your way," Wellman said, smiling.

It made sense that the first role Lyle would play in Hollywood was a gangster. Warner Brothers, the studio where he had, to his surprise, landed on his feet, the studio that would be his home for most of the decade, was also the home to more gangster movies, prison pictures, and topical social dramas than any other studio. In 1932, Darryl Zanuck drafted an article for *The Hollywood Reporter* in which he described the Warners specialty as the "headline type of screen story. . . . Somewhere in its makeup it must have the punch and smash that would entitle it to be a headline on the front page of any successful metropolitan daily." The studio run by the four feuding brothers, the sons of a Jewish cobbler from Poland, secured its future by becoming the first studio to embrace sound. And the sound that the studio gloried in was that of the modern city and its rougher streets: squealing tires, drumrolls of gunfire, the wisecracking, sped-up dialogue of shyster lawyers, smart-ass newspapermen, gangsters, molls, chorines, chiselers, chanteuses, and street kids. All the studios could turn out a little of everything, but each had its signature style, too. MGM was the glossy, prestige studio, celebrated for its adaptations of plays, its women's pictures, and its firmament of highly paid stars. Paramount had a particular flair for comedy, from the Marx Brothers to Ernst Lubitsch. Universal was the specialist in horror films like *Frankenstein* and *Dracula*. And Warner Brothers was the studio that turned out movies like *The Public Enemy, Little Caesar, Five Star Final, Wild Boys of the Road, I Am a Fugitive from a Chain Gang*, and *20,000 Years in Sing Sing.*

A Warner Brothers screenwriter named Jerry Wald remembered being called in by his bosses and given the instructions that "we could not compete with Metro and their tremendous stable of stars, so we had to go after the stories, topical ones, not typical ones. The stories became the stars. . . . We would say, 't-t-t: timely, topical, and not typical'—that was our slogan. . . . We were all searching frantically, looking through papers for story ideas."

With marching orders like these, Warner Brothers became the studio that most often depicted working people and underdogs, and that dealt—especially in movies such as Wellman's *Wild Boys of the Road* and *Heroes for Sale*—the most forthrightly with the pain of the Depression. Neal Gabler in his book *An Empire of Their Own* argues that the distinctive Warner Brothers amalgam of "energy, suspicion, gloom, iconoclasm and liberalism" grew out of the particular

Warner Brothers Studios in Burbank, 1935.
The Bruce Torrence Hollywood Photograph Collection

experience of the brothers themselves. They saw themselves as restless outsiders in American culture and, furthermore, were fiercely divided—by profound personality differences and by their very different commitments to Judaism. Of all the Jewish movie moguls, the Warners, Gabler contends, offered the version of America that was the "least assimilative. Reflecting the divisions within the family itself, what Warner Brothers films acknowledged was that there were deep divisions—divisions of class, of roots, of style, of religion, of values."

It was a vision that depended on directors like Wellman and Mervyn LeRoy, who could make pictures that were fast-moving and blunt, without a lot of close-ups, and with a flair for fight scenes. Or like the Hungarian-born director Michael Curtiz, who was at ease with a shadowy, menacing aesthetic that anticipated film noir. It depended, too, on actors like Cagney and Bogart, because they were so good at embodying city-boy characters who were, as Gabler describes them, "low-born, cocky and self-sufficient," and showed "what one can accomplish against all the odds and outside the traditions." And it depended on a group of writers the studio kept on the lot in the early 1930s, many of whom were raffish types who'd kicked around Chicago or New York and gotten an earful of urban argot and cynical storytelling.

John Bright, for instance, was a young reporter who had written a muckraking, Menckenesque biography of a spectacularly corrupt Chicago mayor. Soon thereafter, he teamed up with a friend named Jacob Glasmon, a Polish-born druggist ten years his senior in whose store Bright had once worked as a soda jerk. Glasmon had picked up a lot of stories at the drugstore—it was on the west side of Chicago and frequented by gangsters—and he had a keen memory for incident and a good ear for street talk. But he couldn't write a lick. For his part, Bright was a gifted if somewhat purple writer, with a fierce social conscience. One day Glasmon rigged a fire at his pharmacy, collected $500 in insurance, and with Bright took a monthlong journey by ship, through the Panama Canal, to Los Angeles. Along the way, they enjoyed themselves thoroughly at various ports of call and arrived in L.A. on Black Thursday 1929 dead broke.

Mining their knowledge of the Chicago underworld, they immediately went to work on a novel they called *Beer and Blood*. "In the ensuing months," Bright later wrote, "it became a rough go—desperate Grubb Street with the unremitting California sunshine as mockery. We learned the bitter pragmatism of hock: suits and suitcases, wristwatches, my new wife's dresses and shoes; we even found a hole-in-the-wall to pawn socks if they didn't smell. Almost everything went but the precious second-hand typewriter." They couldn't find a publisher for their novel, but through a friend, they managed to sell the screen rights for *Beer and Blood* to Warner Brothers, who paid them $1,800 and offered them $100 a week to work for the studio. They "leaped like spawning tuna" at the chance, Bright recalled.

In a burst of sentimental nostalgia for his Jewish family, Glasmon changed his first name to the Yiddish diminutive Kubec. The title of their story was changed somewhere along the way, too. Darryl Zanuck got very enthused about the project, and though Bright regarded him as "vain and imperious, a tin-pot Mussolini," he admired the fact that Zanuck, "indigenous to Hollywood, and with no baggage from any other art form," knew "movies must *move*." Wild Bill Wellman was pegged to direct. The tall, boyish actor who was meant to play the lead was replaced by the pug-faced, wound-up James Cagney. And the movie that emerged in 1931—*The Public Enemy*—turned out to be remarkable then and now for its harshness with its characters, its iconic lines and moments (the scene in which Cagney shoves a grapefruit into Mae Clarke's face; Cagney muttering, "I ain't so tough," after he's been fatally shot; the final scenes in which his gauze-wrapped corpse topples through his front door), and its willingness to poke around in the sociological seedbed of crime. At Warners, especially under Zanuck, "the writers were respected," John Bright once said. "Treated like shit, but respected."

Another writer on the lot whose own story was more colorful than any he concocted was Wilson Mizner, a singular character who'd done a little of everything, very little of it reputable, on his way to a screenwriting gig at Warner Brothers in the early 1930s. With his brother, Addison, Mizner had swindled miners during the Klondike gold rush, bilked wealthy investors during the Florida land boom, and sold overpriced Guatemalan relics. On his own, he'd married a millionairess nineteen years his senior, written plays, and run a hotel in New York (a sign he hung in the elevator read "GUESTS MUST CARRY OUT THEIR OWN DEAD"). He had been an opium addict and a prizefight manager and in Hollywood had ended up as a co-owner and manager of the Brown Derby restaurant. Through it all, remarked his biographer, Alva Johnston, "his hope of finding new suckers to trim never deserted him."

A friend had gotten Mizner a job as a writer during the first flush of sound films. Though employed by Warner Brothers, Mizner was, in Johnston's words, "a writer who never wrote." Not that he didn't contribute. It was just that his "method of collaboration was unique. At the studio he slept most of the time in a huge red plush chair, which so closely resembled an archiepiscopal throne that he was called the Archbishop. When Mizner's literary partners needed some lines or ideas from him, they would shake him gently and start him talking. After half an hour or so, they would order him back to sleep while they sat down at their typewriters and worked up his conversation into script form." And his conversation was worth it. Among the bons mots attributed to Mizner: "Be nice to people on the way up because you'll meet the same people on the way down," "Treat a whore like a lady and a lady like a whore," and "Faith is a wonderful thing, but doubt gets you an education." Actually, my personal favorite is his assessment of his job: "Working for Warner Brothers is like fucking a porcupine: it's a hundred pricks against one."

At Warner Brothers in the early 1930s, Darryl Zanuck's modus operandi was to move quickly to buy hot properties, stories that were talked about and controversial. In 1931, the studio bought the rights to *I Am a Fugitive from a Chain Gang*, the memoir of a World War I veteran, Robert E. Burns, who had been caught up in a minor robbery and dispatched into the hell of Georgia's prison-gang system. The studio lost no time turning it into a fine, and very bleak, movie. My father remembered that Warners hid Burns on the lot—he was still a wanted man—ordering in meals for him while he consulted on the film. Zanuck snatched up Warden Lewis Lawes's bestselling account of the progressive reforms he'd introduced at Sing Sing prison in upstate New York, *20,000 Years in Sing Sing*. And by the end of the 1930s, Warners was on to the most topical story of all: the rise of Nazism. In 1939, the studio bought the rights to a book called *The Nazi Spy Conspiracy in America*, written by an FBI agent who had helped crack a Nazi spy ring within a German-American organization. The Warners took a drubbing for it: the German chargé d'affaires in Los Angeles issued a formal protest; isolationists in Congress sputtered about the malign influence of immigrants in Hollywood; Nazi sympathizers burned down a theater in Milwaukee where the movie *Confessions of a Nazi Spy* was playing.

Warners also had a reputation for being cheap and fast. "MGM was the studio that spent," recalled one Warner Brothers executive at the time. "It was a studio of white telephones. Warners had black telephones"—the basic model, nothing extra. The studio was so notoriously penny-pinching that Harry Warner himself was known to go around turning off the lights in the bathrooms. (And players like Cagney, Bette Davis, and even my father waged regular skirmishes over their low-balled salaries.) Writers, as James Cagney recalled, "were pressed to crank out their stuff by the yard . . . doing the best they could under perpetual rush-rush conditions." For many years, this reputation seemed to undermine appreciation of the films themselves. Even Jack Warner wondered in a 1934 memo to Zanuck's successor Hal Wallis whether "we are cutting our pictures too fast and making them too snappy—you can't tell though, maybe we are right." But in the last couple of decades, those snappy pictures have been rediscovered and admired—in large part for their brusque energy. As the film critic Andrew Sarris wrote, "Movie for movie, Warners was the most reliable source of entertainment through the thirties and forties, even though it was clearly the most budget-conscious of them all." To Sarris, "the razor-sharp cutting and frantic pacing look inspired to the point of absurdism. Not for Warners were the longueurs of MGM and the polish of Paramount. A Warners B picture seldom ran more than seventy minutes. MGM and Paramount Production values padded their Bs to the eighty- and ninety-minute mark without adding anything of substance or originality."

It was a shooting schedule that certainly shaped my father's life. Lyle, like all the contract players at Warner Brothers, worked all the time. He made nine movies in 1932, twelve in 1933. He worked six days a week, often twelve hours a day, sometimes acting in two or three pictures at a time. He'd ride his bicycle between soundstages, carrying two or three scripts in the front basket for pictures he was currently acting in, and two or three in the rear basket for pictures he was signed up to make. "Each studio was a kingdom unto itself," Lyle recalled years later. "Each one had its number of players; we had probably sixty actors under contract at Warner Brothers. We were all called stars. You weren't a movie actor; you were a movie star. You practically lived at the studio; it was like your home. You had your own dressing room and your own chairs with your name on them. If there were any personal things to take care of—like when you got a traffic ticket, and probably up to murder—the studio would take care of it." It was cozy in its way, but it could also be oppressive, as my father would find within a few years. At first, though, and with the Depression casting its shadow, the steady work was a tremendous relief.

Chapter 5

❧❦❧

GANGSTERS, GRIFTERS, AND GOLD DIGGERS

For many years after my father's death and long into my adulthood, most of the first movies he made with Warner Brothers were very hard to find. They were pre-Code movies, produced before July 1934, when the motion picture industry was strong-armed into strictly enforcing the moral strictures it had agreed to four years earlier. In the 1960s and 1970s when I was growing up, those movies were considered too racy for television. Even when I was in college and graduate school in the 1980s, going to revival houses and film festivals in Berkeley and San Francisco, Cambridge and Boston, it was rare to see a pre-Code film. With the exception of a handful of the great gangster movies like *The Public Enemy* and *Scarface*, early Marx Brothers movies, and the occasional Busby Berkeley musical, the films of the early 1930s were terra incognita. Many of them had been out of circulation since after their first run, languishing in studio vaults or carefully preserved in university archives, seen only by the hardest-core movie nerds.

When I discovered those movies, my father's and others, from the early 1930s, I wanted to know where they'd been all my life. I was hardly alone in my curiosity. It wasn't that they were such great examples of cinematic art, though a few were. It was that they were so different from the Hollywood movies that came after them, ragged and breathless and tough, studded with references to subjects like lesbianism and dope addiction that people my age tended to think our forebears scarcely knew let alone talked about. It was like opening a trunk in your grandparents' attic expecting to find family albums full of sepia-toned portraits and discovering a bunch of raunchy magazines instead.

And so I read everything I could find—luckily quite a bit of scholarship has come out since the early 1990s—about the story of the pre-Code era. The first thing that strikes you when you start to delve into it is the rather startling fact that movies, unlike other American art forms, were subject to legal censorship for much of their history. In 1915, the Supreme Court ruled that "the exhibition of moving pictures is a business, pure and simple, originated and conducted for profit"—and therefore exempt from First Amendment protection. Not until 1952, when the Court reversed itself and ruled that movies were, in fact, "a significant medium for the communication of ideas," were they granted free speech protections. Movie industry *self*-censorship remained in effect—though in dwindling force—till the adoption of the alphabet ratings system in 1968.

By the early 1920s, Americans recognized that movies represented a new and unprecedented phenomenon in entertainment. Unlike many other forms of art or amusement, movies were consumed by people of all ages and social classes, in small towns and big cities alike; their appeal was visceral and often overwhelming; they had the power to shape, and often inflate, people's expectations of beauty, sexuality, family relationships, self-fulfillment. Many Americans would have agreed that some control had to be exerted over such a force or it would inundate them, washing away some of their most dearly held assumptions and values. The question was: Who would exert that control, and on what authority? In 1934, moviemakers and the forces that wanted to censor them reached a settlement that would prove politically durable and artistically fruitful. But it was a struggle to get there, one that revealed the cultural divide between Hollywood and much of the rest of the country. And that struggle left behind odd and intriguing traces in the form of pre-Code films.

The Code that the industry adopted in 1930 was both a high-minded, philosophical statement about the power and duty of film to promote moral values and a prim and particular checklist of forbidden words and images. It opened with general principles: "No picture shall be produced which will lower the moral standards of those who see it. Hence, the sympathy of the audience shall never be thrown to the side of crime, wrongdoing, evil or sin." "Correct standards of life, subject only to the requirements of drama and entertainment, shall be presented." "Law, natural or human, shall not be ridiculed, nor shall sympathy be created for its violation." The Code's authors wanted audiences to be led inexorably to the proper conclusions. Hence, "no plot should be so constructed so as to leave the question of right or wrong in doubt or fogged." Bad guys, in other words, could not get away with it.

Under "obscenity and profanity," the Code prohibited a raft of colorful slang, and even sounds: "chippie" and "fairy"; "God, Lord, Jesus, Christ" ("unless used reverently"); "hot" ("as applied to a woman"); "goose" ("in a vulgar sense"); "toilet gags"; Bronx cheers and raspberries. (Words more outré than those—"fuck" or "shit" or their derivatives, for example—were so beyond the pale as to need no addressing.) It completely forbid the presentation of some things: the illegal drug trade; most kidnapping; miscegenation (specifically between blacks and whites); nudity; "excessive" kissing and "lustful embraces"; "sex perversion" or hints of it; allusions to abortion, venereal disease, or birth control; scenes of childbirth; and the presentation of ministers of

religion as comical or villainous characters. Brutality and gruesome-
ness were to be kept to a minimum, and there could be no flaunting
of guns by gangsters, no details showing how a crime was committed, and no scenes wherein agents of the law died at the hands of
criminals.

Other dicey matters could be broached, but only with extreme
caution. Adultery, if it had to be presented at all, could not be presented
as attractive, alluring, or justified, and could not be treated as a laughing matter. Rape could never be more than suggested, and "then only
when essential for the plot." The court system could not be presented
as unjust, though an individual court might be. Bedrooms could be
shown but not in comedies. (The infamous use of twin beds for husbands and wives in Hollywood pictures of the Golden Age was not
actually dictated by the Code; it was a concession to the British market.) The Code acknowledged that "scenes of passion are sometimes
necessary to the plot. However they should appear only when necessary and not as an added stimulus to the emotions of the audience."
(How such scenes, played halfway competently by beautiful actors and
actresses, would not stimulate *some* emotion is a bit of a head-scratcher.)
"Pure love, the love of a man for a woman permitted by the law of God
and man, is the rightful subject of plots. The passion arising from this
love is not the subject for plots." Drinking was to be kept to the absolute minimum necessary for the story. Scenes of undressing—a favorite
ploy of late 1920s and early 1930s movies—were to be avoided. Dances
of the type known as the Kooch or the Can-Can were a no-no.

All in all, the Code was a pretty good précis of what conservative,
middle-class, mostly white Americans considered nice or nasty in the
1930s, a reliable map of conventional sensitivities and prejudices. It
was also a representative document of its times in that its authors could
invoke terms like "decent society" and "correct entertainment," and a
general, unspoken agreement about what constitutes vulgarity, without worrying about backlash or misunderstanding. It's both a record

of the comparative ease of building a consensus on what people should and should not see in their popular entertainment—imagine trying to do that today—and a reminder of whom the consensus left out without asking.

From March 1930 to July 1934, though this grand moral plan was formally in place, its enforcement was much weaker than it would be afterward. When the Motion Picture Production Code office made recommendations for cuts, producers frequently ignored them or negotiated compromises that favored raciness. The movies that came out of that period, now known by the slight misnomer "pre-Code," have a distinctive feel to them. They are more cynical than anything before film noir in the 1940s, more irreverent than many movies before the 1960s. They're pumped full of what my grandparents used to call "fresh talk"—smart-alecky slang and vinegary put-downs. They are more matter-of-fact about sex, and particularly about its use as a tradable commodity for women, than most movies that came after them, at least until the end of the Code era; and despite the warnings of the Code and the fact that Prohibition was in effect till 1933, they are awash in alcohol. They accommodate broad ethnic stereotypes but also an easy sense of immigrant cultures bumping up against one another in prickly familiarity; in pre-Code movies, especially those by Warner Brothers, you could hear Yiddish words like *goniff* and *shiksa* coming from characters who were Jewish and those who were not. Pre-Code movies are steeped in the struggles of the Depression, peopled with characters who skitter along the edge of flat-out penury and who scam without shame and with few sentimental plays for our sympathy, characters who work all the angles with a verve that just barely varnishes their desperation.

Yet as dark as some of them are, pre-Code movies can also be brightly, brassily vulgar. "Am I gonna stink pretty!" shouts an ebullient James Cagney, as he soaks in a scented bath in *Picture Snatcher*. In *The Purchase Price*, a gaggle of ribald mail-order brides whoop it up as they look at photographs of their future husbands. "You know what they say about men with bushy eyebrows and a long nose?" says one, pointedly brandishing the banana she's eating. "Oh, Queenie," hoots her companion. "I can tell you've been married before!" "What's wrong with you?" a woman asks her unhappy gal pal in *Bed of Roses*. "You look like you had a bad pickle." The pre-Code era produced only a few really great talking pictures—*The Public Enemy, I Am a Fugitive from a Chain Gang, Duck Soup*. But many more have a rough energy that draws you in and rattles your teeth like a fast ride over potholed city streets.

The story of Hollywood, the Code and the pre-Code, goes back to the 1910s, when across the country, states and cities began setting up their own censorship boards to review movies and make cuts before the pictures could be shown in their jurisdictions. The boards varied in what they most cared about. New York and Chicago went hard on depictions of official corruption. By contrast, as the screenwriter Courtney Terrett noted, censorship in Maryland, Virginia, Kansas, and Ohio had "been concerned principally with the moral flavor of pictures. Kansas censors could view with equanimity a scene showing a New York copper getting his lumps from some hoodlums, but grow frothy around the lips at the most delicate suggestion that human beings ever climb into bed for any purpose other than sleeping." Pennsylvania was notoriously strict across the board on politics and on morals, and on any allusions to pregnancy or childbearing.

Local censorship was a costly nuisance for the studios. They had to pay a fee when the boards made cuts, the movies came back to them as damaged goods with bits hacked out, and some movies couldn't be shown at all in some parts of the country. The edicts were inconsistent and, for the producers, maddening. But they were also legal; the Supreme Court had authorized them with its 1915 ruling.

Over time, though, tensions developed along the seams of this patchwork system. The censorship boards, and the church and women's groups that supported them, increasingly saw themselves as locked in battle with a business willing to put just about anything on screen in order to lure audiences. They saw themselves as upholding American values—though it would be more accurate to describe them as small-town Protestant values—that an industry run largely by Jewish immigrants from big cities was all too willing to flout. Anti-Semitism would prove to be a remarkably persistent thread in the Hollywood censorship story. A Mrs. Rufus Gibbs, of the Citizens League of Maryland for Better Motion Pictures, put it this way: "Motion Pictures are already controlled by a little group of men who are without moral standards; for the most part composed of agnostic Jews, who as a class are becoming a great moral menace to this country, and who have no sense of obligation to the youth of the Nation." The early 1920s was a moment of anti-immigrant panic—the resurgent KKK was particularly focused on immigration, for instance—and the anti-film crusade battened off such sentiments and fed them in turn.

Still, the censorship system might have stayed more or less in equilibrium if not for the Hollywood scandals of 1921–1922, which gave a major boost to the forces that wanted to see national censorship of the movies. What they were now learning about Hollywood convinced its critics that it was indeed a roiling cesspool of iniquity, and that its denizens could hardly be trusted to clean up their act without the sol vents and scrub brushes provided by more virtuous citizens. The most notorious case was that of Roscoe "Fatty" Arbuckle, a bulky and beloved silent-era comedian. On Labor Day weekend, 1921, Arbuckle hosted a wild party at the St. Francis Hotel in San Francisco. A few days later, one guest, a twenty-six-year-old actress named Virginia Rappe, died of peritonitis resulting from a ruptured bladder. Arbuckle was charged with manslaughter, and though he was never found guilty of anything—even after three trials—rumors persisted that he had caused Rappe's death. The reigning, rather dubious theory was that, as large as he was, and as sexually perverse as he was imagined to be, he had somehow fatally injured Rappe while having sex with her.

Subsequent investigations of the case have revealed just how flimsy it was: the allegations against Arbuckle had been made by a woman who was a professional blackmailer and procurer of girls for parties; the unfortunate Rappe had a history of medical problems, and may have been suffering from complications of the several abortions she had undergone; and the San Francisco D.A. who prosecuted Arbuckle was a grandstanding type who "had tried the case," as one film historian put it, "on practically no evidence, as an anti-Southern California vice crusade." The third jury to hear Arbuckle's case even apologized to the moonfaced comedian, saying, "We feel a great injustice has been done to him. . . . Roscoe Arbuckle is entirely innocent and free of blame." Still, the scandal, eagerly stoked by the Hearst newspapers, transfixed the anti-Hollywood constituency and ruined Arbuckle, who could not find acting work again and whose films were pulled from circulation. (His friends in Hollywood helped him to get some directing jobs, which he took under the pseudonym Will B. Goode.)

In the wake of the Arbuckle case, a new wave of anti-Hollywood rhetoric drew on the notion that actors didn't know how to behave themselves because most of them had come from the lower classes. They were like overindulged, ill-bred children, stuffing themselves with gooey sweets and stomping all over propriety. "At Hollywood, Calif., is a colony of these people, where debauchery, riotous living, drunkenness, ribaldry, dissipation, free love, seem to be conspicuous," declared Senator Henry Lee Myers of Montana on the floor of Congress. "Many of these 'stars,' it is reported, were formerly bartenders, butcher boys, sopers, swampers, variety actors and actresses, who may have earned $10 or $20 a week, and some of whom are now paid, it is said, salaries of something like $5,000 a month or more."

In January 1922, the studios turned to Will Hays, Warren Harding's postmaster general, to help them save their reputation and reassure their Wall Street investors. Hays's official title was president of the Motion Picture Producers and Distributors of America (MPPDA), a newly formed trade association. He was popularly known, though, as the movie czar (or by some wags as the Czar of all the Rushes), and his office as the Hays Office. Hays was a skinny, jug-eared native of Sullivan, Indiana—a conservative Republican, a teetotaler, and an elder in the Presbyterian church. But he was also good-humored (he asked photographers to take his picture with "an ear-reduction lens") and pragmatic, and he got a few things done quickly that were very helpful from a public relations point of view. He saw to it that studios included morals clauses in their contracts with performers, ensuring they could fire any who got caught up in scandals. He persuaded studio publicity departments to muffle the tales of sybaritic luxury that Hollywood stars enjoyed; and for a time, the studios dutifully pumped out home movies of stars like Marion Davies (the mistress of the media titan William Randolph Hearst) dusting her living room, or Alma Rubens (a beautiful dope addict) chatting sedately with her aged mother. He tried to do something about the problem of would-be actresses stranded in Hollywood, prey to hunger and vice—a problem much fretted about in the 1920s—by establishing Central Casting to help register extras and monitor their treatment.

Meanwhile, two more scandals convinced the producers they were lucky to have Hays in place. In February 1922, William Desmond Taylor, a natty, lush-living director, was murdered in his home on Alvarado Street. Taylor had been having an affair with two actresses—the ingenue Mary Miles Minter and the comedienne Mabel Normand, and possibly with Minter's mother as well—when he was found dead of a bullet wound to the back of the head. Both the actresses were suspects for a time, but the crime was never solved.

And in late 1922, the wife of the athletic young matinee idol Wallace Reid publically confirmed the rumor that Reid was addicted to narcotics. A month later, the actor died in a sanatorium where he was trying to kick the habit. Reid's story, unlike Arbuckle's or Taylor's, was treated with some sympathy in the press. Mrs. Reid told reporters

Will Hays, Hollywood's savior?

that her husband had become addicted after he'd been involved in a train accident while making a film in 1919. A doctor hired by the studio had plied him with morphine so he could go on working. Hers was a prescient attempt at framing addiction in a way that would make the addict sympathetic and vulnerable, in part because the confessor—here the wife on behalf of the husband—seemed to be speaking directly to fans. This is standard practice today for celebrities in rehab, but it was novel at the time. "I am being criticized severely by some of our acquaintances for having talked so much," Mrs. Reid told an interviewer, "but I feel that if the public knows the truth, it will not condemn Wally any more than I have condemned him." Will Hays visited Reid at his bedside and vowed to fight the scourge of narcotics.

But if Hays was soon enjoying some success in remaking the image of the Hollywood colony, he was having much less in cleaning up what was shown on screen. In late 1929, he called in a prominent Catholic layman and a Jesuit priest to draft a new and ambitious Production Code to help the moviemakers behave themselves. The authors of the new Code informed their labors with an overarching theory: movies differed from other art forms, such as literature and painting, and could not enjoy the latitude they did, both because movies operated on the senses in a more visceral and all-consuming way and because they were seen by "the masses: the cultivated and the rude, the mature and the immature, the self-respecting and the criminal."

Despite its ambitions, though, the enforcement powers of the new Code were weak; in agreeing to accept it, in March 1930, the studios made sure they were. By 1933, *Variety* opined that "producers have reduced the Hays Production Code to sieve-like proportions and are deliberately out-smarting their own document." Feeling now that they'd been hoodwinked by Hollywood and even by Hays, and angrier than ever, the morals troops mustered again, and this time, they won. In October 1933, a new organization called the Legion of Decency, an offshoot of the Catholic Church, announced that it would be launching a movie boycott. At masses across the country, priests urged their parishioners to take a pledge condemning "vile and unwholesome moving pictures" as a "grave menace to youth, to home life, to country and religion" and promising to boycott such films. Three million people signed the pledge in 1934.

As the boycott grew—attracting Protestants as well as Catholics, shaking movie exhibitors, and triggering calls for federal censorship of films—the producers decided they'd finally have to take their medicine, not just pretend to. "When the protests began to mount and most of Hollywood ignored them, the New York men"—the investors and distributors—"found it necessary to assert themselves," *The New York Times* reported. "They recognized, when the crisis arrived, that a single studio, with a single off-color picture, might plunge the $2,500,000,000 industry into a morass of political censorship and sectarian boycott, with bankruptcy for many the inescapable result." So, in July 1934, the producers agreed to abide by a new regime, one that would reform the system and ensure that it stayed reformed. "Hollywood, when scared, is something like a herd of elephants having a simultaneous chill," the *Times* went on. "Usually the chill passes quickly. Hollywood has found it easy in the past to meet criticism by enunciating, and later amplifying, a code of ethics—and then proceeding blithely to ignore the code." More than once, the motion picture industry had "promised, with tears in its eyes (some of them later turned out to be of the glycerine variety), to be good." But this time around, the moviemakers really were "a bit shocked, considerably bewildered, and openly contrite."

The Code's enforcement regime, now under the auspices of the pugnacious Irish Catholic and former newspaperman Joseph Breen, acquired teeth. Decisions could no longer be appealed to a pliant jury of the producers' peers, for example. Instead, those who objected to proposed cuts and other changes would have to take up their case with an appeals board in New York, not Hollywood. All the major studios and most independent producers would need to go through the review in order to release their movies with a seal of approval. Movies were first to be reviewed as scripts—well before they were actually made.

Breen would stay in his post till 1954, embodying a fascinatingly contradictory role in Hollywood history. He was a domineering, dogmatic man, capable of nasty eruptions of anti-Semitism, and loyal to a nearly unreconstructed Victorian morality. Yet he helmed a censorship regime under which some of Hollywood's finest films were produced. He had taught himself a great deal about movies. He knew how to suggest changes in language that producers understood. Though some in the industry resented the Code from start to finish, many others came to regard it more as a professional code of ethics than a form of censorship and to work with it and around it in fruitful ways. Certainly, their compromises did nothing to lessen the romantic charge of a *Casablanca*, the subversive daffiness of Preston Sturges comedies, the warm rush of civic feeling that was, somehow, not entirely platitudinous in Frank Capra movies, the existential heebie-jeebies of film noir. Appropriately for the era of America's great enamorment with psychoanalysis, movies of the 1940s and 1950s found covert metaphors for desire and deviance. The Code was a kind of repression, a bureaucratic equivalent of the psychological version that allowed meaning to seep around the unspoken. Compelled to deal in displacement, ambiguity, and suggestion, many of the filmmakers of the Code era learned to do so brilliantly. Some, like Alfred Hitchcock, were better working within the strictures of the Code than they were later without.

Still, the Code regime and Breen's lace-curtain autocracy could not last forever. Buffeted by changing mores, by the postwar invasion of (more daring) foreign films, by competition from television, and by the willingness of directors like Otto Preminger (and his studio, United Artists) to defy Breen and release movies without the official seal of approval, the Code began to crack in the 1950s and to disintegrate in the 1960s. Elite public opinion had begun to shift against it, too. In 1952, the Supreme Court would hear a case brought by a New York film distributor who had been screening a Roberto Rossellini movie called *The Miracle*, to which Catholic groups objected. The Court sided with the film distributor. In so doing, it reversed its 1915 ruling that "the exhibition of moving pictures is a business, pure and simple," and tossed out nearly forty years of laws and practices that excluded movies from First Amendment protection. In 1968, the Production Code would be replaced by the movie ratings system we still have today (although some of the classifications have evolved). The ratings system took as its premise the idea that you could differentiate among films on the basis of their appropriateness for certain age groups, rather than assume that any movie might be seen by any child and that all movies had to be crafted with that possibility in mind.

In the meantime, the movies that had been made between 1930 and 1934 when producers felt much less constrained by the Code—all of my father's first movies, as it happened—languished in obscurity. Breen had particularly hated Warner Brothers. He called them the "lowest bunch we have." Of the sixty-three movies that the Legion of Decency had banned its members from seeing in the spring of 1934, twelve had been made by Warner Brothers. Only Paramount had as many on the list, while MGM and Columbia had just five each. After 1934, when Warner Brothers began applying to Breen's office for the right to reissue their pre-Code movies, they were routinely turned down. Some pre-Code movies were lost entirely—to studio fires and more or less purposeful neglect—and others remained only in expurgated form.

Since the 1990s, though, pre-Code films have been rediscovered. Scholarship on Hollywood censorship and the films of the early 1930s has boomed. Turner Classic Movies began showing more and more pre-Code obscurities, some of which had hardly been seen since their first release, and soon they were less obscure. Archives and revival houses began putting on pre-Code festivals. DVDs of some of the films have been released with alluring packaging and titles, as with TCM's "Forbidden Hollywood" collection. Blogs and websites have trained hipster tastes on pre-Code movies. The cynicism and raciness of these movies struck new viewers as fresh, even startling. Watching them, you felt you'd found a peephole into the early years of the Depression; the view was narrow but vivid. And the movies were intriguing because they seemed to reveal a secret lineage of licentiousness, a kind of curatorial stamp of approval for whatever transgressing we might be doing today.

So I was lucky. By the time I started researching this book, there were movies of my father's available to me that I had never been able to see before. I could immerse myself in the pre-Code world of harsh

Lyle fixing for a fight with Humphrey Bogart (actress Sheila
Terry between them) in the typically lurid and still
very watchable pre-Code Big City Blues.

and jagged story lines, of lippy retorts and ethnic jokes, of men and women forever sizing each other up to see who "was on the level," of gangsters and grifters and independent gals with sex on their minds and in the syncopated swing of their satin-clad hips. I could spend time in the company of actresses whose work I knew well, like Barbara Stanwyck and Bette Davis. And of those I knew much less about, in part because much of their best work had been pre-Code: Joan Blondell, Glenda Farrell, Kay Francis, and Ann Dvorak. I could see my father squaring off against a young and very menacing Humphrey Bogart.

And I could catch glimpses of my father as a young man with an erotic charge to him, a man who was best at playing sexy but weak types, who projected a particular combination of tenderness and sensuality and a certain hollowness at the core.

The female characters, and the actresses who played them, surprised me. It's true that the representations of women are more complicated and contradictory in Hollywood films—even in the classic "women's films" of the late 1930s through the late 1950s—than they are sometimes given credit for. As the film scholar Jeanine Basinger writes, those films often undermine the very stereotypes of women that they seem to embody. But it is also true that the pre-Code era gave us some images of women that are quite at odds with what came afterward and with our own stereotypes of the past.

A few of my father's pre-Code films, for instance, centered on the sisterly stratagems of gold diggers. The term "gold digger," meaning a woman who married for money, first appeared in print around 1915, but it wasn't widely used as slang until the late 1920s. And the 1930s saw the launch of a cycle of gold digger films, including the Busby Berkeley musical *Gold Diggers of 1933* and its sequels. The characters—our heroines—were often astonishingly duplicitous and calculating. They weren't like poor, sweet Marilyn Monroe in *Gentlemen Prefer Blondes*, and they weren't merely setting their caps for rich bachelors. In the pre-Code gold digger movies, the gals were often engaging in blackmail. They'd set married men up, for instance, making it look as though their hot-to-trot victims had been fooling around on the side when they hadn't—at least not yet. But two things make these characters tolerable and even lovable: the movies were played for laughs by excellent comediennes, and these were gold diggers who really needed the gold. It was the Depression and they were sometimes in out-and-out danger of going hungry. "Chorus girls used to get pearls and diamonds," says Joan Blondell in *Big City Blues*. "Now all they expect is a corned beef sandwich, and they yell if they don't get it."

Take *Havana Widows*, a movie my father made in 1932 with Glenda Farrell and Joan Blondell. These two actresses, who were close friends in real life, made a great snap-crackle-and-pop pair on screen. Farrell played the tougher, more strategic, and sarcastic pal; Blondell, the sweeter though still sassy one. Glenda Farrell was a platinum blond with a wide mouth full of big square white teeth. When she talked fast, as she almost always did, it was like the strident *clackety-clack* of a typewriter; you half expected her to ring at the end of a sentence. She was slim and wore clothes beautifully. Blondell looked a little like Betty Boop—she was saucer-eyed, with bow lips, a curvy little figure, and a good-natured pep to her performances. In the early 1930s, she always seemed to be showing off a little more of her lovely breasts than the Code allowed, especially when she wore satin evening gowns. ("We must put brassieres on Joan Blondell," Jack Warner pleaded in a 1933 memo to production head Hal Wallis, "and make her cover up her breasts because, otherwise, we are going to have these pictures stopped in a lot of places. I believe in showing their forms, but, for Lord's sake, don't let those bulbs stick out.")

Havana Widows is a wised-up, sharp-elbowed little comedy. Farrell and Blondell play Sadie and Mae, two hardworking chorus girls dancing in a burlesque show whose headliner, "direct from Russia," is called "Iwanna Shakitoff." The opening scene, where the women in their skimpy polka-dot costumes are duly shaking it (though not quite off) and exchanging wisecracks, carries a whiff of earthy realism. The girls look bored, overheated, and out of breath. That night, the show's manager tells Mae he's sending her over to Passaic to entertain at a smoker. "After it's over, I want you to do a dance, you know, show 'em something." "Is it a benefit?" she asks. "Yeah," he fibs slowly, figuring she'll say yes if it is. "It's a benefit." "Then I'm out," Mae snaps back. "My conscience wouldn't let me. What I'd show 'em wouldn't benefit any of 'em."

Mae is fired for insubordination and Sadie gets herself sacked in solidarity. Broke but resourceful, Sadie and Mae haul themselves to Havana, where, they've heard, there's money to be made by fleecing men who can be entrapped in compromising positions. Their first target is the married Deacon Jones, played by Guy Kibbee, the fat and foolish, or sometimes fat and kindly, old man in many, many Warner Brothers movies. The fact that Mae's new love interest is Jones's son— a debonair young fellow played by Lyle—gives her a twinge of conscience, but only a twinge. With the help of a false story and a drunken chiseler of a lawyer, Mae and Sadie lure Deacon Jones to an inn outside town. There, a couple of hired thugs strip him of his clothes down to his union suit (a sight that's always good for a laugh in these movies, especially if the man in question is portly). Mae arrives, boobs sloshing around in her sexy black satin gown, prepared to seduce Jones into the blackmail-worthy pose in which he'll be photographed. The poor duffer runs around shouting hoarsely for help and clutching a gingham tablecloth as a cover-up, while Mae chases him, and a crowd gathers below, hooting and howling.

The peculiar thing is that this sadistic little spectacle is soon tied up with a cheerful ending in which our gold diggers, far from being punished, are enjoying their spoils. Deacon Jones's wife is grateful to the blackmailing women because she's been trying to get a divorce from him for years and now can. Sadie marries her boyfriend, a gangster's gofer who crows, "Nobody's been married legal in my family for the last three generations!" And Mae marries Lyle's character, the son of the man she framed, who promises her, in lieu of eternal love, "caviar and champagne three times a day."

It would all feel a bit sour if it weren't for the central relationship— which is between Sadie and Mae. Female friendship was the heartbeat of these gold digger pictures. The lead characters can be snarky about other women in their general orbit, especially those who get too hoity-toity. ("Why, that moth-eaten little skirt!") But to each other, the gals at the center of these films are unfailingly loyal. They strategize, commiserate, make each other laugh, buy each other drinks, dress each other up and admire their handiwork, refuse to let their friendships be torn asunder by cops, boyfriends, or producers. Surprisingly, to today's audiences, they are often shown sharing a double bed.

The late 1920s and early 1930s were a heyday for female comedy teams: in addition to Glenda Farrell and Joan Blondell, who went on to make five more movies together after *Havana Widows*, there were Marie Dressler and Polly Moran, ZaSu Pitts and Thelma Todd, and Thelma Todd and Patsy Kelly. What's striking about these partnerships and their films, as the cinema scholar Kristine Brunovska Karnick observes, is that the humor in them "is not primarily at the women's expense." Though the gal pals are sexy and (often) blond, they are not dumb-blond characters; they're smart and they can talk their way out of a whole lot of trouble. They're also independent and resourceful and they work for a living, even if their line of work is often the chorus line, with its convenient opportunities for dressing room scenes and thigh-baring high kicks. In a movie called *Girl Missing*, another female-comedy-team picture with Lyle as the male eye candy, Glenda Farrell's friend warns her at one point not to get tough. "I don't have to get tough," she replies, "I *am* tough."

By the mid-1930s these movies were out, and screwball comedies in which women were still funny and mischievous but mostly with their male romantic interests, and mostly in domestic settings, eclipsed the female buddy picture. By contrast, as Karnick argues, the female buddy pictures showed women out in the world, women as adventuresses, plucky and piratical. And unlike later women's pictures, in which the beautiful but unfunny lead has a funny but far less glamorous sidekick (often a maid, sometimes a friend), in these movies the two women were equally attractive and equally wisecracking, and occupied equal time on screen.

During the pre-Code era it was easier than it would be for a long time afterward to make movies in which fallen women were not roundly punished for their sins. In *Blonde Venus*, Marlene Dietrich becomes a hot nightclub entertainer, the mistress of Cary Grant, and ultimately a prostitute, but ends up happily reunited with her husband (whose medical treatment her labors paid for) and their little son. In *Red-Headed Woman*, the gleefully home-wrecking Jean Harlow ends up having her cake and eating it, too—married to a wealthy old marquis in Paris, while playing around with his handsome young chauffeur. Sure, the women in these films endure their humiliations and setbacks, but they end up very far from the gutter.

Several of my father's films from the period offer interesting twists on the theme of feminine punishment and redemption. *Ladies They Talk About* is an odd little film in which plausibility and motivation take it on the chin. But it has its piquant, pre-Code moments. Barbara Stanwyck plays Nan Taylor, a bank robber in a gang of guys led by Lyle, looking unusually buff. Though he made only two movies with her, and neither of them was particularly good, Barbara Stanwyck was my father's favorite actress to work with. She was such a professional, he said, always came to the set prepared, always knew her lines, never made a fuss about it. Like those good sports Carole Lombard and Marion Davies, she was also a star who had an easy rapport with everyone on set, including the crew, whose wives and kids' names she always remembered.

Many of the great Hollywood actresses of the 1930s, 1940s, and 1950s came from lower-class origins, but Stanwyck's background was striking for its sketchiness and rock-bottom struggles. The roles she played in the early '30s weren't so far from the life she'd led in the early '20s, when, as she once recalled, she "just wanted to survive, and eat, and have a nice coat." Stanwyck had been born Ruby Stevens in Brooklyn in 1907, the fifth child of a frequently unemployed laborer and his wife. When she was two years old, her mother, while pregnant again, was killed by a drunken stranger who knocked her off a streetcar. Stanwyck's father ran away to Panama to work on the canal, and she never saw him again. She was raised in foster homes, from which she was constantly running away. As a teenager, Stanwyck got by on her own, taking jobs as a typist, a pattern cutter, a chorus girl on the midnight-to-seven-a.m. shift, and a taxi dancer at a speakeasy, before being discovered on the New York stage as the gifted actress she was. Though she was a beauty, with a lithe, graceful body, a perfectly straight nose, and glimmering eyes, she was not a creamy, luscious type. She seemed to be built for quick escapes and tight corners. Her face was delicate and shrewd, and her acting suggested an incisive native intelligence. She could summon a bitterness and a hysteria that contorted her features and made her look almost ugly. But she was also uncommonly deft at revealing the surprising softness inside a character's brittle shell, and that was what made her great. As the critic Wendy Lesser notes, Stanwyck's characters did not seem as though they were helplessly surrendering up their vulnerability: they seemed to be making a courageous choice to let it show.

In *Ladies They Talk About*, the most memorable scenes take place in prison. After participating in a bank heist, Nan almost evades a prison sentence when the crusading district attorney, David Slade (Preston Foster), takes a shine to her. *Ladies They Talk About* was based on a play by the actress Dorothy Mackaye, who had herself spent two years in San Quentin for concealing evidence in the beating death of her husband (her lover, a young actor she later married, had done the beating). It wouldn't be quite right to say that Mackaye's firsthand experience of prison life made for a *realistic* movie. The prison in *Ladies They Talk About* looks an awful lot like a girl's dormitory at a rather nice boarding school, and the inmates seem to have plenty of silky undergarments and frilly bedclothes. This is a movie too focused on showing what its audiences could be presumed to want—titillating glimpses of women behind bars plus the wish-fulfilling spectacle of a woman who'd made a mess of her life, enjoying the adoration of a good and good-looking man—to bother much with plausible plot development, let alone realistic portrayals of institutions. Still, the inmates' maneuverings around one another, the shabby specificity of their alliances and fights, are sharply rendered.

Prison pictures, like war pictures, offer a studiously diverse cast—high and low, black and white, Jewish and Gentile thrown into un-accustomed proximity—and this movie is no different. Because it's pre-Code, however, the different types and their attributes are coarser and more unabashed than we expect from old movies. There's a dispu-tatious black inmate named Mustard who holds her own against a society dowager in for poisoning her husband; there's a mannish, cigar-smoking woman in a bow tie and short slicked-back hair ("Watch out for her," Nan's friend warns her. "She likes to wrestle"); there's Aunt Maggie, a blowzy, bawdy madam who's a "grand old soul," according to Nan's friend; and there's a David Slade–following religious fanatic named Sister Susie. (She tells Nan there's no punishment too harsh for her, a threat that elicits my favorite riposte in the movie: "Yeah? Well, being penned up here with a daffodil like you comes awful close.")

While at San Quentin, Nan tries to help her friends, my father's character, the suave con Don, and his partner, Dutch, escape from the men's prison next door. When the plot is foiled and the men are killed, she blames David Slade, the D.A., and after her release shoots him. She only wings him, he forgives her, and—sure, why not?—asks her to marry him. *Ladies They Talk About* inverts one common formula: rather than the love of a good woman saving an errant man, it's the other way around. Yet Nan, unlike many a reformed man in the movies, does no swearing to go straight, and other than a perfunctory "I didn't mean to do that" to Slade for shooting him, no real apologizing. The only impassioned speech she delivers is about the grisly fate of the guys from her old criminal gang: "And the two kids they got! Their brains are in alcohol in little jars for curious visitors to gape at, property of the state!" If we like her, it's because, as she says more than once, she's no stoolie; she stays loyal to her friends, bad'uns though they are. Unlike

Sister Susie, she's no true believer, either—just a practical-minded survivor.

Heat Lightning, another of my father's pre-Code women's pictures, this one directed by the capable Mervyn LeRoy, is a better movie, though, morally speaking, more twisted. Aline MacMahon and Ann Dvorak play sisters who run a roadside gas station and diner in the desert. The actresses are convincing as sisters—both tall and dark, with long faces and a tendency to smudginess under the eyes, though Dvorak is gorgeous and MacMahon more interesting-looking. The sister MacMahon plays, Olga, is older and dresses like a man, in coveralls, with a bandanna concealing her hair. She's also the mechanic around the place and gratifyingly competent at her job. Dvorak's Myra is younger, dreamier, and more restless; she's the waitress in the diner but longs for nights out on the town with Steve, a man whom Olga thinks is a bad egg.

Their lives are turned inside out when one hot day—they're all hot days out there—a couple of bank robbers on the lam walk into the diner, squinting from the glare of the desert sun. Preston Foster plays the hard case, George, and my father plays the weaker partner in crime, Jeff, a guy whose queasy combination of conscience and fear of the hot seat are making him as jumpy as a cat. When Jeff says to his partner, "Yeah, you did the shootin', and I've been regrettin' it ever since," George replies: "Those boys were born to be drilled at two o'clock Tuesday and that's when they got it." *Heat Lightning* ends up with a shooting by a woman, too—this one fatal but also unpunished.

It's a fun movie to watch now, in part because of its sense of place—my father remembered shooting it on location in the Mojave Desert, the rare Warner Brothers film made outside a soundstage in those years. It has a fine sense of atmosphere: the Joshua trees and flashes of eponymous heat lightning on the horizon; the diner, with its slamming screen door, checkered tablecloths, and bottled soda pop; the Mexican family whom Olga lets camp out on the property singing boleros in the velvety darkness. And the supporting cast offers up a matter-of-fact pre-Code tawdriness—portraits with an acid tang to them. The divorcees, played with caustic high spirits by Glenda Farrell and Ruth Donnelly, are warm for the form of their nebbishy chauffeur ("I told them I got a wife in Flatbush," he protests feebly to Olga, "but that only seemed to encourage 'em"), and one of them ends up spending the night with him. A respectable-looking geezer stops by the gas station with two hard-faced, hitchhiking hotties in tow on their way to Hollywood. He calls them his nieces, and everybody had a laugh about that. "It's your turn to sit up in the front with that old thigh-pincher," one tells the other as they leave the diner. "You go your way," the other one calls out to George and Jeff, "and we'll go the way of all flesh."

Heat Lightning was released in the spring of 1934, so it just snuck in under the last months of the looser Code enforcement regime. The Studio Relations Committee had won a few concessions—when George leaves the cabin where he's disappeared with Olga, he's fully clothed, for instance. But plenty that the committee had suggested should be expurgated remained in *Heat Lightning*—phrases evoking the geezer's lechery, references to Myra's night with her boyfriend and to Olga's affair with George, an obvious search for the bathroom when the two hotties arrive—and as a result, the film could not be reissued after Code enforcement began in earnest.

Despite its amusing touches, though, *Heat Lightning* is actually kind of a bleak movie—especially when it comes to limning women's prospects. Olga initially looks like a strong character, and in a way she is. She's good at her job—a man's job—and she's brisk and no-nonsense. But ultimately, she's someone who is so vulnerable to the dubious charms of a seductive loser that she's had to isolate herself in the desert and renounce sexuality altogether. It might have been a last resort that some women in the audience could relate to, but it's still a last resort.

By contrast, one of the pre-Code women's films my father did surprised me with its portrayal of a warmly sexual and loving woman who excels at a man's profession. This was *Mary Stevens, M.D.* (1933), a Warner Brothers quickie to be sure, with the slight attention to character development you'd expect but with a vein of real feeling nonetheless. Kay Francis and my father play newly minted doctors who go into practice together. Mary Stevens (Francis) has to deal with naysayers, but she is a calm, resourceful type, and has the support of her pal and nurse, Glenda, played by Glenda Farrell, and—after his fashion— her colleague Don, played by my father. "You said a woman couldn't do it," Mary tells Don on their graduation day from medical school. "A woman couldn't," he replies. "But you! You're a superwoman." Don believes in her as a doctor but—cliché alert—can't see her as a desirable woman and marries a blond society girl (Thelma Todd) before coming to his senses. (Absurd, of course, since the audience can see from the get-go that Francis is a tall, shapely stunner with wide-set gray eyes and luxuriant blue-black hair.) My father liked Francis; they called each other "cuz," and he thought her lisp was cute. They were never lovers, though both got around, but their chemistry works pretty well here—not so much in the laughable scenes where they're doing something vaguely medical but in the private moments when he shows her a tender sympathy. He could play tender—his natural sweetness and affection for women shone through in those moments.

Lyle had several roles like this: the playboy doctor with a drinking problem. It was kind of a stock character at the time. Why, I wonder. Surely there weren't that many doctors pounding back hip flasks full of hooch between patients, even in an era when it was easier for doctors to shield themselves from oversight. Maybe the rich and reckless doctor unleashed on powerless charity cases made a suitably disturbing metaphor for all the authority figures—from bank presidents to the president of the United States—who had let Americans down in the early 1930s. When Mary tells Don she's disgusted with him, it's a relief for the audience.

Later in the film, when the admirable Mary realizes she's pregnant by Don, she makes the decision to have the baby on her own. "Take a good grip on that desk, plant your feet firmly, and prepare for the shock of your life," she tells her friend and nurse, Glenda. "I'm going to have a baby. . . . What's so funny about it? I didn't invent the idea. Women have been having babies for a long while." Glenda asks, "It is Don's?" ("Of course, you goose," Mary replies) and asks her whether she's happy. "Walking on air," Mary tells her. "Well then, darling," says Glenda. "So am I." As the film critic Mick LaSalle notes, "It would be a long time before such a reasonable exchange between single ladies would again be possible in American film."

There are a couple of striking things about the portrayal of women in *Mary Stevens, M.D.* One is that Mary sticks with her career. The last scene shows her in her new offices, practicing medicine with Don as a partner (and husband; Glenda opens the door to reveal the couple in a clinch). True, she has not emerged unscathed; her baby has died and her grief has been exposed, movingly. But there's no reason to think that Don and Mary won't have more children together. Don not only loves her but exalts her career: "Your work is important," he tells her. "Hundreds, thousands of children need your skill, your knowledge." As LaSalle notes, "The movie ends up with an affirmation of her both as a woman and a professional." That would be, for many years to come, an unusual affirmation indeed. Women doctors (and lawyers and other professionals) were comparatively sparse in films— as they were in real life—for most of the 1930s, 1940s, and 1950s. And when they did turn up, they often renounced their careers in the last frames to please their new husbands, as Margaret Lindsay did in *The Law in Her Hands* (1936) and Ann Harding, playing a psychiatrist, did in *The Flame Within* (1935).

The other striking aspect of the picture, though, involves Mary and her baby. It's not just that she is comfortable with having a baby as a single mother. It's also that her interactions with him show the sensual delight that mothers take in their babies, something that is not all that commonly portrayed in movies even now. She lies down on the floor with her baby, brings her face playfully close to his, nibbles on his chubby, bare foot. She seems natural, relaxed, and besotted. It makes the scene when he dies all the more wrenching. The movie manages to convey this sensibility against the will of a censorship regime that was weirdly squeamish about babies. James Wingate, of the Studio Relations Committee, came down unusually hard on this aspect of *Mary Stevens, M.D.*: "From the standpoint of censorship generally, we would recommend that you consider trimming very considerably the various discussions about babies and their expected arrival," he wrote in a letter to Jack Warner. "As you know, the question of pregnancy and childbirth is a touchy one with many censor boards and a large part of the public."

You can understand why the movie censors and conventional opinion might be nervous about depictions of illegitimate births and pregnancies, but often it was birth and pregnancy in general that they were chary of. The Pennsylvania censorship board, for instance, didn't even allow baby clothes or diapers to be shown in movies. It was as though any references to how children actually came into the world and what they might need and do in the first early months were in themselves distasteful. Knowing the attitudes this cut-rate little picture was defying made me like it more and want to defend it from the prissy *New York Times* review that ran when it came out (Kay Francis is "a woman physician who has a startling amount of trouble preserving a professional detachment toward the primitive emotions") and from the oblivion it was consigned to when the Breen office denied its re-release.

Many pre-Code movies do not end as the authors of the Code wanted, and as American movies almost always did from 1934 till the mid-1960s: with virtue rewarded and vice punished. Sometimes, in the pre-Code era, this made for endings that were bleak and deeply effective—endings like that of *I Am a Fugitive from a Chain Gang*, which refuses to find a happy resolution for its hunted hero, a victim of the judicial system and of the Depression. Sometimes, it made for endings that are refreshing because, as in *Mary Stevens, M.D.*, they do not chastise their sexually unconventional heroines. And sometimes the endings are just strange. The resolution of *Love Is a Racket*, the first film my father made in Hollywood, has a handsome young newspaper columnist—the movie's hero or at least its main character—covering up a murder committed by his girlfriend's dowager aunt. He's trying to protect the girlfriend, who's a heartless little minx, and he succeeds, getting off scot-free and apparently guilt-free as well.

In *College Coach*, a gleefully venal college football coach named James Gore (Pat O'Brien) not only hires ringers to play for him, and fixes their grades so they can remain eligible for the team, but instructs them at one point to play so rough that they end up mortally injuring a boy on the opposing team. (He also finagles a dirty real estate deal.) At the end of this blusteringly cynical William Wellman film, though, the coach is still a rich, successful, happily married man who neither suffers nor repents. His beautiful wife (Ann Dvorak) resents all the time he spends at work but apparently has no objection to his complete absence of principles. As the movie reviewer Glenn Erickson writes, "The fascinating thing about 'College Coach' is that Gore isn't a villain, but a guy who knows the score and plays the cards as he sees them. . . . A film produced under the Code would likely insist that 'cheaters never prosper.'" This one does not.

I like *College Coach*; it's fast-moving, the cast is top-notch (in addition to O'Brien and Dvorak and my father, it has Dick Powell, several of the excellent Warner Brothers character actors, and an uncredited cameo by a young John Wayne), and the details of the university's financial woes, real estate deals, and football cheating scandals are still fresh today. My father, getting a break from the gangsters he so often played in those years, is very funny as Buck, the vain quarterback who

Lyle in William Wellman's College Coach,
with John Wayne (left) and Dick Powell (center).

romances the coach's wife. (This was the movie in which Wellman had
encouraged the college football players to pile onto the unsuspecting
Lyle.) But there's no doubt that it's an odd film. It plays like an exposé
of gridiron corruption, but it doesn't end that way.

20,000 Years in Sing Sing, one of my father's favorites of his own
movies, at first seems like it will come to a more conventionally just
conclusion. The cocky gangster played by Spencer Tracy is executed.
But it is punishment for a crime he did not actually commit, and it is
meted out at a prison whose warden, the movie's hero, hates the death
penalty. This was a movie that critics at the time liked and praised for
its realism. "In this rapidly paced film," read the *New York Times* review,
"there are some extraordinarily interesting glimpses of prison routine."
Variety called the prison scenes "near perfect," and added, "There's

everything in this picture to make class entertainment." My father, who played Tracy's fellow con, remembered the movie fondly, too, in large part because it stood out for its backstory; even with his excellent memory, it was hard, fifty and sixty years later, to keep straight all the movies he had made in rapid succession in the early 1930s. The film is based on the story of Lewis Lawes, the crusading warden of Sing Sing prison in upstate New York from 1919 to 1947. Lawes was an anti–death penalty progressive, with a strong faith that the right sort of prison, one that treated all inmates humanely and rewarded them for good behavior, could redeem people. At Sing Sing, he improved the food, health care, and recreation; promoted liberal parole and probation policies; built airy new cells; encouraged inmates to make and tend a garden and greenhouses; and provided other meaningful work. To show how much he trusted his "boys," Lawes let inmates take care of his daughters, and submitted himself to a daily shave at the hands of a prison barber who had once cut a man's throat.

Lawes was a technical adviser on the movie and allowed some of the scenes to be shot at Sing Sing, with real prisoners in them, which did indeed give parts of the movies a touch of documentary verisimilitude. And Lawes was fairly pleased with the finished product—especially the performance of Spencer Tracy as the dapper gangster who enters Sing Sing impudent as can be but develops a grudging respect for the fair-minded warden. Of course, the script took plenty of liberties, too. It was a melodrama and it was written by Wilson Mizner, the confidence man turned screenwriter. My father admired Lawes, though, and was proud to be in a film about his reforms.

Michael Curtiz, the Hungarian-born director who went on to make *Casablanca*, concocted an effectively gloomy atmosphere out of the location shots he got, the shadows cast by prison bars, and the song "Happy Days Are Here Again" played for ironic counterpoint on the harmonica. My father, like a lot of actors, found Curtiz overbearing and intimidating, and was alternately baffled and amused by the

Lyle and Spencer Tracy, in 20,000 Years in Sing Sing.

director's fractured English. "Bring on the empty horses," was Curtiz's way of asking for riderless horses in a scene. On the set of *20,000 Years in Sing Sing*, Curtiz once barked at Lyle: "Come when I don't say stand still!" a piece of direction that had him perplexed for a long moment.

My own favorite of my father's pre-Code movies, though, is a movie called *Three on a Match*, in which he appeared with Joan Blondell, Warren William, Ann Dvorak, and Bette Davis. In his book *Sin in Soft Focus*, the film historian Mark Vieira calls *Three on a Match* "the quintessential Warner Brothers film of 1932, cramming head-lines, history, sociology, sex, alcohol, drugs, adultery, kidnapping, blackmail and suicide into 63 busy minutes." To me, it's the quint-essential pre-Code movie, remarkable for its frankness about drug addiction, its sympathy for the sensuality and frustration of the doomed wife, its upending of the clichéd fates it seems to set out for the three women at the center of the film (the reform school bad girl turns out to be the happiest and most moral of the three women; the refined rich girl, the most miserable), and an ending that still has the power to shock.

A Warner Brothers picture rarely risked boring an audience with psychological exposition, but for that reason the emotional states of characters were often telegraphed with a concision that bordered on the absurd. The performances in *Three on a Match*—particularly those of Ann Dvorak as the straying wife and Lyle as the handsome low-rent chiseler she strays to—are excellent, and they add an emotional shading you don't often get in the Warner Brothers movies of the era. There's one scene in particular that is a model of potent, emotional brevity. It shows us, eloquently if not graphically, that Vivian, the Ann Dvorak character who has left her wealthy straight-arrow husband for Mike, my father's character, is a woman who is now having satisfying sex, probably for the first time in her life. The opening of the scene cuts from a shot of the abandoned husband, played by Warren William, his large white hands twisting in distress as he talks about his missing wife and young son, to one of Lyle's hands wrapped around a cocktail shaker. The camera pulls back to show a hotel room in which Vivian is lying on a sofa wearing a filmy peignoir, a dreamy, postcoital smile on her face. When her little boy toddles over and says, "Mommy, I'm hungry," Vivian's besotted satiety leaks into her response. She coos ineffectually at him and gestures to a decimated tray of hors d'oeuvres. "I don't like those anymore," whimpers Junior. "Can't I have bread and milk?"

At this, a small spasm of conscience passes over Mike's face. Lyle does something subtle with his expression that is not quite a wince, not quite an admission of shame—something shifty-eyed—and is a very nice piece of acting. We see in an instant that as weak and hedonistic as Mike is, he isn't heartless. But Vivian is too blissed out to notice. "C'mere," she murmurs to her lover, then pulls him to her on the couch and whispers something in his ear; a cigarette burns between her long white fingers as they kiss.

In her autobiography, Bette Davis remembered *Three on a Match* as a "dull B picture." Her role, as a dutiful stenographer and friend, was certainly thankless. In 1932, Davis was a contract player at Warner Brothers, doing what she was asked but already beginning to chafe at the restrictions. In *Three on a Match*, she has scarcely any memorable business other than the requisite pre-Code scene of a woman getting dressed or undressed with blithe irrelevance to the plot. (In this one, Davis as the prim stenographer happens to be wearing a skimpy nightie and pulling stockings up over her bare thighs during one important conversation.) Nor did Davis particularly impress the film's director, Mervyn LeRoy. "They gave me three unknown girls in that one— Joan Blondell, Bette Davis, and Ann Dvorak," LeRoy wrote in his autobiography. "I made a mistake when the picture was finished. I told an interviewer that I thought Joan Blondell was going to be a big star, Ann Dvorak had definite possibilities, but that I didn't think Bette Davis would make it. She's been cool to me ever since."

Of the three women, it is certainly Dvorak's Vivian who haunts you. Dvorak was as unusual an actress as Davis, and in a way just as rebellious. If she'd had as long a career, she might have enjoyed Davis's stature instead of having her greatest moments remain in pre-Code movies like *Scarface* and *Three on a Match*. Her beauty was sophisticated and vaguely Eastern European; she looks like an art student— slender, eternally modern, and hip, a girl you'd see in a coffeehouse in Prague or Vienna, nibbling at a Sacher torte with a table full of argumentative intellectuals. Dvorak brought a skittish intelligence and a yearning sexuality to her best performances. With her pale

Lyle on the set of Three on a Match, *with Ann Dvorak, the director Mervyn LeRoy (holding the script), and cinematographer Sol Polito.*

complexion, unruly hair, and tendency to dark circles under her eyes, Dvorak was also one of the few actresses of the period who could look persuasively strung-out. But she defied the studio by fleeing Holly-wood for England and a yearlong honeymoon with her British hus-band. Her career never really recovered, and she retired from the screen in 1951.

In *Three on a Match*, Dvorak and Lyle infuse their mutual down-fall with a palpable sense of panic. Hitting up an old friend for money, Dvorak wears a black suit rubbed shiny in places, taps her scuffed shoes, and picks at her cuticles; all the languor is gone. Her skin has a milky-blue pallor, and she somehow manages to make her refined slenderness look more like gauntness. Lyle, who owes money to a mobster and concocts a nasty scheme to kidnap Vivian's son after the boy has returned to his father, develops a convincingly clammy sheen and an expression compounded of terror and childish ingratiation.

When he brings the boy home to Vivian, who knew nothing about this kidnapping plot, it's clear that she has become an addict. It could be heroin she's hooked on, but it's probably cocaine. She's jumpy; and she wipes her nose compulsively with her knuckle—a gesture that one of the gangsters who is now hanging around, angling to get in on the ransom money, cruelly imitates. (He's played by a cold and menacing young Humphrey Bogart.) When one of the other thugs asks Bogart's character, "Did you get anything for her? She's clean out of it," he snaps back, "How could I? I tell you the heat's on enough to curl your shoe leather."

Meanwhile, the police are looking for the boy, and the dragnet is closing in. Vivian is trapped in the bedroom of a run-down tenement apartment. Junior, who is locked in the room with her, looks grimy and neglected. Mike is holed up in the outer room with a few of the thugs. Early 1930s movies didn't generally use much musical underscoring to cue emotion; if you hear music, it's usually being played on a phonograph or radio and heard by the characters as well. (In Warner Brothers movies, it's often "St. Louis Blues.") So in this scene all that we're hearing are ambient sounds, and they are stark. Sirens wail. Vivian is in withdrawal and you can hear her moaning from behind the closed door.

In short order, Bogart's character decides the kid will have to be killed, then the gang will flee and still try to score the ransom. This is a rather amazing plot development, particularly in the same year that the Lindbergh baby was kidnapped and found dead. Jason Joy of the Code's Studio Relations Committee was certainly taken aback. "I'm frank to say I'm at a loss what to say about it," he wrote to Darryl Zanuck at Warner Brothers. "While there has been no signed agreement among the studios not to make child-kidnapping pictures, the general impression here has been that no one would follow the Lindbergh tragedy with a picture dealing with the kidnapping of a baby for ransom." The state censorship boards were up in arms over the picture, and New York investors were worried it would kick off a cycle of similar movies. In any event, *Three on a Match* was released in 1932, and with few changes—evidence of how weak the system was before Joseph Breen took it over. But in 1937, Breen would deny permission for it to be re-released and nixed a proposed remake, despite its softer approach. Indeed, kidnapping, especially child kidnapping, would for many years be an entirely forbidden subject in films. So would drug addiction, for that matter.

In the final, sad, and suspenseful scenes of *Three on a Match*, Mike dies resisting the Bogart character's order to kill the boy and Vivian dies to save him. Having scrawled her son's location in lipstick on her chest, she leaps from the window to the sidewalk below. At the close of the movie, Junior is seen with Warren William and Joan Blondell, the good bad girl to whom he's now married, saying his bedtime prayers and remembering his mommy in heaven. What's unexpected, and touching, is that his father and stepmother have not tried to expunge her from their story or from the boy's memory. The film scholar William K. Everson, who calls *Three on a Match* "a vivid little picture," "splendidly cut and paced," suggests that it was the kind of movie that offered audiences of the early Depression years a surprising solace: "Like so many early '30s movies, the milieu is realistically that of the Depression, but it offers a kind of inverted escapism by showing that the rich have more than their share of woes, and that real problems spring more from human weaknesses than economic ones." If so, it made those points with more bitterness but also more compassion than most movies of its ilk.

In the years to come, it would be rare indeed to see a major studio release as dark as *Three on a Match*. In part that was because such an outlook would not pass muster with the Code enforcers. But that wasn't the only reason. When Franklin Roosevelt won the presidency in November 1932, it brightened the outlooks of many Americans— not least the Hollywood producers, and among them, none more than the Warner brothers, whose commitment to Roosevelt and his New Deal was passionate and sudden. It was true that Warner Brothers was the studio whose films displayed the most social conscience. But much of that came from the writers—"Schmucks with Underwoods," Jack Warner called them—newspapermen and novelists, many of them New York Jews. As Neal Gabler writes, "poor young educated Jews growing up in New York in the twenties and thirties," which so many of the screenwriters were, came to Hollywood hardwired with sympathy for the underdog. At Warner Brothers, they were especially likely to thrive, and to inflect their scripts with their political conscience. Still, the Warners themselves had been Republicans, as were most Hollywood producers at the time. Gabler thinks that as first- or second-generation Jewish immigrants, they were anxious to ally themselves with the moneyed WASP establishment in this country. In Los Angeles, they tended to take their political cues from the conservative newspaper magnate William Randolph Hearst. They rallied to defeat Upton Sinclair's 1932 campaign for governor—a populist movement known as End Poverty in California—going so far as to create fake newsreels that showed Sinclair-loving hoboes overrunning California and a disreputable-looking, thickly accented Russian immigrant declaring his support for the progressive novelist.

It's a little hard to account for the Warners' embrace of FDR. Maybe they were convinced he was the man to fix the economy; maybe they merely spotted a winner and saw a chance to get on the inside track and become the political machers in Hollywood they'd never really been. In any case, in 1932, Jack's brother Harry called him to

New York for a meeting with advisers to then Governor Roosevelt, along with Joseph Kennedy, Al Smith, and John Raskob, the former General Motors chair and now chair of the Democratic National Committee. Roosevelt's people had identified the Warners as the disgruntled outliers in the Hollywood establishment and saw a chance to win them over. Jack recalled looking at his brother for some clue to this political switch and getting this reply: "The country is in chaos. There is revolution in the air, and we need a change." Jack thought it wasn't a very original battle cry, but he had to admit, as he put it in Warnerese, "The Depression had a half nelson around the nation's already scrawny neck." He dutifully went home to try to muster the Hollywood troops for Roosevelt. In September 1932, the Warners paid for a spectacular electrical parade and sports pageant at the Coliseum, where Roosevelt was the guest of honor and some 75,000 people turned out. "Roosevelt Thrilled by Dazzling Pageant of Filmland," trumpeted the headline in the *Los Angeles Examiner*.

After Roosevelt was elected, Warner Brothers pictures often came equipped with endings in which the New Deal swept in at the last minute to save the day. In William Wellman's fine movie *Wild Boys of the Road* (1933), middle-class teenagers become rail-hopping hoboes after their parents lose their jobs. Out on their own, they endure hunger, rape, pitched battles with the police, the destruction of their peaceful encampment, and a train accident that leaves one boy an amputee. At the end, they are brought before a judge who turns out to be a sympathetic figure, and who is shown with the National Recovery Administration eagle behind him. He refuses to put the kids in jail and reassures them that "things are going to get better all over the country." In another 1933 film, Wellman's *Heroes for Sale*, the protagonist is a World War I veteran who endures a calvary that begins with a rich friend's claiming the military honors that rightly belong to him, and proceeds through morphine addiction, unemployment, a machine-smashing uprising by his workers when he briefly rises to be a factory boss, and baseless hounding by the Red Squads. The last scene finds him a hunted man and hobo, taking refuge with others like him in a dark, rain-swept gully. But unlike the character in *I Am a Fugitive from a Chain Gang*, he offers hope: "Did you read President Roosevelt's inaugural address? It takes more than one sock in the jaw to lay out 120 million people." In the musical *Footlight Parade*, the chorus holds aloft flash cards that form the shape of the NRA eagle and of FDR's smiling face.

It was this kind of spirit that put Lyle on a train bound from Los Angeles on February 21, 1933, to the inauguration of Franklin Roosevelt in Washington, D.C. The train was a magnificent thing—covered in silver and gold leaf, decked out with electric lights that burned continuously and spelled out "Better Times" and "The 42nd Street Special." The movie *42nd Street*, which had just come out, was a Busby Berkeley musical about an imperious producer hit hard by the stock market crash but rallying himself and his cast to put on a fabulous show. It was the prototype of all future backstage musicals, complete with the plucky chorus girl called to stardom when the leading lady collapses. It was also an obvious, if somewhat peculiar, Depression parable: "a giddy extravaganza about economic desperation," as the writer James Traub describes it. Lyle had a small part in the movie that was cut from the final version. His main contribution to the film was doing the excitable voice-over for the preview. But no matter: he was on the train anyway, along with the actors Bette Davis, Glenda Farrell, Leo Carrillo, Preston Foster, Laura LaPlante, and Claire Dodd; the comedian Joe E. Brown; the cowboy star Tom Mix and his horse, Tony Jr.; the Olympic swimming champion Eleanor Holm; the boxer Jack Dempsey; and twelve beautiful chorus girls (the latter the kind of group that is inevitably described as a "bevy"). The train would be stopping in thirteen cities, and it would arrive in Washington, D.C., on March 4, in time for the stars to join the inaugural parade and attend an inaugural ball or two.

The 42nd Street Special was the brainchild of Charles Einfeld, the irrepressible head of publicity for Warner Brothers, and its scale and success set the standard for Hollywood junkets ever after. "What a layout!" a reporter for *Variety* effused. "The dream of every publicity man come true. $1,000,000 worth of some of the grandest exploitation that ever flashed across the horizon of show business laid out right in your lap and nothing to do but sit back and take it—and like it." Einfeld not only saw the possibility of tying together the inauguration and the movie—a New Deal in entertainment!—but also went after and got the sponsorship of General Electric for the train. GE, in turn, made the train a rolling metaphor for a bright new tomorrow, illuminating it with wreaths of lightbulbs and arc lights. The company also promoted its own products in World's Fair style by making one of the train cars into a model kitchen displaying all the latest GE appliances—including the brand-new electric dishwasher. GE supplied sunlamps for the train's Malibu Beach Car, a re-created beach complete with sand and palm trees, so the "stars"—they were all billed as stars in the press materials and accounts—could lounge just as though they were in the real Malibu. There were staterooms for all the human performers, and a separate, hay-filled car for Tony the horse. Speakers blared the songs from *42nd Street* when the train pulled into a station ("Come and meet those dancing feet / on the Avenue I'm taking you to / Forty-second Street"). "A Cinderella train," *The Washington Post* called it. "A flying meteor" that "flashes through the nights," waxed the *Boston Herald*.

A herald of hope in desperate times, the 42nd Street Special also represented something new: a recognition that Hollywood and its celebrities carried a cultural power beyond their ability to distract and entertain. "We Americans must find some hat rack to which we can hang our national affection," wrote one observer. "At this moment celebrities are the number one vote getter. To be sure we haven't much choice. What with Big Business turning its naughty face in the drawer and turning out to be a boring lead-headed princess, there is nothing left for us to idealize except the clan of pretty boys and girls who live on the rhinestone shore of Hollywood." As the film historian Lary May writes, both the "train and the film signaled the incorporation of politics and the popular arts into remaking the nation" with a mass culture that would be more "modern and inclusive."

For Lyle, this journey from the rhinestone shore back into the heartland was an adventure he would treasure all his life. The schedule was certainly all-consuming. On a typical day, he and his fellow performers would arrive in a city about noon, entertain the crowd waiting at the station, and sometimes march in a parade as well. Then they'd attend a luncheon with local dignitaries, do press and radio interviews, and visit a GE showroom where they'd feign deep interest in the wares on display (actually, Lyle, who was kind of a gadget freak and liked to cook, might not have had to feign it). As evening fell, they'd check into a hotel, shower and dress, and head for the local Warners-owned movie palace where they'd sign autographs and appear onstage in a musical revue, then slip out the back door while *42nd Street* screened, drop into a nightclub if they were lucky, haul themselves back onto the train, and roll through the night till the next stop.

EVERYWHERE THEY STOPPED—thirteen cities in seventeen days—the crowds were staggering. In Denver, "the streets around the depot were jammed for blocks," *Variety* reported. In Indianapolis, the 42nd Street Special helped avert a bank riot when worried depositors massing to withdraw their money were diverted by the news that Tom Mix had arrived with his horse. In Pittsburgh, police estimated that the parade attracted between 200,000 and 300,000 people, a bigger crowd than the one that had turned out for Charles Lindbergh a few years earlier. ("42nd St. Comes to Pitt," read the headline in *Variety*, "and Town Goes Nerts.") In Boston, despite a driving rain, mounted police had to be brought in to manage a larger-than-expected throng of men, women, and children at the train station. My father remembered a marching band playing at the station there and how the tuba players would stop periodically and turn their instruments upside down to pour the water out. He kept thinking, "Why are all these people getting soaked just to see us?" In Kansas City, 175,000 people greeted the train; in Toledo, 25,000. A Toledo newspaper described the scene: "The crowd massed on the sloping banks that go down to the railroad tracks from Summit Street, occupied the tops of freight and passenger cars standing on sidings, stooped on top of adjacent buildings, on the roofs of the station itself and overflowed onto the tracks." In New York, when Tom Mix on horseback led a parade on Forty-second Street—"naughty, bawdy, gaudy, sporty Forty-second Street," as the song had it—20,000 people lined up to watch, and a Goodyear airship accompanied the spectacle. "Bette Davis never knew where we were," my father said years later. "She'd speak from the platform and say, 'It's great to be here in Cleveland,' and we'd be in Detroit."

Davis wrote in her autobiography that the 42nd Street Special was where she "learned once and for all how much movies mean to the American people. The reaction of the public in every city convinced me of the miraculous power of the motion picture. There wasn't the slightest doubt that Hollywood's stars were America's royalty and their subjects the most devoted in the world. If in moments of despair I had been uncertain that the world that I had chosen was a sane one, I knew now that my chosen field could be Elysian." Lyle had a similar reaction, though he focused more on his sheer good luck in being where he was. "Lyle Talbot in the car made over to represent Malibu Beach," wrote the reporter for *Variety*. "Talbot is sunning himself under one of those California sun-ray lights and you chew the rag with him about things and stuff. Talbot seems a pretty regular guy. Made a quick jump upward in film circles, but hasn't let it stampede him. Gives all the credit to lucky breaks." One of the things about that trip, my father used to say, wonderingly, was that the 42nd Street Special enjoyed the right-of-way over every other train across the country. That impressed him, probably because he was a veteran of cheap train travel and of all the little branch lines on which traveling actors could get stuck. What a luxury to keep forging ahead through the night and the rain, lighting up fallow fields and the rims of little towns, never stopping till you were in a city surging to see you.

In Yuma, Arizona, when the train stopped in the middle of the night for a quick meet-and-greet with the locals, a woman in the crowd handed Joe E. Brown her baby to hold. Standing on the rear car of the train, Brown cradled the baby while the mayor made a speech. When the train took off, Brown was still holding the baby. It turned out that the mother had fainted in all the excitement and didn't see the train leave. Brown and his pals figured out what happened, and someone alerted the engineer, who backed the train into the station to restore the infant to his overwrought mother.

"Hollywood in those days had a small-town atmosphere," my father recalled many years later, when he was almost ninety. "You went to a regular barbershop, walked down the street freely, there were no hassles with tourists. Hollywood was like this separate world; it seemed so far from the East Coast, which you could only get to by train, really from anywhere else in the country. We were working six days a week at the studio and we didn't think much about what we were doing. I thought I was lucky to have a job. It was the Depression and people were broke, but still they were going to the movies. And we were this new phenomena called movie stars—movie stars who talked. So here I was out of Hollywood for the first time since I'd arrived there, and I was amazed that every time we stopped in a city we were mobbed."

Inside the gleaming train, conditions were deluxe. The studio had hired the head chef from the Ambassador Hotel in Los Angeles to cook on board. The menu on one of the first nights featured a choice of entrees: "Filet of Halibut, Sauce Remoulade, Brace of English Lamb Chops, au Cresson, or Roast Jumbo Squab, stuffed with Wild Rice,

Guava Jelly." The side dishes on offer were "Romaine and Pineapple Salad," "Bermuda Potatoes in Cream," and "Yellow Bantam Corn Sauté." For dessert, there were "Fresh Strawberry Ice Cream, Petits Fours, and Roquefort Cheese."

Between cities, Lyle favored the lounge of the Malibu Beach car, where the ceiling was painted like a cloudless Southern California sky and the gaily striped chairs were wide and cushy. He'd hang out smoking, doing the crossword puzzle, and reading the Hollywood trade papers or the local dailies with Mix, Carrillo, and Brown. They were all good company—downright chatty as men go. Brown, a onetime circus tumbler and baseball player turned vaudevillian and Broadway star, was famous for his mile-wide grin and rubbery face. Carrillo, though he'd found a niche in pictures by playing up a ridiculous bandito accent, was in fact a college-educated former political cartoonist, the scion of a prominent old California family, and in time, a pioneering conservationist of the California shoreline. Carrillo had "an intelligent comeback for anything you threw at him," observed the *Variety* correspondent. He amused himself and his fellow passengers by sketching caricatures of them. Mix was born in 1880 and had enjoyed most of his success in the silent era. But he was still a popular figure, instantly recognizable to his fans with his comically outsized Stetson hats and elaborately studded or embroidered white suits. Though he grew up in Pennsylvania, not out West, he really was an expert rodeo rider—the "Jackie Chan of cowboys," Jeanine Basinger calls him, "with his breakneck pace, his action just for the sake of action, and his amazing stunt work."

Once he made it in Hollywood, Mix lived life large but had a sense of humor about it. He collected fancy guns, cars, and shoes and had his initials embossed on all of them. He married five times. He would die in 1940 in an auto accident while driving eighty miles an hour on a desolate stretch of Arizona road. My father liked Mix very much. He remembered him as the good-natured elder brother of the

trip, and appreciated his sentimentality about his horses, past and present. He was a wild guy, no doubt about it. But he also had a touch of
what passed for gravitas on the 42nd Street Special. Unlike the rest of
the stars, Mix had been to an inauguration before: that of Teddy Roosevelt, where he had ridden his first horse, Tony, in the parade, along
with Roosevelt's Rough Riders. This time around, he was the only one
who seemed more interested in endorsing Franklin Roosevelt than promoting his own career (perhaps the Warners had chosen him, a folksy,
beloved cowboy, to be their designated political spokesman). "You
know, without taking any bows, an actor's a pretty good person to esti-
mate a man in politics," Mix told a reporter, in what still stands as a
sound assessment of Roosevelt's personal appeal. "Some of them are
afraid they'll be criticized for knowing show people. That type gets
stiff as a sprained ankle. The other kind tries to condescend and be
'natural.' They remind you of a cub bear handling an alarm clock. Mr.
Roosevelt is easy and not condescending, friendly without losing dignity. He's the real McCoy. He doesn't need to deliberately simplify his
language to make a cowhand understand him."

If Mix was the Stetson-wearing elder statesman of the trip, then
Lyle was its young heartthrob. As a Kansas City paper noted, not only
was he "the sole eligible young man onboard," he was also a "new 'find'
as a leading man," "handsome as hell. And as likeable as a collie." Lyle
had pinned his own romantic hopes on Bette Davis. They had just
made *20,000 Years in Sing Sing* together, and Lyle, unlike the studio
execs and directors who downgraded her sex appeal, thought Davis
was plenty cute. True, "she wasn't endowed particularly with the
breasts or things like that," my father would tell a radio host in San
Francisco when he was a very old man. But she radiated an almost
naively serious-minded approach to her work, an ambitiousness about
her craft that Lyle, being made of lighter stuff himself, admired. Not
that it didn't confound him sometimes, too. When they did a movie
called *Fog over Frisco*, a very minor picture that Davis was inexplicably

fond of, she would practice her lines off by herself in a sort of trance, Lyle told an interviewer in 1960. It was "as though she'd been handed a Shaw or Shakespeare assignment," he recalled. "Her absolute dedication was unnerving. Her self-involvement came on to me as a kind of selfishness—true, she worked well with other players, and the crew, but I always felt her mind was solely on herself and the effect she was producing."

Still, none of that would have been a deal breaker for the Railway Romeo. The presence of a husband he hadn't known about was another matter. When Bette got on the train in Los Angeles, she brought Harmon "Ham" Nelson, the shy musician she'd known back home in Massachusetts and married six months earlier. Because of her busy work schedule, they'd never had a chance to take a honeymoon, and this was to be it, though as she would say later, "what with waving on the observation car at 2:30 in the morning to wide-eyed movie fans," and the like, it wasn't much of one. "Our stateroom," she recalled, "was only used for lying in state." Davis, it was clear, was on her way to stardom. On this trip, she could afford to laugh with reporters about how the studio had relegated her to "nice, dowdy little gal" roles. If "the hero was supposed to so much as glance in my direction they insisted that it just wouldn't do," she told a reporter in Chicago. No man would be crazy enough to fall for Davis. Now, though, the newspapers agreed, she was having the last laugh, getting the better, sexier roles she deserved. And they singled her out, with loving descriptions of her clothes: bright yellow lounging pajamas and green sandals in Chicago, polka-dot gloves in Kansas City, a brilliant blue tweed suit in Indianapolis.

As for the other ladies on the train, well, Eleanor Holm, the swimmer, liked a good time. Three years later, en route to Berlin, she would be thrown off the U.S. Olympic Team for drinking champagne and breaking curfew with sports reporters. Glenda Farrell was a pal, though much more modulated and ladylike in real life than the brassy gals she played on screen. But she was trying to catch up on sleep the best she could, recovering from a grueling filmmaking schedule over the previous six months. More fun were the game and hardworking chorus girls, with their "hair like spun taffy" and their "long black eyelashes," as one paper described them, young women who "twinkled back and forth in the crowd, basking in the obvious admiration of the fans." My father remembered Toby Wing particularly fondly. She was a platinum blond with a soft, round face who was often billed as the most beautiful chorus girl in Hollywood (and who got more fan mail in her prime than the big stars at her studio, Marlene Dietrich and Claudette Colbert). Davis recalled a less glamorous detail about the chorines: they "were always popping into opera hose and tremendous white polka-dot halters and white coats. The poor girls had one costume apiece. They were not the most attractive sight at the end of the tour. White on a train for sixteen days!"

Everybody got a little rambunctious at times. One night, Lyle and a few of the other actors raided and trashed the GE model kitchen. They tried to make waffles on the electric waffle iron, an object none of them had ever seen before. The batter oozed out like lava when they weren't looking—they were all a little soused to begin with—and everything went kerflooey from there. It was like a kitchen in a cartoon that had turned on its owners. Like penitent children, they stood there in the morning, barefoot but still in evening dress, and took a scolding from their Warner Brothers chaperone. In Pittsburgh, a well-oiled Tom Mix rode his horse onto the dance floor of a nightclub.

When the 42nd Street Special stopped in Chicago, Lyle had an unexpected visitor. His name was Edward "Spike" O'Donnell, and he was a bootlegger and the head of an Irish gang known as the South Side O'Donnells. His deputies were his brothers, and fortunately for him, he had a lot of them, since they had a tendency to get themselves killed. In his history of the Chicago underworld, Herbert Asbury

*Lyle crowding in with chorus girls on the 42nd Street Special,
offering "a New Deal in Entertainment!"*

describes him this way: "A criminal since boyhood, Spike O'Donnell had been sneak thief, pickpocket, burglar, footpad, labor slugger, and bank-robber; he had shot half a dozen men, had been twice tried for murder, and had been accused of several other killings. He was also deeply religious, and not even the prospect of a good murder or a holdup could keep him from attending Sunday Mass at St. Peter's Catholic Church." In 1925, in the midst of the so-called Chicago Beer Wars between rival bootlegging gangs, O'Donnell had the distinction of being the intended target of the first machine-gun attack in American history. He was standing in front of the J.J. Weiss drugstore when an open touring car approached. The rival gang leader Frank McErlane shouted out, "Hel-lo, Spike," then sprayed the storefront with bullets from a Thompson submachine gun, World War I's gift to gangsters, also known as a tommy gun. McErlane didn't really know what he was doing, and lucky Spike emerged unscathed. He would survive multiple attempts on his life. As he put it once, "Life with me is just one bullet after another."

Lyle had met Spike O'Donnell once before, when the bootlegger was visiting the Warners lot and stopped by to watch the filming of the bank robbery sequence in the movie *Ladies They Talk About*. Maybe he was feeling homesick. In any case, he liked what he saw. Lyle was the lead robber and Spike told him he admired how he'd pulled it off—with style, he said. In the heist scene, Lyle says things like "First one that sets off the alarm, I'll blow your insides all over the wall" (a line that censorship boards in New York and Pennsylvania, among other regions, tried to have removed). He tells his cohort to go for the big bucks, "never mind the chicken feed." And he looks sharp; he's chewing gum in a self-possessed sort of way, and he's wearing a well-cut suit. Spike liked to project that kind of an image himself. He was a natty dresser, with a penchant for spats and homburgs and polka-dotted bow ties. He was a good-looking guy, too, who prided himself on his gallantry to women and children. He liked to pal around with actors of Irish lineage—like Spencer Tracy and James Cagney—who either didn't know about or politely overlooked his sociopathic side. In 1931, he even claimed that he himself would be pursuing an acting career in London and that his first role would be a Chicago gangster or else Robin Hood. No acting career materialized, but O'Donnell's fondness for actors was undiminished.

As far as Spike O'Donnell was concerned, Lyle, bless his Irish soul, had shown the world what a stylish gangster looked like. O'Donnell approved of him in *Ladies They Talk About* and had nice things to say about his turn as a dapper bootlegger in an earlier movie, *The Purchase Price*.

So when he arrived in Chicago, O'Donnell wanted to do the actor a favor. He turned up unbidden at his hotel room, trailing a couple of bodyguards he introduced as Dingy and Babe. Dingy, O'Donnell told Lyle with a flourish, would be his escort while he was in Chicago. Dingy would take Lyle anywhere he wanted and wouldn't let anyone bother him. Lyle did not particularly want an escort—if he did, she'd be more along the lines of the chorus girl Toby Wing. He felt he didn't have much choice in the matter, though. "I got along with Spike fine," my father told me once, "but being with him was always a little nerveracking since I knew his brother had been gunned down standing next to him." As he left, O'Donnell gave my father a little token: a pearl-handled derringer, loaded. A few hours later, he brought his wife and children to the premiere of *42nd Street*.

That night, Glenda Farrell drove with Lyle in the studio car when they went out on the town. Farrell may have "played all sorts of tough dames in gangster movies," as my father would recall, but that night, "she took one look at Dingy and the gun he had in his pocket and she nearly peed in her pants." They rode in the car to O'Donnell's gambling joint, which was whimsically designed to look like the New York Stock Exchange, complete with ticker tape. When the 42nd Street Special left Chicago at midnight, Dingy and Babe were there on the platform, waving good-bye. Lyle unlocked his compartment, relieved that his escorts would soon be back to protecting real gangsters. When he opened his luggage, he found, nestled among his clothes, twenty-four pints of bootleg whiskey wrapped in burlap—a going-away present from his admirer, Spike. He never knew how Spike and Dingy had gotten into the locked compartment, and if the porter knew, he wasn't telling. Lyle never saw Spike again—though he would have had the possibility, at least, of doing so. O'Donnell was one of the few gangsters of the Capone era to live a long life, make money in legitimate business, and die of natural causes.

Maybe, in the contrast between the luxury on the train and the penury outside, there was something a little eighteenth-century, a little obscene. Bette Davis thought so in retrospect. "Factories were closed, millions jobless," she wrote, "and we really should have been publicizing the musical Let 'Em Eat Cake." But the entertainers were not entirely immune from the ravages of the Depression. In New York, they learned that all studio employees were to take a 50 percent pay cut. And the bank holiday FDR declared on March 5, 1933, meant they couldn't cash the checks they had.

My father would not have had the reaction Davis did: he was essentially apolitical at that time and not subtly attuned to historical ironies. Even much later in life, when he had emerged under my mother's and his children's influence as a liberal Democrat, he probably wouldn't have seen the experience in class terms. Then again, with that sort of temperament and outlook, he took the bank holiday and the pay cut in stride, too. "Lyle Talbot, who is young enough to take things as they come, and good-natured enough to laugh when they don't come," wrote a reporter for *Cinema Digest*, "got plenty of laughs out of the experience." Lyle told the reporter, "There's plenty of precedent for being stranded. But the orthodox way for an actor to go broke is to sit on his trunk on the station platform. I'll bet we were the first troupe in history to be stranded in a gold train. If my screen career is ended I think I can do pretty well going through life as a moocher. I've had experience. With no checks accepted by the banks, we mooched free entertainment and free meals at all the stops east of Washington. I must have been good. In one hotel, they gave me the plate for a souvenir. That's the first time I've ever heard of the waiters tipping the diners."

If he did not take the Depression itself as seriously as he might have, he did take seriously his duty to entertain people during it—to look the part for the crowds who came out to catch a glimpse of glamorous show folk. In a film clip of the 42nd Street Special's send-off from Los Angeles, Lyle comes out on the platform of the train to say a few words. He is wearing a black shawl-collared coat and a white silk scarf. He tells the crowd this is going to be a "grand trip," and then says, with conspiratorial charm, that he can't talk too long because actually he's a stowaway. The *Indianapolis News* declared him "smooth and nonchalant, the perfect movie man-about-town."

At the inauguration, FDR told Americans, "If I read the temper of our people correctly, we now realize, as we have never realized before, our interdependence on each other, that we cannot merely take, but we must give as well, that if we are to go forward, we must move as a trained and loyal army willing to sacrifice for the good of a common discipline, because without such discipline, no progress can be made, no leadership become effective."

That speech may not have resonated with Lyle all that much. He and the other entertainers aboard the 42nd Street Special were so tired by the time they got to D.C. that several of them slept through long stretches of the inauguration ceremony. Unlike my mother, who was just five at the time but who would remember that speech, admire Roosevelt all her life, and tell her children time and again that there was nothing to fear but fear itself, my father heard more to inspire him in the speech given by the producer in the movie *42nd Street* than the one he witnessed in Washington, D.C., that cloudy day in March. He'd heard the *42nd Street* speech many times, while hanging around the set, providing the overheated narration for the trailer, watching the movie at premiere after premiere. In it, the producer, Julian Marsh, is exhorting Peggy Sawyer, the young chorus girl who must step in for the injured leading lady:

"Sawyer, you listen to me, and you listen hard. Two hundred people, two hundred jobs, two hundred thousand dollars, five weeks of grind and blood and sweat depend on you. It's the lives of all these people who've worked with you. You've got to go on, and you've got to give and give and give. They've *got* to like you. *Got* to. Do you understand? You can't fall down. You can't because your future's in it, my future's in it, and everything all of us have is staked on you. All right, now I'm through, but you keep your feet on the ground and your head on those shoulders of yours and go out, and Sawyer, you're going out a youngster, but you've *got* to come back a star."

Now these for Lyle were words to live by, words to stir himself up with as he brushed his long black coat, polished his wingtip shoes with a chamois cloth, stared at the rivulets of rain shimmying down the train windows, caught a glimpse of the crowd outside that seemed to be shivering in unison, with cold and anticipation both. Yes, he thought. Yes. And out he sallied to give and give and give.

Chapter 6

─◦◦◦─

MAN ABOUT TOWN

When Lyle arrived in Hollywood, nobody made him over. He did not get his hairline altered, his nose refashioned, his teeth capped, or his ears pinned back. Hollywood was a pioneer in plastic surgery, and by the early 1930s, it was not uncommon for actors and actresses to undergo some sort of corrective procedure, often on studio orders. The theater world Lyle had grown up in would never have made such demands, but the close-up and the plastic surgeon were natural allies. "Would you like a new nose?" asked a headline in the August 1930 edition of *Photoplay* magazine. "Over 2,000 of our stars and near-stars have had their faces shuffled and re-assembled." An article in the September 1932 issue of *Modern Screen* confided, "In Hollywood today, features are subject to change without notice. For there is a group of reputable and skilled surgeons, who are able to and do perform miracles for the sake of the camera." Ten years earlier, they couldn't or wouldn't have. Now, articles like these even named names, accomplishing the seemingly contradictory task of glorifying Hollywood beauty while demystifying it—yes, these gods and goddesses of the screen were extraordinary, but they weren't necessarily born that way. If you weren't, either, maybe there was hope for you yet—or, conversely, some consolation in knowing that extraordinarily good-looking performers had been given artificial advantages you had not. "You'd be surprised," claimed *Photoplay*, "at the famous names whose screen beauty is synthetic, who have had nose corrections, new chins, pinned-back ears, facelifts"—a concept the article had to define—"deep acid peels, fat removal and other operations at the hands of these specialists in putting beauty where it isn't." Tarzan actor Johnny Weissmuller was "physically perfect" and "could swing from tree to tree," but "a screen test revealed a defective lump in his nose," *Modern Screen* explained. "Did he give up in despair? No, he went home, talked it over with his wife, and decided to go to Dr. Josef Ginsberg, who has performed over 1,000 operations on the film famous in the last two years." George Raft had his ears pinned back; Clark Gable, despite the rumors, did not, although he used adhesive for close-ups. Rita Hayworth had her hair dyed and her hairline, which sat a bit low on her forehead, raised with electrolysis.

Some performers were unveiled as is. They looked about as good as they needed to look. Lyle was one of those.

True, he wore makeup on screen—everybody did in those days. His was applied most mornings at the studio by Percy Westmore, one of the dynasty of makeup artists who dominated Hollywood. (The patriarch, George Westmore, was a barber from the Isle of Wight, who had immigrated to California and founded the first movie makeup department at Selig studios in 1917. George Westmore fathered twenty children; the six sons who survived to adulthood, an inventive, mercurial, rivalrous bunch, all became Hollywood makeup artists, each at one time heading the department of a major studio.) But that was it, and unlike today's stars, Lyle did not spend hours with a personal trainer resculpting what nature had given him. Aside from Tarzan and the well-oiled sybarites in biblical epics, male actors didn't usually appear bare-chested in movies. When Clark Gable took his shirt off in *It Happened One Night*, and revealed—yowza—no undershirt, it caused a national sensation and a serious dip in undershirt sales. But bare-chestedness being the exception, and gym-wrought fitness not yet the beau ideal, a six-pack was not required. A slim guy who looked good in a suit would do just fine. If he was on the tall side, which my father, at five-feet-eleven, was considered to be (then, as now, the average American male was about five-feet-nine), he got extra credit.

These aesthetic standards served my father well, since he was no athlete. In those days he golfed if dragooned into it, and played handball occasionally because it was a popular pastime with the Hollywood crowd in the 1930s. He played tennis, but only if summoned by the likes of William Randolph Hearst on weekends at San Simeon, and in that case, you were supposed to let the old man win. Not a problem for Lyle. He bicycled, but in a sort of European city-dweller way—it was just how he got around sometimes, especially on the Warner Brothers lot. We grew up with a good-sized backyard pool, but in all my life, I never saw my father dip so much as a toe in it. He had never learned to swim.

When Warners launched Lyle, it didn't even give him a new name. Those were the days of rampant name changes. Ever since the silent era, when Theodosia Goodman, a nice Jewish girl from Cincinnati, became Theda Bara, an anagram for "Arab Death," Hollywood had been rechristening its performers with names that were sexier, classier, less ethnic, or differently ethnic. Exotic and hard-to-trace worked; Ellis Island–ordinary and hard-to-pronounce did not. Lucille LeSueur became Joan Crawford. Another Lucile—this one with the double-barreled last name of Vasconcellos Langhanke—acted under the much tonier and more concise Mary Astor. Archibald Leach was reborn as Cary Grant. Greta Gustafsson launched her acting career as Greta Garbo. Emanuel Goldenberg, who had been born to a

Yiddish-speaking family in Bucharest, achieved fame as the solidly WASPish Edward G. Robinson (even if the role that made his career was Rico, the Italian mobster in *Little Caesar*).

But Lyle, like James Cagney and, more surprisingly, Humphrey Bogart, got to keep his own name. It was a name that did the trick. "Lyle" was soft and caressing and a little bit different. French, perhaps? "Talbot" was firm and aristocratic; it started and then snapped shut with the same consonant, like a bedroom door clicking closed. Of course, they had to drop that silly *s* from "Lysle," the spelling he sometimes used during his theatrical career. But it was silent anyway, so Lyle could hardly have missed it. In fact, what happened to Lyle's name was almost the opposite of what usually happened to actors' names: he kept his real one, but studio publicity and the resulting press claimed he had not. That was because they preferred the story that was almost true—which was that his real name was Lyle Hollywood. Convinced that no one *in* Hollywood would believe it, the young actor had changed it. Of course, Hollywood *was* a family name. It had been his grandmother's maiden name—and it was his grandmother, after all, who had raised him. But Talbot was her married name, and though she was widowed when she kidnapped and adopted Lyle, Talbot was the last name she gave him. (Henderson, his father's last name, was never an option while his grandmother was around.) His young parents had not bothered to give Lyle a middle name, but now, if someone asked him for one, Lyle took to using Florence, or just the letter F, after the mother he had never known.

As it did for any new actor deemed to have star potential, the studio publicity department set out to craft a persona for Lyle—a collection of alluring biographical details that accreted into a story the public would, with any luck, respond to. A persona worked best if it borrowed liberally from the facts, just as lies are usually easier to stick to if they're plausible. Newly signed performers were always asked to fill out a questionnaire about where they'd been raised and what they did for fun, about their fathers and mothers, their first jobs, their phobias, and—this was a popular one during the Depression—their "pet economies" (cheap socks, bologna sandwiches). Then the studio PR department would write up a biography based—though sometimes quite loosely—on the answers, and these sketches would go out to the fan magazines, the wire services, the newspapers, and the trade press. "The studio bio was all a game," writes the film scholar Jeanine Basinger, "a story-telling game, a shrewd tool that helped suggest to fans how to see the star." It was never comprehensive, it burnished and embellished with impunity, but it had a relationship with the truth.

The 1930s marked a peculiar era in the history of movie publicity because it combined old-fashioned, shameless ballyhoo that wouldn't have been out of place in the Walter Savidge carnival with more subtle attempts at lodging particular movies and their stars in the public's mind. A film yearbook aimed at theater owners proposed that for showings of horror movies like *Dracula* and *Frankenstein*, they should have a nurse conspicuously in attendance, supposedly to attend to any viewers who might be overcome, along with a shill in the audience who would faint and have to be taken away by ambulance. The promotional materials that studios sent out to film exhibitors were often full of such brash, corny-sounding ideas, some of which were put into practice. For a movie called *Murder in the Clouds*, an aviation-themed thriller in which Lyle starred as a daredevil pilot opposite Ann Dvorak, the glossy promotional guide produced by the studio suggested that theater managers could: organize a parade of kids lofting model airplanes; hide a PA system somewhere in the lobby from which a mysterious voice would issue saying, "Watch it, folks! Look up! There's been a murder in the clouds!"; pay for a plane to hover overhead, since people still "look up at an airplane" circling; hire two small boys with "leather-lungs" to yell across the street at each other about the swell movie they're going to see that night. "The lads take a trip around the block, and start same spiel again for new passersby. Stunt doesn't look like a plant"—if they say so—"and the exhibitor who used it swears by it." But in the same years, studio publicity people were also crafting more subtle stories about actors and actresses, incorporating calculated glimpses of their divorces and other private sorrows, their surprising hobbies, their physical flaws, and their "secrets" for correcting them.

In Lyle's case, the bones of his story, like those of his face, were good. He'd been a magician and a hypnotist's assistant—the PR guys loved the story about how he'd had rocks broken on his chest. He'd been a theater actor, which was a favorable calling card in the early 1930s, when the advent of talkies led to a vogue for stage actors. What one film historian calls "Hollywood's raid on Broadway" began in 1928, and by 1934, *Variety* was reporting that "Hollywood is now 70% dependent on the stage for its film acting talent in those brackets where performers get screen credit." Silent actors, many of whom had done their first acting for the cameras, were thought to lack the voice training and requisite timbre to make it in talkies. They'd have to study voice or give up. Even a middle American newspaper like the Wayne, Nebraska, *Herald* had gotten with the program, noting in an article about Lyle, "The days of picking a nicely profiled youngster off the streets and training him or her to register a few emotions are at an end—voice control and stage experience are necessary." This didn't turn out to be strictly true. Lots of silent actors did make the transition successfully, but those who failed to do so, like the heartthrob John Gilbert, became legendary for it. Stage actors were definitely garnering more than their share of love in the Hollywood of the early 1930s. One of the studio bios that Warner Brothers compounded for Lyle boasted that "Talbot is a product of the stage. He was practically born on it, his mother and father both being on the stage. He has never known anything else."

Other tidbits about Lyle in the studio bios and the press combined the true with the ought-to-be-true. He'd grown up in a little town that was almost all Bohemian (that was true) and spoke fluent

Czech (that wasn't). He was bright and liked to read (that was true) and had attended the University of Nebraska for two years (that wasn't). He was so sentimental about animals that once when he was playing golf in South Dakota, and his ball had conked a sheep on the head, he had driven the sheep seventeen miles to the nearest vet, delaying the start of the play he was appearing in that night. (That was true-ish; he *had* gone to the aid of the downed sheep, but once he saw it back on its feet and tottering off, he headed for the theater. He would never have been late for curtain.)

The persona devised for him fit him in many ways. The studio did not, for instance, try to turn him into a man's man or a rugged outdoors type—not seriously anyway. There is one unfortunate batch of publicity stills that show him fly-fishing, standing in a stream in waders and grinning madly. It wasn't repeated. Clark Gable had not grown up as an outdoorsman, but he wished he had, so when the studio biographies made him over in that mold, he took to it. He started actually hunting and fishing, just as he was supposed to have been doing all his life. His was, as Jeanine Basinger notes, "a bio success—life imitating art." Lyle, on the other hand, had grown up in a small town and remained fond of it all his life—from a distance. He was an urban creature, really. He liked going to restaurants and the theater, to movies and clubs. And when he was older and more domestic, he liked to read a good daily newspaper first thing in the morning and save the crossword puzzle for the evening, to shop for and cook ambitious meals. Hunting? Not for the man who hovered tenderly over a sheep he'd beaned. Camping? Not with his grooming habits and fondness for well-ironed sheets.

A number of articles in the early 1930s declared Lyle a star-in-the-making. A spread in *Motion Picture* magazine named Katharine Hepburn the female star of tomorrow and Lyle Talbot the male star. And many of those articles identified him as a Clark Gable type—skilled at playing what was known as "light heavies," like the gangster

*Lyle in a publicity photo, playing up his image as a clotheshorse,
or in this case shoehorse.*

who was also a playboy. But the bios took, wisely perhaps, a different tack. "Really, he's nothing at all like any of the roles he's played. He's tall and well set up, with straight brown hair and well-cut features—good looking enough to play with anyone from Garbo down," one of his studio bios enthused. "He's not a tough—I've already said he's no Gable. His interest is in the stage and books, and he's a collector of the latter. He's modest, lives simply, and works hard. He could perhaps be compared to Fredric March for knowledge, ability and application to his job."

His persona was that of a sophisticated yet boyish and playful indoorsman, a collector of first editions, which he liked to have specially bound, an enthusiast of games like charades and concentration, a "devotee," according to one profile, of Ernest Hemingway, William

Faulkner, and Carleton Beals. (Well, that was a bit of a stretch—he did always have a lot of books and he read. But he preferred newspapers and magazines, and he was never a "devotee" of literature.) He liked the idea of Esperanto and thought he might learn it in case there was ever an international theater. He disapproved of Prohibition—no kidding, the way he drank—took little interest in politics, wanted to live in London someday because people seemed to enjoy life more there, and preferred to buy his clothes in Hollywood. He liked children but didn't have any. He liked pets and did: a black Scottie, and a couple of cocker spaniels, one of them a gift from the actress Fifi D'Orsay. He drove his own car, because he liked to drive, but as for pet economies, he had none. He was fond of ballroom dancing, filet of sole, and silk pajamas. He entertained frequently, and when he did, he mixed the drinks for his guests himself. A squib in one of the L.A. papers said he had developed his own cocktail for the spring months that he called the Peacherino—a ripe peach mashed with powdered sugar, "a drink of dry gin," and a "half drink of cream," mixed with shaved ice and seltzer in a highball glass. He scrambled eggs for his guests if they found, in the wee hours, that they'd drunk too much and needed something in their stomachs. He sang and whistled in the car and forgot to stop when he was waiting at an intersection.

He liked to give theme parties—a Christmas Eve gathering where the guests, who included the actors Dick Powell, Mary Brian, and Wallace Ford, had to bring one another presents they'd purchased at Woolworth's; come-as-you-are parties, a fad of the 1930s, at which invitees had to appear in whatever they were wearing when they received a summons (with any luck, some of the invitees might have been in the shower); parties that involved activities that looked a lot like what actors did all day, the sorts of things you might expect they'd be weary of—but, like children, they were not.

Charades were big with Lyle and his friends. So were elaborate memory games. "Concentration, favorite parlor game, took a heavy toll of participants at a party at Helen Ferguson's home," a 1935 item in the L.A. *Times* noted, "with Glenda Farrell, Lyle Talbot, Mae Clark, the Johnny Mack Browns, Addison Randall, Alden Chase, and various others demonstrating their phenomenal memories. . . . The game proceeds along this line: 'I am going to Europe and I am going to take with me a hatrack, a Schnauzer pup, a lumberyard, athlete's foot, a Chinese pagoda etc. etc.,' each person contributing some new and generally fantastic exhibit to the traveler's impedimenta and each being required to recite the growing list from beginning to end."

Lyle moved often—the habits of the road were hard to shake, and he felt for many years that Hollywood and his film career were as fragile as soap bubbles, kept aloft mainly by pure but fickle luck. Still, he picked lovely homes to rent while the luck lasted, and his progression reflected the migration trends of the movie crowd, many of whom settled first in Hollywood, then Beverly Hills or Malibu, and still later, the San Fernando Valley.

The first place he moved after he got his Warner Brothers contract and left the Ravenswood Apartments was the actors' enclave of Whitley Heights. The neighborhood was nestled in the pine and eucalyptus-clad foothills of the Santa Monica Mountains, across Highland Avenue from the Hollywood Bowl. In the 1910s, its developer, a Canadian named Hobart Johnstone Whitley, had sent an architect to Italy for inspiration. The result was a picturesque cluster of houses in that Mediterranean style that would become so influential in Southern California—big, arched windows, wrought-iron gates and balconies, sunken living rooms with terra-cotta floors, walls of ocher or dusty pink or whitewashed stucco. The streets of Whitley Heights were narrow and winding, lush with trailing bougainvillea and heavy swags of wisteria, with cedar and lemon and olive trees. The houses, with their red-tiled roofs, were banked on top of one another, and flights of stairs connected the different levels of streets. "From my second-story veranda," recalled the actress Marie Dressler of her house

Lyle and his father and stepmother, Ed and Anna,
in Whitley Heights.

there, "I could see acre upon acre of green California grass and bright-hued California flowers. I could watch whole regiments of royal palms march down white avenues." The L.A. *Times* once dubbed Whitley Heights "the Palatine Hill of the Golden Age of Hollywood."

Whitley Heights was close to the studios, but it seemed secluded, and the combination made it popular with silent-era actors. Besides Dressler, its residents included Harold Lloyd, Charlie Chaplin, and Wallace Reid. Rudolph Valentino had a house there, and "could often be spotted, clad in riding togs, walking his two mastiffs and his

Dobermans along the narrow road," says the Hollywood historian David Wallace. By the time my father moved to Whitley Heights, to a house on Wedgewood Place, many actors had switched their allegiance to the newly chic Beverly Hills. But there were still those who preferred the supposedly fresher air of Whitley Heights—Bette Davis, Maurice Chevalier, Jean Harlow, and Carole Lombard all lived there at one time, as did William Faulkner. In the mid 1950s, about a third of Whitley Heights was razed and the neighborhood bisected to make way for the Hollywood Freeway. But even today, if you walk around what's left of it, you feel something of what Southern California must have felt like before the postwar development boom. You can see how somebody had the idea to build a replica of an Italian hill town in the middle of Hollywood.

There is a photograph of my father at his Whitley Heights house that I have always been very fond of. He is sitting, in profile and partly in silhouette, on the iron railing of a wide window. He's wearing a white dress shirt and a tie, and his gaze is pensive. Behind him, tile roofs, palm and cypress trees, and sepia-colored hills recede into the distance. He might be in Tuscany. Except that you can also, though just barely, make out a sign in the far hills: the white letters, shivery like a heat mirage, that spell out "Hollywoodland." There's an Expressionist elegance to his pose, and looking at the landscape behind him, you get an elegiac sense of a lost and smogless L.A.

After a year or so, Lyle decamped for Beverly Hills. There he rented a little house that he loved, a Tudor-style cottage with a rustic wooden gate and shuttered windows, on Rexford Drive. We used to drive past it sometimes on our way to Beverly Hills, to Nate 'n Al's deli or to my orthodontist, and my dad would always point it out. That house was the one that got away, the bargain investment he could have landed if only he'd been smart like some of the actors. Guys like Bing Crosby, Gene Autry, and Bob Hope, he'd say, had seen not only that the movie industry in Southern California was going to last, but that

The Mediterranean splendor of the Whitley Heights house.

buying up land and media outlets there was the way to go. Then he'd sigh a little and change the subject. His attitude about money-making was fatalistic and insouciant at once. Sure, there'd been chances to invest, sure, he'd been dumb about them, but money wasn't what mattered. What mattered was that you kept working; what mattered was that you had fun and shared the fun with people less fun than yourself.

He rented the house on Rexford Drive for $125 a month, which included furniture, dishes, silverware, even the gardener's fee. There was a Filipino man who had worked for the previous resident as cook and valet, and though my father liked to cook, he was happy enough to keep the man on: he wore a neat white coat and a black tie at all times on the job, and taught my father how to make perfect rice. The monthly rent counted toward purchase of the house; my father had that in mind for a while, but he eventually transferred to a friend the Rexford Drive house and the down payment he'd made thus far, and made nothing on the deal. "I didn't think about making money that way," he said, looking back. "I didn't think of a house as an investment. I bought a lot of clothes and I lived high and all that sort of thing."

His grandmother came to visit when he lived in that house. Mary Talbot was still running the hotel in Brainard, and would do so until shortly before she died in 1937. She was still fierce, still hardworking, but she could not conceal her pride in her grandson. While staying with Lyle in Beverly Hills, she made her own way to Hollywood Boulevard. It was December, and the studios had decorated the lampposts with silver wreaths holding tinted portraits of their actors and actresses. Mary found Lyle's and sat herself down on a bench under it. Wearing a long black dress and a hat that marked her as a visitor from somewhere colder and older, Mary would return to that same bench each day of her visit. Perhaps some of the passersby who saw her thought she was an extra from a movie, some period piece set on the frontier. All afternoon, to anyone who listened, Mary would point to Lyle's picture and say, "That's my grandson."

In 1936, Lyle decided he wanted a bigger place, and moved to Toluca Lake, a bucolic corner of the San Fernando Valley that Amelia Earhart had helped to make fashionable when she moved there to be close to the Lockheed airplane plant in Burbank. Lyle picked the particular house he did, according to an article in the *Chicago Tribune*, because it had a living room big enough for all his games. "Parlor games are Talbot's weakness. He has installed a ping-pong table, three

Lyle and his grandmother Mary Hollywood Talbot.

marble games, and endless tables for checkers, chess, backgammon, and cards in the living room. He has room for a miniature archery set. The garage houses his three bicycles and the patio he turned into a court for playing badminton."

When Lyle arrived in L.A. to take up this life in a series of rented houses, he was freshly divorced from his first wife, Elaine Melchior, who'd elected to stay behind in New York. Lyle explained to a fan magazine that there had been "nothing dramatic" about his divorce. It was just that they were both busy and ambitious; they didn't get to see each other often, since they were each traveling with shows, and when they did manage to get back to New York at the same time, they stayed with her mother in a rather crowded setup. Theirs was a story that would have resonated with a lot of Americans. Between the turn of the century and 1928, the nation's divorce rate had climbed from about one in fourteen marriages to about one in six. The divorces of actors and actresses were often discussed in those years, less as examples of scandalous excess than as experiences like those of many young people—unfortunate, perhaps, but not scarring or shameful. Stories of Hollywood divorces in which actors and actresses appeared to be speaking frankly and with feeling helped normalize the idea of divorce, just as the articles about the stars' cosmetic interventions did for plastic surgery. By the 1930s, an early divorce—especially one that could be attributed not to adultery but to the divergent paths of a childless young couple like Lyle and Elaine—no longer carried the stigma that all divorce once had. Hollywood had helped make it so.

It didn't take long for the single Lyle to suss out his excellent dating prospects in Hollywood. He was thirty when he arrived (though studio publicity shaved two years off), handsome, and in line for stardom. He loved the company of women, relied on their judgment and taste, and particularly appreciated those who showed spark, intelligence, and a strong will. The studios themselves were like dating agencies. By day, they threw beautiful young people together for long hours. By night, they prodded their contract players to go out on dates with head-turning actors or actresses from the home lot and others (and sent studio photographers along to snap so-called candid pictures, which the studios provided to the newspapers).

In a period of a little over a year, gossip items in the columns of Louella Parsons and Walter Winchell, among others, linked him with a veritable chorus line of actresses. "Lyle Talbot with a pretty blonde at the Club Ballyhoo." "Lyle Talbot, new and very good-looking leading man, chatting with Wynne Gibson at the Garden Room at the Biltmore." "Jayne Shadduck is heaving big sighs over Lyle Talbot at the moment." "Estelle Taylor and Lyle Talbot, the newest screen Apollo, are very much 'that way.'" "Fifi D'Orsay is the latest to go nightclubbing with the ubiquitous Lyle Talbot." "Loretta Young and Lyle Talbot at the opening of the play 'The Devil Passes,' at the Pasadena Community Playhouse." Wynne Gibson and Lyle Talbot, "seen everywhere together. They were dancing again the other night to Stanley Smith's music at the Biltmore Garden Room." "Hollywood romance rumorers now say Lyle Talbot can't decide between Loretta Young and her sister Sally Blane. Lyle seems to be getting over in the city of shadows that talk." "Devoted twosome at the Derby: Estelle Taylor and her latest admirer, Lyle Talbot. Eddie Cantor and Al Jolson telling stories at the dinner table." "Alice Faye and Lyle Talbot—you can't keep that fellow away from a gal long—went to the Cotton Club Sunday night." "Lola Lane and Lyle Talbot, no less, watching the moon from Mulholland Drive." "Lyle (Don Juan) Talbot is putting on the rush act with Helen Mann, a pie catcher from one of the comedy lots."

An article in the *Illustrated Daily News* made a show of mining his childhood in Brainard, which it insisted on referring to as the "village" to account for his charms: "He was a favorite, almost from the beginning with the Bohemian girls in the village, who came to visit him and showed him their bright scarves and let him cut his teeth on their ear-rings and necklaces and bracelets. This popularity seemed to presage a similar happy affinity with their kind in his later life in Hollywood, where he has squired most of the available girls to the town's social and theatrical gatherings, at one time or another—and sometimes oftener."

When the publicity machine wasn't humming about Lyle's Don Juanish dating habits, it was promoting him as a man who really wanted a wife. That was always an attractive notion for fans: the man-about-town who threw himself into a frenetic round of dating was, underneath it all, a romantic who longed for just one good woman. And the thing is, there was a glimmer of truth to that in my father's case. When he talked wistfully about the woman he was looking for, some of what he says sounds as though it was massaged by deft studio hands, but some of it sounds a lot like a description of what he did eventually find in my mother. The two qualities he looked for above all in a woman, he said in one article, were intelligence and a sense of humor. The latter quality was "more precious than beauty, wealth or talent put together," and more likely to keep a couple out of divorce court. You want a girl you can "sit and talk with and exchange ideas with and have for a companion. No man wants the choice between taking a girl to a nightclub or theater every night and being bored." He was attracted to a girl "who gets a kick out of life, is musically inclined and likes to read because I like to read a good deal myself." She "didn't necessarily have to be a raving beauty"—charm was better and "beautiful girls are not always the most interesting." He wasn't wild about athletic girls: if they were awfully serious about their sport, they were too cliquey and talked only about it, he claimed. He did not believe that men should dominate in relationships. a "girl with some give-and-take, the spirit of fifty-fifty, would please me more than a submissive person." And, he concluded, "if I'm going to marry her, I hope she'll be fond of children."

Interviewed about the prospects for marriage, he said he saw so many separations around him in Hollywood that it was beginning to make him nervous. But he took heart from a few couples he'd known when he was younger—including his father and stepmother. "My father and mother married when they were both in their teens," he recalled, "and my mother died when I was two months old. When I was two . . . my father married again and he and my stepmother are ideally happy. They're congenial, they're really suited to one another and absolutely satisfied with their bargain." Another union that encouraged him was that of two actors he'd known from his tent show days. "Oddly enough," theirs was "a combination we're often told is fatal—the wife is 20 years older than the husband," he remarked to the reporter. "Yet they are so completely happy that you can't be with them for ten minutes without feeling something of their pleasure in each other. They've always worked together, first on the stage and then in the hotel business, and if anything happens to break up their family, I'll be a cynic for life."

Often, these articles elicited letters from women who offered to marry him. When he mentioned in one such piece that he sought a wife who would make people feel comfortable in their home, he received a letter from a young woman who told him, "I love my home, love to have friends in it, and I am a good cook. Please do not think I am taking advantage of your offer because you happen to be a movie star. It doesn't make any difference to me how much you have. Even if you were broke and placed an ad in the paper stating your ideals and requirements as they are, I would welcome the chance to tell you they are mine also. Just give me a chance and I'll make you happy." Lyle's views on marriage, wrote another, "make me feel as if life is worth struggling through after all, for there must be some men who still think there is a right and wrong." Another was surprised that a Hollywood actor could sound so "sane and delightful" on the subject of men and women. Lyle felt guilty when he got these letters from women he could only disappoint: his declarations on marriage were heartfelt but theoretical. While some part of him liked the idea of marrying a sweet, small-town girl who knew nothing of acting, increasingly he felt he could never do that. The marriages he most admired were those of the old troupers he'd traveled with—including his father and stepmother—and they were grounded in the camaraderie of a shared love for show business.

Meanwhile, in Hollywood, which was less sane than it was delight-ful, some of the women Lyle went out with were just for show—they were dates to go dancing with, illuminated by the flashbulbs of roving photographers. Some were genuine flings. Loretta Young, the preternaturally beautiful actress, was in that category. She was sweet and elegant and hardworking, but her life was complicated. In 1935, she'd had a baby daughter out of wedlock with Clark Gable, given her up to an orphanage, then adopted her when the child was a little over a year old. Yet Young was an ardent Catholic and so averse to swearing on the set that she made her coworkers pay a fine each time they let a profanity slip. One day when the naturally profane William Wellman was anticipating a particularly rough day on the set, he told Young he'd need to pay upfront.

Lyle enjoyed hanging out with both Loretta and her sister Sally Blane at their home. He was also quite taken with Alice Faye for a while. She was a platinum-blond band singer who was breaking into the movies, and he loved her voice, a soothing, toffee-smooth alto.

But there were three women he had more serious relationships with in the first half of the 1930s. All three were what he would call characters, and you or I might call them pieces of work. Estelle Taylor was the first. When my mother was alive, my father never talked about any of these women—not around us anyway. But after she died, and people interviewed him about his past, he was a bit more forthcoming. Taylor had been a star in the silent era, and had been married from 1925 to 1930 to the world heavyweight champion Jack Dempsey. She was born Estelle Boylan, in Wilmington, Delaware, to a working-class family that was mostly Irish and partly Jewish. At fourteen, she won a beauty contest and left home to marry a banker. Four years later, Estelle ditched the husband and moved to New York, where she enrolled in drama school, modeled nude for artists, and danced in the chorus of a couple of Broadway musicals. Transplanted to Hollywood, she also forged a successful acting career, with a special line in wanton exotics. In Cecil B. DeMille's *The Ten Commandments*, she played Miriam, the sister of Moses, whose most memorable scene involves a lot of heated stroking of the golden calf just before Moses breaks up the orgy. In the 1926 *Don Juan*, the first movie to feature a synchronized score and sound effects, she played Lucrezia Borgia. As my father said, she "wasn't much of an actress," but she was "beautiful, sexy, attractive."

There are actresses from the silent era whose appeal is hard to see today: Theda Bara with her chubby cheeks and masklike aura of sexual menace, for instance. There are those who have a classic beauty that would be admired in any era, such as Greta Garbo. And then there are those in between, like Taylor. In photographs today, Taylor has a dated look about her: her lips are bow-shaped and very dark, her eyes are ultra-smoky in that 1920s way, and her eyebrows are plucked to sinuous threads. But you can also see her allure. Her dark hair is lush and wavy; she seems sensual and very comfortable sidling up to her costars, draping herself on them, running her hands over their chests and shoulders and arms.

Taylor actually made a creditable transition to talkies, turning in a poignant performance in the surprisingly fine 1931 film of the Elmer Rice play *Street Scene*, about two dramatic days in the life of a New York tenement. Taylor plays an emotionally neglected wife and mother (the moments with her sympathetic grown-up daughter, played by an irresistible Sylvia Sidney, are especially tender) who takes up with another man and is killed by her husband. Taylor didn't stay long in the movie business after that; her heyday was over and she wasn't the type to be content playing mothers.

As a person, she was, in the word of Dempsey's biographer, Roger Kahn, "a driving, ambitious, sexually charged woman of the world." Or, as the champ's manager said on reading the detective's report he'd ordered up on her, "Dempsey wasn't getting no maiden."

If Dempsey wasn't, then Lyle, who came next in line and was eight years younger than Taylor, certainly wasn't. But Lyle got a kick out of Estelle and relied on her savvy about the business. He regarded her as "a fabulous character." He was drawn to women who would say the kind of outrageous things other people, including himself, were too polite or modest to say. And Taylor had a knack for commanding respect, even obeisance, from men. Dempsey lived with her in a bedroom swathed in silk and taffeta and decorated with dolls. When the sportswriter Paul Gallico saw the champ ensconced in it, he was reminded of a circus tiger "dressed up for the show in strange and humiliating clothes." She talked Dempsey, who had a good-looking if somewhat rough-hewn profile, into getting a nose job from the same Hollywood surgeon who'd bobbed hers. When Dempsey's fortunes soured at the beginning of the Depression, she left him in a hurry and ended up with their grand house on Los Feliz Boulevard, plus three of their cars and $40,000 in cash.

In later years, Dempsey mostly referred to her, respectfully, as Miss Taylor. And he sounded wistful about her in his interviews with his biographer, though she'd pretty well cleaned him out. Miss Taylor, on the other hand, enjoyed recounting stories about how she had played Dempsey, how easily she'd tamed the champion of the world. She told Lyle, for example, about a time when Dempsey was courting her and far more smitten with her than she ever would be with him. She had invited him over for supper and had ordered her cook to go out and buy the toughest piece of steak he could find to serve the champ, while she had a tender piece of filet mignon on her plate. Dempsey was chewing and chewing and couldn't talk for long stretches, while she nibbled delicately at her food and looked at him in feigned puzzlement. She liked putting people off balance like that. You get the impression that she was avenging herself on men. When she ran away from home in her early teens, perhaps she was fleeing an ugly home life, or sexual abuse. In any case, she relished her ability to make strong men weep—and to tell less strong men, like Lyle, all about it.

Not surprisingly, the liaison didn't last more than a year. One month, Walter Winchell was proclaiming that "Lyle Talbot and Estelle Taylor were plenty goona-goona," and the next month their boldfaced names were no longer linked. There was a new woman at Lyle's side, a countess no less. Dorothy di Frasso was a woman of large appetites and the resources to satisfy them. Flamboyant, fabulously rich, ridiculously well connected in both society and Hollywood circles, di Frasso was in between her most notorious affairs—with Gary Cooper and the gangster Benjamin "Bugsy" Siegel—when she amused herself with Lyle. She had grown up privileged in Watertown, New York, Manhattan, and Palm Beach, a frequent ornament to the society pages. Her father was a wealthy leather merchant turned financier from whom she would one day inherit millions of dollars; her brother became the youngest governor of the New York Stock Exchange.

As a young woman, Dorothy had married and divorced a swashbuckling British aviator, and at thirty-five, she made a marriage of mutual convenience to a much older Italian count, Carlo Dentice di Frasso. It was an old story: he wanted the money; she wanted the title. All very amiable, she always told my father, and it did seem to be. With part of her inheritance, she and the count bought and restored an extraordinary sixteenth-century property called the Villa Madama, which had been built by Pope Clement VII and designed by Raphael. The count stayed there, with occasional visits from his wife, until the villa was seized by Mussolini. No thanks, alas, to any anti-Fascist resistance on the part of the merrily amoral di Frassos; they had entertained the dictator and his minions more than once, and indeed "seized" may be a bit of a postwar exaggeration. They may have given Il Duce the villa, just because he expressed an interest. The di Frassos' friends in Italy were the sort of people who when they woke up and noticed there was a war on were annoyed that their footmen had been called to military service.

In 1931, when Gary Cooper made a visit to Europe, he met the Countess di Frasso, who immediately sized up his possibilities.

On the set of the pre-Code movie Registered Nurse:
*Lyle with the actress Bebe Daniels (wearing a fur coat over
her nurse's uniform), and the Countess di Frasso.*

She slept with him, bought him a new wardrobe, introduced him to society, and followed him back to Hollywood. Di Frasso was no beauty—in photographs she looks gimlet-eyed and a bit jowly, like a more matronly Wallis Simpson. But her wealth and generosity endeared her to good-looking men—as, to be fair to them, did her adventurousness and sense of style. When Cooper seemed to be straying—as he would often, and soon definitively—di Frasso arranged to take him on safari to Africa, with stops in Rome and Milan first to buy some new outfits for the cowboy actor turned big-game hunter. (Said one Hollywood wag: "I've always wanted to go to Europe on the Countess di Frasso.")

In Beverly Hills, the countess lived in a house done up by the society decorator Elsie de Wolfe, in a fantasia of chinoiserie, mirrored paneling, and trompe l'oeil bamboo molding, all rendered in a palette rich with jade and aquamarine. There she hosted a who's who of Hollywood guests. "In spite of her unconventional tastes and overgrown sense of humor," the writer Adela Rogers St. John observed of her, in the early 1950s, "Dorothy di Frasso was—and is—the most popular of all Hollywood favorites who don't actually belong in The Movies." With a gleam in her eye, she amused her many friends with stories about Cooper, and his implacable simplicity. Once, on safari, she said, "The sun was setting. Gary was sitting by himself with an elbow on his knee . . . looking down on the ground. It was one of the most beautiful pictures I had ever seen. 'Oh darling,' I said. 'What are you thinking?' He looked at me for a minute and said, 'I've been wonderin' whether I should change my brand of shoe polish.'"

Given how much she liked to spend money, especially on her men, di Frasso was always finagling to turn her $12 million fortune into an even bigger pile. During her stint as the mistress of Bugsy Siegel, the ruthless blue-eyed gangster who charmed Hollywood in the late 1930s and early 1940s, di Frasso was especially drawn to bizarre get-richer-quick schemes. In September 1938, she and Siegel set sail on a wooden schooner called the *Metha Nelson*, headed for the Pacific coast of Central America. They were in search of treasure—rubies, diamonds, and gold doubloons—that was supposed to be buried on an uninhabited island off Costa Rica. The FBI suspected that Siegel was also trying to pick up a fugitive mobster who'd been hiding out somewhere in the vicinity, and may have planted the captain aboard to keep an eye on the proceedings. It was an expedition worthy of *The Maltese Falcon*, and it ended even more ignominiously for the dramatic personae, with the schooner's destruction in a gale, a mutiny by two of the crew members who claimed the captain was an anti-Semite who abused them, and no treasure.

Then there was the time that di Frasso and Siegel tried to peddle a new kind of explosive to the Italian military. Siegel had met a couple of chemists who'd developed something they called Atomite, which Siegel was convinced would replace dynamite and make him a fortune. Di Frasso arranged to have the stuff demonstrated at the Villa Madama for a contingent from the Italian military. As it happened, her husband's other guests at the villa that weekend included Josef Goebbels, the German propaganda minister, and Hermann Göring, the head of the Luftwaffe. Siegel evidently had no problem consorting with Italian Fascists, but he did bristle at the Nazi bigwigs. In fact, he told Dorothy he was going to kill "that fat bastard Göring" and "that "dirty Goebbels," too. "It's an easy setup the way they're walking around here." Di Frasso talked him out of it, fearing what would happen to her count if his Nazi houseguests ended up dead. The explosive test was a bust, and di Frasso and her mug headed for the French Riviera. Thanks to the countess, Siegel had missed out on making the one defensible hit he'd ever have committed

Di Frasso died in 1954, at sixty-six, in her compartment on a train from Las Vegas. She was found by the actor Clifton Webb, one of a group of friends with whom she was traveling. She was alone, and probably died of a heart attack, but Dorothy being Dorothy, she was wearing a black dress, a mink coat, and several hundred thousand dollars' worth of jewelry, including a diamond necklace. None of her schemes had panned out, but she had kept her fortune and lived large.

For Lyle, as for Gary Cooper, she was an odd sort of mother hen—fourteen years his senior, worldlier and wealthier than anyone he'd ever known. A few days before they were to spend vacation together at Hearst Castle, the countess sent him a set of calfskin luggage, buttery-soft and monogrammed. On the appointed day, she picked him up in her Rolls-Royce, with a chauffeur, and a bar in the back. But when they arrived, there was a telegram waiting for Lyle from Warner Brothers ordering him back to the lot. "They told me I had two weeks off," he complained to Dorothy. "Well," she said, "nuts to them. You're not going to go back." Dorothy urged him to tell Marion Davies, Hearst's mistress and their hostess, to send a message to Warners that the couple hadn't arrived yet. The studio reps sent a telegram back saying to inform them when they *did* arrive. This went on for five days or so. The powerful gossip columnist Louella Parsons was also at Hearst Castle that week, and di Frasso, who was a friend of hers, said, "Now look, Louella, you haven't seen him." "Certainly not," Parsons assured her, "neither hide nor hair." The role the studio wanted him back for was completely unsuited to him—a cop, and much older. So Lyle figured he was right to duck out, but normally he'd be too well behaved to do so, and too worried, as many actors are, about never working again. The studio did suspend him without pay for two weeks. Di Frasso complained to *The Hollywood Reporter*, which obliged her by printing an editorial about studios' oppressing their contract players. Lyle found it thrilling to be in the hands of a woman too rich and too gutsy to worry much about anything.

She could be kind in a breezy, imperious style. When Lyle's father, Ed Henderson, and stepmother, Anna, were visiting from Omaha, the countess made sure that her friend Mary Pickford gave a tea in their honor. Pickford invited them back the next day for dinner, and the Hendersons of Omaha were surprised to find themselves hobnobbing with assorted European aristocrats, including a Swedish baroness and a count of some sort. After the meal, cigarettes were passed around on little silver trays, and Ed accepted one to be sociable even though he never smoked. He took a couple of puffs, then set the cigarette down and forgot about it, till he noticed a big hole in the tablecloth. He put an ashtray on top of it, and on the way home confessed to di Frasso, saying he hoped that since there had been no place cards, his hostess wouldn't know who had done it. Well, she couldn't set his mind at ease on that front. The truth was that though the seating arrangement looked spontaneous, the guests had all been maneuvered into place according to a seating chart in the kitchen. But it didn't really matter, she went on: the tablecloth was insured for $1,000. Every morning of the Hendersons' twenty-six-day visit, di Frasso sent Anna white gardenias, one more for each day.

Neither a diamond in the rough like Cooper nor a rough with diamonds like Siegel, Lyle couldn't have lasted long as a di Frasso project. Perhaps she tired of him first; perhaps it was the other way around. In any case, they both got busy quickly—she with Siegel and he with a number of young actresses, most especially Lina Basquette.

Like Estelle Taylor, Basquette was dark-haired, dark-eyed, pint-sized, and sexy—a look that tended to get her cast as Gypsy girls and Egyptian temptresses. And like Taylor, too, she was a narcissistic live wire, only with even more voltage. Basquette grew up in San Mateo, California, and discovered a talent for holding people's attention while dancing in her father's drugstore to music from the new Victrola that he was the first in town to demonstrate. Her beloved father committed suicide when Lina was nine, and the precocious girl was left to her mother, with whom she did not get along, and a budding career as a dancer—first in her own series of filmed featurettes. Admirers were saying she was the next Anna Pavlova. But Lina went a different direction: at sixteen, she became a featured dancer with the Ziegfeld Follies. One night Sam Warner was in the audience for a Ziegfeld extravaganza called *Louie the 14th* and fell in love with Lina over the footlights. He sent an orchid corsage backstage, along with an invitation to the girl and her mother to dine with him. Sam was almost twice her age, and the eighteen-year-old Lina had no interest in marrying him, but her ambitious mother insisted she accept his offer when he proposed.

It wasn't as bad a deal as it first appeared to the fun-loving, young Lina. Sam was the nicest of the Warners—especially compared with his boorish, hard-nosed brother Jack. By most accounts he was the smartest, too. When the family was living in Youngstown, Ohio, in the early part of the century, and scraping by in the shoe-repair and grocery businesses, it was Sam who first saw a primitive movie projector and excitedly urged his brothers to get into the movie business. Sam was also the first Warner to become enamored of sound, and to push the studio to experiment with it. Harry was famous for saying, "Who wants to hear actors talk?" (Actors like my father used to repeat that line to one another for years afterward in Harry's blustering cadences.)

Basquette was a showgirl, and a Catholic to boot, and the Warner family did not approve of her. But despite their inauspicious start, she and Sam were surprisingly happy together, she told Lyle. Lina was a virgin on their wedding night but found Sam to be a gentle and patient lover. Moreover, he had no problem with her continuing her acting career in Hollywood while he stayed in New York producing the first Vitaphone movies—shorts featuring vaudeville, opera, and other musical acts with sound. In October 1926, Lina and Sam had a baby girl, Lita.

Sam was working intensely in those years, overseeing the production of the Vitaphone shorts, then of the feature-length *Don Juan*, and finally of *The Jazz Singer*. He was also suffering from frequent, debilitating headaches. On October 6, 1927, *The Jazz Singer* was set to debut. But Sam Warner, the man who had done the most to make it happen, was in the hospital. The headaches had been the sign of a chronic sinus infection that eventually spread to his brain. He died of a cerebral hemorrhage on October 5, 1927, at forty years old.

Basquette was shocked by Sam's sudden death, and she missed him. But she was also young and almost alarmingly resilient. She liked to work and she liked to play, and she was soon doing both with her usual tigerish enthusiasm. In January 1928, she started work on a film called *The Godless Girl*, Cecil B. DeMille's strange and fervid saga of young atheists on the rampage—or "rebels throwing spitballs at the

Rock of Ages," as the intertitles have it—then spectacularly brought to heel. Basquette starred as the teenage leader of the atheist society at her Los Angeles high school—a dishy firebrand who has her followers pledge their allegiance on the head of her pet monkey. (It was an era when you could always count on anti-evolutionists deploying a monkey to make their point.) The Atheists, led by Lina's character, and the Christians, led by a handsome boy, square off in a Sharks-and-Jets-like gang rivalry, complete with a riot that lands both the sexy godless girl and her devout rival in the reformatory. In the final reel, they reconcile and are rewarded by a message from God: as they clasp hands through the fence that separates the girls' and boys' sides of the reformatory, their palms are burned with the sign of the cross. The movie was not a success in the United States—the theme was peculiar, it was a movie about teenagers at a time before teenagers were recognized as a demographic, and it was silent (though DeMille did tack on a few sound sequences) at a moment when talkies were the talk of Hollywood. But *The Godless Girl* became a sensation in the Soviet Union—where the last reel was cut, and it played as a celebration of atheism and a denunciation of the American criminal justice system. (DeMille visited the Soviet Union in 1931 and, to his chagrin, was treated "something like a national hero for having produced" the movie.) It, and Lina herself, also made a positive impression on Adolf Hitler, who, according to Basquette, sent her a fan letter in 1930.

While filming *The Godless Girl*, Lina fell into a passionate love affair with DeMille's cinematographer. She ran around town with Clara Bow, Carole Lombard, and Jean Harlow—a threesome who called themselves The Bad Girls. When baby Lita was three, the Warners decided that Lina was an unsuitable mother, and essentially bought Lita from her—offering her a $100,000 settlement and a $300,000 trust fund for her daughter, who would henceforth be raised by Harry Warner and his wife, with their three children, in Mount Vernon, New York. Lina was excoriated in the tabloid press as a heartless hussy who traded her baby for "thirty pieces of silver." In later years, she would say that she had been devastated by the decision. The newspapers reported that a year or so after she gave Lita to the Warners, she attempted suicide by taking poison.

When he dated her, my father took her part and felt she couldn't be blamed for succumbing to the Warner onslaught. But it's fair to say that Lina was not an especially nurturing person, and never would be. "She's a character, and I can see why the family didn't want me to live with her," her grown-up daughter once said. "With Lina I would have had a wild life. It wouldn't have been the greatest thing in the world to have been brought up by her."

"Wild" seems a fair word. Lina got married a total of eight times, twice to the same man, Jack Dempsey's trainer, Teddy Hayes. (She divorced him the first time because he was already married, the second time because he had become abusive.) She had affairs with Nelson Eddy, the Metropolitan Opera singer Lawrence Tibbetts, the gangster Johnny Roselli, and Jack Dempsey himself. (With Dempsey she appeared in a touring show, "Jack Dempsey's Knockout Revue," along with a thirty-piece, all female orchestra.) To Barry Paris, a writer who profiled her in *The New Yorker* in 1989, she described herself in those years as a bitch, and in her present incarnation, as "a recovering nymphomaniac." She also told Paris, and my father, that Hitler had tried to seduce her during a visit she made to Berchtesgaden in 1936 in the company of a German baron she had met. She said that Goebbels and Hitler had wanted to make her a star in German movies, and that she had been tempted since her career in Hollywood was suffering, in part because she was on the outs with the Warners. It's hard to say how much of this was true. There is no independent corroboration of the Berchtesgaden episode. Still, her stories do tend to check out, even if they've been filigreed. In any case, Lina maintained that when the Führer made his move during an evening stroll in the garden, she kneed him in the groin. When that wasn't sufficient to repel him, she told him, truthfully, that her grandfather had been Jewish. That did the job.

Before the misadventure with Hitler, Basquette and my father had a stormy romance. My father remembered feeling very protective of her and of her young son by Teddy Hayes, Eddie. He felt she had gotten a raw deal from the Warners and felt sorry for any mother who'd had to give up her child. And Basquette was lovely to look at and full of energy and sass. "At first the main bond between us was our mutual hatred of Jack Warner and the brass-knuckling tactics that pervaded the Burbank studio," Basquette writes in her autobiography. "However, in short order, our bond escalated into a full-blown romance." Still, they were happy together in a household that was probably a little too domestic for Basquette's taste. They maintained separate residences for appearances' sake, but essentially lived together. When he wasn't drinking too much, "Lyle was an intelligent gentleman with impeccable manners." He and Eddie "adored each other," Lina's judgmental German maid approved of him, and "for a while, life could not have been sweeter nor more amiable or domestically stabilized. We were a nice young couple, going steady, with the fragrance of orange blossoms in the offing."

One night on a date they stopped off at Warner Brothers, and Lina waited in the car while Lyle ran in to do an errand. When he came back to the car, he was "grim-faced, with fists clenched" after an encounter with Jack Warner in which the studio executive had derided Lina and told Lyle to steer clear of her. He drove in a fury for a while, then Lina pleaded, "Stop this car. You'll kill us both." Lyle pulled over. "He was in tears, his handsome face mottled with emotion. He turned to me and grabbed my hands. 'I won't give you up, angel. You're the best thing that ever happened to me.'" Seeing how upset he was, Lina talked Lyle into letting her drive, with the practical argument that neither of them could afford "to be disfigured or arrested." Lyle insisted, though, on stopping at Travaglini's, a restaurant on Sunset

Boulevard known for its "thick steaks" and "generous sized drinks." It was "a masculine haven where dirty stories were swapped along with telephone numbers." As Basquette tells it, Lyle got so drunk at the Travaglini's bar that evening that he was muttering darkly and close to passing out. A suave, well-spoken—and sober—British actor named Henry Mollison was also at the masculine haven that night. When he approached Basquette, she asked him to help her pour Lyle into the car and drive him home. Mollison obliged, then set to seducing Lina, pronouncing sagely that "marriage and alcoholism make a wretched combination" and cold-cocking Lyle when he stumbled down to the living room to see what was going on. It never took much to convince Basquette there was a more intriguing man in the wings, and this time Mollison was it.

Many, many years later, when my father was ninety and Basquette was in her mid-eighties, she turned up in his life again. She had made her last movie in Hollywood in 1943, and had launched a second career as, according to *The New York Times*, "one of the best-known breeders and handlers of champion Great Danes in American dog-show history," and as the author of several books on dog breeding. She was still a good-looking woman, silver-haired and trim. Our father mentioned casually to my siblings and me that Basquette would be coming from West Virginia, where she lived, to San Francisco, where he then lived, alone, for a visit. We wondered, with a little trepidation, whether they would resume a romance. To Barry Paris, she had described herself this way: "I never thought I'd reach this advanced threshold in one healthy piece of mortality. But I have managed to stay ahead of the grim reaper and I'm damned lucky to retain blooming health, a perverted sense of humor, a fair amount of facial pulchritude. Arms, legs, and thighs a bit scraggly, the boobs not as firm as they once were, but what-the-hell. I'm spry, alert, working, fiercely independent, live alone and like it, still smoke but never have inhaled. I stay away from doctors, except my dentist and veterinarian, drive an average of 30,000

miles per year, still can read without glasses, and have not had anything uplifted, tucked-up or sliced off." Paris had dubbed her "the
last of the red-hot mamas." My father was still a handsome man with
an active memory and an affectionate temperament. They were both
lively conversationalists—even if most of the conversation was about
themselves. That could be a problem, we figured—dueling vanities.
Who would listen raptly to whom? Paris had said in his profile that
Basquette could easily talk about herself for eight hours. Well, so could
Lyle if it came to that.

But that didn't turn out to be the stumbling block. What doomed
their romantic revival was a teakettle. My father had always been tidy
and a little compulsive—especially in the kitchen, his special domain.
In his dotage, he was even more so. He still liked to cook for us when
we visited—especially breakfasts, which he looked forward to every
morning of his life with undiminished enthusiasm. But frankly, he'd
rather you didn't enter his kitchen if you weren't going to put things
back where you found them. Lina Basquette made the fatal mistake of
leaving the teakettle on and letting the water run out, scalding it
beyond repair. We felt kind of sorry for her when we heard. Lyle
endured the rest of the red-hot mama's visit with a polite, put-upon
aloofness. And he never saw her again.

Chapter 7

—◦◦◦—

EMPTY BOTTLES

A s far as I can tell, my father didn't drink much before he arrived in Hollywood. Acting on the stage kept him occupied at least part of every evening, and the people he looked to as examples, his own father and stepmother and some of the surrogate parents he met in the theater troupes, were teetotalers or close to it. But in Hollywood, he developed the habit of going out most nights, or staying in and entertaining generously. There was always plenty of alcohol around, and he turned out to be very, very susceptible to the bonhomie it enveloped him in, the lift it imparted to the end of a long and tiring day on the set. Lyle was not an anxious person, so he wouldn't have been using liquor to soothe jitters. But he did like to be in fine form when he went out, to be jolly company always, and I imagine that he became dependent on the help alcohol gave him with that. He may have been genetically vulnerable to alcoholism as well. His father, Ed, was never a drinker. But his grandmother's brother, "Happy Jack"

Hollywood, the saloon keeper and killer, certainly drank to excess. Perhaps the other Hollywood brothers had as well.

In any case, the sheer surfeit of liquor in his new milieu would have been hard for anyone with his inclinations to resist. Hollywood in the 1930s was a little like Pottersville in the movie *It's a Wonderful Life*. Pottersville, you may recall, was the town that wholesome Bedford Falls would have become if evil Mr. Potter had been allowed to run everything. It was still a small town, where everybody knew everybody, but it was also full of jivey, jazzy music, honky-tonk bars, and winking neon. Hollywood was like that, too—simultaneously cozy and debauched. If you were an actor like Lyle, you went out on a regular basis and with a regular crowd to pretty much the same round of nightspots (the Cocoanut Grove, the Cotton Club, the Biltmore Bowl) and the same restaurants (both Brown Derbys, Musso & Frank, Victor Hugo). On Friday nights, you attended the fights at the Hollywood (American) Legion Stadium and then often headed to the dance marathons out at the Santa Monica Pier. On Sunday nights, the place to swing by was the Trocadero, an elegant nightclub on Sunset Boulevard owned by Billy Wilkerson, an inveterate gambler who also owned *The Hollywood Reporter*. That was the night when newcomers could audition in front of Hollywood insiders, one of whom would serve as emcee for the evening's entertainment. The moguls would come out on Sundays at the Troc, too; Louis B. Mayer and the Warner brothers all had their regular tables. Antiquated blue laws prohibited dancing within the city of Los Angeles on the Sabbath, but the Troc, like many of the Sunset clubs, was in the county, which made it extra appealing on Sundays.

However elegant, these places still held a flicker of danger that alcohol fanned. The Cocoanut Grove—the splendid ballroom at the Ambassador Hotel—was the site, for instance, of frequent liquor-sparked fights. The Grove had opened in 1921 as the first really swanky place for the stars to hobnob on a grand scale. It was a big room with a hardwood dance floor rendered exotic by the several hundred prop palms that adorned it, leftovers from the Rudolph Valentino movie *The Sheik*. Chinese lanterns bobbed between the palms, and fake monkeys clung to them. In the 1920s, the Grove was famous for Charleston contests at which Joan Crawford and Carole Lombard shimmied for trophies and attention. By the 1930s, the Grove had an elaborate new Moorish décor and a floor show that featured crooners like Bing Crosby and showgirls arrayed on floats that looked like giant wedding cakes. One evening's entertainment included a fashion show of ancient Egyptian costume. Another night the Grove displayed a nude girl encased in what appeared to be a solid block of ice. (Luckily for the girl, the center of the giant ice cube was in fact hollow and heated.) As my father recalled, "The Cocoanut Grove was just the place to go. You saw everyone you knew there, especially on Tuesday nights. It had all the name bands with all the name singers. And that was a whole evening. You really dressed up in Hollywood then. You almost put on a tuxedo automatically. And for a premiere, tails! With a top hat! I still have my top hat—the kind that folds up so you can put it under the seat in your car. And topcoats! I can't believe it ever got cold enough in L.A. for us to wear them, but we did. We needed coats long enough to cover the tails."

For all its twinkly trappings, the Grove was also something of an informal boxing ring. It was not alone among Hollywood nightspots in that respect. Something about the alchemy of free-flowing booze, revved-up hormones, distended egos, and youthful impetuosity made actors—and even actresses—peculiarly prone to fisticuffs. Actors decked their ex-girlfriends' dates or columnists they thought had been insufficiently admiring. Bands struck up frenetic fox-trots to cover the noise and get people back on the dance floor. You didn't have to worry as much about paparazzi in that era—and not at all, of course, about embarrassing photos winging around the Internet.

At the Cocoanut Grove, showing off a date, Peggy Watters.

Most of the photographers at the nightclubs were semi-official: either on the payroll of the studios or working for newspapers and magazines that depended on the studios for access. So maybe actors in the 1930s and 1940s felt freer than celebrities today to booze and brawl with impunity.

Even my father, definitely a lover not a fighter, nearly went at it with Clark Gable one January evening in 1936. The occasion was the White Mayfair Ball at the Victor Hugo restaurant in Beverly Hills. The evening was hosted by Carole Lombard, and all the guests were supposed to wear white. (The imperious Norma Shearer famously spoiled the effect by wearing a scarlet dress.) It was the evening that ignited Gable and Lombard's affair, an unhappy turn of events for Lyle. He had a major crush on Lombard, with whom he had starred in a movie called *No More Orchids* a few years earlier when she'd been married to William Powell. Not only was she gorgeous, she was one of those sassy, potty-mouthed women he so appreciated. And unlike the versions of those he dated in the 1930s—the Lina Basquettes and Estelle Taylors—Lombard was good-hearted as well. He could see that, and he liked it. Lombard was a practical joker and a natural democrat who palled around with all kinds of people working on a set, no matter how humble their jobs, and who was beloved in return. When Gable left the party for a drive with Lombard that night, according to the couple's biographer, he tried to get her to come up to his apartment at the Beverly Wilshire. She blew him off with the line "Who do you think you are—Clark Gable?" Gable tore back to the Mayfair Ball and headed for the bar. There he ran into Lyle, who couldn't resist making a snide remark about his quick return. They were squaring off for a fight when Lombard intervened.

Though fights broke out at all the Hollywood watering holes, the Cocoanut Grove was unusual and perhaps unique in that it actually worked the slugfests into its publicity. By 1937, sixteen years after it had opened, the club's management was claiming that it had been the scene of 136 major fights.

One of Lyle's favorite hangouts—because he loved the music there—was the Cotton Club, a West Coast version of the Harlem institution. Like its East Coast counterpart, the Cotton Club in Culver City showcased black entertainers but rarely admitted black patrons—a depressing irony that was not lost on Lyle. At least the Cotton Club gave black musicians and entertainers steady work. The owner of the club was a genial fellow named Frank Sebastian who aimed to make the place feel posh but relaxed. On New Year's Eve, he

Lyle and Carole Lombard, romantic leads in No More Orchids.

always threw an all-night party, with dancing till dawn, and a ham-and-egg breakfast for as many as two thousand. It was a good gig: the dressing rooms for star performers were plush and private; the band-stand and acoustics were tip-top. In 1930, Louis Armstrong moved from New York to Los Angeles, and took a seven-month stint at the club. Fats Waller, Duke Ellington, Lionel Hampton, Cab Calloway, and Les Hite all played there, under a vast ceiling draped with vivid silks, like a sumptuous Bedouin tent. Once, when Duke Ellington was performing at the Cotton Club, Lyle invited the musician to a party at his house. He used to tell us that, to his keen embarrassment, Ellington asked if he should come to the back door.

The Cotton Club was a mellower scene than other L.A. night-spots, maybe because you went there as much for the music as for the preening, and maybe because the intoxicant of choice at the club, at least for some of the performers, was marijuana rather than alcohol. In November 1930, Armstrong was arrested, along with his white drummer, Vic Berton, for smoking reefer in the parking lot of the Cotton Club, and they spent a night in the Los Angeles County jail. But Armstrong got off lightly in the end, probably with the intervention of Sebastian, who, like most successful L.A. club owners, knew how to make arrests that interfered with business go away. Besides, the cop who interviewed Armstrong and Berton at headquarters was a fan. "The judge gave me a suspended sentence and I went back to work that night—wailed like nothing happened," Armstrong said later. "What struck me funny, though—I laughed real loud—when several movie stars came up to the bandstand while we played a dance set and told me when they heard about me getting caught with marijuana, they thought marijuana was a chick. Woo boy—that really fractured me." Lyle could have been one of those; marijuana was not in his ken.

Sometimes the Hollywood crowd took its more uncouth entertainments straight up. In September 1932, the *Los Angeles Times* ran an article with the headline "Stars Turn Rubbernecks to Relieve Humdrum Life," in which the writer tried to shed some light on the attractions of slumming and blood sport for Hollywood celebrities. "When they step off the stage or set, the excitement generated during the acting period must be continued. So these people seek out events that fill this need, including trips to the fights, wrestling matches, auto races, flying, horse races and dance marathons."

Lyle was never a gambler, but he liked the Friday-night fights. Hollywood enjoyed a romance with boxing on screen and off. The boxing picture was a recognizable genre, even in the early 1930s; Lyle had already played in one such picture, *The Life of Jimmy Dolan*, with Douglas Fairbanks, Jr., and Loretta Young. On Friday nights, just after dinner, the Brown Derby reliably emptied out as a mob of picture people headed for the Hollywood Legion Stadium to see the fights. The actress Lupe Vélez was famous for championing the Mexican boxers. Sometimes the only thing stopping her "from climbing into the ring and socking her favorite's opponent," according to the *Los Angeles Times*, was "her escort or the ropes around the squared circle."

The dance marathons enjoyed a shorter but weirder vogue in Hollywood. Dance marathons had started in the 1920s as part of the national craze for endurance contests of all kind—flagpole sitting, hand holding, gum chewing. The endurance fads of the 1920s offered a comparatively easy shot at fame. Like the clown who does his own version of the acrobat's stunts, endurance contestants were performing wacky, democratized versions of the record-breaking athletic feats people followed so closely then, such as Channel swimming and long-distance airplane flights. In the early years of the Depression, though, dance marathons hung on after flagpole sitting and its ilk had lost their appeal. And they had become a much darker spectacle than they had been earlier. Now many of the contestants were joining less for a lark or a chance at celebrity than for food and shelter. For six to twelve weeks, twenty-four hours a day, with typically fifteen minutes of rest per hour, contestants shuffled around on leaden feet, dragged each other across the dance floor, kicked and slapped each other awake, propped each other up—it was often the women who did the propping—in the skein-thin hope of being the last couple on the floor and the winners of a couple of hundred dollars. A marathon might start with a hundred couples, but within a few days the numbers would usually be winnowed down to twenty or so. Spectators tossed coins at the contestants they liked. Every once in a while, to stir things up, marathon judges would put the dancers through sudden, brutal elimination rounds—heel-and-toe races, sprints in which a man and a woman would be taped together, or something called "zombie treadmills," in which couples were blindfolded. Judges might declare a "cot night," when the contestants would have to take their brief naps in full view of the audience, instead of backstage.

The appeal of the marathon for most spectators was visceral and emotional but often practical, too. The price of admission—usually forty cents or less—could buy an out-of-work person a warm place to sit all day and indeed all night. For another thing, it was a spectacle of grueling endurance, punctuated by moments of pain and humiliation and, less often, of affection and pleasure, which served as a kind of microcosm of Depression life. "For forty cents, if you are cold and lonely and out of a job on a raw winter's night," a chronicler of the marathons noted in *Esquire* magazine, "you join an audience composed of people who appear to have every right to feel as wretched as yourself, and with them you get the thrill of being able to feel sorry for someone."

But what about the movie stars? They flocked to the marathons at the Santa Monica Pier, and they weren't out of work or wretched. In an article in the December 1932 edition of *Modern Screen*, the columnist Jimmie Fidler described the scene: "Row upon row of benches pyramided away from the dance floor, almost disappearing into an obscure background. The air was heavy with tobacco smoke, the eyes of thousands occupying the seats were bleary from watching, and the faces of the four dancers were haggard, almost like skulls." After 1,200 hours—more than seven weeks—two couples remained, who "struggled around and around that dismally small floor—two mad females clinging hopefully to their males, two wild-eyed men supporting the tired bodies of their weaker partners." The dancers' faces were "raw and red from hard slaps and iced towels," their mouths hung open.

Fidler's article said that the directors William Beaudine and Tod Browning were probably "the first Hollywoodites to notice the marathons"—maybe because they lived "at the beach, conveniently near the ballroom." (Or maybe because Browning, the director of the movie *Freaks*, had a fascination with people in extreme states.) "They invited their friends, who in turn invited others, and very abruptly, and for no reason at all, Hollywood went marathon-mad. Everybody of consequence appeared at the ring-side. An entire section was roped off by the promoters who hung overhead a huge sign 'CELEBRITIES.'"

In 1935, a writer named Horace McCoy published a novel based on his experiences working as a bouncer at the Santa Monica Pier during the marathon craze. Today, people are more likely to know the 1969 movie version of *They Shoot Horses, Don't They?* But the novel, a grim work of hard-boiled existentialism, is still a compelling read. "The marathon dance was held at the amusement pier at the beach in an enormous old building that once had been a public dance hall. It was built over the ocean on pilings, and beneath our feet, beneath the floor, the ocean pounded night and day. I could feel it surging through the balls of my feet, as if they had been stethoscopes." Like *The Day of the Locust*, it's a chronicle of the darkness lurking at the edges of the Hollywood dream. In McCoy's evocation of the marathons, the arrival of a celebrity contingent each night is all irony. It's an echoey *whoosh* of applause in the recesses of an exhausted dancer's consciousness, a coruscating hologram from a Los Angeles as inaccessible as the Emerald City. Gloria, the desperately unhappy partner of the blank, boyish narrator, bristles with jealousy of the Hollywood crowd. She's one of the dancers who's actually trying to break into pictures, but the reader knows from the start she never will. "You're goddamn right I'm jealous. As long as I'm a failure I'm jealous of anyone who's a success, aren't you?" Lyle was one of those people who used to arrive in a big, laughing crowd of people, bearing their own flasks of booze to swig while they watched since it was still Prohibition.

To be fair, the picture folk didn't only gawk. One night, director Robert Z. Leonard offered to donate $5 to the contestants fund if Polly Moran sang "Sonny Boy," and Groucho Marx promptly offered double the amount if she didn't. The Hollywood crowd amused itself, callously sometimes, but at least the contestants made some money from it—more than $100 a week, according to Fidler. They even contributed to the entertainment. The comedian Andy Devine entered the marathon one night, but quickly pretended to faint, and was carried off the dance floor to the tune of the funeral march, wearing a dunce cap. Mary Pickford showed up—to the surprise of fans who considered her above such a spectacle—and left with tears in her eyes, having made a large contribution. "Charlie Chaplin sat for an entire evening, seldom taking his staring eyes from the four humans who stumbled over the floor," Fidler wrote. "When he departed, he left plain white envelopes for each dancer."

The truth was that some of the celebrities probably identified with the dancers; some of the stars watching knew it was only the scrim of luck that separated them from the men and women drooping like storm-bent stalks of grass on the dance floor. The contestants were putting on a show, too, for much of what they did up there was contrived: there were staged fights and staged marriages. On the other hand, for some of the stars this was as close to the privations of the Depression as they could really get, and they studied it with fascination and dismay.

One evening, William Beaudine, Tod Browning, the beautiful silent-screen star Ruth Roland, and her husband, Ben Bard, spontaneously reenacted the making of a movie. The dancers, shuffling past, lifted their heavy heads to watch. Bard, playing the director, shouted instructions to Roland and Beaudine: "Now you're on Hollywood Boulevard, walking towards each other, and you've never met." Roland and Beaudine fell into each other's arms for a swoony embrace. A few of the dancers hooted appreciatively. "Good old Hollywood," cried Bard. Roland would die of cancer five years later, at age forty-five. Browning, whose intense and disturbing *Freaks* fatally damaged his career as a director, would by the end of the decade become a recluse, living Norma Desmond–like until his death in 1962. Surely some of the dancers, desperate though they might have been that night, led happier lives.

When he was in his late eighties, my father was interviewed by a film historian and in-law of ours named Don Peri. Lyle brought up the business about the marathons. He'd actually never mentioned them to us, though I can remember watching the movie of *They Shoot Horses, Don't They?* on TV with him once. "When you think about it, what peasants we were!" he told Don. "It was like watching the Romans throw the slaves to the lions. In modern times, it really was. They were awful, really. But we'd go to these things and the big stars would have their boxes with their names on them. We'd go out there at about eleven at night and sit there for two or three hours watching these people just dance falling over, and holding one another up. When I think about it, I hate to admit that I went to those things."

Like a lot of people of his era, I think my father had a mild streak of sadism in his humor. When life is harsher, as it was during the Depression, senses of humor tend to be correspondingly darker. In some people who grew up in small towns on the prairies in the early years of the twentieth century, places where you saw a lot of rough business and learned to move on, that streak was much more pronounced. My father was gentle and sympathetic in most ways—softhearted toward animals and children, respectful of women. His views on race were tolerant and unfussy. He had black friends in the entertainment business whom he greatly admired, and I never heard him make a racist remark. When it came to gay people, he was a bit less enlightened. He had gay friends, but he preferred not to think about them as gay, and if he suspected you did, he'd insist before you could say anything that so-and-so was "a very manly man." Over the years, my siblings and I met several manly men who sang and danced in the chorus of various musicals with our dad and who looked for all the world like flaming queens. My dad was one of the few men I've known who praised other men as "sweet." "Such a sweet man," was one of the things he said about kind people like Arthur Landau, his first agent in Hollywood, or Mock Sad Alli, the magician he'd worked for as a teenager.

Still, he did retain his fondness for spectacles like boxing and dance marathons and for pranks, when he was young. His early experiences with carnivals and sideshows stuck with him. Lyle was a lifelong lover of cartoons, clowns, and circuses, but his fascination with them was not deep or dark. Their slapstick humor with a crust of meanness was funny to him somehow. Maybe he just realized that such entertainments, with their glimpses of people knocked down by life who stagger up again, got at something about what it is to be human, and that it was better to laugh ruefully at it than to suffer over it.

I remember a story he used to tell about a Borscht Belt stand-up comic he'd known in the 1960s. Harvey was his name, and he had married a much younger, much more attractive woman named Lois. Harvey was crazy about her—he even praised her cooking to the skies, though my father said the onion-soup-mix casserole she once made him was the worst thing he'd ever tasted. Lois, it was clear, had married Harvey for his money—which was not a lot, but more than she had. Still, both got what they wanted, till one day, while entertaining on a cruise ship, Harvey dropped dead of a heart attack. Lois solemnly declared that what Harvey had always wanted was to be buried at sea—a wish that Harvey's friends had never heard and which they found highly implausible, suspecting that Lois was really trying to avoid the additional cost of bringing his body home and having him buried in New York. To my father this was a rueful but very funny story. He felt for Harvey, but being a vain man himself, and susceptible to the charms of younger women, he saw the ridiculous places these tendencies could take you, and he laughed about them.

This sort of sensibility—fatalistic, willing to be amused by a certain amount of cheerful vulgarity, though you were too gentlemanly to generate it yourself—made Lyle feel quite at home when he hung out with what he called the Irish crowd in Hollywood. Spencer Tracy was the first of those he knew. They had met in Chicago when they were doing plays in adjacent theaters, and they used to go to a club there owned by Al Capone. "It was a very unimposing two-story building that looked like it needed a paint job. You went up what I seem to remember as rickety steps and you opened the door. And here was this nightclub that wouldn't stop. It wasn't that fancy, but it was huge and it had a big bar. You'd see the cops and detectives there. Spencer was a pretty good drinker and there were some Irishmen in the company, so we went there a lot. One night he'd gotten a telegram to come out to Hollywood; they'd picked up his contract. We were staying at the Sherman Hotel, and some of his pals had the baker, for a joke, bake a big loaf of bread in the shape of a penis and testicles.

"You couldn't buy a drink in the place. It was all free." Capone wanted actors served in the house. "Tell an actor that—and well, you're going to be seeing him a lot."

In Hollywood, the regulars in the all-male Irish crowd included Lyle, Spencer Tracy, James Cagney (though he didn't drink), and Pat O'Brien; an ex–theater actor they called Bill Stage Boyd (to distinguish him from the Hopalong Cassidy actor whose name was also Bill Boyd); an actor named William Gargan, who usually played Irish cops, priests, and reporters; and Walter Catlett, a bespectacled character actor who made a specialty of playing meddlesome, bombastic little men. "We had Sundays off, so on Saturday nights we'd go to Bill Gargan's house at the end of Fairfax across Hollywood Boulevard," my father recalled. "You'd run into his garage and he had a bar in there. The Irish crowd would all gather there. Sometimes there'd be fights. There was a midget known as Little Billy who'd get drunk and want to fight. So you'd set him up on a chair and go over to him, and he'd take a poke at you. One time Walter Catlett was leaning against the bar and he gave me his false teeth to hold so he wouldn't get them broken by Little Billy. 'Here, kid, hold these.'"

Catlett lived with a beautiful former showgirl in an apartment nearby. On occasion Lyle and some of the Irish crowd would end up there after they left Gargan's garage. Though Catlett worked steadily all his life, he was fearful, like a lot of actors, that no next job would materialize. So periodically he'd take all his money and stock up on groceries and booze, which he'd stash in hiding places around his apartment. "He called them his wolf chests; he was keeping the wolf from the door, you see," my father said. Often, though, Catlett couldn't find the booze he'd stashed, and once they had to resort to some he'd stored in coconuts into which he had drilled holes he then plugged up. "It was nasty stuff. It'd knock you cold," said my father, who evidently drank it anyway.

IF YOU WERE A CONTRACT PLAYER in the thirties, you didn't get out of town much. Your work schedule didn't allow it, and location shooting—especially at any real distance from L.A.—was an unusual occurrence. Like a lot of actors in those days, my father used to quote the motto attributed to the penny-pinching producer Sam Goldwyn: "A rock's a rock; a tree's a tree; shoot it in Griffith Park." Sure enough, Griffith Park—a swath of eucalyptus groves and scrub-covered hills in the heart of L.A.—came to stand in for all kinds of exotic locations.

Once, while shooting a film called *Mandalay* in 1933, Lyle did get farther afield, to the Sacramento River Delta. *Mandalay* was a steamy pre-Coder directed by Michael Curtiz. Warners was banking on its being a successful women's picture, and had decided to invest in a location shoot to re-create a tropical atmosphere. The movie starred Kay Francis as a fabulously dressed prostitute named Spot White who plies her trade in a Rangoon nightclub, Ricardo Cortez as the gambler boyfriend she ends up killing, and Lyle as the doctor kicking a drinking habit with whom she goes off in the end, seeking a redemption for two. In Sacramento, my father recalled, "We lived on a boat called the *Delta Queen*. It was all mahogany, and very beautiful. There were Chinese people living all along the river there at that time. The film crew didn't have to do much to make it look like a port in the Orient. The actors all slept on the *Delta Queen* and ate there. But at night the crew would go off and eat in the Chinese places and gamble, and the Chinese would take them for everything they had."

But mostly, when Lyle went out of town, it was to the Hearst Ranch at San Simeon. Visits to the Shangri-La overlooking the Pacific were kind of a standard perk for Hollywood stars in those days. The actress Marion Davies, William Randolph Hearst's longtime mistress, was one of the most sociable of stars, and the newspaper magnate himself was one of those fundamentally shy people who love to be around extroverts, especially performers. "Together," writes Hearst's biographer David Nasaw, "he and Marion were assembling a new California aristocracy of the amusing, witty, beautiful and accomplished that included Marion's old friends from the *Follies* and her new friends from MGM, prominent studio executives, established and on-the-make stars and starlets, reporters, publishing tycoons, politicians, bankers and writers."

My father recalled that the Hearst hospitality worked this way: "Marion's secretary would call you and say Miss Davies and Mr. Hearst would like to have you as a guest at the ranch in a week's time. A limousine would pick you up at your house and you'd usually go up on a train called the Midnight Lark. You'd have a compartment, a sleeping car, and then a limo would pick you up in San Luis Obispo and drive you to San Simeon." The roads there were rough, dirt for part of the way, and often shrouded in fog. But when you got there, it was breathtaking: coastal plains tumbling down to the vast blue Pacific. "You went through three gates, and as you drove in, along the way, there were animals grazing: llamas, buffalo, and deer. Hearst had the largest private zoo in the world at that time, and some of the animals roamed free, though there were others—like a panther—that were enclosed, of course. There were several guesthouses they called cottages, but really they were two- and three-story Mediterranean-style houses, filled with antiques. I stayed in one called the Del Monte. Only the real VIPs, those very close to Hearst himself, slept in the castle. Outside of the castle, and the guesthouses, you'd always see these big wooden packing cases. He was constantly acquiring new bric-a-brac from Europe.

"The wonderful thing about being a guest there was that you could wander around all day on your own"—swim in a mosaic-lined pool overlooked by slender marble statues, go for a long, rambling horseback ride, or maybe even an overnight camping trip led by one of the in-house wranglers, play billiards, read in the library, visit the zoo. Lyle, a foodie *avant la lettre*, loved the kitchen—a vast place with copper pots and pans hanging everywhere and walk-in refrigerators. "The only time you were expected was at dinner, which was served at eight. Men never wore dinner jackets, because Hearst didn't. But Marion would send out word to the women that she was going to dress formally or casually. And all the other women would dress accordingly. You'd sit at his long refectory-style table that would seat maybe fifty people. It was like something out of a medieval banquet, except one thing that I always remember is that there were bottles of ketchup set out. It was so formal and old-world, but Hearst liked his ketchup."

Some of the Hollywood visitors found conversation with their host to be heavy-sledding. Compared with the warm and vivacious Davies, Hearst was stiff, reserved, and imposing, with, as Nasaw notes, "a life-long habit of staring unblinkingly at his interlocutor." But Lyle, not being of judgmental temperament or psychological bent of mind, was prepared to like him without puzzling over him. Hearst was certainly hospitable, and that was enough to earn him an unexamined regard from Lyle. On a couple of occasions, Hearst recruited Lyle to play doubles tennis. Lyle's tennis game had nothing to recommend it, but he could hardly say no. The first time, Lyle was on Hearst's team. "The old man was a big guy, not really fat but big, with long arms. Still, he was pretty agile. Of course we won." Remembering Lyle's skills no doubt, Hearst placed him on the opposing team the next time

At Hearst Castle. Lyle is seated on the ground next to William Randolph Hearst.
Joan Blondell is in slacks, Mary Astor is in the middle of the back row,
and Marion Davies wears the hat.

they played. Left alone with the tycoon a few times during the cocktail hour, Lyle gamely tried to get a conversation going. He knew nothing about decorating or architecture, but he did love newspapers, after all. "Gee, Mr. Hearst, my people in Omaha sure were happy to know that you had bought the *Omaha Bee*." Lyle rattled on happily a bit about the columnists and cartoonists in the *Bee*. Hearst nodded once, gravely, then walked away without saying anything. "Hey Talbot, you put your foot in it," said an actor acquaintance of Lyle's who was standing nearby. "That Omaha paper's a money loser; the old man's trying to unload it." Lyle was touched by Hearst's fondness for animals and did sometimes find common ground there. "Before dinner, Hearst would go out and feed this one deer he'd sort of tamed. He loved dogs and he had these long-haired dachshunds—I'd never seen them before, but gee, were they cute! Anyway, the old man was crazy about them, and he'd let them sit beside him at the dinner table."

Of course, Lyle liked his hostess, Marion Davies, better. She had a winsome personality, blond curls, and a blue-eyed, china-doll prettiness. "She was really kind of a simple, little Irish girl from Brooklyn, very down-to-earth, and such a dear lady" and seemed to Lyle to "respect and admire Hearst," whom she had met when she was a teenage chorus girl and he a very rich and long-married stage-door Johnny in his late fifties. He never did get a divorce, but his relationship with Marion would last till his death. He was crazy about her; she was devoted to him, even bailing out his business with a no-questions-asked gift of a million dollars at one point. Alas, for Davies, the image many people have of her is that of the talentless—not to mention shrill and unpleasant—Susan Alexander, the character that was supposedly based on her in *Citizen Kane*. Alexander cannot sing, but Orson Welles as the arrogant newspaper tycoon pokes and prods his mistress into becoming a singer anyway.

Marion Davies, on the other hand, *was* talented, particularly as a comedienne. She was the sort of actress who doesn't mind making herself look goofy and even unattractive on screen, and she was an excellent mimic of her fellow actors—a flair that is put to particularly good use in the charming silent comedies *The Patsy* and *Show People*, both directed by King Vidor. The film historian Jeanine Basinger makes a persuasive case that Hearst did his mistress a disservice out of love for her and a need to see her treated in the movies with the dignity that their own unconventional relationship sometimes denied her in society. He was always getting Davies to do costume dramas and sentimental romances, when her real talent was for comedy. Once, Vidor and his screenwriter drove up to San Simeon to tell Hearst and Marion about a new script that called upon her to do "comic imitations and get hit with a custard pie in the face. Marion said, 'I like it,' but Hearst was silent. He finally gave consent, but only if Marion did not get hit with the custard pie." The truth was that Davies herself was also self-deprecating about her acting skills, almost as though she bought the Susan Alexander version, hurt as she must have been by it. In any case, at San Simeon among her friends, her mimicry and her self-mockery were all given free rein.

As if staying at San Simeon weren't one big party enough, Hearst and Davies were always whipping up actual parties—picnics on the beach and costume parties, frequently with a western theme. If a guest happened to have a birthday while at San Simeon, Davies would summon musicians and throw a party. Like a mother trying to ensure her children's fondness for one another, she would get presents for the other guests to give.

There was one patch of darkness in the Hearst–Davies idyll, and that was Marion's drinking. But at the time, Lyle, like many of her guests, was not inclined to see it as a shadow. Marion drank too much and that was naughty and had to be concealed from W.R., but the concealing was fun! There was a lot of giggling involved. They were like kids sneaking candy at a slumber party under the nose of the pater-familias. In time, Lyle's own drinking would become a disaster, but in the 1930s, and especially amid the splendor of San Simeon, he was far from seeing it that way. Still, even he was aware that Hearst worried about Marion and liquor. "You could see that he tried, somewhat, to limit everybody's drinking." That was how he tried to limit Marion's. "Before dinner," my father recalled, "cocktails were set out: two big silver decanters, one was a gin drink and the other was whiskey sours and little glasses. You had one drink and then they were cleared away. In the silent era they'd had a bar. It was Prohibition, but they had every kind of booze you could think of. Lew Cody, a fabulous silent-era actor and big drinker, and his friends got into a fight one night and the old man heard about it and took the bar out.

"At night there was always a movie, usually one we hadn't seen yet because it was just out, and you'd watch it in a beautiful little theater. But before that Marion always managed to get somebody to sneak in booze for her in a thick water glass, an old-fashioned tumbler. She would gather her drinking friends—I happened to be one of them—and we'd assemble in a little nook behind some columns off the dining room. She had a butler who was her ally, and he would often be the one to bring in these tumblers that were supposed to be inconspicuous. Other times it'd be one of her guests. I remember one time Chaplin was there with the drinkers. He was married to Paulette Goddard at the time, and she was the only one of his wives who could tell him off. She called him on a house phone and you could hear her through the receiver from her quarters yelling, *Get your ass over here!* We would wind up, some of us, feeling no pain."

The longest visit Lyle ever made to the Hearst ranch was with the Countess di Frasso, the time she persuaded him to tell Warner Brothers off when the studio wanted him to come back earlier. It was Christmas, and it would have been especially disappointing to cut the visit short. "Hearst would never cut down a tree on his own property, though he had about twenty-five thousand acres. The tree came from Arrowhead, and it was huge, like the Rockefeller Center tree," standing right at the entrance to the main hall and lavishly decorated.

"Gosh," said Lyle to the countess as they were dressing one night, "what do you give these guys for a Christmas present?" And she said, "Oh, nothing, darling. You're not expected to." But the guests all received presents—for Lyle, it was a Sulka silk tie.

"When you worked with Marion you got presents, too. If you were on the crew, an actor, whatever. She'd hear that a cameraman's wife was going to have a baby or one of the grips totaled his car, and she'd give the most lavish presents. She was a very generous person." By the time Lyle worked with her, Davies had moved from MGM to Warner Brothers, and had moved her dressing room—really a fourteen-room villa—along with her, broken up and placed on ten flatbed trucks, to the lot in Burbank. When Lyle did a movie called *Page Miss Glory*, a light, mildly amusing Cinderella story with Davies, Dick Powell, and Mary Astor, Davies gave him a Patek Philippe watch. "Platinum with diamonds and rubies. I wouldn't even wear it. I put it in a vault."

The thing was, there were times when Lyle would have been happy to put a lot of the fanciest trappings of his new life into a vault for a while. He was still a guy, would always be a guy, who loved getting the blue plate special at a decent diner, reading the newspaper on his own couch while he smoked a pipe, listening to the ball game on the radio while he folded his handkerchiefs and matched his socks. He could get a little of that cozy feeling from certain Hollywood establishments—the places where he went several times a week and ordered the same comfort foods from the same waiters and waitresses whose names he quickly learned and used. By the time I was growing up, he was the sort of person who read the name tags of waitresses and salesclerks and then called them by name throughout the transaction. Not constantly, but just enough. And he did it without sounding smarmy—something I've tried and failed at. The trick, I think, is doing it without air-quotey self-consciousness, and that's the part I can't get. He just figured that most of us like to be called by our own names—especially by a handsome actor—and it turns out he was right. He wouldn't have put it this way, but it makes us feel seen.

The Brown Derby restaurants were the main places like that, especially the original one, shaped like a big hat set down on Wilshire Boulevard with its neon sign on top entreating people to "EAT IN THE HAT." Inside, it was rather plain-looking, with booths set flush against cream-colored walls, but from the time it first opened in 1926, the Derby was chockablock with picture people, who appreciated it in part because it was open till four a.m. for breakfast, lunch, or dinner, and the kitchen would make you anything you wanted—sponge cake soaked with ketchup for Wallace Beery, a supposedly low-calorie grapefruit cake invented for the dieting Hedda Hopper. Lyle liked to order the corned beef hash; it was a specialty of the house and would become a specialty of our house. One of the owners of the Brown Derby was Wilson Mizner, the wag who had just switched from real estate swindling in Boca Raton to desultory screenwriting for Warner Brothers. Lyle often found Mizner holding court from his usual booth, in his own acerbic style and reedy voice. It was hard to keep a straight face around Mizner. To producers he'd say anything: "I've seen your picture," he told one, "and the heroes aren't on the screen. They're in the audience." But for moochers, and characters like himself, he was a soft touch—always willing to empty his pockets.

Sometimes Lyle missed home—not the one he'd grown up in, but the home that was life on the road and nights on the stage. That was not an uncommon longing for people like Lyle who'd come from the theater, especially perhaps for those from the repertory companies that became so much like family for many of them. It was a relief to be paid a weekly salary and not have to worry about a company leaving you stranded somewhere. But for theater actors it could be hard to get used to the choppy discontinuity of moviemaking, performing scenes out of order and sometimes shooting more than one movie at once. At times, you might not even meet most of the actors who were in a film with you, and there was much less feeling of solidarity. "There was a class system—a caste system, you might call it—that existed in Hollywood in the silent days, before we even got there," my father would recall later in an interview. "There was the star, and the featured player, and so on. We didn't have that in the theater. If you were in the play, maybe there was a guy who had only two lines, but he wasn't ever looked down upon. He could be your best friend, your pal. All actors, generally speaking, cooperated. It was an ensemble and you felt that. You were together all at once in the theater, for rehearsals, for performances. In a picture that wasn't necessarily so. You might have scenes in a picture with someone you hardly knew. There was less of that ensemble feeling. The star—now, I'm exaggerating a little here, but still—might not speak to the featured player, the featured player might not speak to the bit player, and the bit player had nothing to do with the extras. Even among the extras, there was a hierarchy: there were the dress extras, the ones who wore the tuxedos and evening clothes, and maybe they didn't speak to the next class, the cowboy types, or whatever they were."

Partly, though, what Lyle and other stage-bred actors got nostalgic for was the adrenaline rush of live theater, when whatever went wrong had to be fixed on the fly, and their youth, when the little successes often mean so much more than bigger ones do later. When you're just starting out as a performer, applause is a drug that works even at low doses; inevitably, you need more of it in order to produce the same charge. As Marion Davies recalled late in life, "My happiest days had been on the stage. I had had more fun onstage than in the movies. Not fun, exactly, but the exhilaration and excitement and the music and the glamour. Of all the things I did, that was what I liked most. That was when I was most insignificant. And that was why I liked it the best. I had no responsibility. I just held up the backdrops."

For Lyle, a visit from those old troupers, his father and stepmother, was often the best cure for incipient homesickness. In June 1933, when Lyle got his first vacation from the studio, he had chosen to spend it in Brainard and Omaha, with short side trips to Sioux City, Iowa, and Wayne, Nebraska, where he'd traveled with the Walter Savidge Amusement Co. and where, the local paper reported, he now "drove down a sunbaked Main Street in his slender, California type sports car." In Brainard, he attended a Saturday-night dance and stayed with his grandmother, enjoying her cooking once again. But one of the Nebraska papers said he was "warm in his defense of the movie-city and resents the Midwestern conception of it as the modern city of sin. It's a place for hard workers, he affirms." Lyle must have felt betwixt and between, tied irrevocably to Nebraska but also alienated by the anti-cinema sentiments he was likely hearing. This was, after all, just a few months before the Legion of Decency launched its boycott of racy Hollywood films. Lyle did not go back to Nebraska for many years. Instead, he brought his grandmother, and even more often, Ed and Anna, out to Hollywood.

The Hendersons were now more or less retired from the stage and living in Omaha, in the apartment building they had bought, renting mostly to fellow performers. They came to California several times during the 1930s. Ed got a big kick out of seeing Lyle in Hollywood, and Lyle got a big kick out of his indefatigably cheerful, puckish dad. To Anna, they always seemed like overgrown boys when they were together, teasing and trying to outdo each other with ridiculous puns. Ed was a down-to-earth, long-married midwesterner, but he was also a showman who appreciated Hollywood's quirks and excesses. He and Anna knit the two halves of Lyle's life together for him. When Lyle was filming the movie *Mandalay*, he took his father and Anna up to the Sacramento River with him and got them bit parts in the movie. Many years later, when he was an elderly man and a widower living in an old folks' home in Omaha, Ed was interviewed by a local reporter. "They once gave me a dressing room between Lyle's and Kay Francis's," he said wistfully. "It was just as luxurious as theirs. You'd have thought I was Jack Warner himself. I've had a wonderful life."

But at a younger age, Ed sounded less reverent, noting wryly, as parents of newly grown-up children often do, how very much more our children apparently know than we do. "We mixed very smoothly with the film folks," Ed told an Omaha paper when he returned from one of the trips he made to Hollywood in the 1930s. "I guess it was because of the lesson of 'don'ts' that our boy gave us when we first arrived. Now folks, don't stare at the stars, don't ask for autographs, don't act thrilled at the sight of them, don't tamper with movie equipment, don't bother anyone on the lot." Ed disregarded some of the don'ts. Once, when he was watching Dick Powell and Lyle in a fight scene during the filming of *College Coach*, he started shouting, "My gosh, that's a dandy. Let her go! Wheeh!" William Wellman, who was directing the picture, turned to him in consternation: "Don't you know you've just ruined thirty feet of film?"

But irrepressible Ed and his sweet-natured wife charmed many of the people they met in Hollywood. After Pickford invited them to tea, at the Countess di Frasso's request, she was so taken with them she had them back for dinner. On a train trip to New York that Ed and Lyle made together, they were surprised, when the train stopped in Chicago, to see a swarm of reporters and photographers on the station platform. "I had no idea they knew I was on the train," Lyle told his father. But when he stepped out to greet them, Lyle realized it wasn't him they were looking for. The press boys had been tipped off that Greta Garbo was on the train. Still, since they had Talbot there and no Garbo in sight, they started interviewing him. Lyle was just reaching the punch line of what he thought was a pretty delightful story when somebody shouted, "There she goes!" and the reporters dashed off in a mob, leaving Lyle "as alone as if I'd been on a desert island," he told his dad. He was mortified at first. Then one of Garbo's assistants took him aside and told him how grateful the privacy-craving star was: Lyle had created enough of a diversion that she had successfully eluded the press pack. Could he do it again at the next stop? Lyle was a little dubious, but Ed reminded him that he would be coming to the aid of a lady. Why, Ed would be happy to help out, too; he had a few jokes up his sleeve, after all. Father and son rose to the occasion, keeping the reporters at bay twice more. Before they got off the train in New York, Garbo summoned them to her compartment to thank them.

IN THE SUMMER OF 1933, Lyle got so lonesome for the stage that he persuaded Warner Brothers to let him act in a play at the El Capitan Theatre in Hollywood, even though it meant reporting to the theater every night after a long day on the set. The play was *One Sunday Afternoon*, a nostalgic Gay Nineties piece with a small-town setting, and in it, Lyle got to dress in natty period clothing—striped vests and straw boaters—and act opposite pretty, blond Lola Lane. He got excellent reviews. The *Los Angeles Examiner* said his performance as Biff Grimes, "the village bully, with a fist of iron and a heart of wax," was "delightful," and won him "vociferous applause after his every scene." The *Los Angeles Times* declared him "splendid" and praised the play for its "haunting overtones of yesterday's life, simple natural incidents that might be anybody's experience" and that were "not disturbed by vulgarity or suggestiveness."

For an L.A. *Times* article in late July headlined "Lyle Talbot Simply Had to Do Stage Role at Any Cost," Lyle explained why. Actors in the movies faced "so many obstacles when it comes to sustaining a certain mood or feeling throughout," he told the reporter. "One works oneself into a marvelous emotional fervor and then the order comes to stop work. You know, it's almost impossible to recapture the thing, that is, the same degree of intensity. And then there's the cutting room! The ogre of the actor. One's best moments are usually cut out."

Even when it wasn't practical for them to be acting in plays, Lyle and some of his Hollywood friends made a point of going to the theater often. It was their way of showing they still felt loyal to the stage, while getting a look at plays that might turn up as screenplays, checking out new talent in town, and cheering on movie colleagues who found the time and energy to do stage work. On occasion, a particular play might acquire a following, and groups of actors would go back to see it night after night. One of the odder such cases was that of a play called *The Drunkard*, which opened July 6, 1933, at the Theatre Mart near Vermont Avenue. *The Drunkard* was a temperance melodrama that had first been performed in 1844 in Boston, and that would become a mainstay of the blood-and-thunder circuit in the nineteenth century. One of around a hundred plays about the evils of drink that audiences flocked to in the nineteenth century, it was probably the most popular until it was eclipsed, in the 1860s, by *Ten Nights in a Bar-Room*. P. T. Barnum featured it at his American Museum in New York in the 1850s. *The Drunkard* resurrected stock characters such as the beautiful orphaned girl, the deep-dyed villain who lusts after her, the well-bred, weak-willed man she marries, who succumbs to demon rum, and their saintly, sickly little daughter. It was the kind of play in which characters speak in loudly whispered asides to the audience, and the eponymous drunkard addresses the bottle this way: "You! Rum! Eternal curses on you! Had it not been for your infernal poison shop in our village, I had been still a man—the foul den where you plunder the pockets of your fellow, where you deal forth death in tumblers, and from whence goes forth the blast of ruin over the land to mildew the bright hope of youth, to fill the widow's heart with agony, to curse the orphan, to steal the glorious mind of man, to cast them from their high state of honest pride and make them—such as I."

In 1933, a couple of arty types from Carmel, Preston Shobe and Galt Bell, bought a theater in L.A. and got inspired to open it with a revival of *The Drunkard*. Given that Prohibition had been repealed just three months earlier, they figured it'd be funny—"campy" would have been the word except people didn't say "campy" in the 1930s—to stage one of the old chestnuts of the temperance movement. Where Barnum had presented the play in utter earnestness, in a venue he called "The Moral Lecture Room," Shobe and Bell would re-create the atmosphere of a music hall with tables for the patrons to sit around and beer for them to drink. They did figure, though, on a short run for this novelty. They had high hopes for staging the classics and a new Russian version of *Uncle Tom's Cabin*, rewritten as an anticapitalist parable.

But to their surprise, *The Drunkard* became an instant and persistent hit. It was still running and filling the house a year later. It would still be running ten years later. Indeed, *The Drunkard* would not close until October 1959. "As the years passed," a retrospective item in the

Los Angeles Times noted, "actors who had begun as children outgrew their roles and had to retire. By 1940, there had been 16 weddings among the cast members." An actor named Neely Edwards, who was seventy-six when the show closed and had been acting in it since Christmas Eve, 1933, said, "I was getting kind of tired anyhow. I can stay home now and relax for a while. Something usually comes along."

In the 1930s, *The Drunkard* was especially popular among picture actors, including Lyle. A squib in the L.A. *Times* about the movie crowd that had been filling the tables at the Theatre Mart noted that "this week among the personages who added gayety were Lyle Talbot who was awarded a gold star for having seen the piece five times." W. C. Fields was so taken with *The Drunkard* that he incorporated scenes from it and actors from the L.A. production into his 1934 movie about a moth-eaten acting troupe, *The Old Fashioned Way*. For Hollywood audiences, it must have felt liberating to smirk at this fusty tribute to temperance at the very moment when the temperance movement's greatest accomplishment had been rolled back and looked, already, quite ridiculous.

But if that knowingness was part of the enjoyment, nostalgia was probably another part. For someone like my father, who had acted in melodramas when he first started out, there were sweetly familiar sensations here: the histrionics and the flowery language onstage, the chummy hissing at the villains and cheering for the heroes from the audience, the elaborately if amateurishly painted scenery. And he wasn't the only one to notice its yesteryearian charms. "The atmosphere of the auditorium, except for the absence of kerosene lamps, is much as it might have been ninety years ago," Philip K. Scheuer wrote in the L.A. *Times*. "A collection of posters, illustrating Barnum exhibits of the period, and carefully reproduced from etchings (and in the single instance of Jenny Lind, from an existing original); ushers in the formal dress of provincial gentlemen; a curtain adorned with cupids and clouds, and falling, when it falls, with a weighted thud; scenery, actors and play—asides and all, conspire to preserve the great moral force of Mr. Barnum's lesson, exactly as it was driven home to the stumbling sinners of his own wicked era."

And maybe one of the reasons Lyle saw *The Drunkard* at least five times was that somewhere in that creaky melodrama of how drink could bring a man low there was a message for him. If he heard it then, it was still very faint. It would be years before he realized that he himself was in danger of becoming a character in his own cautionary tale—the man with looks, talent, charm, and a real yearning for a happy home, who came very close to squandering it all.

Chapter 8

❧⟡❧

UNIONIZING ACTORS,
UNITING FANS

I t wasn't the money that propelled Lyle into uncharacteristic rebellion. He was earning $300 a week at Warner Brothers in the early 1930s, and that felt like plenty. He never had an interest in making money for the sake of making money. When he had cash, he liked to spend it—there were always lovely things in the world to buy or experience—but he never yearned for piles of it. And it wasn't the job security, either, because he didn't exactly expect that. For many years after he came to Hollywood, Lyle felt, moving lightly beneath the surface of his working life, a vertiginous sense of impermanence. On Fridays the paymaster at the studio would come around with an accordion folder and hand employees their checks, and Lyle would hurry down to the Bank of America on Highland and Hollywood to cash it, in the grip of a suspicion that the check might not be good by Monday. Some of this feeling was symptomatic of the Depression; some was the superstitiousness of actors. Some came from the sense that talking pictures were still a novelty, a little too gimmicky to last; some from the atmosphere of L.A. itself. Sure, Lyle and his actor friends always told each other, "Don't buy anything you can't put on the Santa Fe Chief," but non-actors said it, too. Maybe it was the whimsy of the architecture, or the region's vulnerability to earthquakes, or the too-good-to-be-true climate, but as the L.A. newspaperman Matt Weinstock put it, "Something about the city seemed psychologically unsound, even impossible." People who moved there "liked the place well enough, but in the ephemeral sense that they liked a circus or a Fourth of July fireworks display. Nothing about it gave any confidence that it was here to stay." The Depression upended that attitude, Weinstock wrote from the vantage point of the late 1940s. Regular people couldn't pull up stakes as easily, and "the economic pressure taught them a great lesson: a person couldn't have his malnutrition in a nicer place than Los Angeles." For actors like Lyle, who were not experiencing economic pressure, it was more a matter of time's passage reassuring them: by the end of the 1930s, they could feel confident that the picture industry was not going to evaporate in the next economic drought.

What launched Lyle into risky and pioneering labor activism were the hours. They were grueling. When he came to Hollywood, there were no rules about how long an actor could work at a stretch or how much time he was allowed between shoots, and the regimen was exhausting. More than that, it signaled an attitude on the part of the studios that Lyle and many others objected to, a sense that actors were disposable, fungible material. In 1933, Lyle became a founder of the Screen Actors Guild, which would grow into one of the most successful and democratic unions in America. He was no firebrand, not even a Popular Front sympathizer. But he had a strong sense of camaraderie with his fellow actors and a fresh memory of a different way of doing things. In the theater, he was used to getting to work in time to dress and make up for the curtain at eight, and he'd usually be done by eleven. "You did the play and that was it," he told David Prindle, a political scientist researching the Guild in the 1980s. "In Hollywood, hours meant nothing. It was a carryover from the silent era when hours had meant nothing and there were no unions at all to regulate anything in Hollywood." (Los Angeles was the least organized big city in America as late as the 1940s.) "They just thought that was the norm. Our objection was we would work fourteen-, fifteen-hour days and then be called back the next morning. Saturday night they liked to work till midnight because you had Sunday off. The Catholic actors, Pat O'Brien and Bill Gargan and Spencer Tracy, would joke that they'd barely get home in time to make it to Mass." The actress Fay Wray remembered working for twenty-two hours straight on *King Kong*. Claire Trevor recalled that with the hours the studios demanded, "you'd be half-awake during an important scene and you'd worry that the stress would take its toll on your career."

Some directors were worse than others when it came to keeping actors on the set: Michael Curtiz, for instance. "We used to say," my father recalled, "that Mike must have hated his wife, because he never wanted to go home." (Or maybe he didn't want to go home because he was happily obtaining sexual favors from bit players, a pursuit for which he was so well known that it inspired a prank. During the filming of *Casablanca*, Peter Lorre supposedly hid a microphone in one of the couches where Curtiz was known to bring his conquests; it broadcast his moans throughout the soundstage.)

The studios were turning out, collectively, on the order of four hundred movies a year in the 1930s, and the pace was frenetic. Those were the years when Lyle took to bicycling around the Warner lot in Burbank, with two or three scripts for movies he was currently working on in the front basket and two or three more for upcoming films in the rear basket. Lyle's friend Glenda Farrell remembered a relentless work schedule: "When I went out there to do *Little Caesar* in 1930, the talkies were still new. Not many actors could talk, so they shoved the ones who came from Broadway into everything. It all went so fast. I used to ask myself, What set am I on today? What script am I supposed to be doing—this one or that one? Up at five every morning, start work at six, work till seven or eight at night. By the time you got home it was nine. Then you had to study your lines, have your dinner and bath, and go to bed. You worked till midnight on Saturday. All I ever really wanted was a day off. Our contracts gave us six weeks' vacation each year, but they got around that by loaning us out to other studios."

With schedules like that, some actors were too busy or intimidated to even read their contracts. "My studio contract was about five inches thick," my father recalled. "You couldn't read it if you wanted to. What it said, basically, was that the actor was totally at the mercy of the studio. You couldn't quit. The only way you could get out of your contract was to be let go by the studio. They had to guarantee you a certain amount of work, but that was never a problem."

The studio was such a wraparound world that you could sometimes forget why you might want to have a life outside it. In that sense, the studios of the Hollywood Golden Age anticipated workplaces like Google today; they were cocoons lined with perks that gave you fewer and fewer excuses to leave work. Studios had their own fire and police departments, commissaries where you could eat all your meals if you so desired, dentists, doctors, barbershops, shoe-shine parlors, post offices, health clubs, and stores. Joseph Mankiewicz, the producer and director, recalled that "you never left the studio for anything. When you were at the studio, you were not only safe from the outside world, you could participate in any part of the outside world you wanted to. If you wanted to register to vote or renew your driver's license, they came to the lot. At Christmastime, the department stores used to bring stuff over to your office to show you."

And the studios provided other, more dubious services as well. As my father remembered it, "The studio would protect you. They would even get a traffic ticket okayed for you. There was a guy by the name of

Blayney Matthews who was hired to kind of look after Errol Flynn to keep him out of trouble. Errol was inclined to get into a lot of different things," my father said, with the kind of polite discretion that could sometimes make him sound to us, his kids, a little clueless. "So they hired a special—well, he wasn't a bodyguard, but if Errol got into a little difficulty, Blayney would see that he got out of it." Especially in the 1930s, under L.A.'s corrupt mayor Frank Shaw, studio publicity agents pursued cozy relationships with the police, ensuring that they'd be called first, and on the q.t., when a contract player got into a scrape. "Studio cops worked hand in glove with custodians of the law outside the studio gates," wrote the gossip columnist Hedda Hopper in her book *The Whole Truth and Nothing But.* "Some days the telephones of the top public-relations men like Howard Strickling at Metro and Harry Brand at Fox rang like a four-alarm call in the firehouse, as police dutifully reported that they had this or that star safely locked up for speeding, drinking, or mixing it up in a public brawl."

Like any workplace that forestalls dissent through a combination of despotism and flattery, the studios were hard places to organize, especially for actors, who didn't necessarily see themselves as workers at all. The studios could loan you to another studio without your permission, work you six days a week, twelve or more hours a day, cast you in any role or film they liked, keep you under binding contract for seven years, and blacklist you with all the other studios if you crossed them. They kept close enough tabs on you that you had to pay attention even to the reading material you brought onto the lot: on the days when there was a bad review of a Warner Brothers movie in *Variety* or *The Hollywood Reporter,* Lyle, who always bought both trade papers, knew to hide his copy of the offending periodical. But in turn, the studio system offered dependable work, a paternalistic bailout if you got yourself in trouble—and, of course, the elixir of potential stardom. All of this made it tough to get an actors' union started in Hollywood, and brave to do it anyway.

A union for theatrical actors—Actors' Equity—had been in existence since 1913. (Broadway producers officially recognized it in 1919.) In the theater anyway, actors had gotten over a reluctance to consider themselves a trade, at least when it came to negotiating with canny producers. For a time, noted a pro-Equity writer for *The New Republic*, actors had tripped over the very idea of a union. "Are artists," they asked, "to place themselves on a level with hod-carriers?" But "while they hugged their romantic pride, the managers gave them the short end of every contract." Eventually they hugged their pride a little less tightly. In the late 1920s, Equity made an attempt to organize film actors as well, but it got nowhere. In part to ward off further such attempts, the movie producers created their own organization for handling labor disputes. It was called the Academy of Motion Picture Arts and Sciences, and is better known today as the entity that oversees the Academy Awards. In the late 1920s and early 1930s, though, the Academy functioned essentially as a company union.

It took a new influx of actors from the stage to revive the idea of a real union for actors. They had experience of what a labor organization could do for them. They remembered what it was like to work more reasonable hours. And they tended to value the ensemble spirit.

In late 1932, an actor named Clay Clement approached Lyle to tell him about a group of fellow actors who were meeting at the private Masquers Club, a wood-paneled, Tudor-style retreat on Sycamore Street, to talk about founding a union. None of them were stars. Clement himself was a Kentucky-born former stage actor a dozen or so years Lyle's senior, and like him, the son of actors. "Look," Clement told Lyle, "these hours are crazy. We have no time to ourselves. If we can't do something about it, to hell with Hollywood, I'm going back to New York." But going back to New York wouldn't have been that easy. Compared with the days of thriving local theater, "the stage seemed like this fabulous invalid about to die," as my father recalled, "and suddenly, we're out in Hollywood, it's three thousand miles away from

New York, and the only way you could travel was by train, or car, no flying, so it was like another world." Lyle preferred staying and making a stand.

Of the twenty-one original Guild members, nineteen men and two women, all but two came from the theater, and several had been active early members of Equity. They were a cultivated, well-spoken lot, mostly past the age when they might have become stars, and they included a generous smattering of Britons. Ralph Morgan had graduated with a law degree from Columbia University before shaking up his wealthy New York family by going on the stage. He became a popular leading man on Broadway, and set an example for his younger brother Frank, who eventually came to Hollywood where he made an indelible impression as the Wizard of Oz. Alan Mowbray was a British character actor whose plummy mannerisms belied his finances; he had $60 in his bank account in July 1933 when he wrote a check for $50 to pay the Guild's first lawyer. Ivan Simpson was a Scottish-born actor who created the Guild's altruistic motto "He best serves himself who serves others." Noel Madison, the son of an actor in the New York Yiddish theater, had been educated in England, where he also played Shakespeare. Claude King, who was known as "the Major" in deference to his rank in the Royal Artillery during World War I, was a pipe-smoking gentleman who brought his dalmatian to every meeting. Lyle was an exception. Though he was from the theater, he was young and still had leading-man potential. He was also the first contract player from Warner Brothers to join the union, and for at least a year, the only one.

Perhaps the best-known of the founding members was Boris Karloff, who was not a star but who had gained some fame for his horror movies. In fact, it was the peculiar demands of the horror genre that had pushed the courtly London-born Karloff into the union. Karloff generally wore greasy makeup that took hours to apply and remove, often with foul-smelling solvents. While filming *Frankenstein* in September 1931, he had once worked for twenty-five hours straight wearing thick makeup, layers of collodion-soaked cheesecloth wrapped around his forehead to make it protrude, and his ridiculously heavy costume—a double-quilted suit with steel rods and struts to stiffen his back and legs, and boots that weighed thirteen pounds each. In the heat of a Southern California September, Karloff was nearly always soaked in sweat beneath his quilted suit and outer garments, as though he were tightly wrapped, he said, in "a clammy shroud."

The restive thespians decided to call themselves a guild rather than a union. "There was an aesthetic sort of feeling about the name," Lyle recalled. "It wasn't snobbery, but it did seem a bit classier." As classy and artistic as they might have felt, they were showing their teeth, and they knew it could get them in trouble. They moved their meetings from the Masquers Club and started gathering in secret at one another's houses. "We liked Beverly Hills because it had a lot of alleys and you could sneak in," my father used to say. "You know, you'd go in the front door and out the back way and then on to somebody else's house. Just to throw the spies off the trail. Because strangely enough, the studio was sending spies out. All they could find out was who was going to the meetings, but that was enough."

Robert Young, who became an early member of the union long before he became the father who knew best, remembered meeting "at night, in private homes, in the basement if there was one. It was like a Communist cell for those of us who were involved in the formation of the SAG. We had to be very careful back then because the actors unionizing was verboten as far as the studios were concerned. It was risky for us. They had spies all over the place, so we were very secretive. If we were identified with the Guild, it could cost us our contracts."

At Warner Brothers, word was soon out that Lyle was one of the mutineers. Bill Koenig, the studio manager, began taking him aside, alternately wheedling ("What do you need a union for, Lyle? You've got everything you need here!") and threatening ("This isn't going to sit well with Jack Warner. Not well at all"). "Because stars constituted the most important component of production," writes the film historian Tino Balio, "the majors waged a vicious public relations battle that ridiculed their demands."

Given such pressures, the actors' union grew slowly at first. Some actors set themselves firmly against it. This was particularly true at MGM, whose head, Louis B. Mayer, was an anti-union Republican and the unofficial kingpin of Hollywood. "All the studio heads were opposed to an actors union, but L. B. Mayer was in particular, and his people, his actors, followed," my father remembered. "He, as a head of a studio, probably had more influence, personal influence, on his actors than any other studio head. And guys like Wallace Beery—he was a big star at MGM—were fiercely anti-union."

But many other actors were just timorous or undecided. Two events pushed them off the fence. In March 1933, shortly after the newly elected FDR declared a bank holiday, the Hollywood producers announced a mandatory 50 percent pay cut for eight weeks. Though the producers eventually backed off the plan, the threatened pay cut added enough insult to injury to impel the gentlemanly crew that had been meeting in secret to launch themselves officially in June 1933. Within months, a handful of more prominent actors—notably James Cagney, the Marx Brothers, and Robert Montgomery—started coming to meetings. Lyle particularly admired Montgomery's gumption since he was under contract at MGM.

Lyle and his fellow Guild members began talking about SAG to other actors on the sets where they were working. "I can remember hearing stories of Boris Karloff and Bela Lugosi recruiting fellow actors on the sets of their Universal horror movies," said the actress Mary Brian. "You can imagine the persuasive spectacle of Frankenstein's monster and Dracula in full makeup bringing you an application and urging you to 'Join the Guild now.'" Still, by September 1933, the Guild had only fifty-four members.

Then that month, the movie producers issued a new body of rules that was meant to govern their industry and to bring them into compliance with the National Industrial Recovery Act. It contained provisions that particularly offended actors—including one that said a studio still had right of first refusal for an actor's services even after his seven-year contract was up, another that capped actors' salaries at $100,000 a year, and still another decreeing that performers' agents had to be licensed by the studios. This last nettlesome condition "would put the actors' representative completely under the thumb of the producer," the Guild maintained, "make every contract a one-sided bargain, and in the end reduce compensation." Hoping to win a victory in the PR war, SAG issued a report showing that the majority of actors were not making anything like the lavish salaries the studio heads were always invoking—and that the producers themselves made. A quarter of employed actors grossed less than $1,000 a year, and one-half made less than $2,000—and this was before the 10 percent that went to their agents and the money of their own they had to spend on clothes.

SAG called a meeting at the El Capitan Theatre on Hollywood Boulevard in October, and this time, several hundred actors, including some big stars, turned out. Ralph Morgan had stepped down from the presidency in favor of Eddie Cantor, a goggle-eyed, high-energy singer and comedian who was then quite popular (he recorded the hit songs "Makin' Whoopee" and "Ma, He's Makin' Eyes at Me"). Cantor had the added advantage of a personal friendship with Roosevelt. And when the actors sent FDR a telegram protesting the new Code, the president invited Cantor to Warm Springs, Georgia, where he took his polio treatments, to discuss their grievances. The president found Cantor and his delegation convincing enough to cancel the offending provisions then and there. Lyle was emceeing a dance at the Biltmore Bowl that night, and Cantor called him to tell him the good news and let him announce it to the soigné crowd. It was the first big victory for the fledgling Guild.

Not that it finished the matter. It would be four years before the movie moguls recognized the actors' union as a bargaining agent. (They took even longer to recognize the Screen Writers Guild and the Screen Directors Guild. Though the writers first organized in 1933, a couple of months before the actors, SAG won recognition first, in 1937, followed by the directors in 1939 and the writers in 1941. The writers' demands were more fundamental—they had to do with creative control and copyright ownership—and its membership more militant. The actors cared mainly about the daily conditions of their work.) By 1935, SAG's membership had surpassed five thousand, and extras had been allowed to join. In 1936, the Guild boycotted the Oscars ceremony to protest the Academy's continued representation of itself as a legitimate voice for actors' interests.

It was work to get organized, but it could be kind of a ball, too. There were fund-raisers called Frolics, for instance (one was evidently a little too frolicsome and ended up cleaning out the Guild's entire treasury). Lyle was a frequent master of ceremonies for the annual SAG balls. At the Third Annual Screen Actors Guild Ball and dinner at the Biltmore, Frank Morgan, Lyle, and Fred Keating shared the duties with the beautiful Mexican-born actress Dolores del Rio. The prima ballerina Maria Gambarelli performed, as did the tap dancer Bill "Bojangles" Robinson. At the Biltmore Bowl on Thanksgiving Eve, 1934, Lyle emceed a big show and fund-raiser for SAG. He sang, along with Dick Powell, Nelson Eddy, and Jeanette MacDonald. The comedians Joe E. Brown, Skeets Gallagher, and Hugh Herbert came out high-kicking in Gay Nineties drag as the "Florodora Girls." The L.A. *Times* noted that it was an evening "open to the public—or as many as can get in." At the World's Fair in San Diego, SAG put on a hearts-and-minds-winning exhibit about Hollywood. Three or four actors would play a scene while a cameraman pretended to shoot it with an empty camera. Crowds would gather, transfixed by the clean smack of the clapboard, and the sense—this was long before the Universal Studios tour or anything like it—that they were getting a peek inside the machinery of motion picture making. Charlie Chaplin loaned his tramp's outfit and Mary Pickford her curls to put on display. Bing Crosby sang. Lyle and his SAG stalwart friends took turns heading down to San Diego on Sunday afternoons to volunteer at the exhibit.

ONE OF THE STRANGER INTERLUDES in the history of the Guild involved a fierce struggle with organized crime. The background is familiar but still striking: the extent to which Hollywood consorted with the mob, especially in the 1930s, before Bugsy Siegel and the Capone organization turned their attention to building Las Vegas. The nightclubs, the see-and-be-seen restaurants, were all embedded in a Los Angeles that was spectacularly corrupt. You didn't have to be a civic reformer to notice; you just had to read the newspapers or go out at night, and Lyle did plenty of both. "Hollywood was wide open when I came here," he recalled. "There was prostitution, gambling. A man named Frank Shaw was the mayor of Los Angeles, and he was a real crook." Shaw, who was mayor from 1933 till he was recalled in 1938, ran a rich spoils system that rewarded cronies and skimmed money from gamblers, brothels, and bootleggers in exchange for protection from law enforcement. People used to say that the crooked cops who manned Shaw's protection racket got a dime for every towel used in every brothel in the city.

But it wasn't just the invitingly rotten power structure in L.A. that attracted gangsters like Bugsy Siegel and Johnny Roselli in the 1930s. Gangsters were also drawn to Hollywood by the prospects of investing in movies and making quick money, by the gorgeous women there, and like the Irish mobster Spike O'Donnell who'd been so taken with Lyle, by the flattering versions of themselves the film industry was pumping out. The bootlegger Abner "Longie" Zwillman kept a room at the Garden of Allah apartments mainly so he could indulge his obsession with Jean Harlow, whom he briefly dated. Bugsy Siegel—though busy conducting affairs with Dorothy di Frasso and his partner in crime, Virginia Hill—found time to date the actresses Wendy Barrie and Marie "The Body" McDonald. Johnny Roselli—the gangster who'd later be known for his role in the CIA plot to kill Fidel Castro—dated my father's girlfriend Lina Basquette. Hollywood had made gangsters look glamorous, and they were grateful for it. When G-men gunned down John Dillinger, aka Public Enemy No. 1, in the summer of 1934, he was coming out of a movie theater where he'd been watching Clark Gable in the gangster film *Manhattan Melodrama*. There was, in the words of the Hollywood historians Christopher Finch and Linda Rosenkrantz, something of a "cultural exchange program between the studios and the underworld." Actors imitated gangsters who imitated them right back. Screenwriters incorporated street argot and made it snappier—and then it filtered back to the street, new and improved. By the late 1940s, Las Vegas had partly replaced Los Angeles as the mecca for mobsters, but before then, as Finch and Rosenkrantz write, "they flourished at all levels—from the neurotic gunmen, crooked club owners and slick-haired blackmailers who inhabit Raymond Chandler's stories, up to the big-time mobsters like . . . Bugsy Siegel."

I always found it peculiar when my father dropped casual references to the gangsters who hung out in Hollywood, making them sound like the slick kids in the schoolyard you had to learn how to appease. "Johnny Roselli was a nice guy—a good-looking guy. I always got along with Johnny," my father would say. "Of course, he ended up floating in an oil drum." At which point I might say, "Well, gee, Dad, maybe he wasn't such a nice guy after all."

My father did know what men like that were capable of. He knew very well, for example, what had happened to an entertainer at one of his favorite hangouts, the Trocadero. The Troc was *the* nightclub of the 1930s in Hollywood. It was a swell-looking place—low-slung, with a long striped awning and a beautiful neon sign spelling out "café trocadero" in small, neat Deco letters. (You can see it in the 1937 version of *A Star Is Born.* Janet Gaynor and Fredric March go there for a party after the premiere of her first movie.) Inside, on the top floor, it had cream-colored walls with gold-tinged molding and a mural of Paris. The downstairs was a clubby bar, done up in red-and-black plaid. An observer at the opening night admired the hatcheck girls—"perfect soubrettes, with eyelashes and chic caps and sheer lawn aprons and a vast expanse of silk stockings with a general effect of being all knees." But the regular entertainer my father remembered seeing most often there was a singing comedian named Joe E. Lewis, whose horrible backstory everyone knew.

Lewis had been a nightclub entertainer in Chicago and had performed in a cocktail lounge called the Green Mill, which was frequented by gangsters and celebrities and partly owned by Al Capone. In 1927, he took a better offer from a club owned by a rival gang, and told an Al Capone lieutenant named Jack "Machine Gun" McGurn what he'd decided. McGurn swore he'd make Lewis pay, and one November morning in 1927 he did. McGurn's thugs burst in on the entertainer in his room at the Commonwealth Hotel. They beat him brutally, carved up his face with a hunting knife, and cut off part of his tongue. Though they left him for dead, Lewis managed to crawl out into the hall, where a chambermaid found him. Capone himself supposedly regretted the attack and helped pay for the comedian's rehabilitation. But, as my father remembered, "Lewis required a long time to even learn to speak again. He had scars on his face and everything. But here he was staging his comeback at the Troc. He was a nice guy. Everybody liked him. We were all cheering him on. But it was gruesome, when you think about it now." On Sunday nights, my father sometimes emceed the new-talent auditions. "You'd arrive at noon to rehearse, and they'd have food set out, and booze." On the Sundays when he performed with Lewis, he found himself downing even more of the booze than usual.

My father did have some standards. Chatting with a violent gangster at a party was okay, enjoying a certain amount of mobster hospitality might be a good self-protective strategy, but he absolutely did not want to give one the keys to anything. The Guild, for instance. He liked to tell the story about how such a thing almost happened, and how the braver souls at the Guild averted it. And it was a good story.

In 1935, a man named Willie Bioff turned up in Hollywood. Bioff was a gangster from Chicago, and he controlled the International Alliance of Theatrical Stage Employees, or IATSE, the union that represented all the so-called crafts in theater and movies, everyone from projectionists to prop men and electricians. Within months, Bioff would be shaking down studio executives for millions of dollars in exchange for his promise that IATSE would not strike (deals that the rank and file of the union generally neither knew about nor benefited from). His reign in Hollywood was heavy-handed and lucrative; for several years in the late 1930s, he had the movie moguls dancing to his bidding, and he enjoyed the spectacle thoroughly. "I've found that dickering with these picture producers goes about the same all the time," Bioff once said. "You get into a room with them and they start yelling and hollering about how they're bein' held up and robbed. That goes on and on. I'm a busy man and don't get too much sleep. I always go to sleep when that roaring starts. After a while it dies down and the quiet wakes me up. And I say, 'All right, gentlemen, do we get the money?'"

Bioff's patient charade nearly always paid off—in thick, brown-wrapped parcels of cash. It took a combination of muckraking journalism by a gadfly columnist, the actions of a brave dissident minority in IATSE, and the Screen Actors Guild's queasy unwillingness to play along to finally bring Bioff down.

Bioff was born in Odessa, Russia, around 1900, and had emigrated with his family and settled in Chicago a few years later. A third-grade dropout who'd gone to work for local gangsters when he was still a kid, he was barely literate, and certainly no charmer. The historian David Witwer describes him as "abrasive, boastful and foul-mouthed, . . . Bioff himself told federal authorities that had he stayed in Chicago, he believed his organized crime associates there essentially would have killed him out of sheer irritation." He was also single-mindedly avaricious—drinking and womanizing never seemed to tempt him—and scarily strong. "Talking to him, I sensed the relentless drive concentrated in his burly body," wrote the L.A. newspaperwoman Florabel Muir. "He told me . . . with pride, that he could lift an ordinary man off the floor with one hand at arm's length, and his yes-men nodded corroboration."

Bioff's first venture into a business of his own involved trying to lock up Kosher chicken dealers into a collusive organization from which he'd skim money. His plan fizzled, but along the way he met George Browne, an Irishman who was trying to lock up the non-Kosher chicken market. For Browne, plucking poultry dealers clean was a mere sideline. His main gig was as a business agent for the local chapter of IATSE. Soon he and Bioff had given up counting their chickens and turned to fleecing Chicago theater owners with threatened strikes by the projectionists. Bioff and Browne had caught the attention of the Capone organization, which maneuvered Browne into the presidency of the national IATSE. Bioff secured his own position by allegedly ordering the killings of several rival powerbrokers in the union, including one Fred "Bugs" Blacker, who won his nickname by dint of a memorable tactic: releasing bedbugs in the theaters of owners who wouldn't do business with him.

Bioff started out in Hollywood by putting the squeeze on the chairman of the board of Twentieth Century–Fox, Nicholas Schenck, and when that worked out to Bioff's liking, he made the rounds of all the studios. "To the Hollywood moguls," notes the film historian Neal Gabler, "most of them Eastern European Jewish immigrants who aggressively promoted the American dream in their films for fear their adopted country might reject them as aliens, this bumpkin, himself an Eastern European Jew, was the American nightmare." If Bioff was mainly interested in the tidy handover of large sums of cash, he hadn't entirely shed the brutality of the Chicago streets, either. At one point, he decided that he didn't like James Cagney. While visiting the set of a movie Cagney was making, Bioff and his associates supposedly came up with a plan to drop a klieg light on Cagney's head. It wasn't clear why: maybe they'd had it with Cagney's loyalty to SAG, which was steadily becoming an annoyance to Bioff; maybe they just wanted to show the sort of mayhem they were capable of. Only the presence of George Raft, an actor who was both close to the mob and friendly with Cagney, dissuaded them.

By this time, Bioff had automatic entrée to all the studios and was rich enough to buy himself eighty acres in the San Fernando Valley with a thick-walled adobe house set in the midst of alfalfa fields and olive trees. He called it his ranch, and named it the Laurie A. after the wife he doted on. He wore bespoke suits and collected first editions he couldn't read.

Like a lot of people living in Hollywood, Bioff wanted a little more of its glamour to accrue to him than was realistic. He wanted the people in front of the camera in his fiefdom, as well as those behind it. And that desire would lead to his downfall, for the actors wanted no part of Bioff. Or not, anyway, after an initial flirtation.

In 1937, the actors, under the leadership of Robert Montgomery, had voted overwhelmingly to go out on strike as a means of getting the producers to recognize their union. The meeting at which the strike vote took place was well attended and sober in mood. "Furs and jewels were not worn by the feminine stars," a newspaper account noted. "The men were informal in slacks and polo shirts. All were grim-faced." As part of their strategy, the actors had made common cause with a union called the Federation of Motion Picture Crafts, a progressive would-be alternative to the mob-ridden IATSE that was already on strike. The FMPC had gotten protection from longshoremen who worked at the San Pedro harbor. And the longies had been engaging in public fist-fights with the men from IATSE, whom Bioff and Browne had provided with Lincoln-Zephyr cars and sinister-looking backup brought in from Chicago.

One morning in early May, a delegation of actors held a meeting with Louis B. Mayer at his beach house. It was a Sunday, and Mayer was annoyed at the interruption of his weekly bridge game. To everybody's surprise, Willie Bioff showed up, uninvited, to argue for the actors. "He boasted afterwards that his barging in threw such a fright into the producers that they promptly granted the actors all they had asked," wrote Florabel Muir.

That very evening, at the Hollywood Legion Stadium, where the Friday-night boxing matches were held, Montgomery told an audience of stars, contract players, and extras that the moguls had finally capitulated: SAG was now the official voice and bargaining agent for the actors. They'd be guaranteed a minimum wage and twelve hours between the end of one working day and the start of another. Lyle was elated, and loved the symbolism of the setting: a fight arena. "I can remember Bob coming out and standing in the ring and announcing that we had won. The place was packed, and it probably seated fifteen hundred people. And we were all on our feet, cheering." At first, the actors were grateful to Bioff, the pudgy tough guy who'd faced down the bullying moguls. The Guild stopped throwing its support behind IATSE's would-be rival, the leftist FMPC, canceled its own plans to strike, and published a long letter in its magazine thanking Bioff for his intervention. But before long the actors were anxious to shed their new friend—and to expose him in the process.

Robert Montgomery was particularly suspicious of Bioff. "I give Bob so much credit," my father recalled, "because he got wise to Bioff pretty soon, and he went after him like a bulldog. He was quiet about it at first, and he was always a personable guy, but at the same time he was relentless. And courageous."

If you were casting the role, you would never have picked Robert Montgomery for the man who faced down the bulldozing thug from Chicago. In person, Montgomery was slim, elegant, and dapper—one profile said he "refused to carry cigarettes because he felt that their bulk spoiled the drape of his coat"—and on screen in the 1930s he was frequently cast as a stylishly intoxicated bon vivant. "The directors shoved a cocktail shaker into my hands," he once said, "and kept me shaking it for years." Clearly, Bioff was counting on Montgomery's being a "frivolous dandy," who could be easily pushed around or manipulated, as David Witwer notes in his history of racketeering in 1930s Hollywood.

In fact, Montgomery was a man with an uncommonly firm backbone. His politics were a bit atypical for Hollywood, where, with a few high-profile exceptions, liberal affinities have always been more in vogue than conservative ones for actors. Montgomery was a lifelong Republican and anti-Communist, who would become an adviser to President Eisenhower (his brief was to help the president look his best in the new medium of television) and a friendly witness in front of the HUAC. But unlike some ritualistic invokers of patriotism, Montgomery put himself on the line. In 1940, while making a film in Europe, he abruptly suspended his acting career to become a volunteer ambulance driver. He distinguished himself evacuating wounded French soldiers under German machine-gun fire and was named to the French Legion of Honor for his bravery. After the United States entered the war, Montgomery became a naval officer, first in the Pacific, where he commanded PT boats, then in the North Atlantic, where he was on the first destroyer to enter the harbor during the Normandy invasion.

If he was a capital-R Republican, he was also a little-d democrat. Though he'd been born to wealth—his father had been vice president of New York Rubber Company—his family's fortune vanished when the father committed suicide in 1922. Montgomery, who was then eighteen, went to work as a railroad mechanic's assistant and then as a deckhand on a tanker. It didn't take long for him to realize, though, that his good looks and privileged origins had equipped him for the pleasanter lot of impersonating the kind of young man he'd been brought up to be.

Maybe his experiences on both sides of the class divide were what endowed Montgomery with his empathy for the little guy and his aristocratic allergy to being told what to do. Both qualities served him well in his capacity as president of a beleaguered new union that lots of people in and out of Hollywood regarded as a lightweight. One of his colleagues in the Guild remembered a parlay in 1938 at which Montgomery, by then a popular leading man at MGM, was negotiating with recalcitrant studio executives over the rights of extras. "Finally Bob Montgomery hit the table, and he said, 'You know, you people should be ashamed of yourselves. You have no compunction about robbing an extra. You won't challenge me, but an extra you will take on like this. You take advantage of the helpless. Why don't you pick on people your own size?'"

Montgomery decided it would be worthwhile to look into the background of the man he and the Guild were up against—especially after Bioff made an official announcement in October 1938 of his plan to fold SAG into one big motion picture union under IATSE's control. Montgomery asked the Guild to appropriate $5,000 for a discreet investigation of Bioff, and said he'd personally refund the money if it didn't turn up anything noteworthy. But it did. "Nobody knew what exactly Bioff had been up to with the studios at that point," my father recalled. "But we knew he was a shady character and we knew he wanted to take over the Guild." The detectives the Guild hired found that Bioff had been convicted of pandering back in Chicago, and that he had mysteriously managed to avoid serving out his sentence.

More important, they got hold of a $100,000 check that Nicholas Schenck's nephew had written to Bioff for one of their transactions, providing the first solid evidence of the extortion racket linking Bioff and the studio chiefs. By late 1939, Bioff's rule was starting to unravel. Montgomery was on the case, and had presented the SAG detective's findings to the Roosevelt administration; so were Westbrook Pegler, a flamboyant conservative columnist who'd been digging into the mob's connections in Hollywood, and a group of IATSE dissidents who called themselves the White Rats.

But Bioff wasn't going to give up his cash cow that easily. Montgomery and the Guild vice president, George Murphy, started getting threats, including one directed at Murphy's children that had Bioff's signature style all over it: his children would have acid thrown in their faces if SAG didn't call off its campaign against him. Eddie Mannix, an executive at MGM who'd had his own dealings with the underworld, warned Murphy to stay out of it. "You're playing with fire. These boys are tough. They'll think nothing of smashing your brains out. They've done it before and they'll do it again." My father recalled that a group of stuntmen volunteered as bodyguards, accompanying Montgomery and Murphy to and from their cars after meetings.

In 1941, Schenck was convicted of tax evasion, a charge that had come to light as a result of criminal investigations into his relationship with Bioff. Hoping to reduce his three-year sentence, Schenck decided to cooperate with the authorities who were seeking Bioff's arrest and tell the full, unsavory story. Bioff and Browne were indicted for extortion, and studio chiefs from Warners, MGM, and Twentieth Century–Fox now all lined up to testify for the prosecution. "The stories they told over and over again of carrying fifty-thousand-dollar payments to Willie's New York hotel room in paper sacks were more fantastic," wrote Florabel Muir, "than any movie scenario written for a B production."

In November 1941, Browne and Bioff were convicted in a New York federal court. Browne was sentenced to eight years in prison, Bioff to ten. That was the end of Bioff's reign in Hollywood, but it was not quite the end of Bioff. In prison, he turned state's witness and told authorities he was ready to reveal everything he knew about the Chicago mafia bosses to whom he'd been delivering, he said, two-thirds of the Hollywood money. In March 1943, the New York attorney general indicted nine men from Capone's organization, including the handsome Hollywood operative Johnny Roselli and Frank "the Enforcer" Nitti, who promptly shot himself in the head. The eight who went to trial were all convicted. At previous trials, Bioff said he had "lied and lied and lied" to the authorities, but now he was telling the truth, and at great length. "I'm just a low uncouth person, a low type of man. People of my caliber don't do nice things."

Nor, generally, do people do nice things to them. One morning in November 1955, Bioff stepped on the starter of his pickup truck and was blown to bits. Bioff had been living quietly in a tract-house suburb of Phoenix, where he represented himself as William Nelson, a retired businessman of modest habits and means. Unassuming though he may have been, "Nelson" had managed to befriend a rising Arizona politician named Barry Goldwater. Goldwater always claimed he had no idea who the dumpy, bespectacled retiree with a keen interest in Republican politics really was. But Bioff's craving for power had not, it seemed, entirely been extinguished.

Meanwhile, by helping to banish Bioff and the mob from Hollywood—it was true they were not gone entirely, but henceforth they were more interested in Las Vegas—the actors had shown themselves tougher than anyone would have predicted. As my father put it, "If we could survive Willie Bioff, that nasty little putz, we could survive just about anybody."

"Five years ago," declared the *Nation* magazine in 1938, "a gag about a Hollywood actor being a union man would have been good for a ripple of horror in Hollywood's drawing-rooms and for a derisive laugh along the embattled labor fronts of Eastern and Midwestern America. Stars were artists. Featured players were artists. The least conspicuous extra was an artist. The hem of Hollywood's epicene skirt was lifted gingerly and superciliously as Hollywood walked over the mud puddles of its labor problems.

"But Hollywood is a town where the least likely things happen. The incredible has now become commonplace. The Screen Actors Guild rules the roost. . . . The stars have stepped down into the ranks to fight for the extras, the bit players, the masses. . . . The result has been a startling betterment of working conditions, somewhat increased pay, and the discovery that the iron heel of the studios is still a heel, but that it is not iron and that it is not, in fact, any more impressive than any other heel."

While the Guild did improve working conditions, it did not transform the relationship between a studio and the actors signed to it. If the hours were more humane, and the treatment of the rank-and-file performer less exploitative, it was still the case that a studio essentially owned an actor for seven years at a stretch, during which time it could drop him entirely at its own discretion. Actors of scrappier temperament and more exalted ambition than Lyle fought the system for better roles and more freedom to craft their own careers. Bette Davis got so fed up with the lackluster parts and forgettable projects Warner Brothers was assigning her to that she left the country to make a movie in England in 1936. Warner Brothers sued her for breach of contract and won. James Cagney, who had grown weary of his typecasting as a "dese-dem-dose" gangster, had better luck with his lawsuit. It was never settled, but the studio did try to accommodate him with roles more to his liking in the late 1930s. It wasn't until 1944, when Olivia de Havilland, backed by the Screen Actors Guild, won her own lawsuit against Warners that a legal ruling reduced some of the dominion studios had over their performers. The so-called De Havilland Law established that seven years means seven calendar years, so an actor was free to leave a studio at that point. It seems like an obvious point, but until then, when an actor was suspended for any reason (refusal to take a lousy part, uppityness over pay), the studio started the clock on the contract all over again; so time off to serve in the military, as many actors did during World War II, restarted the clock as well. The effect was to extend an actor's service to the studio indefinitely, whether he wanted it or not.

In Lyle's career, the big fight had been for the union itself. Beyond that, he was content to take the roles the studio gave him, as a story he used to tell about Humphrey Bogart and himself makes clear. In 1932, both he and Bogart were newly hired contract actors at Warners. They acted together in *Three on a Match* and in *Big City Blues*, both minor roles for Bogart, who snarled convincingly but had not yet latched on to the melancholy tough-guy persona that would make him unforgettable. When the time came for the studio executives to renew Bogart's option, they declined. Lyle was baffled, but "Bogart didn't care," my father said. "He seemed happy." In 1930, he'd come out from New York where he'd been on the stage, "and a lot of the theater guys didn't like it in Hollywood. They wanted to get the hell out of there. Me, I liked the security, and I liked to work. Bogart went back to New York and I never heard anything much about him. New York was so far away and I wasn't reading the New York papers then."

Then one day in the late summer of 1935, Lyle was cast in an upcoming movie called *The Petrified Forest*. "So I read the script and it's a good part—Duke Mantee—and a good script. And regardless, I'm going to play the thing. You're under contract and you do what they tell you to do. Several weeks later the casting director says, 'No, Lyle, you're not going to play it after all.' I wasn't upset; I'd still be working, still getting paid, just in something else." But Lyle did ask why and was told that Leslie Howard, who had played the lead in the New York stage production of *The Petrified Forest*, had insisted on bringing his costar from the play out to Hollywood with him. "'Guy's name is Humphrey Bogart.' I say, 'Bogart's back?' And the casting director says, 'What do you mean, *back*? He's a new actor—Jack Warner just told me so—Warners just signed him.' I say, 'Well, go up and look at the stills from a couple of pictures three years back. Don't embarrass yourselves.'" Bogart, of all people, had failed to make a lasting impression on the studio execs. "So he arrives on the set and I see him walking towards me, and he's holding up the middle finger. 'That's not for you, Talbot. That's for Warner Brothers. Did I let 'em have it. I didn't want to come back here, you know that. And when it's over, I'm going back to New York.'" An actress who worked with Bogart on Broadway once said that he reversed the usual order of things: he was kind when he was on top of the world and "an absolute son of a bitch" when he was on the bottom. There was a bitterness about him when Lyle knew him as a drinking companion in the early 1930s. From his first days in Hollywood, Bogart had a proud sense of deserving better that Lyle did not. Lyle felt he'd struck it big just being where he was—and he never forgot it.

Still, my father sometimes used to say, late in his life, that he thought he'd paid a price in his career for having been one of the founders of the Guild. He didn't regret it, but he thought it might have held him back. That may have been true, but only in part. It was true that his union activism did not make him popular at the studio. He was the twenty-first of the initial twenty-four SAG members, and the first actor at Warners to join. He was just starting out in pictures, so he had no star stature to protect him. There were plenty of ways a studio could be vindictive: casting an actor in lesser or manifestly unsuitable parts, loaning him out to other studios against his will, or, conversely, blacklisting him with other studios. But Lyle's romance with Lina Basquette, Sam Warner's scandalous little widow, probably didn't help, either. Basquette recalled how angry Lyle had been over the Warner family's treatment of her—he was particularly incensed that they had taken her baby to raise—and how hard he found it, in his misguided (and sometimes drunken) gallantry, to keep his anger to himself. My father felt that he'd been blacklisted at Warners, and in fact, he never did work there again as a freelancer after his contract was canceled.

It would be difficult to prove any of this, and the fact is that there were other reasons why Lyle did not become a star. There was, for example, his lack of pickiness about parts. By his own account, he never turned down a job. Ever. That's not quite true; he did refuse to come back from Hearst Castle that time to play a Brooklyn cop—a ridiculous piece of casting—in a picture. But that was less out of professional vanity than an inclination to hang out at Hearst Castle for a while longer (who can blame him?). Even so, he still needed the urging of his steely girlfriend, Dorothy di Frasso, to ignore the studio's telegrams.

There was a lovely aspect to his approach—an affable graciousness about slipping into smaller roles, a game enthusiasm about working in an ensemble cast. In 1935, when a reporter asked him how he felt about playing featured roles more than leading ones, he said, "Well, it bothered me at first. I had always played leads in stock, and I couldn't understand why they didn't let me do them in pictures. Now I don't mind anymore. I feel that I've become essentially a character actor. And as long as they keep on giving me nice meaty parts—even though they don't carry the whole picture—I'm satisfied. As a matter of fact, I'd rather jog along this way than become one of those overnight stars whose years in pictures are numbered. I've seen too much unhappiness on this account, right here on my home lot."

You can see this attitude buoying Lyle's supporting role in a Mae

West movie he made in 1936. *Go West Young Man* isn't her best movie. More than any other performer in Hollywood, West had had her wings clipped by the enforcement of the Code. But the movie is still quite funny. West plays Mavis Arden, a zaftig, ultraconfident star who scoops up most of the good-looking men in her path and shamelessly ogles the rest. ("My, what large and sinewy"—she pronounces it "sinoo-ey"—"muscles," she purrs when she gets a glimpse of one farm boy. "Ooh, Sitting Bull," she enthuses, peering at beefcake pictures in a little stereoscope viewer. "Not bad for a guy who's been sittin' all his life.") Warren William, as the manager who loves her, is tasked with putting a crimp in her style—ostensibly because her contract says she's not supposed to marry for seven years, but really, we get the feeling, because her sexual appetites are a little too anarchic. Lyle had a smallish role as a politician, Francis X. Harrigan, who is an old flame of Mavis's, a stuffy young man who goes weak in the knees for her.

For Lyle, it was pure fun. He was no longer afraid of West as he had been when he tried out for her play *Sex* years before. Now he found himself admiring her command of the picture—West was the only actress in Hollywood who wrote her own jokes and took a powerful role in shaping her movies—and delighting in the ease with which she could crack him up. Yes, she was ridiculously infatuated with herself, but she was also creative and endlessly amusing, and she liked him. Her current boyfriend and personal trainer, Johnny Indrisano, played a role in the movie (Mavis Arden's chauffeur), so for Lyle there was no thought of turning his friendly banter with Miss West into anything more, even if he'd been so inclined. One afternoon when they were waiting for a romantic scene to be set up and lit, Lyle told West the story of how he'd auditioned for *Sex* and been so scared when he'd gotten the part that he fled town. "She thought it was the funniest thing she ever heard. She said, 'You don't feel that way about me now, do you?' And I said, 'Of course I'm not afraid of you. You're terrific!'"

In the scene they were shooting, she and Lyle's character are meant to be canoodling in the moonlight on her balcony. "She said, 'I tell you what. In this scene we've got, to hell with the dialogue we have. Let's you and I just look at each other and mumble our lines. Let them imagine what we're saying.' So they were getting ready to shoot and the soundman said, 'I can't understand what they're saying!' And she said the hell with it! Henry Hathaway was the director. He was a tough guy, but he never got tough with Miss West. She was the boss; it was her picture and whatever she said went. . . . So she said, 'Roll 'em!' And that's the way the scene is in the picture."

After the movie, West had plans to take a little play based on the movie on tour, and she picked Lyle to play the part of her manager and chief love interest. "I had a line where I come up to her room, and I say, 'Miss West, there are about twenty-five newsmen down in the lobby waiting to see you.' And she would look at me and do this thing, and it would just break me up. And she'd get angry. She'd say, 'Now look, Talbot, you're not supposed to laugh there.' And I'd say, 'Miss West, when I look at you and you say that line—"Send 'em up." Long pause. "One at a time"—I can't help it.' And she really talked that way. She'd say, in that voice, 'Where are you gonna have lunch? I think I'll have a hamburger,' and she'd sound, you know, like Mae West."

Not all of West's young male costars felt as affectionate toward her as Lyle did. Cary Grant, who had played opposite her in *She Done Him Wrong* a few years earlier, thought that the actress one contemporary called "the greatest female impersonator of all time," used all the male actors around her as "feeders." As he told a writer for the *Los Angeles Times*, "With Mae West, that word 'chattel' about which the suffragettes of yore would snort does sort of creep into the picture, what?" Grant was not yet a big star and he acknowledged that being in a Mae West picture gave an actor a "magnificent break," but still. "Haven't you ever met a man that can make you happy?" his besotted character asks West's Lady Lou. "Sure. Lots of times," was the famous reply. That sort of said it all about West and her persona.

Lyle canoodling with Mae West in Go West Young Man, *1936.*

WHAT ELSE HELD LYLE BACK? Well, there was charisma, the ineffable star quality. It's a cliché, but we all know there's something to it. And he didn't have it—not the screen-commanding you-know-you-can't-stop-watching-me kind. When he first came to Hollywood, fan magazines and newspaper columnists quickly anointed him the next Clark Gable. His bosses at the studio had that comparison in mind, too. In 1934, after Jack Warner watched *It Happened One Night*, the big hit from rival studio Columbia, he dashed off a memo to Hal B. Wallis saying that Lyle "should grow a mustache just like [Gable's]. It gives him a sort of flash and good looks."

*Lyle with a dubious Shirley Temple
in a scene from* Our Little Girl, *1936.*

Lyle dutifully grew a mustache, but it didn't endow him with Gable's he-man sexiness. (And it soon disappeared.) Instead, Lyle often conveyed a bit of foppishness, a juvenile quality, with a faint trace of the feminine in it, that sometimes played as inadvertently goofy. He seemed like an urban type, but he was not one of the edgy new city boys like Humphrey Bogart or James Cagney or John Garfield. Then, too, he lacked the paradoxical quality that often makes a star—the elegant beauty who can show an earthy sensuality or the "Aw, shucks" all-American with an angry streak. Nor did he have the adorable imperfection—jug ears, a crooked smile—that will often seal the deal with fans. He did not project a large and distinctive personality that surrounded him like an aura from role to role. He possessed neither the soaring ambition nor the bottomless desire to be loved by the crowd that propels many stars. He had a small amount of both, because all performers need some, but he did not have them in the quantities of somebody, like, for example, Joan Crawford, who could declare that she remembered "every one of my important roles the way I remember a part of my life because at the time I did them, I *was* the role and it *was* my life for fourteen hours a day."

In retrospect, he thought he would have fared better at a studio other than Warners, one like Paramount or Columbia, which turned out a lot of light romances. In 1932, on loan to Columbia, he'd starred in *No More Orchids* opposite Carole Lombard; that was the sort of amusing lover's role he felt he had a flair for, and the genre in which he'd made the best impression onstage. But the truth is, though he's capable in that role, he's also a little stiff. His best movies, actually, are the early Warner Brothers pre-Code pictures, with their crowded casts of stock players in small, vivid roles, and fidgety pacing. In those, he did particularly well playing weak-willed malefactors, not hard-ass ones: a dissolute actor who hangs himself after accidentally killing his party-girl date in *Big City Blues*, the oleaginous freeloader turned reluctant thug in *Three on a Match*, the preening, skirt-chasing football player in *College Coach*. All three movies are tight little exercises in cynicism and urban verve, as bright and winking as polished spoons.

Starting in the mid-thirties, and even after Warner Brothers dropped his contract in 1936, Lyle worked steadily, often in the Other Man role. Sometimes he was the husband whom the heroine married on the rebound from the right guy who briefly looked wrong to her (*Second Honeymoon*, with Tyrone Power and Loretta Young). Sometimes he was the hometown boyfriend left behind (*Second Fiddle*, with the ice-skating champion Sonja Henie—whose dimples do most of her acting for her—and Tyrone Power again) or *One Night of Love* (with the Metropolitan Opera star Grace Moore). Sometimes he was the tempting, but ultimately resistible, alternative to an importantly distracted husband (*Our Little Girl*, where we know he will never really take Rosemary Ames away from husband Joel McCrea—not only because the Code would not allow it, or because his character has the Euro-trashy name "Rolfe" to go with his idle habits, but because Ames

On the Twentieth Century–Fox lot, in 1936: from left, Marjorie Weaver,
J. Edward Bromberg, Claire Trevor, Lyle, Loretta Young, Tyrone Power.
Lyle looks like he's still striding into a starry future here.

and McCrea play the parents of Shirley Temple, for goodness' sake).
He was attractive enough to be a plausible rival and funny enough to
squeeze some amusing moments out of his befuddlement when he's
thrown over (the audiences have seen it coming for miles; the Other
Man never does).

One Night of Love, in particular, did very well—surprisingly, given
its generous dollops of actual opera. Serious music lovers allowed
themselves to hope—in vain, as it turned out—that the movies were
launching a long and respectful romance with classical music. Lyle did
not care for Moore. The blond Tennessee native was a "beautiful girl
with a glorious soprano voice," my father recalled. For a diva in that
era, she was slim, too; her studio contract held her to a weight of

135 pounds and required weighings—which, reasonably enough, she refused. "But she wasn't much of an actress; she was so used to projecting outward," my father said. "Victor Schertzinger, the director, would say 'You're supposed to love this man! How about looking at him?' Or he'd have to tell her, 'Don't worry: I'll get the camera around to you.'" Besides that, Moore, it was rumored, refused to appear on any bill that included a black performer, which disturbed Lyle. Neither Tullio Carminati, her other costar, nor Schertzinger found her at all easy to work with. Still, they were all delighted when *One Night of Love* became an unlikely box-office hit—in Australia, it played at one theater for a full year—that was also nominated for four Oscars and created a short-lived fad for importing opera singers to Hollywood.

Writing in the magazine *Films of the Golden Age*, Laura Wagner summed up Lyle's appeal and his liabilities in those years: "He played everything well. His leads were marked by an affable nature that made him valuable . . . he lightened the heaviest productions. Lyle Talbot's sure-footed, but light handling could brighten anything." And again: "His style was likeable, easy-going when needed, menacing when called for, but he did not possess the larger-than-life presence of the big stars."

Then there was his drinking. Drinking itself—even heavy drinking—didn't disqualify you for much in Hollywood. Not as long as you showed up for work, which Lyle, always the professional, did unfailingly. He might have been hungover, but he was always sharply dressed and finely groomed, always had his lines secure in his head. If your star was already on the wane, though, public drinking and its consequences could muddy your ledger.

And Lyle was getting into car accidents that were obviously the results of drunk driving. One night in October 1933, he totaled his car in a crash that also bashed in a corner of a house on one of the narrow, winding streets in Whitley Heights. He ended up in the hospital with a concussion, a possible skull fracture, and lacerations. In the papers, he credited the derby hat he'd been wearing with saving him from worse injury. He and Dorothy di Frasso had attended a costume party with a Gay Nineties theme, Lyle as a Bowery dandy and di Frasso as a barroom girl. His hat, he said, had served him like "an iron lid." In March 1935, he pled guilty to charges of having been "drunk on the highway," and was fined $150 and ordered "not to take a drink of liquor for 90 days." A columnist in the *Los Angeles Times* crowed that the "lowdown on the arrest of Lyle Talbot in Beverly Hills is too tempting a morsel not to print. A member of a nightclubbing party, Talbot was advised strongly against attempting to drive in his own car home. In fact, taxicabs were ordered for him several times by well-meaning friends. One of them, fearful for the worst, sneaked out and took the keys from his auto. And so it was that when he was nabbed by traffic officers the engine of Talbot's machine wasn't functioning. Lyle had persuaded a member of his party to push him home with another automobile."

Certainly there were Hollywood partyers who did far worse damage while drunk. In September 1935, for example, Busby Berkeley was driving one of the cars in an accident that killed two people and seriously injured five. The Breathalyzer test would not be adopted by law enforcement until the mid-1950s, and even its more primitive precursor, a contraption called the Drunkometer, was used only sporadically starting around 1938. Without that kind of proof, it was easier to fudge whether someone was actually intoxicated—though cops and witnesses would often report smelling liquor on a reckless driver, and that observation would sometimes make it into the papers. That was the case with Berkeley, who was nonetheless acquitted of second-degree murder charges after three trials (the first two ended with hung juries), and even managed to make a successful return to pictures.

Savvy studio PR people could sometimes perpetuate an ambiguous interpretation of what caused an accident. In the absence of blood-alcohol content or Breathalyzer tests, they could often prevent rumors of an actor's drunkenness from hardening into something more like moral sanction. Sometimes, they could even create a spin for our sympathy. When Lyle was recovering from the accident in October 1933, he was photographed looking wan and vulnerable, his head fetchingly swathed in bandages like a doomed doughboy in a World War I melodrama. Lyle confessed to a reporter that he'd thought the accident would end his career because he'd sustained scars that would rule out even character parts. He found himself wondering what he could do instead, and thinking he could go back to Memphis where an old friend would give him a job in his drugstore or else to Omaha where he could be a night clerk in a hotel. Poor guy! Surely there were fans weeping into their Wheaties over that prospect.

Meanwhile, the papers were reporting that Lyle had received more "wires from more different girls than any patient ever" hospitalized at Cedars of Lebanon. The Countess di Frasso, whom he had dropped off at home just before the accident, was sending flowers and calling daily. And he was receiving regular visits from Judith Allen, a toothsome actress and former model with whom he had not previously been linked. Allen was the recently divorced wife of a football player turned professional wrestler named Gus Sonnenberg, and Sonnenberg was telling reporters that he was still in love with her but could not compete with "professional lovers" like Lyle. Allen didn't seem to harbor any such tender regard for her ex: she had divorced him after four months of marriage while he was in the hospital recovering from a heart attack. When it came to ministering to ailing men, she evidently preferred them in Lyle's barely, and rather rakishly, unsound condition. "That statement of [Sonnenberg's] about professional lovers makes me angry," she sniffed to a reporter. "It was most unkind but I can't do anything about it. Lovers are born not made anyway. Perhaps if some were more considerate, they might get farther." Ouch. Lyle, she proclaimed, "is the nicest boy I know."

In October 1938, a fire broke out at Lyle's Beverly Hills home and gave him a chance to show just how nice he could be. It's not clear what started the blaze, but Lyle was at the house with his drinking buddy Franklin Parker, an actor he'd known in Nebraska who was struggling to make it in Hollywood. Parker had been too soused to go home and was the only guest still there after a late-night party that had trickled into the early-morning hours. And Lyle, it seemed, had rescued him. "Lyle Talbot played a real hero's role today which may blight his screen career," said the AP account of the fire. "His hands, neck, arms and head were burned so severely in a $50,000 fire that he may never again appear before a camera. Witnesses saw Mr. Talbot, trapped on the second floor by flames that started at ground level, trying desperately to drag Mr. Parker, who was unconscious, out on a porch roof from a bedroom. Choking with smoke, his pajamas aflame, he finally got Mr. Parker to safety and then leaped twenty feet to the ground." Lyle was hospitalized again, but his burns turned out to be less severe than originally reported, and certainly did not blight his screen career.

One person who was not so impressed with Lyle's actions that night was his wife of just under two years. On March 28, 1937, Lyle had married for the second time. The new Mrs. Talbot was a petite, dark-haired New York socialite named Marguerite Cramer, whom he had known for only three months when they married. My father never said anything about her. Not to his children—though that was a given, because his previous marriages were never spoken of in our household. But apparently not to anyone else, either. In articles and interviews in the 1930s and early 1940s, Lyle did occasionally mention his first wife, Elaine Melchior. Later in life, he talked about Lina Basquette, Estelle Taylor, and the Countess di Frasso; sometimes he referred to them, delicately, as "friends," but he clearly got a kick out of his memories of these formidable women and of others he'd flirted with but never gotten into bed—like Carole Lombard. But he never spoke about

Marguerite Cramer. Maybe the habit of discretion about his former wives was too ingrained, and maybe in her case, he didn't trust himself to say anything kind.

Cramer did "rush to his bedside" in the hospital after the fire, but she had been staying elsewhere that night and she wasn't at all happy about the loss of some of her furs and jewels in the conflagration. (One thing the couple apparently had in common was a passion for clothes. The AP reported that firemen had managed to save "scores of her costly gowns," along with "forty suits, 100 shirts and about 400 neckties" of Lyle's.) When Cramer sued for divorce, she cited her husband's reputation as "a nightclub Romeo." Cramer told a Los Angeles judge that Lyle "didn't seem to care about me or our home. He liked to go out to nightclubs without me. Frequently I heard reports about his attending these clubs in the company of other women."

The fact was that whatever the combination of forces working against stardom for Lyle—the drinking, the early union agitation, a certain something lacking in the animal magnetism department, a failure to be cast more often in the romantic comedy roles he thought he was best at—the odds for all actors were against a successful leap into the stratosphere. It was extremely rare to get noticed and signed by a studio; it was almost as rare, once you were signed, to become a star. An article that appeared in *Motion Picture Daily* in January 1934 gives a good idea of the chances. Of the one hundred newcomers signed by eight studios that year, seven went on to become stars: Ida Lupino, Fred Astaire, Claude Rains, Nelson Eddy, Ethel Merman, Charles Boyer, and Margaret Sullavan. About the same number worked steadily, though not usually in leading roles: Mona Barrie, Claire Trevor, Gail Patrick, Alice Faye, Buster Crabbe, and Frances Lederer. The rest are names that an Internet search will turn up very little for: Neysa Nourse, Chick Chandler, Earl Oxford, Ellalee Ruby, Dean Benton—the list goes on. Some of them continued to play bit roles in movies for years to come, and to be fair, they may have been signed to do supporting roles in the first place. Some disappeared from the business altogether.

Probably Lyle knew, by the late 1930s, that he wasn't going to be a star. He must have been disappointed, but he wasn't saying so. And maybe his disappointment wasn't deep; what he'd always wanted, after all, was to be a lifelong working actor, and at that he still had a chance.

One group that did not accept this concession to reality—and for whom Lyle always kept up a gamely glamorous face—was the Lyle Talbot Fan Club. He may have been a nightclub Romeo to his wife, a fading commodity to his studio, and a danger to himself and any-one else on the road at the same time, but to his fans, Lyle was still a star-in-the-making.

Fan culture had changed a great deal since the earliest days of film, when viewers successfully pressured the studios to release the names of the actors and actresses who were initially uncredited and anonymous. People had been watching performers on screen since 1898, but at first they knew the leading ones only by the names of their studios. Soon moviegoers were writing letters addressed to "the Bio-graph girl" or "the Vitagraph girl." Producers had been unprepared for the intense curiosity about the people in pictures, but they quickly saw its worth. In 1910, the producer Carl Laemmle revealed the name of his new leading actress, Florence Lawrence—and then cooked up a bit of publicity for her by spreading a phony report that she'd been killed in a streetcar accident—and the reign of namelessness was over for good. Fans were free to adore the actors and actresses they set their hearts on, to imagine lives for them beyond the screen, and to find out as much about those lives as they could.

For a while, that wasn't much. The first movie magazine, *Motion Picture Story*, came out in 1911, but it was, for several years, a compara-tively staid affair, devoted to running story adaptations of films. Later in 1911 it was joined by *Photoplay*, which became the most famous of the fan magazines. By the early 1920s, there were perhaps a dozen others, catering to what was by then a familiar term and phenomenon: movie fans. The word *fan*, short for *fanatic* and connoting an enthusiast of some popular spectacle, came into widespread use in the late nineteenth century, applied mostly to male baseball lovers. By the 1910s, it was at least as commonly deployed to describe ardent moviegoers, who were more often female than male. Not only *Motion Picture Story* itself but virtually all of its successors had adapted to new readers and new desires, running more of what we've come to expect from the fan genre: squibs about forthcoming movies, articles about the stars' childhoods, love lives, and tastes in interior decorating, along with Hollywood-tested beauty, fashion, and grooming tips.

Over time, some fans found these sources suspect, or at least unsatisfying. The articles, they soon figured out, were based on biographical material furnished and sometimes manufactured by press agents and studio publicity departments. They distrusted "bunk" and "ballyhoo" and wanted to know more about their favorite actors' actual lives, to assess for themselves the distance between the roles they played or the personae they represented and their non-acting selves. Like Reformation Protestants seeking a direct relationship with God, these fans wanted a conduit to their favorite performer that was unmediated by another entity.

The 1930s saw the growth of fan clubs that arose from the grass roots, independent of the studios and often devoted to one particular actor or actress. Younger performers and those who sang as well as acted—Shirley Temple, Deanna Durbin, Bing Crosby—were particularly popular magnets for fan clubs, which linked fervent and knowledgeable moviegoers within neighborhoods and cities and across the country. They saw themselves as lobbyists—or boosters—for the performer of their choice, since a big part of what club members did, in addition to socializing and often publishing a newsletter, was to write letters to the studios demanding better or more suitable parts for him or her.

They also sought, and often achieved, a relationship of some kind with their admired performer: exchanging letters and presents, and in some cases being invited to meet the star on a studio tour in Hollywood or when the star visited a club president's hometown. In *America at the Movies*, a 1939 study of movie audiences, the anthropologist Margaret Thorp made special note of the new fan club phenomenon. Thorp described what she said was a common scene, but one that is almost impossible to imagine today, when the scale of celebrity and the coverage of it have become so much bigger and more unwieldy. "When the star visits New York or some other city," wrote Thorp, "the local fan club members make it their duty to act as her bodyguard. They follow her about the streets and into shops, attracting as much attention as they can from a populace who might otherwise remain in ignorance of the glory passing in their midst."

The fan clubbers were often quite opinionated and not so awestruck by the Hollywood glamour machine that they withheld pointed commentary. An article in the *Los Angeles Times* in 1934 drew attention to a new boldness on the part of the more savvy fans. "Back in those dear, dead days of the silent screen, nine out of every ten fans' letters would read: I think you are swell. Please send me your picture." But now, the article went on, letter writers were just as likely to be critiquing a star's new hairstyle or offering advice on the roles she should take: "People write a much more critical epistle now." Whereas fan mail had once gone almost exclusively to actors and actresses, now it was often addressed to studio executives as well. Fans chided executives for miscasting or neglecting their favorite performers, or suggested books and news stories that ought to be adapted for the movies. The article even offered the (somewhat suspiciously precise) claim that "last year alone, forty-two productions were made because fans requested or suggested them."

Moreover, while fan clubbers were intoxicated by their chosen honoree, they could snap out of their reveries if he or she let them down. They gave themselves credit for supporting and promoting performers, and expected some respect and attention in return or they would switch their allegiances. Thorp tells an anecdote about the 150 members of a Jane Withers fan club who showed up at the actress's studio, Twentieth Century–Fox, and were barred at the gates. When Warner Brothers PR people heard the tale, "they hurried down to capture the delegation and entertain them on their own lot." The club decided on the spot to rechristen itself after a Warner Brothers actress.

One big reason these more insistent and knowing fans were coming to the fore was that conditions of spectatorship had changed and given movie viewers a greater feeling of command and intimacy. Hearing performers speak fostered a new connection: however beautiful and glamorous, the performers on screen seemed more human, less hieratic and distant, than they had when they beamed their charisma at audiences in mysterious silence. All the more so if they had Brooklyn accents or cracked their gum or squeaked a little when they talked.

Movie theaters in the 1930s were different, too. The silent era and particularly the 1920s had been the apotheosis of the movie palace: the grand, imposing theater with the vast lobby and sweeping staircase, often designed in an exotic or self-consciously historical style—Moorish or Gothic or "Oriental." The ostentatious architecture had been an answer to moviemakers' anxieties about whether their product was an art form, one that could attract viewers beyond the mostly working-class patrons of the early nickelodeons. (If you watched your movies in a palace, then surely they were art.) By the 1930s, that particular anxiety was largely laid to rest. People of all classes were going to the movies, whether the movies were art or not.

The movie theaters of the 1930s reflected a new architectural and social vision, one best articulated by the young architect Ben Schlanger, who designed theaters all over the country. (His first was the Thalia, on the Upper West Side of Manhattan, which opened in 1931.) These theaters were smaller, with 500 to 800 seats, as opposed to the

1,500 to 3,000 of the movie palaces. They were being built in suburbs and neighborhoods, not just downtowns, where most of the movie palaces had been. In design, they were often Art Moderne—or in any case, simpler, more streamlined, and more likely to feature industrial materials like chrome and aluminum. Instead of offering box and loge seats that cost more, as the movie palaces had, in imitation of legitimate theaters, the new theaters sold tickets at a uniform price and provided seating on the same level.

What they sacrificed in luxury, the new theaters made up for in comfort. In the early 1930s, theaters started selling popcorn (candy came next, and soft drinks in the 1940s)—a practice that had been thought too déclassé for the movie palaces. By the late 1930s, most movie theaters had air-conditioning, too—they were among the first public spaces you could count on for a blast of cool air on a hot day. There's a great Ben Shahn photograph that shows a movie theater in a small Ohio town in 1938. The passersby are formally dressed in that 1930s way—suits, ties, and hats on the men, dresses and stockings for the women—though it must be hot outside. The marquee of the theater advertises the movie *One Wild Night* and its stars: Lyle Talbot and June Lang. But beneath the marquee and in much bigger letters is one intoxicating word—*COOL*—that clearly refers to the temperature inside, not the film being shown.

Together, the advent of talking pictures and the new theaters made for a more intimate, relaxed, and democratic moviegoing experience, and it probably gave spectators more of a sense that they could talk back. In any case, it was certainly good for moviegoing. In 1939, 85 million people a week were going to the movies, out of an American population of 130 million. Some of those people may have been repeat viewers, so that, in Margaret Thorp's estimation, perhaps "not more than" 40 million people were seeing movies twice a week. But "not more than" seems the wrong phrase here. The numbers had been climbing since 1912, when 16 million Americans went to the movies each week, reaching 40 million in the early 1920s, and taking a dip, as we saw, only in 1933. Most people could get to a movie theater fairly easily—with the notable exception of black Americans, who were still banned from many theaters, and not only in the South. With 17,000 cinemas in the United States, in small towns as well as big cities, movie-going was no longer chiefly an urban pursuit. As Thorp wrote, "It is not surprising to find theaters, big and little, in the cities, but there are more than three thousand small towns, numbering their citizens by hundreds, which have moving picture theaters." These were the towns where my father had once entertained in tent shows and theater troupes, and movies had largely replaced those. Along with radio, the movies had created a national market for entertainment, a mass culture. You were as likely to know about Shirley Temple or Mae West—or Lyle Talbot, for that matter—if you lived in Walla Walla, Washington; Enid, Oklahoma; or New York City.

Lyle's fan club and his relationship with it were emblematic of the new fan culture. The Talbot club had members all over the country—from Bangor, Maine, to Oakland, California, but its executive officers were two sisters, Lillian and Frances Kerzner, who lived in Malverne, on Long Island. The Kerzners published a newsletter called *The Talbot Tabloid*, with articles written by club members, and the tone of it was wry, chatty, and modern. The members were mostly women, many, it seemed, in their twenties and thirties. (The *Motion Picture Herald* said a typical fan club member fit this profile: a woman between the ages of sixteen and forty-five.) There were fewer teenagers than you might think, and they come across as more levelheaded than you'd expect them to be. They're smitten with Lyle, but they poke a bit of fun at themselves for it. *Three on a Match* was such a sordid picture it gave club member Helen Raether "the orks" to think of; she liked Lyle "slightly tough, but in a perfectly nice way you understand."

The women who wrote for the newsletter remind me of the kind of wisecracking, self-respecting best friends who would be played in the movies by Eve Arden or Celeste Holm. In almost every issue, one of the members writes a profile of another of the members, appropriating the style of fan-magazine star profiles. They had clearly learned the lessons about the self that Hollywood taught: that people were an accretion of piquant details to be sifted through and selected for public presentation, that those details should be particular but not bizarre or eccentric, that apparent paradoxes made for a more intriguing persona, that it was important to project youthfulness and vivacity and that these could help make up for deficiencies in natural beauty, and that we all express something vital about ourselves through our shopping habits.

Though they were to some extent imitating a new formula—the superficial celebrity profile—there is also genuine, teasing warmth in what they say about one another. They write admiringly about each other's slim figures and natural curls and surprising talents. They make note of one another's pet likes and dislikes. There was Irene Lubkeman, whose father ran a delicatessen in Brooklyn where she sometimes helped out—and happily noshed on everything in sight—when she wasn't taking a typing course at business school. Irene played basketball "like a professional," her fellow fan club member offuood, and loved to "dance and dance and dance." Alice Walls of New York City was the young mother of three sons, but she was still awfully fond of "jazz, candy and clothes" and couldn't stand to sit still, even under the hair dryer. Lillian Kerzner, said her sister, had "more pep, energy and vitality than any other six persons I know. Her pet likes are Chow Mein and Chocolate Layer Cake—at different times, you dumbbells!!" Frances Kerzner, a beautician, hated Long Island and spent "a good part of the day reading. One day it will be the works of Shakespeare or Tolstoi and the next day it will be a ten cent love story magazine." In some ways, these squibs anticipate Facebook posts—except that in these, the women are writing about their friends, not themselves. In fact, the *Talbot Tabloid* writers devoted about as much space to touting one another and securing their friendships as they did to saluting Lyle, and it's touching to see how these ordinary but game women built one another up.

When they weren't writing brightly about their daily activities, or reminding one another how delightful the namesake who'd brought them together was, fan club members were bemoaning the lack of good roles for Lyle. "Seriously," wrote one, "hasn't it been hard to see Lyle in such poor roles, knowing his capabilities? Most of his parts, until his work with Universal, didn't have anything desirable. I'm not in favor of having him continually cast, from now on, as a toothpaste-ad hero; far from it. I only mean that he should have varied roles. A villainish part that provides a chance for characterization is every bit as good a role as that of a hero." They had a healthy sense of their own importance as fans: "I wonder if you ever stopped to realize just how much you owe to your fans?" Violet M. Platzer wrote in an open letter to Lyle. "We all realize you have what it takes to get across, but how many others have that and yet get nowhere. The answer is plenty, and the reason is that they have no fans." They crafted funny little tributes to Lyle like this one: "To you and Only you: on his birthday. The wishes we're wishing / The thoughts that we think / would blister the paper / and sizzle the ink: So out in the open / all that we dare say is Many More Happy Returns of the DAY."

In return, Lyle wrote them regularly, telling them how "clever" they were and how "grand" their writing was: "The new Tabloid just came and it's perfectly swelegant." When they sent him gifts, he was delighted: "I am very happy with my cigarette case and lighter. I had several cases but none that I could wear with evening clothes, so it's just what I needed." He was "tickled to death" when they sent an album of snapshots of all the members: "I feel as though I know each and every one so much better now." When Warner Brothers declined to renew his contract, he wrote the club members about it right away, sounding and perhaps truly feeling hopeful: "It was all quite amicable, but anyway I'm free now. It's a grand feeling after all these years." Like many clubs devoted to one performer, the Lyle Talbot Fan Club enlisted the endorsements of other celebrities. Joan Crawford was the honorary vice president and Warren William the honorary secretary. Crawford wrote to the Talbot club, sending personal updates on what she was working on and wearing. (In an upcoming movie: "My clothes are all of an extreme tailored design—even the evening clothes—and I think you will be interested in seeing them.")

One memorable afternoon in June 1935, Lyle himself showed up to visit the Kerzner sisters. He called from the train station in Long Island, with his father in tow, and Mrs. Kerzner went to pick them up. When they got to the house, Lillian Kerzner wrote, in the most sensational *Talbot Tabloid* dispatch ever, "we were all jabbering away as fast as we could and Mother flew to the kitchen to get the good ole coffee pot a-percolating. Evelyn made highballs, in which she forgot to put the ice. But still n' all, she knows how to mix 'em." Ed Henderson "came into the kitchen and kept us busy laughing while we were getting together a light repast. I dimly recall cutting up some delicious pickles and then going to work on a cake. But I came into my senses again when I missed the cake and cut my finger. After the proper amount of sympathy from Mother, which was 'Forget it!' I got busy again.

"While we were eating, I was sitting across from Lyle and I wish you all could have seen what I saw. He has the largest, clear blue eyes I've ever seen. They are the kind that seem to see right through you, if you know what I mean. A more handsome man you wouldn't want to meet, and girls, don't you love that tiny widow's peak that you can't help but notice whenever you look at his picture?"

And Lyle put his keyed-up fans at ease, too. He ambled over to the piano, noticed a framed picture of himself sitting atop it, and said, "Who's this guy?" He got down on hands and knees and played with the Kerzner family hound dog, Spunky. He told the gals about his and his father's brush with Greta Garbo on the train, how he'd been foolish enough to think the reporters gathered on the platform were there for him, and how Miss Garbo had asked him to go ahead and act as though they were to protect her. He warned the ladies to watch out for his father; he seemed like a nice old gentleman, but he liked to crawl under the table and nip people's legs.

By that time, two other fan club members, Della Feil and Gladys Hiltonsmith, had heard the rumor that Lyle was in their midst and hurried over to take a peek. "I wonder if Gladys has gotten over it yet," Lillian Kerzner wrote, and you can practically hear her chuckling to herself. "While Mr. Henderson was having a second cup of coffee with Mother, Della and Gladys, Gladys was stretching her neck to see Lyle, who was in the living room with the girls, and saying such things as 'Isn't he grand So handsome too, etc.' Poor Lyle blushed all over the place. I wonder if he realizes that he did. Then Grace Wilson came down the block and I'm surprised she wasn't running after the way she pushed her boyfriend out of the car when she heard Lyle was here. Her boyfriend was peeved and said, 'What's he got that I haven't got?' Grace didn't even stop to answer."

GRACE AND THE KERZNERS and their friends were at once harbingers of the future and relics of the past. In the decades to come, it would be less and less likely that a well-known actor would drop by a fan's house or encourage a pack of fans to trail her on a shopping expedition. The connection between celebrities and their audiences would become more distant, more mediated. (One could argue that celebrities who tweet are creating a more direct line of communication with their fans—but many of their tweets are written by staff, and they go out to thousands or millions.) They were also learning to be modern media consumers—to be charmed by movie stars but not overwhelmed by them, to live in the world of celebrity without either turning their back on it or becoming unstrung by the fact that they themselves were not celebrities. As the film historian Samantha Barbas writes, in *Movie Crazy: Fans, Stars, and the Cult of Celebrity*: "Fans joined clubs and wrote fan letters not only to praise their idols but to become individually involved in what seemed like a distant, impersonal form of mass entertainment. Fans barraged studios with advice and suggestions not merely out of selfishness but from a firm conviction that they were valued Hollywood consumers whose opinions deserved to be acknowledged. Hard workers and great dreamers, fans tried diligently to create a democracy of entertainment in which audiences, as much as studios, had a say in the filmmaking process." Sometimes producers did pay attention—and tailor publicity campaigns or consider casting choices in the light of fans' comments. But generally, "the story of film fandom is the story of an education: how fans learned to exert their power as activists and consumers, but also how to accept the limitations of their influence." In the end it was a matter of conceding the territory to the glamour specialists, while retaining an upbeat willingness to be entertained, combining delight with a sense of irony and critical perspective. That, it turns out, was how to live in the world of celebrity and mass entertainment, and fans like the Talbot club members, fond of Lyle as they were, seemed to be learning it.

Chapter 9

—◦◦◦—

BROADWAY AND
B MOVIES

T he critics were not impressed with *Separate Rooms*, a new play that opened on Broadway in March 1940. In one of the kinder notices, *The Hollywood Reporter* called it "a lightweight bit of farcical risgayety." *The New Yorker*, meanwhile, predicted a quick demise. *Separate Rooms* packed in "more gags than you would think possible"—a definite strike against it, according to the magazine's sophisticated correspondent, especially since "a good average one" was "'Butlers should be seen, not *ob*scene.' If you're still interested, you'd better hurry." The play was a brittle bauble that told the story of a spoiled actress; the clueless, besotted playwright she marries when he writes her a hit, only to ban him from the bedroom after the vows; and the playwright's brother, a Walter Winchell–like columnist who threatens to expose the actress's past indiscretions unless she becomes a real wife to her frustrated husband. It was, said *Billboard*, "the sort of thing that the stage tossed upon the Flushing dump about 20 years ago—a little farce that is utterly meaningless and discouragingly unfunny" except for some "genuinely amusing lines" in the last act "that must have crept in in disguise." *The New York Times* concluded disdainfully that if you were the sort who liked "the joke the boys are telling," then you would get a "nice dirty laugh."

Most reviewers did pay grudging tribute to the show's stars— Lyle, Glenda Farrell, and Alan Dinehart. Farrell was nice to look at, the *Times* magnanimously pointed out, and as for Lyle, even the appalled *Billboard* reviewer allowed that "saddled with the terrible role of the playwright, [he] really tries hard and does surprisingly well with it." Still, things did not look at all auspicious for *Separate Rooms*. Glenda Farrell, Lyle's old pal from Warner Brothers, had been playing a motor-mouthed reporter named Torchy Blane in a seven-movie series back in Hollywood. Farrell certainly had the fast-talking thing down pat—in one of the Torchy movies, she delivered a four-hundred-word speech in forty seconds—but she had been hoping that the New York stage would let her show she "could do more than talk out of the corner of my mouth." Now she figured she wouldn't be in New York long enough to change anybody's mind about her. Lyle was tired of playing heavies and cops in forgettable movies—the latest was *Parole Fixer*, a film made by Universal with the cooperation of J. Edgar Hoover, part of a series based on FBI files. It earned him the slightly creepy admiration of Hoover (who sent him a highly flattering portrait of himself in charcoal) and a trip to Washington to try out the FBI firing range, but not much in the way of better roles. Lyle had escaped from Hollywood hoping to stay for a while in the quickening air of Manhattan, energized by the crowds and the clamor and the smart talk, thrilled to be acting in front of a live audience again. Then the reviews came in for *Separate Rooms* and he assumed he'd soon be heading back to the West Coast, and not in style.

But a funny thing happened on the way to the Flushing dump. *Separate Rooms* began selling out the theater. At first, it managed this feat through gimmickry. The show's desperate press agent gave out two-for-one tickets all over town. He booked the three leads on every radio show he could find, had them doing ads for toothpaste, cold cream, sheer silk stockings, and Melofelt hats. A few weeks into the show's run at a Thirty-ninth Street theater, the audiences were coming on their own, paying full price, and laughing uproariously, especially in the busy last act. Soon after that, the show moved to a bigger, more prestigious Broadway venue, the Plymouth Theatre on Forty-fifth Street.

This was the spring of 1940. Hitler and Stalin had signed their cooperation pact; the Nazis had annexed Austria and Czechoslovakia, and occupied Poland; in June, they would be marching down the Champs-Élysées. However reluctantly, Americans were gearing up for war. But Broadway offered comparatively few plays dealing with themes of war or fascism. And of those, hardly any were successes. "With the exception of a few noble failures, such as Lillian Hellman's *The Searching Wind*, which attempted to damn isolationists for all time, and modest successes such as John Hersey's *A Bell for Adano*," writes home-front historian Richard Lingeman, "Broadway failed to mirror the larger real-life drama convulsing the world. . . . Indeed, it appeared that Broadway, becoming increasingly prosperous as war money flowed into the box office, became more and more escapist as the war went on." The plays that did particularly well just before and during the war were comedies and musicals; one of them, Irving Berlin's *This Is the Army*, was about military life, but only in the most lighthearted and rollicking way. ("This is the Army, Mr. Jones! / No private rooms or telephones!") *Oklahoma!* debuted in 1943 and became an immediate and understandable sensation. Harder to credit was the popularity of *Harvey*, a play about a man and his outsized imaginary rabbit that did boffo box office, as *Variety* would say, in the 1942–1943 season.

A play like *Separate Rooms* may have been devoid of meaningful, socially engaged themes, but it probably reminded audiences of some of the pre-Code movies that had distracted them during the

Depression. They liked the Deco penthouse set, the beautiful, form-fitting gowns, the barrage of cheerful double entendres. And they liked seeing actors from the screen on the stage. It was a relative novelty then for movie actors to make the trek to New York to act in a play, even though many of them had started there. Critics were often dismissive of these "Hollywood refugees." Actors in Hollywood might "moon, pant and sigh for the legitimate stage," the critic of one Chicago newspaper complained in an article headlined "Sunkist Actors: A Bit Overripe," but "too few of them bother either to equip themselves for it or to pick plays that justify their leaving the Coast, which cans salmon and films with equal facility." When Leslie Howard appeared in *Hamlet* and Katharine Hepburn in *Jane Eyre*, "each drew to the theater crowds of movie-goers, eager to see their gods in person," but neither had chosen a suitable vehicle. "Miss Hepburn was wooden" and "did little more than impress critics with her determination to be an actress someday."

Theatergoers, on the other hand, relished the chance to see Sunkist movie actors in three dimensions, even if some of those actors were trying to jumpstart moribund Hollywood careers. As a writer for *Gotham Life* magazine noted, *Separate Rooms* had the distinction of being a virtually all-Hollywood cast. (Dinehart was a character actor in the movies, as was Jack Smart, the funny big man who played the butler in the play.) Word got out that movie people were going to see the play. "Every visiting screenite heads first for *Separate Rooms*," claimed *Gotham Life*, "to chin about the play and about mutual friends." The actresses Mary Brian, Constance Bennett, and Simone Simon had all been to see it and to hang out backstage. Celebrities drew more celebrities from different fields. Mayor La Guardia was in the audience one night, as were former mayor Jimmy Walker and young Winthrop Rockefeller. If you bought a ticket, there was always a chance you might be sitting next to a star or a scion.

On August 18, 1940, *Separate Rooms* played its 171st show

(generally, a Broadway show was considered a success if it made the one-hundred-show mark), an occasion *The New York Times* marked with a hat-tipping, head-shaking article called "Saga of a Play That Was Brave Under Fire." The show's "peculiar elixir of life" consisted of "a public which finds the show immensely funny even if critics did not," and "the superior showmanship" through which the production reached that public. *Separate Rooms* would go on to play 613 performances, during which none of the three principals missed a show, and would not close till September 1941.

It was a lively and eventful run. One night, Farrell sprained her ankle backstage between acts and the stage manager made the proverbial call for a doctor in the house. The man who answered it was Henry Ross, a West Point–educated staff surgeon at New York's Polyclinic Hospital. He was a bachelor. Farrell was thirty-six and had been a single mother, raising her son from a youthful first marriage, for more than a decade. Doctor and patient took an immediate liking to each other, began dating, and married in January 1941 (in the afternoon so she could do the play that night). They would remain together till Farrell died in 1971.

One evening in August 1940, a man who tried to hold up a store on Eighth Avenue fled on foot, exchanging shots with a policeman and pursued by a crowd. The fugitive, described by *The New York Times* as a "slender, sallow man with a small mustache," dodged between taxicabs, and at one point tried to commandeer one. The cabdriver shoved him out and drove off at high speed. Waving his pistol, the man dashed down Forty-fifth Street between Eighth and Broadway till he got to the Plymouth Theatre and tried to muscle his way through the stage door a few minutes before the curtain rose on Act One of *Separate Rooms*. James Mitchell, whom the *Times* referred to as the "Negro porter at the Plymouth," managed to block the gunman but took a bullet in the foot. The fugitive, who was later identified as Julio Lima, the son of a Cuban army officer, shot himself in the temple after being shot in the leg by a policeman. Lima fell dead across the threshold of the stage door. The show went on that night, and the cast took up a collection to pay for the porter's medical expenses.

Though Dinehart was a cowriter of the play, he and the other stars knew they weren't exactly doing Kaufman and Hart. (They weren't even doing Abbott and Costello.) Given that *Separate Rooms* wasn't likely to enter the canon and the words weren't indelible, they figured they might as well have some fun ad-libbing. The Broadway audiences would be savvy enough to see what they were doing and get a kick out of it, and they would keep themselves from getting bored. Lyle, in particular, liked puns, and deployed them merrily. Moreover, even if the audience didn't want serious war-related material, they responded to topical references. "Dinehart had no shame and I didn't have any shame about getting a laugh," Lyle would recall years later. "We did not moon the audience, but we did just about everything else, and we would try to top each other. . . . We did ridiculous things that worked." They made jokes about the small privations of war preparedness. Gas stations were now open only limited hours, so when Jack Smart was called upon to run across the stage in one scene, Lyle ad-libbed. "He has to get to the gas station by eight o'clock." The audience laughed, more out of a collective sense of recognition than anything else. "We had a matinee on the Fourth of July and somebody shot a firecracker out on Forty-fifth Street, and Glenda had just made an exit. I said, 'She left with a bang,' and they howled. We'd do shameless things, really awful."

For the year-and-a-half run of the play, Lyle lived at the Royalton on West Forty-fourth Street. It was then a residential hotel, built in 1898, and rather grand in an understated way, with a red-and-yellow-striped awning at the entrance and a handsome brick facade adorned with Romanesque arches. The Royalton was the longtime home to a number of actors, actresses, and theater reviewers, including George Jean Nathan, the dean of New York drama critics. When Nathan panned *Separate Rooms*, Lyle tore the offending page from the newspaper, scrawled "You stink, too!" on it and stuck it under the critic's door. But—and this was typical of Lyle—by the next day, sober again no doubt, he thought better of it. He'd been childish, the man was entitled to his opinions, and besides, why antagonize him? So Lyle threw on his dressing gown and dashed downstairs to retrieve the message. Luckily the maid was there. She'd found the message first, and she liked Mr. Talbot. He was so kind and so well turned out, and he'd learned her name right away. Mr. Nathan wasn't in—he was traveling, in fact—and she was happy to restore the defaced review to its sheepish defacer. Not that the caustic and urbane Nathan would have given a second thought to an insult of the caliber "You stink, too!" Imagine the theater critic Addison DeWitt in *All About Eve*, a character based on Nathan, reacting to such an outburst, and you get the picture. "I drink," Nathan once said, "to make other people interesting."

Lyle, meanwhile, was loving life. In a column titled "Broadway Stage Proving Life Saver for Film Stars," Louella Parsons wrote that she'd caught up with him and that he kept saying, "Isn't New York wonderful?" Who could blame him? There he was, living at the elegant Royalton, with his extensive collection of jazz and swing records, and his two dogs, a cocker spaniel and a German shepherd. A reporter for *Gotham Life* magazine who interviewed him over frozen daiquiris one night at the Circus Bar, noted that Lyle cut short the interview, saying, "My gosh, I have a few friends at home waiting to go for a walk with me. They've been home since before tonight's performance and I'm pretty sure they are anxious to go for a little walk by now. Excuse me, I must hurry. Even thoroughbreds can't hold on forever."

In the evenings, he made the short walk to the theater, sometimes stopping for a frankfurter or a warm jacket potato from one of the vendors. He loved the blue velvet of dusk as it settled over the city but did nothing to muffle its symphonic din. He loved the candy-apple red of the neon signs, the sunflower yellow of the cabs, and the unexpected privacy of walking under a black umbrella in the rain on a busy New

York street. He loved the way the porter greeted him every night at the stage door, with an ironic bow, and how Glenda, looking chic and radiant, gave him her soft, powdered cheek for a kiss, and he loved knowing that when the show was over that night, the night would really only just have begun.

Lyle was certainly making himself at home in the stylish nightclubs and eateries of New York. Now close to forty, he had put on weight, but he dressed, as always, with great care, and the New York papers often ran squibs about his look for the night. ("Style flash: Lyle Talbot at Bill Bertolotti's, in a gray sharkskin suit striped with green and red, blue shirt with white collar, and blue and silver figured tie.") He was seen at La Conga, the Rainbow Room, the Stork Club, El Morocco, and Ben Marden's Riviera, the nightclub perched high above the Hudson River, just across the George Washington Bridge in Fort Lee, New Jersey. The Riviera was a splendid place, with an Art Deco design reminiscent of an ocean liner, portholes and all. It had a terraced ballroom, a serpentine bar, and a revolving stage. The carpets were plush, the leather smoking chairs were the latest in comfort, and the walls glowed with brilliantly colored murals by the painter Arshile Gorky. It had its own barbershop, masseur, and shoe-shine stand. And best of all, the Riviera's domed roof retracted to reveal the night sky and splash the revelers with moonlight.

At Manny Wolf's Chop House, the restaurant's newsletter reported, "Lyle Talbot [could] go four fast rounds with anything from a set of pork chops to breast of baby pheasant." For late nights, he liked the brash and noisy Leon and Eddie's on Fifty-second Street, an establishment that was less exclusive than some of the swanker clubs—it catered to out-of-town businessmen and even families as well as celebs—but also less likely to attract the gangster element. The show at Leon and Eddie's was like *The Ed Sullivan Show* with a burlesque component and no rock 'n' roll. It featured troupes of midgets, jugglers, hoofers, ventriloquists, harmonica duos, stand-up comics, and blue patter and songs from the club's host, Eddie Davis ("Myrtle Isn't Fertile Anymore" was a perennial favorite), who always got the crowd to sing along. Leon and Eddie's also employed two rather special resident strippers. Sherry Britton had broken into the business with a gimmick in which she balanced a glass of water on each breast. She was well spoken and kind of elegant—she favored chiffon evening gowns and a Tchaikovsky score for her act, and had a remarkable eighteen-inch waist. "I used to strip down to an itsy-bitsy G-string and nothing else," Britton recalled years later. "Not even pasties. I did this in the evening during the dinner hour when lots of children were in the audience. Please remember that this was March 1941. But my body was so perfect and I did it with such good taste that no one ever thought of complaining—quite the opposite!" (She was sometimes billed as "Great Britton—the stripteuse with brains.") Then there was Lois De Fee, who was six feet tall and had started out as a bouncer at the club, where she would later be known as the "Queen of the Glamazons" or the "Eiffel Eyeful." Sunday nights were celebrity nights, and you never knew who would stand up to do a spiel—it might be Milton Berle, Henny Youngman, Danny Kaye, or Jerry Lewis. There were four shows a night, the first starting at eight p.m. The last, which started at three a.m., was popular with actors like Lyle who had been working in the evening, then eating a late supper at some quieter spot (though he liked the "Boston Caviar"—otherwise known as baked beans—at Leon and Eddie's).

Of course, being Lyle, he did not go to these places alone. During his stay in New York, Lyle squired around a beautiful blond showgirl from the Riviera named Ann Staunton, a twenty-one-year-old actress named Linda Brent, and the comedienne Judy Canova, among others. Dorothy Kilgallen, the journalist who was then writing a column about Broadway for the Hearst papers, dubbed him "the dream prince," and kept her eye trained on him. In one column she observed that "Lyle Talbot sat on the ringside with a new blonde (are there any new blondes left?), but I would say from the number of times he was called to the telephone that quite a few of the old blondes were trying to get in touch with him." In another, Kilgallen suggested that "some feature writer with a lot of time and patience really ought to follow Lyle around for a week and do a play-by-play piece on him. . . . The whole town— at least the gossip-oriented section of the town—seems more interested in his romances than in anything else in life." When Lyle was seen on the town with Canova, Kilgallen professed a bit of confusion. Canova was plain-looking, with a line of comedy that ran to corn-pone dorkiness. She had started her career as part of a vaudeville singing trio, the Three Georgia Crackers, with her siblings Annie and Zeke. She yodeled. She frequently wore her hair in braids, often performed barefoot, and had, as Kilgallen noted, "short, straight eyelashes." But there she was at Leon and Eddie's, with her hair bobbed and waved, "charming the playboy who's been charmed by the experts." What Kilgallen didn't realize was that Lyle really appreciated a funny girl.

Another newspaper columnist reported that Lyle Talbot must have been running out of dates, because he'd been seen "march[ing] into the Royalton around 4 a.m. one Saturday, accompanied by a midget, a bearded lady, a 550-pound fat man, and an 8'6" foot giant" (surely not that tall!), whereupon he announced that they must all stay and meet Robert Benchley, the *New Yorker* humorist who lived at the Algonquin, across the street. True? Some version of it, perhaps. He'd come of age around sideshow types, he loved the circus, and he might have gone one night, made some friends, and invited them for (more) drinks. Maybe hanging out with them took him back to his days with the Walter Savidge Amusement Co.

On the afternoons when he didn't have a matinee, Lyle and some of his cast mates would head over to the World's Fair. It had opened in 1939 in Flushing Meadows, Queens, and was still going strong in its second season. With its slogan "Dawn of a New Day," the 1939 World's Fair was the first expo with a futuristic theme. The fair's two iconic structures—the enormous round Perisphere and the triangular spire known as the Trylon—were gleaming white and boldly geometric. The fair itself offered a vision of the near future transformed by innovation and brimming with technological wonders. The portentous optimism with which this vision was unrolled must have been especially welcome in the aftermath of the Depression. Forty-five million people came to Queens over the fair's two seasons to see such marvels as the first displays of television ("the technical term for seeing as well as hearing radio"), efficient new electric dishwashers (one exhibit featured a dishwashing contest between "Mrs. Drudge," who was still scrubbing hers by hand, and "Mrs. Modern," who stood idly by while the machine handled hers), and a seven-foot robot named Elektro, the Moto-Man, endowed with a regular-guy sense of humor and an eye for the ladies.

The most popular of all the dawn-of-a-new-day exhibits, though, was Futurama, the GM-sponsored model of an America circa 1960, crisscrossed by motorways and populated by contented car owners who glided home from their streamlined office buildings to houses set in impossibly neat and clean suburbs. The cars-and-highways part of this vision mostly came true—in part because it was in the interest of GM and the other car companies that had made it look so marvelous. In 1939, there were only 237 vehicles per 1,000 Americans; by 1960, the figure was 410, and the United States had a national system of highways. Futurama spectators could take an aerial trip over this "Wonderworld of 1960" in seats that moved along a track Disneyland style (though Disneyland itself would not be with us for nearly two decades).

The World's Fair had exhibits with a more basic and eternal appeal, as well. There were carny-style rides and sideshows, and dazzling lighting on the midway described as "flashing pinwheels." When the fair opened for its second season in 1940, its board chairman sounded a homey note: "The World's Fair of 1940 is simply a great big edition of the county fairs and State fairs that are as much a part of our tradition as fried chicken and ice cream and cake." And let's not forget the tradition of displaying women who were naked or nearly so! The fair's planners certainly had not. Interest in a replica of a Buddhist temple had been lackluster till the second season, when it was reconfigured as "Forbidden Tibet," a girlie show in which a Tibetan lama was "tempted by a symbol of desire" but saved in time by a ballet representing the "Triumph of Good over Evil." The fair's first season also offered, bizarrely, a surrealist fun house designed by Salvador Dalí called "Dream of Venus." *Life* magazine assayed a puzzled description: "Girls swim under water, milk a bandaged-up cow, tap typewriter keys which float like seaweed. . . . A sleeping Venus reclines in a 36-foot bed, covered with white and red satin, flowers and leaves. Scattered about the bed are lobsters frying on a bed of hot coals and bottles of champagne. . . . All this is very interesting and amusing." You didn't need to be a connoisseur of Surrealism to take an interest in the Dalí installation of the "living liquid ladies" swimming languorously, bare-breasted, in a big tank. The underwater exhibit was just as popular, if not more so, when "Dream of Venus" was replaced by "Twenty Thousand Legs Under the Sea," featuring Oscar the Obscene Octopus. Dalí had nothing to do with Oscar, a man in a rubber octopus suit who pulled the bathing suits off women with his tentacles.

Lyle's favorite stops at the fair were Billy Rose's Aquacade and the RCA Hall of Television. (Oh, and the smorgasbord at the Swedish Pavilion. He always liked a new word and a nice spread of cold cuts.) For pure showmanship, the Aquacade was the most spectacular thing going at the fair. It starred champion swimmers like the Olympians Eleanor Holm, who had been on the 42nd Street Special with Lyle, and Johnny Weissmuller, who played Tarzan in the movies and had an amazing physique, of which he was exceedingly proud. Against a curtain of water forty feet high, in a gorgeous Deco amphitheater and pool built for the occasion, the performers undertook feats of diving and of elaborate, Busby Berkeley–like synchronized swimming. In the late 1940s, this kind of chlorinated extravaganza would become the basis for the hugely popular movies of Esther Williams, "the million-dollar mermaid," but in 1939 they were a dizzying novelty.

Lyle also took an interest in the new phenomenon of television—in part because in 1936, he'd starred with Mary Astor in a movie called *Trapped by Television*. It's a little surprising to watch this very slight caper movie today and see that its premise is the competition among broadcasting companies trying to put out the first "television machine." (The executives and inventors all take for granted that companies that fall behind will be out of business altogether—this at a time when there were only about two hundred televisions in the whole country.) Lyle, who'd played an eager young inventor, remained intrigued by the possibilities of television—and hey, they'd need people to act for it, wouldn't they?

On the opening day of the fair, RCA broadcast a speech by FDR—the first televised presidential speech in history, though it could be watched only on sets within a fifty-five-mile radius of the Empire State Building. Lyle missed that, but like hundreds of thousands of other fairgoers, he stood transfixed in front of the small sets in the RCA Hall of Television that broadcast live shots of the fair itself. It was neat, all right, though a lot of people who saw those first demonstrations of broadcast TV were not persuaded that television would become a staple of everyday life in the future. "The problem with television," wrote Orrin E. Dunlap in *The New York Times* the month the fair opened, "is that the people must sit and keep their eyes glued on a screen: the average American family hasn't time for it. . . . Radio can flow on like a brook, while people listen and go about their household duties and routine. Television, on the other hand is no brook; it is more of a Niagara, a spectacle for the eyes." He was wrong, of course—as off base in his skepticism about the new technology as the cock-eyed futurists sometimes were in their optimism. But Dunlap also had a point: the qualities he attributes to radio listening—its compatibility with other activities, such as driving or cooking—are a big reason that radio is still alive today despite television, the Internet, and other blandishments.

L YLE HAD PLENTY OF STAMINA, and he loved to work, so when he wasn't onstage at the Plymouth or at play in some nightspot or at the fairground, he kept himself busy with personal appearances. He got his own radio show, *Hollywood Footlights*, on WHN. Three times a week, he played songs by Judy Garland and Cab Calloway and Jimmy Dorsey in between Hollywood gossip and interviews with visiting movie people. (It all went smoothly—he had a breezy, enthusiastic, still boyish style—except for the time he embarrassed himself when he was handed a bit of war news that he described as a "late-breaking communique," pronouncing it without the accent, so that it rhymed with "mystique." For some reason, he was still mortified by that flub years later.) He did benefits for the Stage Relief Fund, which helped indigent actors; the Milk Fund, which supplied milk for poor children; and the Red Cross War Relief Fund. He visited the Botany Worsted Mills in Passaic, New Jersey, where, snappily dressed in a double breasted suit and two-tone wingtips, he listened with what I'm sure was genuine fascination—he loved clothes and he loved gadgets— while two factory workers named Sophie Sonowski and Helen Dukich explained how they made ties. ("Lyle Talbot Thrills Girls at Botany" read the headline in the Passaic *Herald News*.) He visited a twenty-one-year-old "crippled girl," as the papers called her, who had written him a letter saying she longed to see him in *Separate Rooms* but was confined at home. He did a dramatic reading of the Bill of Rights to commemorate the state of New Jersey's Bill of Rights week. He appeared at the Apollo Theater in Harlem, on a bill with Duke Ellington, Billie Holiday, Ella Fitzgerald, the Ink Spots, and Jack Benny and Rochester, in a "benefit for the needy." He joined Gene Autry and the boxer Max Baer in a rally to raise money for the British Ambulance Corps. Kids turned out, said one of the newspaper accounts, "in aid of their schoolmates across the ocean whose entertainment consists chiefly of fleeing death-dealing bombs."

Somehow Lyle managed, amid this rather taxing whirl, to find himself a third wife. Abigail "Tommye" Adams was a twenty-one-year-old brunette model and aspiring actress from Greensboro, North Carolina. As a student at the University of North Carolina, she'd been picked as the "Typical American Girl" by a modeling agency scout; the prize was a trip to New York and a two-week gig as a decorative asset at the Stork Club, where Lyle presumably met her. In January 1942, Adams left her first job, in the chorus of a musical called *Sons o' Fun*, and joined Lyle in Kansas City. They were married there by a justice of the peace, with only Lyle's parents and the leading lady from the touring company of *Separate Rooms* in attendance. Lyle had picked out a ring for his bride, but she'd lost it, so she had to borrow his stepmother's for the ceremony. Three months later, they separated, and in September 1942, Adams asked for either a divorce or an annulment on the grounds that her consent to the marriage ceremony had been obtained by fraud. What that fraud would be is a little hard to imagine; Adams didn't say, and my father, obeying the unwritten law in our household of never even alluding to his former marriages, certainly never explained the breakup of this one—a quickie even by his standards. Adams did ask that he financially support her henceforth.

With nobody at home to attend to, no particular desire to pay a big chunk of his salary to an ex-wife he'd been with for less than three months, and no great film prospects, Lyle was visited by an unexpected wave of patriotism. Two days after Adams asked for an annulment, he enlisted as a private in the air force. It is a testament to the mood in the country, and especially in Hollywood, that somebody like Lyle, a less-than-fit forty-year-old bon vivant with a decidedly non-martial temperament, would feel he had something to offer the U.S. military, and that offer it he must. The movie industry had signed up relatively early for the war effort, producing films about the Fascist threat in Europe such as *Confessions of a Nazi Spy* in 1939, and in 1940, *The Mortal Storm, Foreign Correspondent,* and in a different vein, Charlie Chaplin's *The Great Dictator.* By 1941, Hollywood's premature anti-Fascism was proving such an irritant to isolationists in Congress that they launched a Senate investigation to determine whether the motion picture studios were improperly using their influence to push America into intervening in Europe. The problem, said Senator Gerald P. Nye (R-North Dakota), was that Hollywood was "swarm[ing] with refugees,"—he singled out British actors and Russian, Hungarian, German, and Balkan directors—"who were susceptible to . . . national and racial emotions," and were giving vent to them in anti-Nazi, pro-intervention movies.

Though the likes of Darryl Zanuck and Harry Warner were called to testify, the hearings fizzled out without much impact. The industry stepped up its war-related production and public opinion softened toward intervention. By mid-1942, six months after Pearl Harbor, "about one-third of the features in production dealt directly with the war," writes the film historian Thomas Schatz, while "a much higher proportion treated [it] indirectly as a given set of social, political and economic circumstances." Hollywood turned out propaganda films and documentaries at the direct behest of the government, but it also quickly retrofitted familiar genres for wartime. "Spy, detective and crime thrillers, for instance, were easily reformulated (perhaps too easily) into espionage thrillers or underground resistance dramas in the early war years. The musical and woman's picture were recycled for war production as well and remained enormously effective throughout the war. The backstage musical was recast to depict groups of entertainers putting on military shows 'for the boys,' while working girl sagas and melodramas of maternal or marital sacrifice were ideally suited to war conditions."

But there was more to Hollywood's enlistment in the war effort than making movies. On the home front, Bette Davis ran the Hollywood Canteen, where soldiers about to be shipped off could come to get a hot meal and dance with actresses like Hedy Lamarr, Deanna Durbin, Betty Grable, Lana Turner, and Marlene Dietrich to the music of the Xavier Cugat orchestra and Jimmy Durante, among others. Actresses also sold war bonds—the lushly beautiful, onyx-haired Lamarr once sold $7 million in a single day, offering a kiss from her for $50,000.

Among the actors, a remarkable number volunteered for active duty. Henry Fonda, who said he "didn't want to be in fake war in a studio," served for three years, first as a quartermaster on a destroyer, then in combat intelligence in the Pacific. Jimmy Stewart got rejected twice for being too skinny, then gained enough weight to be drafted into the army as a private. He eventually piloted bombers over Germany, rose to the rank of colonel, and received a Distinguished Flying Cross. Tyrone Power became a transport pilot in the South Pacific. Clark Gable, whose beloved wife, Carole Lombard, had just been killed in a plane crash on her way home from a tour selling war bonds, joined the air force and operated machine guns and a newsreel camera in bombing missions over Germany. "By October of 1942," notes the historian Otto Friedrich, "some 2,700 Hollywood people—12 percent of the total number employed in the movie business—had joined the armed forces."

By contrast to Montgomery's or Stewart's service, Lyle's was more like the future president Ronald Reagan's. Reagan had helped make army training films in Culver City. And Lyle was assigned to the Army Air Corps flying school near Merced, in the flat Central Valley of California, where he organized entertainment for the troops. To be fair, even if he'd been the heroic type, he really wouldn't have been fit for combat duty. Lyle came from a line of Scotch and Irish immigrants, coal miners and farmers who'd reinvented themselves in the United

States as saloon and inn keepers, traveling actors and acrobats—a raffish bunch with no military service to show among them. Unlike, say,
Bogart (who was rejected from service because he was too old), he was
not a veteran of World War I. He knew next to nothing about fire-
arms. The base had him listed as a "bicycle mechanic," because he
happened to mention that he liked riding a bike, but it didn't take long
for somebody in charge to realize that Private Talbot would serve his
country better if he was in charge of entertainment for the base. From
then on, Lyle, who was quickly elevated to sergeant then staff sergeant,
put on variety shows and plays at Merced, flying down to L.A. to bring
back whatever talent he could rustle up.

"We'd fly over the Tehachapi Mountains in basic trainers down to
Hollywood," he recalled. "They had the open pits, and you'd sit behind
the pilot—they only fit two people. You were supposed to wear headphones and a parachute. But one time, I had a hangover and a headache,
so I took my headphones off. Well, apparently the pilot lost rudder
control. He's saying so, and saying *May Day! May Day!* over the headphones, but I can't hear a thing. He managed to put the plane down
anyway, and the next day there are these headlines in the paper: 'Heroic
Landing by Actor.' I didn't even know! No idea!" He would always
remember the enthusiastic reaction of one young soldier from a small
town in the Central Valley who saw a play for the first time on the
base: "Sarge, I've never been round actors before."

B UT BACK IN HOLLYWOOD after the war, Lyle felt "like nobody
knew me. It was like a different town." He'd been away since 1940,
first in New York, then touring with *Separate Rooms,* then in the air
force. A new wave of younger actors had arrived, as a new wave always
does, and for the first time, Lyle was having a tough time getting a job.
Danny Kaye, whom he had known in New York, helped him get a role
as a blustery sergeant in the first movie Kaye starred in, *Up in Arms,* a

patriotic musical that generously showcased Kaye's gawky, frenetic comedic style and featured a charming Dinah Shore. The producer Samuel Goldwyn had plucked Danny Kaye from the nightclub circuit, but worried that in screen tests, Kaye's long schnoz made him look too Jewish for Middle America. According to Goldwyn's biographer A. Scott Berg, the producer decided the former Borscht Belt comic would be more palatable if he dyed his red hair blond, and Kaye did as he was told. The movie was distributed to troops overseas, and at home turned into a commercial and critical hit, earning $3.3 million for the studio and making Kaye a film star. But *Up in Arms* didn't open any big doors for Lyle. When he did get offers, most of them were schlock, but he said yes anyway—to Saturday-morning cliffhanger serials, B-grade noir, and exploitation films about the menace of marijuana or, ironically, of alcohol.

In some ways the westerns were the biggest challenge for him—mainly because he was a lousy horseman and convinced that horses knew it. "I got thrown one time. It was one of those scenes where there's a big posse and the posse is supposed to go one way, and I'm supposed to go another on my horse. And my horse wouldn't go. These horses that work in westerns, they know whether you're a good horseman or not the minute you start to mount. If you have to call for a stool to step on, they know. But the moment they hear those clappers, they take off, and if you're not ready, you're left behind on the ground. Well, I wasn't ready." He usually wasn't ready. When Lyle had to ride a horse, the scene would start with him, as he put it, "pre-mounted." Or better yet, they'd cast him "as the banker, in the stage coach, which was great."

Lyle found work, too, in the two new comic book–based serials that came out after the war: as Commissioner Gordon in *Batman and Robin* and as Lex Luthor in *Atom Man vs. Superman*—the first actor to enact a screen version of Superman's mortal enemy. These were cheap productions, heavily reliant on stock footage, on not-so-special effects, and on ill-fitting, goofy costumes (Robin's had a big R sewn on the vest). But Lyle didn't mind doing them, and tried as always to give audiences their money's worth—especially since these audiences were mainly kids who went to the movie theater on Saturday mornings, gobbled up the serial chapters, and came back the next Saturday and the next to see whether the villain was ruling the world yet or Superman had managed to get ahold of whatever that atomic-cyclonic gizmo was. Ken Weiss and Ed Goodgold, fans who wrote a book about serials called *To Be Continued . . .* , remembered going to a movie theater in the Bronx at nine-thirty on Saturday mornings, and for a dime, getting a comic book and a candy bar, then watching five or so cartoons, the morning's feature (usually a western), and finally their favorite: the serial. It might be Flash Gordon or Captain America, Congo Bill or Son of Zorro. That would mean it was nearly noon, and at that point, "the theatre would begin to take on the aroma of salami and cream cheese and jelly as sandwiches were taken from brown paper bags and removed from wax paper wrappers." You could stay to watch another feature film, if you liked, usually a classic like *King Kong* or *The Thief of Bagdad,* and then the serial would be repeated again, and after that, at about three-thirty, the show was over, your dime about as well spent as a dime could be.

"The serials were a world of their own," wrote Weiss and Goodgold. "For approximately twenty minutes, you were totally involved in a series of hair-raising escapes, spectacular battles, mile-a-minute chases, hidden treasures, secret plans, and diabolical scientific devices, all being held together by a plot that was at once highly tenuous and at the same time complicated almost beyond comprehension." You could always count on the "consistent stupidity of both the hero and the villain. Deep down in his heart of hearts, every kid sitting in the movie theatre knew that he was smarter than the hero. Each kid could anticipate the villain's moves and knew when the hero was walking into a trap. How come the hero never seemed to *learn?* . . . And the villain

Lyle as Commissioner Gordon in Batman and Robin.

was no smarter. There he was, supposedly the cream of the villainous crop, and it was obvious that he couldn't organize a game of hide-and-seek, no less dominate the world."

Though serials had been around since the early 1930s, telling stories that stretched over a dozen or more chapters, and mostly produced by the smaller independent studios like Republic and Universal, they relied more on comic books for material after the war. During the war, the popularity of superheroes and all comics had mushroomed. "Sales rose from twelve million copies a month in 1942," notes historian Allan M. Winkler, "to over sixty million a month in 1946. Eighty percent of the population aged six to seventeen read comic books during the war; a third of people from eighteen to thirty years of age did the same." Many cartoon characters were shown in combat, but Superman was not. His creators worried that if Superman went to war he would make it look too easy, misleading or demoralizing real soldiers.

So reporter Clark Kent was 4-F: his X-ray vision caused him to fail the vision test when he read the chart in the next room. After the war, though, the Man of Steel's fans were happy to see him scoping out technological advances that had fallen into enemy hands: radiation, for instance.

I don't think Lyle made a great Lex Luthor. He played him too rationally; there wasn't enough of the unhinged in his performance. But some Superman fans give him more credit than that. "Wearing an uncomfortable plastic bald cap, Talbot made an impressively stern Luthor as he fiddled with a laboratory full of futuristic equipment," writes Les Daniels, an authoritative historian of Superman. Lyle said later that he always tried to play Luthor with "total conviction, as if he really existed." He didn't think it was fair to kids in the audience to camp it up or play the part with a knowing wink.

"Oh, all the dials we had in that one set there!" he remembered. "Those were just things that they'd gotten from the phone company or somewhere, and they put them on the wall with a lot of lights behind them. You had a sense of humor, and you'd laugh about certain things, but our approach was never to kid it. This had to be for real." Between takes, Lyle and Kirk Alyn, the broad-shouldered former dancer who played Superman, exchanged recipes. Each was delighted to find another man who liked to cook. Lyle thought Alyn was a "wonderful, quiet fellow" and a good actor, but after the serials died out—they couldn't last long after TV—Alyn found he'd been typecast as Superman and couldn't get other roles.

Some of the schlocky movies Lyle did in the 1940s are of sociological interest today. They're lurid and marginal, but they reflect larger social concerns. A movie he turned up in called *Are These Our Parents?* was part of a small wave of immediate postwar movies that fretted about juvenile delinquency. (There would be more and better movies about teen trouble in the 1950s; this wavelet anticipated them.) A movie called *Strange Impersonation*, a B noir that was an early effort by the director Anthony Mann, gives a creepy twist to the postwar push to discourage career women. Brenda Marshall plays a research chemist named Nora Goodrich who's working on a new anesthetic. Nora is in love with a fellow scientist, Stephen Lindstrom (William Gargan), but also destabilizingly dedicated to her work: Stephen wants to marry her, but she keeps putting him off till her experiment is complete. ("Enough science," he admonishes her when they're alone together.) On the night when Nora administers the anesthetic to herself at home—sure, why not?—her jealous lab assistant, Arline (Hillary Brooke), engineers an explosion that leaves Nora's face horribly scarred. While poor Nora is recovering in the hospital, Arline inveigles Stephen away. Eventually, Nora steals the identity of a dead woman and gets plastic surgery. (Like Humphrey Bogart's facial reconstruction in *Dark Passage*, another film noir of the period, this one is rendered by an elderly solo practitioner, with implausibly excellent results.) Her new face—which actually looks just like her old face since she's played by the same actress, but never mind—allows her to insinuate herself back into the lives of the now married Stephen and Arline, who think Nora is dead and, unlike everyone in the audience, don't recognize her. Things get even weirder from there, and Nora finds herself in a very noirish catch-22: under interrogation as the lead suspect in her own murder. Lyle plays the cop, with a pencil mustache and a world-weary relentlessness.

In the end, when it all turns out to have been a dream induced by her anesthetic, Nora wakes, comes to her feminine senses, and tells Stephen she'll marry him right away. But Nora's nightmare is a lathered-up version of an understandable anxiety, a potboiler vision of a real trap for women. Nora is a convincingly intelligent woman who hopes to accomplish something in science. Her bad dream reveals that however confident she appears on the surface, subconsciously she fears that her professional ambitions will make her repellent and lonely. And the film agrees with her subconscious; unlike Mary Stevens, M.D., almost twenty years earlier, Nora Goodrich, research scientist, has to be shut down. Marshall is quite good in it, and in its sleazy little way, *Strange Impersonation* is a haunting movie.

The same cannot be said for *"She Shoulda Said 'No'!"* aka *Wild Weed*, a screechy cheapo about the marijuana menace, in which Lyle did another turn as a glowering cop. *"She Shoulda Said 'No'!"* was your basic exploitation movie. Eric Schaefer, a film scholar who has written the definitive history of such films, notes that they "often played in grind-houses, theaters located in that physical space between the commercial areas and the skid row districts of many major cities" or else in "neighborhood or small-town theaters in between runs of regular Hollywood pictures." The producers and distributors of these "ragged little films" liked to present them as though they were educational quasi-documentaries—cautionary tales that wallowed in the lurid behavior they were cautioning against with their doom-laden, pedantic voice-overs. ("This is the story of tea, or tomatoes, the kind millions, through ignorance, have been induced to smoke.") Exploitation producers evaded the Production Code, distributing their movies in theaters that were not owned by the major studios, and turning the lack of a PCA seal of approval into an explicit selling point. If you saw a movie made between 1934 and about 1965 that dealt with birth control, childbirth, venereal disease, or illegal drugs, or that showed any kind of nudity, then you were most likely seeing an exploitation film. It was probably shoddily made and hysterically acted, but it would at least offer some acknowledgment that these realms of human experience existed.

"She Shoulda Said 'No'!" was an exploitation film with an interesting backstory. Very early one morning in September 1948, at a cottage in Laurel Canyon, the actor Robert Mitchum was arrested for smoking marijuana. Also arrested were Lila Leeds, an actress he'd been hanging around with while his wife and he were taking a break, and two friends. Pot was not widely known at the time. Back in the 1930s, there had been a brief gust of public concern about it, much of it

preoccupied with the concern that marijuana smoking would promote the mingling of races in "sensuous" environments like jazz clubs. Still, when Cab Calloway sang "Reefer Man," and Sidney Bechet did "Viper Mad Blues," most Americans had no idea what they were on about. The classic exploitation film *Reefer Madness* was released in 1936, one of a triumvirate of movies that emerged from this early law-enforcement concern with marijuana. But it disappeared for decades until it was rediscovered by pot-smoking college students in the 1970s, who liked to giggle their way through midnight showings. In 1948, as Otto Friedrich points out, *Time* magazine's editors felt it necessary to explain the following, in the magazine's report on Mitchum's arrest: "Marijuana, a drug made from Indian hemp, is . . . said to produce a state of exhilaration."

When Mitchum was booked, he gave his occupation as "Former Actor." But he actually survived the scandal nicely. Mitchum served sixty days in jail, and he worked it for a certain street cred. When trailers for his upcoming movie, *Rachel and the Stranger*, started showing in theaters after his arrest, audiences cheered, and when the movie came out, it became the number-one box-office hit in the country. Maybe not enough people were worried about marijuana—which, whatever the dire voice-over of *"She Shoulda Said 'No'!"* might be saying, did not seem to be cutting a wide swath through the malt shop or the sock hop. It seemed too exotic to pose a threat to middle-class youngsters. Besides, Mitchum was a star—and a new hep-cat, cynical-type star, at that. He didn't have to keep his image soapy clean to retain his fans. He was doing just fine as a heavy-lidded bad boy.

For Lila Leeds, it was another story. Leeds was a runaway from Iola, Kansas, by way of Clovis, New Mexico. In L.A. she'd gotten work as a carhop and then as a hatcheck girl at Ciro's, though she was always getting groped there and forgetting the names of producers who were big stuff or thought they were. She was blond and gorgeous— people kept telling her she could be the next Lana Turner, and it wasn't always to get her in the sack. She liked her reefer, a habit she'd picked up hanging out with jazz musicians, but she had some ambition, too. She left Ciro's, started studying acting, and landed some bit parts in decent movies, one of them *Green Dolphin Street*, with Lana Turner herself. But the only role she found when she got out of jail was in *"She Shoulda Said 'No'!"*—a movie crudely designed to cash in on her arrest, something she was really hoping to put behind her. She must have found the movie's depiction of the effects of dope smoking pretty ridiculous. As she said, marijuana made her feel dreamy and sleepy, not much else—it was relaxing. But the marijuana smokers in *"She Shoulda Said 'No'!"* get very seriously whack—they dance with conveniently licentious abandon, hallucinate like subjects in a poorly managed LSD experiment, let loose with gales of crazed laughter, and generally divest themselves of any shreds of personal dignity. When Leeds's college-kid brother in the movie discovers she's been smoking and selling marijuana sticks, he wastes no time in hanging himself.

Yet strangely, Leeds's own story unfolded much like a cautionary tale in an exploitation movie. Life, it seems, sometimes imitates schlock. After she made the movie, Leeds drifted around the Midwest, working in nightclubs, doing jail time, getting addicted to heroin. When she finally got clean, in the mid-1960s, she returned to California, as Mitchum's biographer Lee Server documents, "sick [and] penniless." She eventually became a lay minister at a storefront church in Hollywood that was known by the acronym SMILE, helping runaways and addicts.

LYLE'S OWN LIFE AFTER THE WAR had begun to seem like something out of one of the B noirs—a stumble down a long, dark alley. He was drinking a lot. His favored drinking companion was a man named Philip Van Zandt, a mustachioed Dutch-born character actor who was often cast as a Nazi, though he also turned up in *Citizen Kane* and a clutch of Three Stooges shorts. Van Zandt had a compulsion for gambling and a tendency to depression, but like Lyle, he loved to work, and he, too, managed to pull himself together when he had an acting job. Lyle was not a depressive. But he was vulnerable, on occasion, to a certain vaporous despair. In my experience—I saw it a few times later—this fleeting melancholy did not express itself as a disappointment with himself or his life, professional or personal, though perhaps that was the well-hidden trigger. It was more like an existential sadness: about mortality, the state of the world, human limits. He treated that feeling successfully by working—hence the willingness, the eagerness, to take any role that came along. When he was working, the essential sprightliness of his nature came to the fore. When people needed him to entertain them, he became entertaining. But if roles were sparse, as they were in the late 1940s, he drank to keep the melancholy at bay.

I think he must have been lonely, too. He was, fundamentally, a very loving person, and yet he'd never been able to sustain a romantic relationship for long. Some of it must have been his choice; he liked women and he liked to play around. Some of it, particularly as he was reaching his late forties, was not. Some of it was finding himself attracted to much younger women who were vital, stubborn, and sometimes troubled and mercurial as well, and who quickly grew restive. And some of it, of course, was his drinking, which played havoc with his natural charm and his judgment.

In 1944, Lyle was acting in a touring production of *A Doll's House*, along with Jane Darwell, a fine character actress he was very fond of, who had played Ma Joad in *The Grapes of Wrath*. The cast also included a young woman named Keven McClure, a dark-haired beauty with wide-set green eyes and strong, sensual features. Though she was only twenty, and Lyle was forty-four, they quickly fell into a romance. In August 1946, Lyle and Keven were married in Tijuana.

McClure was, by all accounts, a rather remarkable person—

intelligent, artistic, resourceful, an endurance swimmer and a speaker of several languages. The daughter of a theatrical producer, she had grown up in Berkeley and attended the University of California, where she wrote a thesis about Ibsen before joining the cast of *A Doll's House*. An article about her in the *Berkeley Gazette* described her as speaking in a "low voice, firm and distinct," saying that she'd wanted to be "a dramatic actress as long as I can remember."

Before Lyle, McClure had been married to another older man. His name was John Carr. His age was varyingly given in newspaper accounts as either forty-one or fifty, and he was a self-described writer, actor, and director with a small financial stake in the show. One night during the run of *A Doll's House*, in Los Angeles, he showed up at the stage entrance of the Biltmore Theater, waving a revolver and shouting, "I'm going to let you all have it." He socked McClure, then aimed a heavy blow at Lyle, and was subdued with a punch from the play's producer, according to an account in the *Los Angeles Times*. That didn't keep him down for long. When McClure took off on foot, Carr jumped on the running board of a passing car, broke its windshield, and brandished shards of glass "to terrify bystanders" the article said. Eventually he chased his wife into the Biltmore lobby, where she "ran screaming into the women's lounge, locking the door." Carr explained himself this way to a reporter: "I just saw red when I saw Keven walking out of the theater arm-in-arm with Lyle Talbot. I blew my top." He said Keven wanted a divorce so she could marry Lyle; Keven denied it to the press, but on that score, Carr was right. Lyle and other members of the cast took her to the hospital to be treated for her black eye. Still, she went onstage the next night with makeup covering it. Carr granted her a divorce soon after, saying, "I must have been nuts to think a guy my age could make a go of it with a beautiful young girl."

Lyle and Keven separated after five months of marriage and divorced soon after. In McClure's complaint, she said Lyle "drank excessively, swore at her in public, and struck her at home." And that he'd once forced her out of the car at four a.m. in the rain. The part about striking her is particularly hard for me to believe, since it would have been so out of character for Lyle. None of his four children ever saw my father strike anybody, let alone my mother. Of course, we didn't know him as an alcoholic. But my mother's brother, who knew him well in these darker years, and was inclined to regard him with suspicion on his sister's account, said he never saw Lyle behave violently even at his drunkest. He remembers him as gallant up to the point when he'd pass out. To establish a claim of "intolerable cruelty" in the era before no-fault divorce, women certainly had incentive to make their spouse's faults sound more egregious than they were. Still, I'll never know for certain: improbable as it seems to me, it's possible that at his lowest, he did slap McClure.

The truth is I know almost nothing about what his relationships with his wives before my mother were like. Almost everything I write here about the women themselves I found out in the course of researching this book. My parents tacitly declared those former marriages irrelevant to our family story, and mostly, I think they were. But that doesn't make the women uninteresting.

After her divorce from Lyle, McClure, who was by then using the first name Eve, would go on to marry the writer Henry Miller, and to make a life and a community for herself in the bohemian precincts of Big Sur. She drew and painted and was an excellent cook. She tolerated Miller's faults and eccentricities, relishing the role of muse to genius. Miller told friends that she reminded him of his old friend and lover Anaïs Nin, in that she "brings with her the feeling of ease and abundance." She was especially kind and loving to Miller's two young children from his third marriage, Valentine and Tony. Valentine remembers her putting on crafts classes every summer in their home, where she taught them and other local kids Indian beading, pottery, and marionette making, and helped them put on shows for their families. McClure acted in the local Big Sur Revue and made costumes for all the children, sewing beautifully with long fingers that were stained with nicotine.

McClure had a drinking problem, though. Eventually it would kill her. And the combination with Lyle's own alcohol addiction was combustible. Moreover, McClure seemed to have a knack for attracting man trouble. Miller praised her for her tolerance and capacity for silence—living with her was "like living on velour," he wrote to a friend. But perhaps that was partly in comparison with extreme cases like his former wife June Mansfield Miller, an emotionally unstable coke-using quasi-prostitute who had moved her lesbian lover into their household.

In any case, whatever soured Lyle's marriage to McClure did so very quickly. Just as I was launching into the research for this book, a commercial photographer in Omaha serendipitously tracked me down through the Internet. He'd been at a yard sale and found a few photo albums that he'd bought because he admired the photographs in them—mostly black-and-white head shots and studio publicity stills from the 1930s and 1940s. After a while, he realized that many of the glamorous, rather haunting pictures were of an actor named Lyle Talbot and his friends, and after doing a little research, concluded that the albums had probably belonged to Lyle's father and stepmother, who had died in Omaha in the 1960s. Eventually, the photographer from Omaha began to think that someone in our family ought to have the albums instead of him, which was kind, and he got in touch with us. I met him in the lobby of the Magnolia Hotel in Omaha one gray afternoon in March 2010, and after he gave me the albums, I sat in the dwindling light and pored through them.

Many of the photos inside were duplicates of ones we had at home, but many—such as a lovely one of Mock Sad Alli, the magician Lyle had traveled with so long ago—were not. One of the pictures was of Keven McClure. On the back, she had written, in a girlish script and green ink, an inscription to Lyle's parents, Ed and Anna: "darlins',

Keven, aka Eve, McClure.

may I make a good addition to a wonderful family—and may your grandchildren be as nice as their grandparents are—I love you two so much—'ya know?" She signed herself "Mac." It struck me that nobody marries without hope—no matter how soon it goes. And here was Keven McClure's hope, distilled and sweet, the dregs at the bottom of a wineglass from a long-forgotten party.

McClure was married to Henry Miller from 1953 to 1960. Toward the end, he was having an affair with his German translator, and McClure could no longer put up with his straying. She left him for a sculptor who also lived in Big Sur. But she and Miller maintained a friendship and a correspondence. She even remained friendly with two of his former wives, June Miller and Janina Martha Lepska, the mother of Tony and Valentine. Once or twice Eve sent a couple of her drawings of female nudes to my father. She was only forty-one when she died, in her beloved Big Sur, from complications of alcoholism.

At least she lived a longer and seemingly more fulfilled life than Abigail "Tommye" Adams, the woman Lyle had been married to just before her. In L.A. in the late 1940s and early 1950s, Adams had become a notorious party girl. She'd been arrested once, for hit-and-run driving, though the charges were dismissed, and once, along with the actor Broderick Crawford, for public drunkenness. She'd been the mistress of the comedian George Jessel, and that relationship seemed to leave her floundering. She floundered a lot in public, and with a certain angry energy that seemed like it might be keeping her alive for a while. After the police were called when neighbors complained about a loud argument between Jessel and Adams, she gave an interview to reporters, the *Los Angeles Times* said, "while curled up on a divan in her den," wearing pajamas and a bright red robe. "She looked quite effervescent for a young woman accused of waking up the neighborhood in the early morning hours." Adams declared that the argument was nothing compared with many they'd had; it was just that Jessel was tired after a twenty-one-day tour he'd been on to benefit the United Jewish Appeal and he wanted to stay home that night while she wanted to go out. "Incidentally," she said brightly, "I'm going to have George put on a benefit for Baby—and Baby, you know, is me." Adams went on: "We'll stop going together and stop arguing when one kills the other. I didn't throw anything at George last night but I've thrown a lot of things at him in my day." She found excuses to let reporters know that Jessel had once given her a diamond ring. In the meantime, Jessel's penchant for getting involved with much younger women made him the butt of fellow comedians' jokes. (That at least was a fate you could avoid if you were Henry Miller, or even Lyle.) *George couldn't*

make it tonight: He had to pick his wife up after school. Or: *His wife is ill—
she's teething.* Adams got so incensed about a young female singer who
was billing herself as "George Jessel's discovery" that she headed over
to the Sherman Oaks nightspot where the woman was singing, and
apparently tore the singer's sequined gown, tried to punch her, and
later drove her car into the side of the nightclub. Her acting career,
meanwhile, had fizzled. Adams had started out in the early 1940s with
roles billed as "College Girl" or "Pretty Girl," but her brief scenes were
often deleted or uncredited, and by the late 1940s, she wasn't getting
any work at all.

One Friday in February 1955, Jessel took her to the races in the
afternoon. He later recounted to the police something he'd told
Adams, his longtime girlfriend, that day: "Girls who don't succeed in
Hollywood ought to go home." Early Sunday morning, Adams was
found dead from an overdose of sleeping pills, after a night of drinking
at Ciro's and the Luau. She was thirty-seven and left an estate of $500
and a bunch of mementos from Jessel that were auctioned off to a
crowd of strangers.

Three years later, Lyle's old drinking companion Phil Van Zandt
was found dead in his apartment on Gower Street in Hollywood. He
had been depressed about his dwindling career and his gambling debts,
and had separated from his wife. He, too, had taken an overdose of
barbiturates.

It was always alcohol with Lyle, not pills. But in the late 1940s,
his path tracked close to theirs nonetheless. He could so easily have
gone the same way.

Chapter 10

— ❦ —

FROM ED WOOD
TO OZZIE AND HARRIET

They say you should never marry a person you mean to reform. Marriage is not a reclamation project. A spouse won't turn himself inside out for you, nor should he. They say that a big age difference between husband and wife is probably not conducive to a long and happy marriage. The older partner will get sick or feeble and the younger one will have to become a caretaker when she—it's usually a she, after all—is still in bloom. Resentments will fester. The relationship will strike other people as weird or a bit ridiculous. As for a man who's been married four times before, each time briefly, well, it goes without saying that he does not seem like a good marriage risk. Add in the information that he is an alcoholic, and no sensible person is going to put odds on that union.

Surely this is sound advice. If my daughter were to someday tell me she wanted to marry a multiply divorced boozehound twenty-six years her senior, I doubt I'd be overjoyed. Yet if my own mother had followed this perfectly valid line of thinking, I would not be here, nor would my three siblings, nor any of our beloved children. Life will sometimes flip over these wild cards, show us these sports of common sense, these dark horses that make it to the end of the race. And how lovely that it does.

It helped that my mother was nineteen when she met my father, barely twenty when she married him. At twenty, you don't know what you don't know. You still find it plausible that people who are cautioning you against this feeling have never felt it. Besides, my mother was a person of uncommon determination and trust in her own judgment, particularly about people. She may have been sparsely educated, ebullient to the point of ditziness at times, blond and sexy and, at a scant five-feet-two, not especially imposing, but she knew her own mind and she knew how capacious her heart was. She knew she was stronger than she looked.

My mother was born in Hackensack, New Jersey, on May 8, 1928, the second of three children of Fred and Margaret Epple. The fact that she was named Margaret—as I would be—tells you something about my grandmother's ego. It's usually only men who pass their names down, but in my grandmother's family, her version of the world held sway. (It was she who insisted, on pain of not speaking to my mother again, that I be named Margaret.) My namesake had been born into a distinguished Philadelphia family, with one Titian-haired wayward sister who brought some kind of disgrace on the family and was institutionalized—a trauma my grandmother still spoke about decades later. Margaret went to college, unusual for a woman born near the turn of the last century, at Bucknell, and became a schoolteacher and a principal. At one of the schools where she worked, she met her future husband, a fellow educator named Emil Frederick Epple, who was the son of German immigrants from Alsace-Lorraine. He thought that Emil was too old-world a name, and asked Margaret to call him Fred. Fred's own mother, Ursula, was so domineering that none of his brothers ever married or left home. Fred managed to break away—but he married a woman as formidable in her own way as Ursula had been.

Margaret lived her life with a brittle sense of having come down in the world. The story she always told was that her father was a ship's doctor who, on a trip to England, fell in love with a music hall singer and brought her home to Philadelphia as his wife. His family thought it scandalous to marry a woman who'd been on the stage and shunted him aside. After he died, when his family would have nothing to do with her, the music hall singer took up with a much younger handyman, whom my mother dubbed "Uncle Eddie Do-Hammer."

My plain but intelligent grandmother took after her father but adored her mother, who sang like a tinkling bell, was blessed with the most beautiful red-gold curls (the wild sister evidently inherited those), and was not terribly interested in motherhood. As my grandmother told it, her father's family, the Abbotts, already cool toward him after he married the music hall girl, were not impressed when their granddaughter married Fred, whose people were immigrants and poor. To me, these Abbotts sounded snooty and unpleasant; who wouldn't choose romance over them? But my grandmother clearly felt that she'd been banished from a golden circle and was as prickly as a hedgehog when it came to perceived social slights. Today I'm sure she'd have some sort of psychiatric diagnosis—borderline personality disorder, maybe, or mild bipolar syndrome. She was prey to gloweringly dark moods, but she could also be lively, generous, and funny, especially with the grandchildren. My mother said she was a "pepper pot," or like a grown-up version of the little girl with the curl—when she was good she was very good, and when she was bad she was horrid.

As a child, my mother vowed very early on to create a family that would be more stable and harmonious than her own. Yet she remained close to my grandmother all her life, and took care of her even when she locked my mother and grandfather out of the apartment and snarled invective at them from the other side of the door. (My grandfather, a much gentler spirit, would call my mother to come over and "do something about your mother.") My grandparents lived a five-minute drive from us all my life, came over nearly every day, regularly accompanied us on our family vacations, and were the only people who ever babysat for us. My mother was a loyal person, and a deep believer in family ties, but her mother intimidated her, too, I'm sure. She was probably the only person who did.

In the household my mother grew up in, her parents had fierce and frequent arguments, often about money, of which there was never enough, or status, which the older Margaret always yearned for more of. They were verbal clashes, but my mother decided then that words—particularly the contemptuous words that were her mother's weapons against her far more mild-mannered father—could do irreparable damage. She called her parents' quarrels "burners" and always found a place for herself and her younger sister to hide when one flamed up. She often had to stake out new hiding places—under the stairs, in a pantry, beneath a lilac bush—because the family moved so often, something else my mother firmly disliked about her childhood. Margaret Epple was restless, mercurial, and ambitious for distinction of some sort. In the 1930s and early 1940s, during my mother's childhood, the family bounced around among Hackensack, New Jersey; New York City; Biloxi, Mississippi; Chapel Hill, North Carolina; and Los Angeles, with summers spent in Atlantic City, where Fred earned extra money managing a hotel on the boardwalk. Money was always tight. My mother and her sister learned the trick of mixing ketchup from the hotel dining room with hot water from the tap to make tomato soup for themselves. The years in Chapel Hill, when my mother was in her early teens, were her favorites. My grandfather had earned a degree in educational psychology from Columbia University Teachers College, and then managed to get an academic post at the University of North Carolina. The family lived in a house with a wrap-around porch and a magnolia tree whose bright, waxy leaves looked to my mother as if they'd been individually polished by fairies, and the college campus was like a big playground for her and her sister. Margaret acted in college plays, and dated a nice local boy named Motley Morehead, whose mother invited her for tea and served rose-petal jam sandwiches, a taste so sickly-sweet she never forgot it.

Though the Epples were intelligent people—and educators to boot—they had a strange notion of child rearing. They cast each child in a very particular role. The roles were certainly based on the talents of the child in question, but they allowed for very little straying from the script. Robert, the oldest, who was very bright and had a gift for mathematics, attended the Cathedral School at St. John the Divine in New York and the Hotchkiss School in Connecticut, and as an adolescent was enrolled at the University of North Carolina. (He finished his education at UCLA and became, literally, a rocket scientist, designing guidance control systems for the space program at North American Rockwell.) The youngest, Liz, was the sweet, innocent, marriageable girl. The middle child, Margaret, was the focus of her mother's stage-struck ambition, and frankly a breadwinner for her family. She had a lovely soprano singing voice. At the age of eight, when Margaret won a voice competition sponsored by the New York City Music Education League, the opera singer Lily Pons presented her with the gold medal. As a teenager, she helped support the family by singing everywhere from army bases to funerals, though after one service, to her chagrin, the bereaved family gave her a huge, white Persian cat in lieu of payment. She could suit her voice to light opera or musical comedy, hymns or blues, but her forte was the mid-tempo jazz standards, songs like "Fly Me to the Moon" and "I Wish You Love." For my mother, an education wasn't part of the script. She sang for her supper and never finished high school.

When she was singing at an army base in Biloxi, she met a young enlisted man named Paul Deaven. They dated a few times, and after he'd been transferred to another base, he sent her a telegram saying he was coming to Biloxi on a weekend leave "if you are willing." My mother, naturally enough, interpreted this to mean "if you are willing to see me." She wired back, with characteristic exuberance, "willing, and thrilled." When Paul showed up at her door, however, it was clear that he had been referring to marriage, and though my mother had never given it a thought, she felt too sorry for him to say no. She was just sixteen, but apparently her parents didn't think to say no, either. The newlyweds had only a few weeks together before Paul was shipped overseas.

Not long after, the teenage Margaret was spotted by a talent scout from Twentieth Century–Fox who invited her out to Hollywood to do a screen test. My grandmother, always up for a new and disruptive adventure, packed up her three children and headed west. (Fred joined them later.) Robert enrolled at UCLA and lived on campus. The two girls and their mother found a place to live off Highland Avenue that was like something out of the movie *Stage Door*—a boardinghouse packed with young women trying to make it in show business. (They included a sword swallower with the memorable name Gloria Dick.) One day a man showed up at the door asking for Margaret; when she ran downstairs, she didn't recognize her husband for several awkward moments. It wasn't that the war had changed him. It was just that she had barely known him beforehand. This time, though, Margaret managed to explain that she really didn't want to be married, and Paul accepted her decision. She never saw him again, but she did keep one important token of their marriage: she adopted "Paula Deaven" as her stage name (or as she liked to say, "Paula Deaven, a little bit of heaven"). The Deaven soon fell away, like the spent booster on a rocket, but Paula became, for all but legal purposes, her name.

The screen test she'd come out for either did not materialize or did not yield up any movie roles, so Paula was relieved when, after answering an ad for an understudy in a touring production of a play called *Trouble for Rent*, she got the part.

The star of the play was Lyle Talbot, a much older man whom she'd seen in a few movies. He wasn't a crush or anything—like her mother, she was an anglophile, and when it came to movie actors, her heart belonged to Laurence Olivier and Leslie Howard. (When I was growing up, my mother would drag me to any revival house in Southern California that happened to be playing *Wuthering Heights* or *Gone With the Wind*.) The leading lady in *Trouble for Rent* was none other than Estelle Taylor, the onetime silent star who had been Jack Dempsey's wife and my father's girlfriend in the 1930s. My mother remembered her as a dauntingly glamorous woman who wore a silk turban, wreathed herself in some spicy perfume, and had nothing nice to say to a young understudy. Once, when my mother was a little girl in Atlantic City, she left behind a much-prized new pair of sandals on the beach. When she ran back in a panic to get them, she found that a lady had spread a blanket and was sunbathing on the exact spot where her sandals had been. "Would you mind moving a little?" Margaret asked timidly. "Little girl," the sunbather drawled, "I wouldn't move if you were the Queen of Sheba." Estelle Taylor reminded her quite a bit of that woman.

Lyle didn't have much to say to the young understudy, either. He was polite, but "he was like the sailor with a woman in every port," my mother told me. "Every place we went—Detroit, Chicago, St. Louis, there'd be some *dear* female friend, sometimes several, at the stage door." Paula was lonely and homesick, and the one night she got to go onstage, she was so nervous that she forgot to put on underwear before she slipped into her dress and spent the entire first act in a terror that someone in the front row would notice.

When she got back to L.A. in the late spring of 1947, her mother told her to write a letter to Mr. Talbot thanking him for all his help. "What help?" Paula asked. "He barely spoke to me." "Doesn't matter," her mother said. "He's a big name, just do it." So Paula dutifully wrote a letter. It happened that when he received the letter, Lyle was about to go out on tour again and needed someone to look in on his house while he was gone. She'd seemed like a sweet kid and she lived nearby; why not ask her? So while Lyle was away, Paula walked over to the little Mediterranean-style bungalow he was living in on Camrose Drive, a winding street above the Hollywood Bowl, took in his mail, and watered his succulents. After a while, she started bringing along her sister, Liz, who was by then studying nursing at UCLA, and they'd raid Lyle's cabinets and lie around reading his *Life* magazines. He always kept a nice supply of smoked oysters, and Paula and Liz were always a little on the hungry side.

After Lyle got home, he called Paula up and offered to take her out to dinner to thank her for looking after his bachelor pad. They ate steaks at Musso & Frank and afterward drove back to his house, where they listened to Sarah Vaughan sing "Tenderly" on the record player with the living room windows flung open to let in the honeysuckle-scented air. They fell in love hard and fast. Paula was good-looking, certainly, with her wavy ash-blond hair, teal-blue eyes, and curvy little figure, but Lyle had known a lot of good-looking women by that point. He had never met anyone, though, who was as bubbly as she was without a single drink. Paula never drank. As a teenage girl singing in clubs and canteens, she'd found that men often tried to ply her with alcohol, and she'd learned to be on her guard and to like the feeling of being the one person in the room who had her wits about her. She was giddy and fun-loving, and a great enthusiast of sex—but she valued being alert and in control too much to enjoy the blurriness of inebriation. In many ways, she was the embodiment of the wife Lyle had said he was seeking in those articles back in the 1930s: someone with musical gifts, a sense of humor, and a mind of her own who knew how to put people at ease. She was earthy and sensual, a little raunchy, firm in her own sense of self, but unlike some of his previous girlfriends who may have had some of these same qualities, she was also a deeply warmhearted and decent person.

My mother always told me that you should only marry someone for whom you had an undeniable passion: that heat would be your secret stash, the way you provisioned yourself against the seasonal vagaries of marriage. You had to start with a generous supply of pheromonal stickiness and genuine admiration between you. It helped, she used to say, if you really enjoyed looking at the person you're married to. Once she told me, "It sounds so simple, but I remember sitting with your father in the car on a date, and just looking at his hands on the steering wheel and his forearms and how strong they were, and thinking, yes, I could look at this man forever." I think my siblings and I were aware for as long as we can remember that they had a strong sexual bond. Not that we walked in on them or even overheard them. (Okay, my brother Steve did once, when he thought my father was having a heart attack in a hotel room next door and burst in to save him.) As my other brother, David, put it, when I asked him about this sense we had: "There was always a little bit of sex in the air. Maybe there was even a sense of something naughty about their relationship, something kinky just built in because of the age difference. But beyond that, it just seemed like they had a love affair. He'd be in the kitchen making breakfast, cooking the bacon, and she'd come in singing, and grab him and kiss him. And of course he had that booming voice, and he'd just sound delighted: 'Well, hi there, honey!' They had a really playful sense of love and marriage. They sort of had this gossipy, secret world between them, too, reading the trades and talking about show business together. Flirting. It made marriage seem more fun than what I saw in other people's households." When I was in college, our mom once told my older sister and me, "You know, your father was into oral sex before it was in." More than you want to hear about your parents, but somehow, after the initial squirm, I was happy for her.

Paula loved acting and she loved the theater, maybe even more than the movies, which were kind of a family religion. We saw my father in so many plays, and we went to lots of other theater, too, and invariably when the orchestra struck up the first notes of the overture, or the lights went down and the curtain went up, my mother would grab my hand and squeeze it with an excitement I found slightly embarrassing then and envy now. After both my parents died, I found a birthday card she'd made for my dad, in which she'd inscribed an unattributed quote: "How wonderful to sit in a theater filled with anonymous people all paying for the privilege of sharing him with me. I would hear the applause, the oohs and aahs, the sighs, the comments, the coughs all around me. At the sound of the familiar, deep voice, I would smile, titillated by the bittersweet pleasure of knowing him in a way no one else could." And she had added, "For all the magic moments in the theater, the intimate days and nights and the lovely years together, I thank you and love you." That was in 1982, by which time they'd been married thirty-four years; she was fifty-four and he was eighty.

I think she also saw something in Lyle that perhaps none of his previous wives or girlfriends had—the essential sweetness beneath the suavity, the hard drinking, and the playboy rep. She used to say that at heart he was a small-town Nebraska boy who really, really wanted a family and secretly feared it was far too late. About the people she loved she was uncommonly insightful—so much so that it could sometimes feel intrusive. She could read my emotional state from the way I said "Hello" when I picked up the phone in my college dorm. "I know, I know. I'm a witch," she'd say. "I read minds." I bridled against it sometimes, but now I miss it every day of my life. My sister said the same thing to me recently. "Mom wanted to be so close—that whole I know what you're thinking. I can feel what you're feeling. It was oppressive sometimes. But I miss it now." There's nothing like being truly known, not just for what you did but for how you felt about it, known and at the same time extravagantly loved. In any case, she was right about my father; he was a simple person in a certain way, he did long for domesticity, and though I don't think anyone but Paula would have predicted it in 1948, he did make a very fine father.

"And they said it wouldn't last," my mother used to say, decades into their forty-year marriage. We'd chuckle indulgently, but when I think about it now, that was surely an understatement. They got married in June 1948, a little over a year after they met. She was twenty, he was forty-six. For some reason my father opted for Tijuana, where he'd launched his last, spectacularly unsuccessful marriage, as their wedding venue. My mother always said they'd gone south of the border to avoid reporters. My father was particularly interested in discretion at that point, to give the marriage a little breathing room and Paula a little privacy. Her family stood up with them. Paula wore a lavender wool suit with a cinched waist and a pencil skirt, and they spent a brief honeymoon at Laguna Beach.

The newlyweds moved into the bachelor pad on Camrose, and in February 1949, their first child, Stephen Henderson Talbot, was born. David was born two years later, on September 22, 1951; Cynthia on April 1, 1953. My parents were smitten with their three healthy, talkative golden-haired and blue-eyed children. When Lyle, in the waiting room for fathers, got a call from the delivery room telling him Steve had been born, he was so excited that he yanked the receiver right off the cord, much to the annoyance of the other expectant fathers in the room. Paula, whose intoxication with her children once in a while produced an off note, had wanted to name my sister Treasure. Fortunately my father talked her out of it, pointing out that Treasure Talbot sounded an awful lot like a stripper. She hadn't seen it as tacky, because *treasure* was so overwhelmingly the right word for how she regarded her children. My mother was one of those people who took to parenting with a warm, natural authority and the conviction that her innate playfulness finally had a legitimate outlet. Though she was still in her early twenties, had not gone much beyond junior high, and was married to a man who was a first-time father at forty-seven, she had definite, and progressive, ideas about how they would do things: she breastfed her babies at a time when bottle-feeding was the norm, and forswore spanking. When a fifth-grade teacher replied to a challenging question Steve asked by saying, "Curiosity killed the cat," Paula, who had spent so little time in classrooms herself, mustered the wherewithal to complain to the teacher in person. Years later, when we were all grown up, she told my sister that before she had children, she would wake up every morning aware that her first feeling was one of vague emptiness, and that after she had children she never felt that emptiness again.

Yet objectively speaking, constructing a family life with Lyle was a bold-faced gamble. Five years into their marriage, she had three children under the age of five, and the family was moving every year, just like hers had, just like she swore she never would. They lived in my father's Camrose bungalow; in a little house off Laurel Canyon with a view, over the palm trees, of a giant concrete ice cream cone and the sign "HOME OF THE MILE-HIGH CONE"; way out in Tarzana, in a tan stucco house with a stubbly lawn like a five-o'clock shadow; and finally in the Highland Towers, a hulking apartment building in the heart of Hollywood that had been put up in the silent era with an eye to grandeur but was now rather tatty. It was not the sort of domestic setting that Dick and Jane from Steve's school readers or any of the families on 1950s television lived in. Steve remembers the Highland Towers as "a literally quite dark, sort of seedy place, full of weird actors and magicians. In retrospect, it was very film noir." One day when Steve was playing in a little park nearby, he was startled to see a boy about his age eating out of the garbage can. "I told Mom about it and she said if you see that boy again invite him home. A few days later, I did and I invited him back to the apartment and she fed him lunch." Hollywood Boulevard was just a short walk away, and that was where Lyle took five-year-old Steve to see the first movie he ever went to, *Prince Valiant*, in the new wide-screen CinemaScope format at Grauman's Chinese Theatre. Lyle bought Steve a sword and shield in the lobby and they walked back to their noir tower of a home, hand in hand.

Lyle was still having trouble finding work—by this point his reputation as a drinker was beginning to hurt him—money was tight, and Paula had set her career aside while the kids were little. Though it was true that Lyle virtually never turned down a job, he might, if he hadn't had a growing family to support, have turned down the ones he took next: working for a director named Ed Wood. Lyle knew Eddie Wood as a peppy young man who had worked as a gofer on a movie he had made a couple of years earlier at Universal. "He was this young, eager-beaver type—a very personable, very nice, very sweet guy," my father recalled. "He'd come to me—he used this same speech with the various actors that he afterwards used when he made pictures—and his pitch was: 'You know, Lyle, you're my favorite actor.' He was sincere about it; he meant it when he said it. He'd say, 'Someday I'm going to make movies and when I do I want you to be in them.' So what do you say? I was an actor who very seldom turned down anything, because I wanted to work. So consequently I worked in all kinds of pictures—good, bad, and indifferent. Anyway, I said, 'Well, sure, Eddie, call me.' Well, two or three years later I got a call from this Eddie Wood. I'd forgotten who he was, but he told me he had this film he was making, and he had a great part for me. He said, 'I don't have much money, Lyle, and I know you get a pretty big salary—but I'll give you just as much as I can.' It amounted to three hundred dollars a day. He said, 'So you know I'll pay you, I'll pay you every day.'"

The movie was *Glen or Glenda*, and like all Wood's movies it was so very bad in so many and such bizarre ways that it would eventually transcend, if that's the right word, the utter shoddiness of its production and become a cult classic. Actually, Wood's work was first rescued from oblivion when the writers Harry and Michael Medved anointed *Plan 9 from Outer Space* the worst film of all time. That was in 1978, two years after Wood died of a heart attack at age fifty-four, depressed and in desperate financial straits after years of eking out a living writing pulp and porn. But after a while, the Internet started showing its capacity to draw together aficionados of the obscure. It rustled up all the arch and ironic film buffs, all the knowing, winking connoisseurs of Bettie Page bondage flicks and the lesser-known films of Val Lewton, and along the way, even some with a secret, sincere fondness for Ed Wood. In 1994, the director Tim Burton made his biopic about Wood, with Johnny Depp playing him as a sincere if absurdly buoyant film lover, and that image stuck. After that, Ed Wood might still be billed as the worst filmmaker in the world, but he elicited a certain befuddled affection, too. Yes, he had made atrocious movies, but he didn't seem to know it—he loved his films!—and that earnest belief in his product seemed like such a delirious act of will that it was almost like art itself.

"I feel the fans must be responding to the love and dedication Eddie had for the business, because even at his most absurd, Ed Wood believed so much in what he was doing," my father told an interviewer in the 1990s, after Wood had been rediscovered. "And he *worshipped* actors like Bela [Lugosi]!" Wood seemed genuinely hurt when Lyle referred to the flying saucers in *Plan 9 from Outer Space* as garbage can lids. They were not, he indignantly assured Lyle; they were hubcaps. "Eddie was serious about his movie," my father would say later. "It wasn't a rip-off. He wanted to keep making them and he wanted to improve. And that's why I don't think you can ridicule the poor little guy."

Then, too, Wood assembled a stock company of players for his movies who were themselves so odd that they constituted at once a realistic rendering of the underside of Hollywood and a sort of living avant-garde performance piece. There was Bela Lugosi, the heavy-accented Hungarian-born actor who'd played Dracula in the 1930s but had since fallen on hard times. Lugosi had successfully fought an addiction to painkillers and was now hoping to make a comeback under Wood's auspices. There was the four-hundred-pound, bald-pated Swedish wrestler Tor Johnson. And there was the ornately mus-cled bodybuilder Steve Reeves, who would go on to become the highest-paid actor in Europe, starring in sword-and-sandal movies in which he never spoke, because they were dubbed in Italian. Wood's girlfriend, the wide-eyed, strangely innocent Dolores Fuller, who went on to some success as a songwriter for Elvis Presley movies, was his leading lady. And for an ahead-of-its-time touch of goth sex, there was Maila Nurmi, a Finnish-born pinup model who'd invented a persona for herself as the hot-and-cold "glamour ghoul" Vampira, a TV host who introduced horror movies. (She had a full-throated scream, a scar-ily tiny waist she showed off in a long black gown, and an acerbic sense of humor married to a disarmingly large ego.) The ensemble also embraced Bunny Breckinridge, an openly gay gadabout and drag queen from a wealthy and prominent family who played the role of the alien leader in *Plan 9 from Outer Space* wearing abundant, incongruous eye makeup.

Finally there was The Amazing Criswell, an amazingly unreli-able mystic who made regular TV appearances where he intoned his trademark line: "We are all interested in the future, for that is where you and I are going to spend the rest of our lives." One of Criswell's predictions was that Denver, Colorado, would be destroyed by "a strange and terrible pressure from outer space" that would "cause all solids to turn into a jelly-like mass." He also predicted an outbreak of cannibalism in Pittsburgh, of all places, for November 1980. Criswell did marginally better when it came to future fashions. He predicted that body decoration would become universal, though in Criswell's version, women would "decorate their breasts with startling colors," while men would "decorate their genitals." Still, if tattoos count, he was on to something. He said nose rings would come into fashion in 1966 for both men and women, and hey, by about 1996 they did!

You had to be pretty seriously weird to register as weird with my father. He'd grown up around carny people, acted with and been directed by every kind of personality you can think of, and basically lived his life in the company of exhibitionists. If you were a nice person (big bonus points if you listened to his stories), then your eccentricities were safe with him. Criswell was one of the few fellow performers I ever heard him describe as "a very strange person." (Hell, he didn't even describe Ed Wood that way.) Criswell lived in the Highland Towers at the same time that Lyle and the family did, and when they ran into him in the elevator, he'd speak to them in the same stentorian tones in which he'd predicted the future enslavement of men by women (not at all a bad thing, in his view) and fix them with that nearly translucent blue gaze (were those contacts?) from beneath that frothy platinum coiffure. Either the guy never broke character or he truly believed in his psychic powers. Both explanations puzzled my father, a performer who was almost never in character when he didn't have to be—that is, when he wasn't actually working—and who'd known too many charlatans in his day to set much store by psychic powers.

In the Ed Wood company, Lyle was the straight arrow. Sure, he might have been a heavy drinker, down on his luck and married to a woman twenty-six years his junior, but in Wood world, he was reliable, presentable, a regular Boy Scout. Wood cast him twice as a police inspector and once as a general in charge of repelling an alien invasion. I don't think I'm bragging when I say that he brought a note of professionalism and a faint hint of rationality to the proceedings, accomplishments that would inevitably be undone a moment later, when say, a loud and inexplicable burst of flamenco music interjected itself on the sound track.

Plan 9 and *Jail Bait*, two of the three movies my father made with Wood, are really unwatchable for me. When I saw them once or twice with friends who were cracking up over them, I just felt sad and queasy and embarrassed for my dad. They reminded me of the cheap, off-brand Day-Glo candy you'd sometimes get in those claw-grabber machines at an arcade. Candy was so good; how could anybody make it so wretched?

When I finally made myself watch *Glen or Glenda*, though, I found it kind of . . . touching. Of course, it was still awful—botched and awkward, and surreal in a style you could be pretty sure was not intentional. (The deployment of Bela Lugosi in this movie's dream sequence, uttering gloomily about "snips and snails and puppy dog tails," is truly bonkers, and not in a good way.) But it was also, in its peculiar fashion kind of a brave and earnest plea for understanding and empathizing with people who didn't conform to their assigned gender. Wood had been hired to make an exploitation movie based on the story of Christine Jorgensen, whose sex-reassignment surgery had been generating headlines in late 1952 and early 1953. When Jorgensen showed no interest in cooperating, he switched gears, producing a movie centered on a man who likes—or as *Glen or Glenda* puts it, "desperately wish[es]"—to dress in women's clothes. The quasi-documentary-style narration, written by Wood, is at once completely ridiculous and emotionally truthful: "Give this man satin undies, a dress, a sweater and a skirt, or even the lounging outfit he has on and he's the happiest individual in the world. He can work better, think better, he can play better and he can be a credit to his community and his government because he is happy. These things are his comfort." You shouldn't send transgendered people to psychiatrists with the goal of punishing them or eradicating their "strange desires," the narrator intones, because "this is their life. To take it away from them might do as great a harm as taking away an arm or a leg or life itself." Honestly, these are beliefs that have only quite recently, and after years of activism on the part of transsexuals and their allies, become more widely accepted.

Glen or Glenda was Wood's own story; he was a devoted cross-dresser who claimed that he had fought as a Marine at Guadalcanal wearing red satin panties and a bra beneath his fatigues. Supposedly his mother had dressed him as a girl when he was little, and he harbored lifelong, obsessive memories of how soft those clothes were and how good they felt to him. Although he was sexually attracted to women (he had girlfriends like Fuller who were very into him, and he was married twice), he was also really, really attracted to their clothes—especially their angora sweaters.

On the set of Wood's movies, Lyle's "A job's a job" attitude got him through, abetted by a certain amusement at Eddie's seemingly guileless chutzpah. Lyle had acted in shabby independent productions before (*"She Shoulda Said 'No'!"* wasn't exactly Academy Award material), so he was used to directors who stole shots, filming on the street without permits. Sometimes a director would see a good shot, and even if it had nothing to do with the movie he was making, he'd grab it, figuring the studios could use it somehow. "So, for instance, one time we're winding up the day's shooting—it was in Long Beach—and here comes this big battleship into port," my father recalled. "And the director says, 'Holy Jesus, we've got to get that,' and he's lining up the cameras and they're having trouble, so he starts yelling at this giant dreadnought, 'Back up! Back up!'"

But "Eddie took stealing shots to a whole new level." He never got permits to film anywhere—he couldn't afford them—so his camera crew was always prepared to pack up and flee at a moment's notice. "We were shooting at a motel on the Sunset Strip," my father recalled, "and he hadn't gotten an okay to do this. We were shooting around the pool when the manager came out and said, 'What the hell is going on here? You better get out!' So everyone—the cameraman who had worked for him before and a couple of the electricians—they'd rush to get the hell out of there and go somewhere else.

"On *Plan 9*, our 'studio'—what a name to call it!—was down an alley off of Santa Monica Boulevard, and it was behind a four-story hotel that mostly housed prostitutes. It was this wooden shack—maybe

it had been a garage or something. It certainly wasn't soundproofed."
And the lights! "The lights were on little music stands and they were
literally tin cans with a bulb in them."

Wood was true to his word, though, when it came to paying Lyle
every day. (The shoots usually lasted only about a week.) "I always got
a large stack of singles, maybe some fives in there, and they were all
sort of wrinkled, as if he'd gathered them in small amounts and stuffed
them into his pockets. He obviously collected them somehow"—Lyle
didn't even want to think about the circumstances—"from different
people." Lyle found it sad, but also—he couldn't help it—funny. And
that was before he even knew that one way Wood had raised money
for *Plan 9* was by getting some elders from a local Baptist church to
chip in, promising that he'd take the money he made from this
sure-to-be-a-hit horror/sci-fi flick to make an epic series of movies for
the church about the twelve apostles. Before they got the money,
Wood and several others from his inner circle, including the big man,
Tor Johnson, had to agree to be baptized. No record exists of what
kind of undergarments Wood was wearing for his immersion.

Then one evening, after the premiere of one of the Wood movies,
Lyle was tasked with driving him home. Wood was drunk and couldn't
or wouldn't tell Lyle where he lived, so Lyle drove to his own place,
parked the car, and left Wood there to sleep it off. At about two in the
morning, Wood knocked at the door and Lyle let him in. My mother
insisted that he stay the night rather than calling a cab, and offered
him the main bedroom. She and Lyle would go sleep in the kids' room.
The next morning, Paula and Lyle were eating breakfast with the little
boys when Wood emerged wearing a filmy black nightgown and a bra
of Paula's that had been hanging in the bathroom. Paula, who had
never met Wood before that night, was momentarily speechless. Lyle,
who apparently thought Wood had only been acting in *Glen or Glenda*
and who was still a little vague on the whole cross-dressing thing, was
furious, and ordered Wood out of his wife's nightie and out of the

apartment. That morning it must have seemed to him that the seediness of Wood's world was encroaching, seeping into the cracks of a home life that must have felt increasingly precious and fragile to Lyle.

And it was—because of Lyle himself. His drinking persisted despite my mother's pleading and her own abstention. "He was not a mean drunk. I don't think he had a mean bone in his body," said my mother's brother, Robert Epple. "But he'd drink till he passed out. He'd drive badly—very slowly, but very badly." One night my mother called Robert. She was crying. Lyle had his friend Phil Van Zandt over at the house in Tarzana and he and Lyle were smashed, with the kids there. She wanted Van Zandt out of the house, but she was holed up with the little boys in their bedroom, because she didn't want them to see their father that way. When Robert got there, he was so angry at Van Zandt, whom he'd decided was a bad influence on Lyle, that he made the first indignant gesture a fundamentally peaceable and rational man like him could think of at the moment: "Van Zandt had this beautiful, fawn-colored suede jacket. I took it and threw it out in the gutter."

In the spring of 1953, just after Cindy was born, Paula gave Lyle an ultimatum: Either he stopped drinking or their marriage, this whole experiment in making a new, family-oriented life, was over. In the summer, she filed for divorce. Lyle moved out, and Paula sent baby Cindy to stay with her parents for a few weeks while she took care of the boys, then five and two, and tried to figure out what to do from there. She had been reading up on Alcoholics Anonymous and on the new understanding of alcoholism that had been gaining purchase in the United States since the late 1930s. Alcoholism was a disease, the new thinking held, rather than a moral failing. Or maybe it was more like an allergy; for people who were susceptible, alcohol was something they simply could not tolerate, even in very small doses. A vow to drink in moderation was not tenable. The only way to regain control was to stop drinking altogether. Lyle, she decided, would have to try this approach.

After several weeks—the papers said two, but I think it was longer—Paula decided to take Lyle back. He must have promised, in a way she found newly convincing, that he wouldn't drink again. "Probably the most unlikely place in the world for romance is the Los Angeles Domestic Relations Court," read the chirpy account in the *Evening Herald-Express*, "but that is where love bloomed again today for Screen Actor Lyle Talbot and his wife, Margaret, who is officially suing him for divorce." The Talbots walked "out of the courtroom arm in arm," the paper reported, "and planned to have dinner together that night." The children, said Paula, "need their father—and I need him, too," adding, "I expect to go back with him. I have every hope the problems we have can be worked out successfully." One of the photos shows Lyle smiling broadly and gripping Paula's hand, while she leans against him looking sleepy and a bit stunned, though her hair is perfectly curled and she is wearing a smart little black dress with a jaunty white collar.

"When I think back on it," my mother's brother told me recently, "I think how really strong she was to do that. Here she was, in her early twenties with these three little kids, and no money. But I also think how strong he was, because it must have been really, really hard, but he did it for her."

Lyle got sober partly through AA. He hardly ever talked about it—and certainly never threw twelve-step lingo around. But when AA did come up in household conversation, both my parents spoke about it with a certain low-key respect. Lyle apparently did do some formal or informal sponsoring of other alcoholics, especially if they, too, were in show business, for some years after he got sober.

When my brother Steve was about ten, the family was spending part of a humid summer in Indianapolis while my father did a play there. They were staying at a big old resort-style hotel in a leafy part of

Paula and Lyle at the Highland Towers, with baby Stephen.

town. The marquee out in front of the hotel boasted Lyle Talbot's name as a guest. But one day, Steve noticed that Lyle's name had been demoted to second billing beneath that of the Lone Ranger, who was in town for a personal appearance. Steve, who was a huge fan of the *Lone Ranger* TV show, ran back to the hotel room to tell the family the thrilling news. "No sooner had I blurted out who was coming," Steve wrote me in an e-mail recently, "than the phone rang and it was the Ranger himself in his unmistakable voice. And even more incredibly, he was coming up to see Dad. I could barely contain myself, though I noticed that Dad and Mom's excitement was muted for some reason I couldn't understand." The next thing Steve knew, the Lone Ranger was at their hotel room door. "And he was not wearing the mask! I was stunned. How could he reveal his identity like that? He was a little bleary-eyed and tired-looking, too. He shook my hand and said hi.

Maybe he slurred his words a little, but he seemed very serious and he wanted to talk to Dad and they went off to another room. Mom told us later that he had a drinking problem and that's why he needed to talk to Dad." Steve remembers other actors calling the house, not famous ones, just names or voices he sometimes recognized, for what he knew somehow was the same reason. After he'd told me this story, he googled Clayton Moore, the actor who played the Ranger on TV from 1949 to 1957, and saw that "he spent the next forty years of his life living off the same role, doing personal appearances, and lived to be eighty-five. So he must have pulled himself together. Guess he had to uphold that image of the honorable law man who lived by a code of justice and propriety."

My parents were involved with an Episcopal church in Los Angeles at the time. The minister was young, liberal and—always an important credit in my parents' eyes—good-looking. The church was integrated and rather hip. Nat King Cole sang in the church choir. Lyle used to like to talk with Father Pratt and found in those sessions during the time he was quitting alcohol the closest thing he'd ever had to therapy.

Mostly, though, he took strength from the powerful motivation of doing right by Paula and their children and being allowed to keep his life with them whole. He was a doting father. From the time they were toddlers, he took the boys to the set—not of Ed Wood movies, of course, but of the TV westerns he was also doing. He let them dress up in the cowboy gear and wander around the dusty streets and push open the swinging doors on the fake saloons. On one set, David made the mistake of shouting in excitement after the director had called all quiet on the set, and the director started haranguing him. "Normally, Dad was very deferential to directors," David said. "He had the actor's thing of almost becoming childlike with the director. But when this guy yelled at me, and I remember thinking this was very cool, Dad turned on him and said, 'Don't you *ever* talk to my son

Family portrait: just after my parents' reconciliation.

that way.'" Lyle was physically affectionate and told his children every day how much he loved them. "I can remember thinking he was sweeter than the other dads," my brother David says. "You know, he'd put his arm around me when we walked down the street, hold my hand. This was in the '50s and early '60s, when dads didn't do that. Of course, it was embarrassing sometimes, especially when I was a teenager! But I also appreciated that he was more affectionate than other dads."

Our mother "became his anchor and his mood stabilizer," as David put it. He still did have his black moods sometimes—actually, I'd call them dark gray—and if in the past he drank to try to break those moods up, now he looked to my mother to buoy him up instead. She was very, very good at persuading people out of their self-doubt or their sadness. Her own willful optimism was partly self-taught. Some of it was in her nature, but some of it was what she had learned, from childhood, to tell herself. Words were talismanic for her, and she became the Scheherazade of comfort talk, resourcefully spinning out a more convincing, more engrossing story than whatever self-pitying version you were telling yourself about your life.

During the forty years he and my mother were married, neither my sister nor I ever saw Lyle take a drink, let alone get drunk. I never harbored an anxiety that he *would* drink. But David remembers coming down the hall once as a small child and seeing my parents silhouetted in the kitchen, my father slumped at the table, his head in his hands and my mother standing over him, lecturing him. At the time, David just felt there was something strange and wrong about the picture, and wanted to get away; in retrospect, he figures it must have been one of the times when my father relapsed.

Both my brothers have told me about the one time they actually saw him drunk. This was some years after my mother had delivered her ultimatum and left my father; David was in seventh grade by then, Steve in tenth. They were both enrolled at Harvard, a boys' prep school a few minutes from where we lived. One evening, Harvard was hosting a father-son sports banquet at which my brothers were to get trophies. My father had been looking forward to it, but he arrived late. And when he got there, it was immediately apparent that something was very wrong.

"I'd never seen him drunk," David recalled, "but I knew what it was. He was staggering. Steve and I were sitting at different tables because we were in different grades, so we didn't even really have each other for solidarity. Dad kind of lurched over, he was slurring his words, and he went over to one of my teachers to say, 'Oh, David just loooves your class.' I was mortified, of course. It was like seeing your dad suddenly turn into an alien—just deeply disturbing. We went home. It was a Friday night and I remember Steve and I watched *Route 66* on TV, just sitting there in this deep silence. I don't think we even said anything about it to each other.

"The next morning Dad came into our bedroom, and if he wasn't actually crying, he was very teary. He apologized over and over again.

He was so pained. And it made it even harder in a way because we'd never seen him that way either, never seen him crying. He said it would never happen again. And it never did."

What I can remember is that all my life, every time we went out to dinner (and I went out to dinner a lot with my parents) and the server would ask if we wanted to order wine or some other alcoholic beverage, my father would hesitate. The pause would seem a shade long to me. Then he would always say the same thing: "Not tonight, thank you." As though there could be a night when he would say, "Yes, bring us a bottle of your best white wine," or "How about a Scotch on the rocks?" I suppose that he might have been tempted each time, might have been steeling himself with each offer to refuse. But I think it was also a case of feeling, somewhere inside, a little embarrassed to be a teetotaler—as though he hesitated before answering, in order to seal his affinity with a more sophisticated tribe he'd had to leave behind. I don't believe that he ever really regretted giving up alcohol. He told us again and again over the years that my mother had saved his life, given him a whole new life. And he must have had that point driven home each time he read about the sad demises of some of the people he was drinking with in the late 1940s—Phil Van Zandt's suicide, the premature deaths of his last two ex-wives. But I do think that in a dark restaurant, with a heavy leather-bound menu in his hand and the flicker of candlelight in a little red globe on the table, he could feel a twinge that was partly real longing and partly the need to perform his role as a gentleman of the world.

One way that my mother ensured he would not feel this twinge more often was to build a social life for our family that was oriented to the kids and built around her own family—Liz and Robert each had married and had three children and were living near Los Angeles— none of whom drank at all. We had a lot of pool parties with our cousins and drank a lot of iced tea. "Mom put her foot down and then she drew that very bright line," as my sister put it. "She created a haven.

My mom and me in Union Square, San Francisco, 1964.

Our family life was very insulated from Hollywood. We rarely entertained people from the industry, or even from outside our extended
family, at home. We'd see them at the theater; Dad would socialize
with them on the set or before a play. But for the most part we did not
invite Hollywood into our home."

T hat attitude extended sometimes to my father's bristly protec-
tiveness when people approached him in public. Usually he was very
gracious when someone came up to him and asked for an autograph,
or said they'd seen him in this or that, which happened fairly often.
He'd ask them where they were from and then say: "Oh, you're from
Kansas City / Cincinnati / fill-in-the-blank? Oh, I love Kansas City /
Cincinnati / fill-in-the-blank. It has some of the best barbecue"—or
steaks or ice cream or whatever it was that city had. Or, barring a specialty he could name, he would always dub it "a great theater town!"
And tell the person that he'd played there in 1923 or 1943 or whenever,
because he'd played almost everywhere and he did know and love his

cities and the tasty items they were known for. But the old joke about people coming up to an actor, maybe a down-on-his-luck actor, and saying, "Didn't you used to be so-and-so?" is actually true. Sometimes people did say exactly that. Or worse, "I thought you were dead!" Or, gesturing toward my mother, "Is this your daughter?" At which point my father would get very icy. These interlocutors hurt his own vanity, but more than that, they embarrassed him in front of his children.

In 1955, Lyle and Paula were able to buy a house, the home where they would spend the rest of their life together, and where I would grow up. The down payment came from the sale of the old Talbot Hotel in Brainard, which was still standing in the 1950s, some twenty years after Mary Talbot had died. My brother Steve remembers the trip to Nebraska to sell the place, stopping in to see Ed and Anna Henderson at the apartment building in Omaha where they lived among other old troupers, and then the long drive back in a rattletrap black car that seemed to him like a Model T. It broke down entirely in Arizona, and to Steve's amazement, the family was rescued by actual Indians from a nearby reservation who came out to tow the car. Back home in California, Paula and Lyle and their three kids moved into a neat, white house on a cul-de-sac at the end of Goodland Avenue, in Studio City, near Coldwater Canyon. Like the Bing Crosby song had it, they were "going to settle down and never more roam, and make the San Fernando Valley [their] home." That same song described the Valley as "cow country," a place to which the singer's mail would have to be delivered "RFD." There were still parts of the Valley that rural in the mid-1950s, but Studio City was not one of them. It was named after the Mack Sennett studio, where they had made Keystone Kops movies in the silent era, and which later became Republic Studios and then CBS. It had a busy little commercial district with a toy store, a Sav-On drugstore and a Du-par's pie and coffee shop and—this was still L.A., after all—a bar called the Queen Mary that featured female impersonators.

"To me," says Steve, "the move from crumbling Highland Towers in Hollywood to suburban Studio City in the mid-1950s was like moving from black-and-white to Kodachrome. It was the big dividing line in my childhood and I think in Dad and Mom's marriage and the life of our family. I had the feeling afterwards that our family was on an upward path." The house was a modest split-level, built in the 1930s, with a sunken living room and three bedrooms. My sister and I, who were eight years apart, shared a room, and my two brothers shared a smaller one, sleeping in bunk beds and doing their homework side by side at the same built-in desk till they went off to college. My parents' bedroom was up a short flight of stairs and down a little hall from mine and my sister's. On nights my sister wasn't in her twin bed yet and I had trouble getting to sleep, I'd call up to my mother, who'd often be reading in bed, and she'd call back that everything was okay, we "were close as two peas in a pod."

When I was growing up there, the house seemed big enough to accommodate everything I wanted to do in it, to meet my imagination halfway. Out back, there was a little sunken courtyard of cracked concrete where I used to play handball against one side of the house, and up a short flight of stairs, an apron of lawn trimmed with zinnias and snapdragons, and up another flight of stairs, the pool and deck that my parents built for us (neither of them could swim), and above that, a tangled hillside of ice plant and wild mustard and leggy purple weeds. There was a sturdy lemon tree that my mom used to send me to, for our nightly iced tea. For a relatively small house, it had a lot of odd little cabinets, built-in bookshelves, unexpected nooks, and deceptively large, mothball-scented closets. It was an excellent house for playing hide-and-seek or for staking out secret reading places. Sitting atop the built-in bookshelf next to a window in my bedroom closet with *Jane Eyre* and a box of Pop-Tarts by my side was the height of luxury for me when I was a preteen. I once reached down into the empty space behind the drawer of my built-in desk and found a yellowing stash of love letters to the teenage girl who'd lived there before me.

Studio City was a regular middle-class suburb, except that so many of the people who lived there worked in what we called "the business." It wasn't a neighborhood where you'd find a map to the stars' homes, though. This was a community of humble, working showbiz types. Our neighbors included stuntmen, TV directors, and cameramen, and a guy who wrote scripts for the TV series *Get Smart*. (He'd give us the scripts they'd already shot, and David would stage productions of them in our backyard, once selling an astonishing number of overpriced tickets to people who must have been hoping that Lyle or some other professional actors would turn up in the cast. No such luck, it was just my scrawny cousins and I playing international men and women of mystery.) Across the street lived Thurl Ravenscroft, the voice of Tony the Tiger on the Kellogg's Frosted Flakes commercials. (Kids were always wheedling him to "do the voice." He never would.) Down the street was the house of Marty Milner, the blond actor who starred in *Route 66* and later in *Adam-12*, iconic TV shows "about two regular guys in a car," as the Wikipedia entry on Milner aptly puts it. (He also played the jazz musician who falls for Burt Lancaster's sister in *The Sweet Smell of Success*.)

We did not live extravagantly in Studio City—no lavish parties, no expensive jewelry for my mom, no vacations abroad, no nannies or babysitters (other than my grandparents), just the one car (a station wagon). But there was enough money to send my brothers to the fancy all-boys prep school across the street (my sister and I went to the perfectly good public schools) and later to put all four of us through college (albeit on three University of California tuitions, a bargain in those days). My father's acting earned him just over $19,000 in 1963, which doesn't sound like much until you realize that only 5 percent of American families had an income over $15,000 that year and the median family income was $6,200. In 1965, his earnings from TV shows and plays (no movies) jumped to $35,000 (and we splurged on a new Mercury station wagon for $4,800). That year, though, was the kind of fluke that freelancers sometimes get lucky with; his earnings settled back down to $20,000 the following year.

The new medium of television had been very good to Lyle, and he made a smooth transition to it—especially once he stopped drinking. Since he'd always been at ease onstage, he was more comfortable than some of his movie-made colleagues with live TV, especially the live drama that was a mainstay of early 1950s broadcasting. Lyle still liked to be at the bright, buzzy center of the culture, an officially designated funmaker. And TV, the powerful novelty that was meant to bring families home and together after the separations and dispersals of war, certainly felt like the centerpiece of the entertainment industry in the 1950s. Lyle was content now with character parts. "You can't go on forever doing leads," he told the columnist Erskine Johnson in 1951. "Being a character man is better. You don't have to watch your waist-line. You don't have to worry about whether you're a handsome guy or not. What a relief!" Fellow actors who still tried to be "dashing and irresistible" at fifty and over were "foolish. Audiences aren't going to continue to accept them." If this smacks of making a virtue of neces-sity, it's still sort of touching to see him so gamely trying to do so. In any case, he found plentiful character roles on TV—those bankers and "Docs" on the westerns, the police commissioners and psychiatrists on the mysteries.

And the next-door neighbors/best friends like Joe Randolph, the character he played on the *Ozzie and Harriet* show. We got to live our suburban idyll in large part because my father was enacting another one on TV. In 1956, he landed a continuing role on *The Adventures of Ozzie and Harriet*, a role he played for ten of the show's fourteen years on television. On the 1950s family sitcom, the parents' (and kids') best friends were often the neighbors. That was an integral part of the ideal of living they represented: the pal next door you could organize a golf outing with at a moment's notice. You didn't have to leave community behind when you moved from the city; it was there in abundance and ready for play.

Around the same time, my brother Steve discovered that he had a hankering to act, too, and my parents decided to let him try. He was talented and a quick study. And he was all-American cute, with his wheat-blond hair, blue eyes, and square little jaw. From the time he was nine till he was fourteen, he got a lot of work, on *The Twilight Zone*, *Perry Mason*, and *Lassie* (he was once bitten by the dog trained to play the "fighting Lassie"—I hate to reveal this, but Lassie was played by more than one collie). He played Dick Clark's ward in the one movie Clark ever made, a sensitive teen movie called *Because They're Young*, with Tuesday Weld as one of the sensitive teens. But his longest-running role was on the family comedy *Leave It to Beaver*, where he played Gilbert Bates, the friend of Beaver Cleaver's who was most likely to get him into hot water. Not that it was ever that hot—tepid, more like it. The classic Gilbert maneuver was to get Beaver to pledge they'd both make faces in their fifth-grade class picture, then not make a face himself, and leave Beaver to mar the photo and take the punishment. Or Gilbert might, as he did in another episode, egg the Beaver into starting a lawn-mowing enterprise, then back out and leave Beaver to do all the work. Or he might talk Beaver and another friend into buying a burro, then renege on his promise to keep the burro at his house part of the time, when his mother gets steamed about it.

No two shows projected the ideal of the 1950s American family as indelibly as *Ozzie and Harriet* and *Leave It to Beaver* did. You could throw in *Father Knows Best* and *The Donna Reed Show*, too, but it was *Ozzie and Harriet* that became common shorthand for a certain kind of family—the male-breadwinner, stay-at-home-mom, white, suburban kind. And when that norm began to be undermined—by the 1960s counterculture, by feminism, by an increase in the number of working mothers, of divorce, and of single-parent-headed households—both its critics and its defenders latched on to the convenient symbolism of the sitcom, producing articles and speeches with titles like "Ozzie and Harriet Don't Live Here Anymore."

June Cleaver, the mother in the Cleaver household, who famously wore pumps and pearls while she did the housework, came to epitomize the 1950s homemaker who was supposed to combine fastidious devotion to a clean and orderly household with an impeccably maintained femininity. Type "June Cleaver" into your Amazon search engine and you'll find recent books with titles like *Even June Cleaver Would Forget the Juice Box: Cut Yourself Some Slack (and Still Raise Great Kids) in the Age of Extreme Parenting* (I like that marketing-friendly "and still raise great kids"); *Not June Cleaver: Women and Gender in Postwar America*; and even *I Killed June Cleaver: Modern Moms Shatter the Myth of Perfect Parenting.* As of this writing, it has been nearly fifty years since *Leave It to Beaver* went off the air (though it did survive in reruns long after), and we're still invoking June Cleaver as the paragon of a certain kind of oppressive domestic perfectionism.

No wonder, then, that when my brother Steve emerged as a student radical at Wesleyan University in the late 1960s, a leader of the campus chapter of Students for a Democratic Society, and a guy who romanced brainy East Coast feminists, he was embarrassed enough about the Beaver years to sort of . . . never mention them. Still, he was going to school with a lot of kids who'd grown up with 1950s TV. It was a testament to the purchase Beaver Cleaver had on the baby boomer subconscious that when a false rumor started to the effect that Jerry Mathers, the actor who played the Beaver, had been killed in Vietnam, it simply would not go away. Even in those easier-to-hide years before Google, there was really no escaping from a televised past, collective or personal. In 1968, Steve was speaking at a New England town meeting against the Vietnam War, along with other SDS members and representatives of the Black Panthers, when someone in the audience stood up and asked, "Hey, weren't you Gilbert on *Leave It to Beaver?*" As Steve recalled in an article he wrote for *California* magazine, "All heads onstage turned to stare at me. One Panther from Newark lowered his shades to get a better look. I felt like an imposter—an alleged college radical exposed as a child sitcom actor." Another time, when Steve had been urging fellow Wesleyan students to go out on strike against the war, he arrived on campus one morning to see a big hand-painted sign that read "GEE, BEAV, I DON'T KNOW," an oft-repeated phrase from the show. Back then, when he contemplated his dad's run on *Ozzie and Harriet* and his own on *Beaver*, Steve some-times thought that if "our roles as sidekicks in the ultimate suburban fantasies didn't exactly qualify as war crimes," still "culturally and aes-thetically . . . we had a lot to atone for."

Well, maybe. But watching a bunch of the episodes from both shows recently (like so many things—maybe everything eventually—they are available on DVD with Bonus Features), I was inclined to give them more of a break. *Ozzie and Harriet* is indeed remarkably bland and corny. But let me give it credit for a few things, besides, that is, supporting my family, and allowing my parents the lagniappe of a late-in-life fourth child—me—for I was born during the middle of my father's well-paid *Ozzie and Harriet* run.

Ozzie and Harriet was the first program on TV to show a married couple sharing the same bed—a breakthrough at a time when it still wasn't common even in the movies. It launched the career of Ricky Nelson, the guitar-playing, dreamy-looking younger Nelson son, a performer with some real rockabilly chops, even though he had to keep them pretty tame when he sang on the show. Incorporating Rick's emergence as a rock musician into the series made it seem like it was possible to rock a little without smashing the family. In some ways, this was a conservative message. "Rather than fracturing domesticity," writes media scholar Lynn Spigel, teen idols like Ricky Nelson "seemed to repair it by bringing the new youth culture, with its threatening Elvis Presleys and Little Richards, into a domestic world where chil-dren sang the latest hits under the watchful eyes of their parents." This image did not seem particularly true to the 1960s, when families tended to be generationally divided in their musical tastes. But it nicely anticipated the era we're living in now, when boomer and Gen X parents send their kids off to rock 'n' roll camp. Ozzie and Harriet lying in bed swaying awkwardly but enthusiastically along as Ricky sings "Hello Mary Lou" on television reminds me more than I'm quite comfortable admitting of my own helpless enthusiasm for my kids' indie rock band.

At times you can even see that *Ozzie and Harriet* was a template for shows like *Seinfeld* and *Curb Your Enthusiasm*. Yes, as many a wiseacre has pointed out, *The Adventures of Ozzie and Harriet* (the show's full title) was a misnomer, since nothing ever really happened on the show. But nothing really happens on many modern sitcoms, and many of them are fueled, as *Ozzie and Harriet* was, by the half-childlike, half-philosophical riffing of a perpetually irked, perpetually befuddled male lead. His children are alternately amused and embarrassed by him, and his sensible wife shakes her head and deftly extracts him from the jams he's gotten himself into. Of course, Ozzie was a gentler, more anodyne version of Larry David (or Homer Simpson, for that matter). Take the episode in which he decides not to get out of bed all day. It's a poignantly small-scale rebellion, not least because it's a Sunday, but of course it goes all wrong anyway. Ozzie wants to make a point about arbitrary conformity; Harriet just wants to make the bed. A parade of visitors refuses to believe he isn't sick, and one, a lugubrious fellow from the "Cheer-Up Committee" at the Moose Lodge who calls him "Brother Nelson" and eats all his bedside snacks, puts him into a hypochondriacal funk. It's actually quite funny.

As for *Leave It to Beaver*, well, the pace seems slow by contemporary standards and the places where we're cued to laugh by the laugh track never seem quite right—a phenomenon that began to strike my twelve-year-old daughter and me as funny in its own right when we'd watched enough episodes in a row. One setup that always gets the big hahas is when Beaver and his brother, Wally, use some kind of contemporary kid lingo at the dinner table—refer to somebody, for instance, as a "creep," an all-purpose put-down that seems to mean something more like "weird"—and their parents, Ward and June, cock an eyebrow at each other as if to say, *Aren't we tolerant to let them express themselves this way?* Also, evidently real rib-ticklers for 1950s audiences and not so much for us: the many occasions when Beaver or other preadolescent kids on the show express utter amazement at the idea that they would ever like a girl. Actually, the way girls their age are usually presented on the show—prissy, with hair curled and sprayed into immobility like their moms', and clad in stiffly starched dresses—you can hardly blame Beaver and his pals.

But there are charming moments, too, especially in the relationship between Beaver and his teenage brother, with whom he shares a room. My daughter and I both found at least some of the situations quite, as they say, relatable. They were the sorts of predicaments of ordinary family life and childhood friendship that never go away: kids losing things and pretending they didn't; friends who try to get you to cheat or who form alliances with your other friends behind your back; the frustration elicited by a smarmy guy like Eddie Haskell who impresses adults but harasses kids when the adults aren't there to see; the many and intricate ways your parents and teachers can embarrass you. At times, I found myself kind of keen to discover how Ward was going to handle this or that dilemma on the home front. Surprisingly, it usually was Ward, not June, who did the heavy parenting, and it turned out I wasn't above taking tips from Beaver's dad.

If you watch *The Adventures of Ozzie and Harriet* or *Leave It to Beaver* assuming that the traditional families they showcase will be predicated on male domination, it turns out to be a little more complicated than that. More than one commentator has pointed out that the fathers in these shows, presumably the breadwinners, display identities that are remarkably detached from their work and subsumed in their fatherhood. Ward Cleaver seems to arrive home at about four-thirty every day, maybe five—it's still daylight and the boys have just gotten home from school. Though he mentions "the office" now and again, he rarely talks to his wife about anything going on there, and never seems to bring work home. If he isn't discussing the boys with June, or dispensing advice to the boys themselves, he's usually reading a newspaper. Ozzie, as more than one wag has pointed out, does not appear to have a job at all. (The comedian Bob Newhart once speculated that perhaps Ozzie was a bookie—he spent an awful lot of time on the phone and seemed to be in a position to support a pleasant lifestyle.) This was a reflection partly of the family sitcom's traditional emphasis on relationships, partly of the reality that men really did work shorter days in the 1950s, and partly of a new cultural preoccupation with fatherhood.

As social historians such as Stephanie Coontz and Elaine Tyler May have shown in recent years, the "traditional" 1950s family was actually a rather novel formation. It was the product of new trends: the sudden postwar drop in the age for marriage and motherhood and the educational attainment of women vis-à-vis men, along with sharp declines in divorce and in the proportion of people who'd never been married. People were marrying younger, living together longer, and having their children earlier and closer together. "The legendary family of the 1950s—was not, as common wisdom tells us, the last gasp of traditional family life with deep roots in the past," writes May. "Rather it was the first wholehearted effort to create a home that would fulfill virtually all its members' personal needs through an energized and expressive personal life." Nothing quite makes the point about the social place of divorce in late 1950s America like the episode of *Leave It to Beaver* in which Beaver's friend from camp, a cute little fellow named Chopper, comes to visit for the weekend. When June learns that Chopper's parents are divorced and his father is remarried, she worries that he's too "sophisticated" a companion for Beaver, who has "never known someone with two sets of parents before." Wally gets a laugh with the line "Heck, I know all about divorces and stuff. I go to the movies." And poor Chopper is called home early by his mother, who's "got the weepies again."

Sitcoms like *Leave It to Beaver*, *The Adventures of Ozzie and Harriet*, and *Father Knows Best* were at once reflections of and advertisements for the new family model. And perhaps for a new vision of fatherhood, in particular. "Fatherhood became a new badge of masculinity and meaning for the postwar man," writes May, "and Father's Day a holiday of major significance. Men began attending classes on marriage and family in unprecedented numbers. In 1954, *Life* magazine announced the 'domestication of the American male.' Fatherhood was important not just to give meaning to men's lives, but to counteract the abundance of maternal care"—thus fending off the dreaded sissification of boys.

The shows' role as display models for the new family values makes you think a little differently about how formally the characters dress. After all, it wasn't just June Cleaver in her crisp shirtdresses, pearls, and pumps who dressed up. Ward and Ozzie are frequently in suits and ties at home; if they're chilling on the weekend, they don the cardigan over dress shirt and slacks look. Beaver and Wally wear suits and ties if the family goes out to a restaurant. Even just hanging out in the neighborhood, they sport neatly pressed plaid or checked shirts tucked into slacks or cuffed jeans with a belt. Wally and the Beav are frequently seen polishing their shoes. Since the characters are dressed at home as though they were at work, the effect is to remind viewers that family life *is* work, the most important work of all. Yes, people did dress up much more in the 1950s—just look at the hats on the men and the white gloves on the women in photographs of city streets from the era—but most loosened up a bit more than the Cleavers do at home. On the show they're staging what family life *should* look like. As the sociologist Nelson Foote noted in 1955, families living in their new showcase homes, with TV families for company, were more aware of themselves as "performers" of family roles than they had been before. (Lynn Spigel points out that this was a common motif of sociological commentary on the suburban family in this period.) "The husband may be an audience to the wife, or the wife to the husband, or the older child to both."

I N HIS ARTICLE FOR *CALIFORNIA* MAGAZINE, Steve recalled the work routine at home during the years when he and our dad were helping to project this new family ideal. "When my dad went to work in the morning, he climbed into the station wagon and drove twenty minutes to General Service Studio, on Las Palmas in Hollywood. On Stage 5, he slipped into the obligatory cardigan and played Ozzie Nelson's stocky, good-natured neighbor. At home he smoked a pipe and was my stocky, good-natured dad. On Goodland Avenue he was never a buffoon, he was my sometimes-imposing father, and his blonde wife was much younger and more attractive than his ditzy TV wife with the whiny voice. Many mornings he waved good-bye on his way to Ozzie's while my mom and I took off for *Beaver*—two sidekicks on their way to work. My commute was shorter: *Beaver* was filmed at Studio City's own Republic, shifting later to nearby Universal. The way my father saw it, we were two professionals doing a job. It happened that the job was acting and it was usually fun and we made good money, but that didn't alter the fact that it was a job with certain responsibilities: know your lines, be on time, hit your mark, listen to the director."

Lyle enjoyed and felt lucky to have the *Ozzie and Harriet* gig. He wasn't close to Ozzie Nelson, but he had respect for him as a businessman who wrote, produced, and often directed the shows; as a college graduate (Ozzie went to Rutgers; neither of his own sons, who were too busy playing his sons on TV, graduated from college); and as a perfectionist, who always insisted, for instance, on having real flowers when flowers were called for in the script. Lyle didn't mind that the show was bland. He seems relaxed in his affable role and his banter with Ozzie. And he liked the routine, the money he could count on, and the fact that it was a show his kids could talk about at school. In one five-year period, he'd gone from Ed Wood movies shot on the sly behind a brothel to a popular sitcom featuring "America's Favorite Family" and sponsored by Quaker Oats. My sister remembers being at a Back-to-School Night with our father when she was in seventh grade and he was still on *Ozzie and Harriet*. As they walked down the aisle of the auditorium, she could hear people whispering eagerly, "There's Lyle Talbot!" When it was time to go look at the individual classrooms, Lyle said to Cindy, "Now, which shall we go to first? Or what do you say we just ad-lib it?" She hoped that other people around them could hear—"It just sounded so chic to me."

When TV production knocked off for the summer, Lyle did live theater in summer stock companies around the country, which he loved—enjoying his star turns and his "as seen on TV" billing, as well as the chance to work with my mother, who often took roles in these productions. She'd pack up the whole family and bring them along, including my grandparents as resident babysitters. "We would travel like gypsies across the country in our station wagon," says my brother Steve. He remembers our grandmother sitting in the backseat sewing pink flowers on my mother's underwear for her appearance in a play called *Champagne Complex*, in which she "played an innocent Marilyn Monroe type who started undressing as soon as she sipped a bit of the bubbly."

Lyle happily touted the virtues of live theater. "That's my first love and it always will be," he told one reporter. "For an actor, nothing matches the challenge and stimulation of performing live. This is where the real rewards of being in the business are found. . . . Everybody knows it's possible to fake a little bit here and there in film work without being obvious about it. But working live is the real test. You

*Lyle on the set of Ozzie and Harriet, with
Ricky Nelson in the background*

either have it or you don't." Asked by another reporter whether it got
boring to do the same part night after night—this was during a production of *My Fair Lady* under a big tent in Sacramento—he said no, it
didn't, "because each audience is like a fingerprint, no two are the
same. Each night is a different experience and a challenge unto itself."
When I was a kid I used to go see him perform three or four nights in
a row sometimes, and it always fascinated me to see the range of audience response to the same lines—how, for example, one guy with a real
guffaw could create a ripple effect. If I had the time and money, I think
I'd go see plays that way now, deriving fastidious pleasure from observ-
ing how the dynamics between audience and performer shift around

from night to night, and how an actor's reading of the same line can be subtly altered. Maybe that's why people became Deadheads (I mean besides the dope). They like immersing themselves in comparative iterations of the same material.

In the late 1960s and the 1970s, Lyle was flying all over the country to appear in everything from revivals of *The Front Page* and serious new plays like *The Last Meeting of the Knights of the White Magnolia* at the Alley Theatre in Houston, to *South Pacific* at Lincoln Center, to frothy stuff like *Barefoot in the Park*, *There's a Girl in My Soup*, and *Never Too Late*, sometimes in stalwart downtown venues and sometimes in suburban dinner theaters where you got to bring home the tacky cup your novelty drink came in. One of the young directors he worked with at the Alley, Robert Leonard, who cast him against type as the wheelchair-bound leader of a Klan-like group, wrote me recently to say that "Lyle was the most honest, collaborative, and supportive actor I ever met." Lyle once told Leonard about having to audition for a road show of Neil Simon's *The Odd Couple* that was to be directed by the playwright's brother, Danny. They met at the San Francisco airport, where Danny Simon was just flying in, and after an awkward lunch during which he put the make on the waitress, Simon told Lyle he'd have to do the audition in the bathroom—it was the only more or less quiet space—and for the part of Felix, though Lyle had been playing Oscar for three years in a different touring company. "So I stood in the men's bathroom of the San Francisco airport and read with this jerk for the wrong role," Lyle recalled. Indignant on his behalf, Leonard asked him, "Did you do the tour?" And, as Leonard wrote me recently, "Lyle replied with a twinkle in his eye, and that mischievous smile, 'Are you kidding? Of course I did. The show paid five grand a week plus per diem. And I was a damned good Felix, too!'"

It was sort of thrilling for us kids to see how cool our dad stayed backstage before a show. "I was in a lot of dressing rooms with him, and he was never nervous," Steve recalled. "He was always doing crossword puzzles, schmoozing with the prop guy. I asked him a couple of times, Do you ever get nervous? And he said, you get keyed up. If you didn't you'd be dead. And you need the energy to perform. But stage fright? Jitters? Never." David remembers "how present he was before a play when we were backstage with him. The stage manager would be coming in, saying ten minutes, Mr. Talbot, five minutes, two minutes. *I'd* start to get nervous. My palms would get sweaty. But he'd be talking to us, asking about school. I remember thinking, What a pro!"

THERE WERE A FEW REASONS why my father proved so happily domesticable—my mother was a lot of fun to live with; she was right about his really wanting to be a father; he was old enough and he'd slept with plenty of women. I sometimes think that he also got some reinforcement from acting a part on one of the seminal family sitcoms. Here he was, convincingly making suburban family life look jolly and rewarding—even dropping in on *Leave It to Beaver* a couple of times to play the role of a "perfect father" Ward Cleaver gets jealous of. And with Paula as his wife, it was easier than it would have been with shrill Clara, his TV wife.

Not that our family life looked much like the Cleavers' or the Nelsons'. Like all families, we took the basic roles and worked our own variation on them, for, with apologies to Tolstoy, families find their happiness in infinitely different grooves. In ours, as my sister said, "Dad was gone a lot, on the road, but when he was home, he was really home. He would do a lot around the house. Make all the breakfasts. Cook half the dinners. *Loved* to do the grocery shopping. They were not a traditional couple of the time." Our mother did the emotional heavy lifting in the family; if you had a problem, if you wanted a heart-to-heart, you went to her. At the same time, as my sister says, "I never experienced Dad as distant. He was very loving, kind, very solicitous and appreciative of us. He always wanted to do something special for you—make you something good to eat."

I was born in 1961, when my sister was eight and my brothers were ten and twelve. My mother was thirty-four and my father was just shy of sixty. Still, I never experienced my father as old, exactly. He had his booming actor's baritone; he did accents and sang a lot around the house. He still memorized parts easily, whispering to himself increasingly large chunks of dialogue as he sat on our den couch with a script, and always arriving for the first rehearsal off book. He sprang out of bed in the morning, childishly eager for breakfast. He took me miniature golfing and bowling. He seemed zippy. The ways in which I *was* reminded of his advanced age were agreeably strange; they connected me to the past, with a thin but real and glowing filament, and I, a kid who loved history books and fantasized regularly about traveling just for a day or two to the 1880s or the 1920s, loved that. There were moments when it felt distancing: how different his life had been. But, especially as I got older, I learned to savor the easy intimacy with the past that my father's advanced age and keen memory offered me. He remembered a time before electricity! He called early sound movies "talkies"! When I tried on the new school clothes my mom had bought me and modeled them for him—a family tradition—he'd say, "Oh, that's a very smart outfit." It was 1930s lingo—"smart" was not how we praised clothes in the 1970s. Yet it was kind of impressive because it was coming from a man who had known some very smartly dressed stunners in his day, a man who'd kissed Carole Lombard and Loretta Young.

An older father—take comfort if you are one or are married to one—is at a gentle remove from Oedipal struggles, from overt generational conflict. It was nice, it was cozy, to be a teenager with a father who was vital but also white-haired and courtly. All through my sister's and my own pimply, braces-wearing adolescences, on through the years when Cindy wore hiking boots every day and refused to shave

*Easter on Goodland Avenue, 1961, with Lyle holding baby me,
and my siblings, Cindy, Steve, and David.*

her legs, and when I had a haircut that looked like Rod Stewart's in the seventies, my father told us we were lovely, which is something that sticks with you. It's shining armor a woman can don when she needs it the rest of her life.

For my mother, the 1960s were a kind of second youth. She once told my sister that her happiest period as a parent was the years when her children were teenagers. Since that's not a common refrain from parents, I figure that it's partly because that's when she got to experience some fun version of adolescence herself. She'd always been so responsible. When she was a teenager, she was working and helping to support her family, not to mention keeping peace between her parents. It wasn't as though she ran wild in her second youth. She was staunchly anti-drug and she still never drank. But going on long barefoot walks after dinner with my sister and her friends, skipping down the street with me hand in hand, cranking the Doors up really loud while she cleaned the house: these were her little youth-culture rebellions, her be-ins, her flower power. When one of the neighborhood teenagers said something intolerant at the breakfast table, she poured a pitcher of orange juice over his head. But when Steve and his friend accidentally put laundry soap instead of dishwashing soap in the dishwasher and the whole kitchen filled with suds, she took one look, started to laugh, and got us all to come play in the bubbles. She had always been a person who made a gift of her own happiness to the people she loved: when she was happy, and especially when you had made her happy, she wanted you to know it right then. She wanted to tell you that you'd "made her heart sing." And in her own way, she resonated with the emotional openness of the time, the spirit of letting the sun shine in. She didn't want to shock people, exactly, but she liked surprising them a lot.

Once she was asked by a radio interviewer if she and Lyle had a song. "Yes," she replied. "Maybe you know it. It's called 'Why Don't We Do It in the Road?'" When my sister missed a day of high school to attend an antiwar demonstration, our mom wrote a note for her that said, "Please excuse Cindy's absence yesterday. She was sick. Sick of War." And she could never agree with the school when they chided Cindy for wearing her skirts too short. The girl had great legs, for goodness' sake!

Some of her schemes were like wacky gimmicks from an *I Love Lucy* episode. One time she got the idea of filling our wood-paneled station wagon with balloons on which she had written risqué messages for my father. I think she'd read about it somewhere, in some article about keeping the spark in your marriage. Unfortunately the first person to get into the car was the very buttoned-down driving instructor from my brothers' school who had come to the house to give David his lesson.

She loved holidays and was especially besotted with Christmas. One year when my father was doing a play in San Francisco during the Christmas week, and we were staying at the St. Francis Hotel, my mother dragged an enormous fir tree through the lobby to put in our room. That was the same Christmas when the stage manager of the play my father was in arranged a cast party that turned out to be at a topless bar. My whole family showed up there—I was five—and my mother took one look, laughed, then sat down at a table with me and ordered us two Shirley Temples. Another year, she decided the way to get the best tree in Los Angeles was to wake up very early and go down to the train station, where retailers from the Christmas tree lots got their trees. She took my cousins and my sister and me, along with a thermos of hot chocolate. It would have turned out fine except that you got the trees by auction, none of us knew what we were doing, and we all bid against one another, driving the costs up wildly.

In the crucible of our 1960s, Paula even transformed Lyle into a liberal Democrat. After he'd stopped drinking, politics was the one thing that continued to divide them—though the conflict flared up mainly during the presidential elections. My mother was a progressive Democrat, and fairly impassioned about it. Franklin Roosevelt was a real hero to her. Whenever I had to write a paper on some great figure in history, she'd press me to write about FDR or one of her other two heroes, Jonas Salk and Louis Pasteur. For presidential debates, she put us all in the car and took us to my grandparents'; they had a color TV before we did. (That's where I went, in footed pajamas, to watch the annual broadcast of *The Wizard of Oz*, too.) In the 1960 election, my mother supported Adlai Stevenson during the primaries, then switched her allegiance to John Kennedy. Lyle was a Nixon man. He even took the kids to the Van Nuys Airport with him—Paula pointedly stayed home—to greet Nixon when he arrived there once. It's hard to say why, except that he was a reflexive Republican and, as my mother always said sotto voce, "from Nebraska."

In the early 1950s in Hollywood, you had to be on one side or the other of the anti-Communist crusade, and Lyle had fallen into the anti side in part out of identification with the Screen Actors Guild. He didn't do a whole lot about that, but he did a few things. When an actress named Anne Revere resigned from the SAG board in 1951, after refusing to tell the House Un-American Activities Committee whether she'd ever been a Communist, Lyle was identified as a neutral party who could take her place—and he did. Steve remembers him watching the televised rallies led by a peculiar figure named Dr. Fred C. Schwarz, an Australian who would take over the L.A. Sports Arena for a few days to work Southern California into an anti-Communist lather. "The whole spectacle had this sort of dark, tacky feel to it. Roy Rogers and other actors would go down and testify. Dad never went, but he'd watch it on TV and get kind of worked up." For a while he was doing a television show, *The Real McCoys*, with the actor Walter Brennan, who was very conservative and would send him home with piles of overheated literature about the Communist threat. Paula would dump the leaflets in the trash.

Gradually, his convictions started to shift. He had always been sympathetic to the civil rights movement. He turned against the Vietnam War—partly, no doubt, because he had draft-age sons and partly because the draft-age sons were so opposed to the war and so articulate about it. In the 1960s my father still liked to hold forth at the dinner table, to tell his long stories about old Hollywood, and David began to chafe against that. "He expected to set the tone, and he told those stories. And if you interrupted them at all, it was like interrupting a play. It was like, Who's this heckler in the audience? So I was kind of a wise-ass and I started to throw out these one-liners, getting everybody to laugh, and I think it began to hurt him. It began to rankle. He was intellectually somewhat un-self-confident, but he was a voracious reader and he had lived a very full life. So one afternoon, he took me into the den, and he said, 'You know I'm not as educated as you are, but I know about the world.'"

He also followed his children's lead. "By the end of the 1960s," as Steve said, "I think he just looked up and saw that his wife and his children, the people he loved best, were all on one side, and he was on the other, and he didn't want to be there anymore." He grew sideburns, clipped cartoons by the liberal L.A. *Times* cartoonist Paul Conrad, drove my cousin and me around to supermarket parking lots where we passed out hand-scrawled leaflets urging shoppers to boycott grapes and iceberg lettuce in support of César Chávez's United Farm Workers. He boycotted grapes and iceberg lettuce himself. By 1972, he was a fervent supporter of George McGovern, about as liberal a mainstream presidential candidate as we've ever had. (It helped that McGovern was a midwesterner.)

When David was a senior at Harvard, the prep school he'd gone to since seventh grade, and his campaign to get the school to drop its ROTC component had earned him the opprobrium of the administration, it was my father who backed him up. One of David's teachers, an inspired educator named Paul Cummins, had left Harvard to become the principal of a progressive new private school called Oakwood. One day, David walked over there by himself and asked Cummins if he'd take him in. When he said yes, David went home and sat my parents down to say he wanted to leave Harvard. Our mother was opposed to it, anxious that he was blowing his education by leaving his prestigious school for some new, experimental one, and in the middle of his senior year, too. "Dad was just sitting there very quietly," David remembers. "And then he said, 'I can see that you're doing this out of conscience. So I think you have to do it.' And that was it."

In 1975, when he was seventy-three, Lyle gave an interview to the *St. Louis Post-Dispatch* in which he explained his transformation, and unlike a lot of people his age, he sounds sweetly, if ingenuously, admiring of the younger generation. "The thing about young people today is that they are much more aware than we ever were," he said. "We came of age when football and Joe College were big even for those of us who never finished school. It was the image that was the thing. Today's kids go to college and they discover that things aren't everything they've been cracked up to be. And they want to do something about it. They want to right their world. My own kids woke me up to what was going on in Vietnam—the sadness and futility of it all. They kept saying, 'Dad, they're lying to us.' And they were. Maybe these kids can do something for our world, each in his own way. At least they're trying."

NONE OF US FOUR KIDS became actors. At fourteen, Steve decided he wanted to focus on school and sports, and my parents supported him in that decision. If they were disappointed, they didn't show it—though we did find it funny that they'd sometimes say, "Acting is something Steve could always fall back on," given that acting is about the least secure way to make a living I can think of. As a kid, David had gone out for a few parts and didn't get them, and my father was very indignant on his behalf. Plus, David was chubby as a pre-adolescent, and Lyle was concerned that he not be typecast as the fat kid. As a young teenager, Cindy thought she might like to act, but my parents were pretty wrapped up by then in the importance of education, so they told her she should wait till she was older, and by that time, she was launched on a different, more academic path. And I had zero acting talent. I get nervous before speaking at a meeting. In the *Post-Dispatch* article, my father affectionately refers to me, at fourteen, as a poetry-writing "women's libber" (feminist, dad, feminist!), determinedly sending my work to publications with names like *Amazon Quarterly*. That gives you an idea of what I was like.

Still, my mom used to say that she figured my sister and I would grow up to be showgirls. We were so tall compared with her! She was five-feet-two, and my sister and I were five-feet-eight and five-feet-nine. If only she'd stuck to her guns and named Cindy "Treasure"! It was sort of a joke and sort of not. I think she actually would have been proud if we'd been showgirls—as long as we were happy non-drug-using showgirls with husbands who loved us. But when it was apparent we were going a different way, working our brains more than our bods—believe me, nobody would have paid to see me as a showgirl—she enthusiastically went with that. Steve became a successful and prolific documentary filmmaker who's won lots of prestigious awards and who hired our father a couple of times to narrate his films; David became an author and editor and the founder of the website Salon .com; Cindy earned a medical degree from the University of California, San Francisco, and a master's in public health from UC–Berkeley and became a family physician who also teaches in a residency program; and I went to graduate school at Harvard, thinking I'd become a history professor, then switched gears and became a magazine journalist. "I got the impression later in his life that Dad was sort of in awe of us," Cindy said recently. (And he certainly was of his "daughter, the doctor.") "It was, like, now how exactly would I have been involved in producing them? He always gave Mom the credit for it."

I SAID THAT HAVING AN OLD FATHER didn't bother me, but in one respect it did. I used to worry that he would die. I mean I knew he'd die, of course, but I worried that he would die sooner than I could bear. In the end, though, it was my mother who died first. Twenty-one years later, that sentence is still very hard for me to write. I don't even want to look at it on the screen.

When I was in elementary school, and the last kid left at home, my mom took a new kind of job. The only paid work she'd ever done was acting and singing, but she had let her career fade in deference to child rearing. If she felt any serious regret about that, I thank her for never showing it. But really, I think she was a person who found tremendous fulfillment—and fun—in raising kids. In any case, now she needed the money; my dad was still working, doing guest spots on prime-time TV and touring with plays, but the work wasn't as steady, and they had tuition to pay. Lacking a high school degree, my mother didn't have many choices. She ended up as a clerk on the dialysis ward at Children's Hospital of Los Angeles. Being Paula, she soon reimagined the job as a kind of ambassador of goodwill. She accompanied scared children to the operating room, holding their hands and singing to them. She became a friend and confidante to an unlikely assortment of coworkers: a dauntingly intellectual doctor who was the daughter of a prominent Marxist theorist and German émigré; a cocky young tech whose father was a big-time Latin jazz musician; a very tall and homesick Dutch female doctor who was doing a fellowship there; a pampered and beautiful Peruvian woman who was shocking her upper-class family by working as a licensed vocational nurse to assert her independence. My mother got them all to tell her their stories. One year, she won the hospital's Humanitarian Award, an honor that usually went to doctors or nurses.

She had gone to a play with a group of these friends from Children's one night in November 1985 and woken up before dawn with a terrible headache. It turned out to be a bleed from a brain aneurysm. She had emergency surgery and survived but with lingering aphasia and paralysis on one side of her body. Still, she was able to live at home with my father, her optimism intact, though it must have been tremendously frustrating for a person who loved her heart-to-hearts not to be able to chat and advise as she once had. Her brain did not heal well, and after a year or so, she started to have seizures and small strokes, and finally, in the summer of 1988, a major stroke. It began to seem clear that my father, who was then eighty-six, could not care for her at home anymore, even with our help. In the winter of 1989, my father sold the house on Goodland Avenue, and we packed him up and moved him to San Francisco, where my brothers and their families lived. My mother was to stay at a nursing home in San Francisco, where my father could visit her regularly. But she died almost immediately after the move, on March 17, 1989, at sixty years old. Lyle was suddenly the one thing a man who marries a woman twenty-six years younger never imagines he'll be: a widower. My mother had been the radiant heart and soul of our family, and my father's personal jar of sunlight, for forty years. We were all devastated by her illness and her death.

Our father seemed hollowed out, lonely, and physically fragile as we'd never seen him. In San Francisco, he lived in a condominium downtown near the Opera House and the City Hall. At first, when my brothers would come to take him out, he didn't want to go anywhere; he preferred to sit among the familiar things we'd brought from Goodland Avenue. Then one week, Steve read in the paper that the beautiful old Castro Theatre would be screening *Three on a Match*. Lyle said he didn't want to go, but Steve finally coaxed him into it. In the darkness of the movie palace, Steve watched our father watch a version of himself sixty years younger, eternally handsome, eternally on the verge of a stardom he'd never achieve. "You know, I'm the only actor in this movie who's still alive," my father whispered to Steve. "And this movie's probably gonna outlast both of us," Steve told him. "Maybe," he said, and smiled a little. "When he rose unsteadily from his seat at the end of the film and raised his arm to acknowledge the audience's applause," Steve said, "I could swear the guy looked ten years younger." "Where are we going to dinner?" Lyle asked when the clapping had subsided. "I'm starved."

It was the kind of moment my siblings and I had laughed at before—the old actor rejuvenated instantly by the elixir of applause. We still laugh about it now. But we were also grateful for the sweet, reliable spark between the entertainer and his audience. We were grateful for my father's unbowed vanity. We knew it rekindled him and, at the same time, that the effect was fleeting. My father could rise to the occasion when the spotlight found him, but it wasn't like it brought my mother back.

I guess we had all come to cherish the old pro in him, the instincts of the workhorse actor, the ability to get out there and turn on the brights for an audience. My father didn't talk much about the philosophy of acting, except to say that he didn't believe in Method acting. He didn't believe you should try to lose yourself in a role, merge your identity with it, access your own buried emotions. You always had to remember you were acting; you could get emotional, but you had to maintain control. If he had a credo, it was a credo of entertaining. You owed something to the people who came to see you. You did a job for them. You kept working for as long as you could, with as much love as you could muster. That didn't make him the best actor, and it didn't make him a star, but it made him a lifelong working actor, a man who raised a family without ever working at anything he cared for less than he did for acting. "I think you can only learn to act by acting," he told an interviewer once. "And if you have to start sitting down and theorizing, it's too late. You don't have time to tell the audience what you're thinking. You can't say, 'Look, when I say this line, here's what I really mean.' You've got to do whatever the script is, and it's got to immediately have an impact with the audience if you're going to act for an audience and I don't know why else you would act. . . . You don't act for yourself."

In the seven years he lived in this world without my mother, he missed her keenly. He often talked about being reunited with her, his dear Paula, after death. But he also revived in San Francisco; life jangled its bells and flashed its beads at him, and he did not turn his back on them. Steve and David and their wives, Pippa and Camille, took him to trendy restaurants he enjoyed dissing, and to some he loved because they served a good hamburger and he liked flirting with the waitresses. He became close friends with a much younger documentary filmmaker who interviewed him for one of her projects, and he got in touch with the few old friends who were still alive, including a handsome charm bomb of an actor named Walter Reed. And he gave other interviews, to reporters and oral historians and obsessive film buffs—several of them devoted, to his astonishment, to the career of the long-forgotten Eddie Wood. He cooked delicious omelettes for himself at breakfast, went to the movies a lot, found a barbershop where they made just enough of a fuss over him. He got to know his grandchildren, one of whom, Steve's daughter, Caitlin, was already continuing the family tradition of staging plays in the garage and who would in fact grow up to be an actress, and another of whom, Steve's son, Dash, went to high school up the street and came by most afternoons to check on Lyle and partake of his snack supply. He stood up with me when I married my husband, Art, on a typically chilly summer afternoon in San Francisco, under the Beaux-Arts domes of the Palace of Fine Arts, and he delivered a fine and funny toast at our party the night before.

He did a couple of things he had never done before, too. He drank wine when we went out to dinner. After all those years, it didn't seem to do much more than make him a little sentimental. None of us had the heart to tell him to stop. And occasionally, to my brothers, though not to my sister or me, he would mention something about one of his previous wives. "Dad had never talked about other women with us, either," David told me recently. "He was never the type of dad who'd ogle a woman when he was out with his sons. He was very respectful of women, gentlemanly. He didn't want to embarrass Mom or to gloat. He was discreet. And he wanted us to think—and he really felt at some level—that his marriage was the beginning of his life." But one time, during those last seven years in San Francisco, he did do just a little bit of gloating. David and he were having lunch at the Zuni Café, and Lyle told him, "You kids think you invented free love in the sixties. You have no idea what it was like to be young and beautiful in the thirties in Hollywood. Everyone was sleeping with everyone."

"Okay," said David. "You win."

WHEN I WAS GROWING UP, I used to spend a lot of time with my father in the car. He'd take me to school and pick me up most days, drive me to after-school activities, take me on errands. And in the car he'd tell stories about touring with the old rep companies through the winter-bound Midwest, about Hollywood in the 1930s. For some reason, I always remember the drive over Coldwater Canyon, when we had been on the west side and were coming home, almost floating home, it always seemed to me, inscribing a lazy zigzag through the hills, like thistle down on the breeze. In my memory, it is sunset, with a rime of orange on the horizon, the smog that turned beautiful at this time of day with the sun refracted through it. We'd drive past Mulholland, past the houses on stilts, their wide windows blazing with late afternoon light. And sometimes I was lulled by his voice, and sometimes I was really amused, and sometimes I was bored and eager to be home.

But over the years, I realized stories were what made my family. Stories were the soft golden net that enmeshed us. My father's stories. And my parents' stories—how they met, how she saved him. It was a fairy tale, really, the brave and lovely young princess who unlocked the cage—but true, too.

My father died on March 2, 1996, when he was ninety-four years old. He died at home, in his own bed—thankfully, for he hated hospitals and feared wasting away. His heart stopped. He was ninety-four, and my brother David was with him. He was lucky. Luck of the Irish.

After that, I found that I wished for those stories again, the stories my mother told us, the stories of Lyle as a magician's boy and a matinee idol and an elegant pre-Code gangster and even a figment of

Ed Wood's imagination. I dreamed my parents were alive but weak, except for their voices. I dreamed I was hearing their stories again.

Tell me.

Tell me one more time.

And I wished so hard, and with such a keen memory of my father, cresting the canyon, drifting into the past and down into the valley, that at last, when I knew I would never hear them again from him, I had to tell them myself.

Acknowledgments

⸺⦵⦵⸺

One of the best parts of finishing a book—the vanilla bread pudding, the peach pie à la mode, or whatever your favorite dessert happens to be—is that you get to thank people you've been waiting to thank. For somebody like me who didn't manage to write a first book till pretty damn late in my career, the reward is even sweeter.

So, thank you, first of all, to the gifted editors who have helped me learn and keep practicing the craft of long-form magazine journalism: Jeffrey Kittay and Judith Shulevitz at *Lingua Franca*; Andrew Sullivan, the late Michael Kelly, and Leon Wieseltier at *The New Republic*; Adam Moss and Katherine Bouton at *The New York Times Magazine*; David Remnick and Daniel Zalewski at *The New Yorker*. Leon was the first person who encouraged me to write about my father and entertainment history, and I'll always be grateful for that opening.

My current journalistic home, *The New Yorker*, is a privilege to work for. I am grateful to David Remnick for keeping a venerable institution lively and indispensable, for his kindness as an editor and the high bar he sets as a writer. Having an editor like Daniel Zalewski to work with makes me feel lucky all the time: his remarkable ability to see both the bones and the heart of a story before its writer does, and often more clearly, amount to a kind of X-ray vision. Dorothy Wickenden and David Grann have been inspiring to me as authors, and wonderfully supportive as colleagues. I've also benefited from the editorial rigor of Amy Davidson, Virginia Cannon, and the magazine's crackerjack fact-checkers.

If there is one person without whom this book would not have been written, it's Sarah Chalfant of the Wylie Agency. It was Sarah who first saw the possibility of the book back in 1998, in a short piece I wrote for *The New Republic,* and she has been unfailingly encouraging and insightful about the project ever since. Her intelligent championship of writers and books is a marvelous thing.

It was also Sarah who brought me together with Riverhead, a very happy match-up from my point of view. Sarah McGrath's editorial guidance was always spot-on, and delivered with grace, patience, and a natural confidence that gave me confidence. It's great to be in the hands of a book editor whose instincts are so steadily right. Sarah Stein has been an anchor—ever knowledgeable and professional. I'm grateful for the lovely and intuitive book design by Amanda Dewey, the smart and thorough copyediting by Sharon Gonzalez and the extraordinary Anna Jardine, which saved me from many errors, and the creativity, enthusiasm, and know-how of Lydia Hirt, Elizabeth Hohenadel, Jynne Martin, and Kate Stark.

Though this is a book that relies to a great extent on personal and family memories and memorabilia, I also benefited from research and interviews done by others. Sarah Yager helped at the end with some swift and efficient fact-checking. Carolyn Dvorak and Sharon Bruner were friendly and informative hosts in Brainard, Nebraska, and shared research they had done about Lyle, as well as their correspondence with him. Valentine Miller replied to my inquiries about Eve McClure Miller with vivid recollections. Jeff Bruner took the trouble to track down my siblings and me to give us a photo album that had belonged to Lyle's parents, which he bought at a garage sale.

Don Peri had the forethought to sit down with Lyle and record many hours of interviews during his last years, interviews that were nicely illumined by Don's knowledge of film history, and which he kindly shared with me. David Prindle, who interviewed Lyle for his book about the Screen Actors Guild, *The Politics of Glamour*, courteously responded to my out-of-the-blue request, and dug out his old cassette tapes. Terry Sanders conducted a long interview with Lyle in 1989 for the Screen Actors Guild Foundation; Edward Guthmann, Bob Stephens, and Jan Wahl did memorable pieces on him for San Francisco newspapers and radio, which I was very happy to have. Articles or interviews by David Del Valle, Laura Wagner, and an unnamed interviewer for *American Classic Screen* magazine jogged my memory and led me to new insights. Martha Vestecka Miller found some tidbits for me in the archives of the Nebraska State Historical Society, where the staff was very helpful to me when I visited as well.

A big thanks to the librarians and archivists at the Margaret Herrick Library of the Academy of Motion Picture Arts and Sciences, the Theatre Museum of Repertoire Americana, the UCLA Film & Television Archive, the Warner Bros. Archives at the University of Southern California, and the Wisconsin Center for Film and Theater Research. Anybody who loves old films is deeply grateful to Turner Classic Movies and to the fine repertory houses that feed that love and introduce those films to new generations of cinephiles. The Castro in San Francisco, the AFI Silver in Silver Spring, Maryland, and Film Forum in New York are especially wonderful theaters where I was able to watch, on a big screen, some of the movies discussed in this book.

Writing is, of course, a solitary endeavor, so it's particularly nice, when you emerge from the attic, or equivalent, to have friends for whom you are eager to change out of your ratty T-shirt who will go out to dinner with you and remind you of the pleasures of conversation. In Washington, D.C., where I live, I am lucky to have close women friends who are very fine writers and truly understand: Ann Hulbert, Liza Mundy, Hanna Rosin, and Mary Kay Zuravleff. Special thanks to Ann for a close reading of the manuscript, and for the sustenance of our morning walks; to Liza for always having my back; to Hanna for picking up the phone; and to Mary Kay for making the discipline of writing feel like fun. Maureen Corrigan came into my life toward the end of this project, and brought a welcome boost of wit and writerly/parental solidarity.

Over the period of time I've been working on *The Entertainer*, Vered and Nathan Guttman and their sons, Shauli, Evyatar, and Uri, have enriched my family's life immeasurably with their warmth, their knack for bringing people together, and their multifarious talents.

Kelly Goode, my oldest friend, is a delightful tie to L.A. and to my childhood, and I am grateful to Kelly and her parents, Fritz and Sheila, for introducing me to cool places in my native city—starting with Beachwood Canyon, where they lived in a mid-century modern house they designed themselves.

A project like this one—family history as history—doesn't go so well if your family isn't on board. I am grateful that mine was. My in-laws, Barbara and Richard Allen, have taken a generous interest in my work since we first met, almost twenty-five years ago. They are also my models of engaged and voracious readers. Nick Allen, Martha Kowalick, Emily Allen, Susie Allen, and Richard DiCarlo have built a solid tradition of annual family get-togethers and have been big-hearted in opening their homes, from Palo Alto to Barcelona, to my husband, my kids, and me. My cousins Robert and Ojeni Sammis gave me a home base in L.A. during my research trips there, fed me and schlepped me around with their usual good humor and loyal family spirit. My uncle and aunt Robert and Ann Epple offered helpful memories and observations.

Stephen, David, and Cindy Talbot share our father's story, of course, and have been great about ceding to me this telling of it. Cindy and Steve undertook family photo searches, and Cindy went online to find a bottle of our mother's old brand of perfume, so I could have a transporting whiff of it while I was writing the last chapter. Steve and David, both excellent journalists and natural storytellers, carefully read the manuscript, correcting and elaborating where it was needed; they are always so fun to compare notes with. My sisters-in-law Pippa Gordon and Camille Peri, who brought so much to my father's last years, listened to me talk about the book, and asked good questions. David, Camille, Joe, and Nat have made San Francisco, and especially Chez Perbot, a nourishing second home for me and my family. My brother-in-law Dave Davis, whose grandfather was Clifford Clinton, the founder of Clifton's cafeterias, has an old L.A. lineage as well; anecdotes he told about his eccentric grandfather are woven into my childhood memories, and one or two turn up in this book.

And finally, I get to thank my own immediate family: Ike, Lucy, and Art, the heart and soul of my life. Ike's refined and interesting aesthetic sensibilities—his fascination with old films, beautiful music, and the history they are embedded in—both overlaps with and transcends my own. His sunny good nature is a constant joy. Lucy's high standards, independent vision, and creative productivity inspire me daily. Her quirky sense of humor makes me laugh just as often. I wish my parents could have known them, but at least I have the pleasure of seeing facets of Lyle and Paula in both of them.

My husband, Arthur Allen, is my companion in everything that matters. I rely on his moral compass, his journalistic ethics, and his editorial judgment, and I love his company. There's nobody I'd rather sit in a darkened theater with, sharing popcorn, or talk about a movie with afterward—I can think of no higher compliment.

Washington, D.C.
June 2012

A Note on Sources

- ∘⟨∞⟩∘ -

bove all, this book depends on my father's memories and
stories, shared with my siblings and me, and the scrapbooks
he kept and left to us, which contain photographs, theatrical
programs and advertising, restaurant menus, hotel receipts and train
schedules, reviews and many other clippings from newspapers and fan
magazines, studio promotional material for individual movies, *The Talbot Tabloids*, publications of the Screen Actors Guild, contracts, letters,
postcards, and telegrams, covering the period from 1919 till his death
in 1996, with a few documents from his early childhood as well.

In addition, my father did several long interviews, the tapes or
transcripts of which were especially helpful. One was conducted by
Terry Sanders in 1989 for a history project of the Screen Actors Guild
Foundation, another by Cliff Ashby in 1976 for Texas Tech University's
Southwest Collection, another by David Prindle in 1985 for his book on
the Screen Actors Guild, *The Politics of Glamour*, and yet another, a quite
comprehensive interview, by Don Peri in San Francisco in 1993. I also
drew on articles about or interviews with my father that appeared in the
following publications in the 1980s and 1990s: *Scarlet Street*, *Films of the
Golden Age*, *American Classic Screen*, *The TV Collector*, the *Los Angeles
Times*, the *San Francisco Examiner*, and the *San Francisco Chronicle*.

I benefited from time spent with files and films at the following archives: The Nebraska State Historical Society, Lincoln; the Brainard, Nebraska, City Hall; the Theatre Museum of Repertoire Americana, Mount Pleasant, Iowa; the Margaret Herrick Library of the Academy of Motion Picture Arts and Sciences, Los Angeles; the Warner Bros. Archives at the University of Southern California; the UCLA Film & Television Archive; and the Wisconsin Center for Film and Theater Research at the University of Wisconsin, Madison.

I took advantage of the online availability of historical newspapers and magazines, including *The New York Times*, the *Los Angeles Times*, *The Atlanta Constitution*, *The Boston Globe*, *Harper's*, *The Nation*, and *Time*.

I also relied on a number of books of history, criticism, fiction, and memoir. The chapter-by-chapter account below is not a comprehensive bibliography, but a précis of books, scholarly articles, and documentaries that I found particularly informative or inspiring or both, and that a reader might consult to learn more about these subjects.

Chapter 1. Learning to Cry

For additional insights into small-town Nebraska, and Brainard specifically, at the turn of the century, I turned to the novels of Willa Cather, especially *My Ántonia*, as well as Thomas Capek's *The Cechs (Bohemians) in America* (1920), and two books produced by the town of Brainard: *Brainard, Nebraska: From Then to Now, the First 125 Years* (2003) and *Brainard's First Hundred Years, 1878–1978* (1978).

For context relating to the history of sexuality and childbearing in the United States, I drew on Joan Jacobs Brumberg, *The Body Project: An Intimate History of American Girls* (1997); Judith Walzer Leavitt, *Brought to Bed: Child-Bearing in America, 1750–1850* (1986); Steven Mintz and Susan Kellogg, *Domestic Revolutions: A Social History of American Family Life* (1988); and Richard W. Wertz and Dorothy C. Wertz, *Lying-in: A History of Childbirth in America* (1979). The diary of Rolf Johnson was published as *Happy as a Big Sunflower: Adventures in the West, 1876–1880* (2000), edited by Richard E. Jensen. For the story of Rosa Petrusky, see Joan M. Jensen, "The Death of Rosa: Sexuality in Rural America," *Agricultural History*, vol. 67, no. 4 (Autumn 1993).

For the history of typhoid fever, I turned to Judith Walzer Leavitt, *Typhoid Mary: Captive to the Public's Health* (1996). For more general cultural context that informed the chapter, I appreciated Michael S. Kimmel, *Manhood in America: A Cultural History* (1996); Tom Lutz, *American Nervousness 1903: An Anecdotal History* (1991); and Megan J. Elias, *Food in the United States, 1890–1945* (2009).

I was able to learn more about the life and milieu of Jack Hollywood from John W. Davis, *Goodbye, Judge Lynch: The End of a Lawless Era in Wyoming's Big Horn Basin* (2005).

For more about the image and history of the traveling salesman, see Timothy B. Spears, *100 Years on the Road: The Traveling Salesman in American Culture* (1995).

Chapter 2. The Hypnotist's Boy

There are some great books about the history of magic, carnivals, and sideshows in the United States. I am indebted to Robert Bogdan, *Freak Show: Presenting Human Oddities for Amusement and Profit* (1988); James W. Cook, *The Arts of Deception: Playing with Fraud in the Age of Barnum* (2001); Rachel Adams, *Sideshow U.S.A.: Freaks and the American Cultural Imagination* (2001); Fred Nadis, *Wonder Shows: Performing Science, Magic, and Religion in America* (2005); and *American Popular Entertainments: Papers and Proceedings of the Conference on the History of American Popular Entertainment* (1977), edited by Myron Matlaw.

Among contemporary accounts, I recommend *"Hey Rube"* (1933), Bert Chipman's memoir of his circus and carnival days; the entertaining and revealing *Secrets of Stage Hypnotism* (1901) by Professor Leonidas; and back issues of *The Sphinx*, where I found the tribute to Mock Sad Alli by Dr. E. G. Ervin (vol. 32, no. 1, March 1933).

For more on immigrant stock characters in repertory theater, see "Ole Olson and Companions as Others: Swedish Dialect Characters and the Question of Scandinavian Acculturation," *Theatre History Studies*, vol. 28 (2008); and Carl Wittke, "The Immigrant Theme on the American Stage," *The Mississippi Valley Historical Review*, vol. 39, no. 2 (September 1952).

Chapter 3. Footlights on the Prairie

For more on the history of tent rep and theatrical stock companies, and the lives of actors who worked in them, see Jere Mickel, *Footlights on the Prairie* (1974), from which I borrowed this chapter's title; W. L. Slout, *Theatre in a Tent* (1972); Solomon Smith, *Theatrical Management in the West and South for Thirty Years* (1868); Don B. Wilmeth, *Variety Entertainment and Outdoor Amusements: A Reference Guide* (1982); and Philip C. Lewis, *Trouping: How the Show Came to Town* (1973).

For more general histories of acting and of audiences, see Benjamin McArthur, *Actors and American Culture, 1880–1920* (1984); Richard Butsch, *The Making of American Audiences: From Stage to Television, 1750–1990* (2000); David Grimsted, *Melodrama Unveiled: American Theater and Culture, 1800–1850* (1968); and Kathryn H.

Fuller, *At the Picture Show: Small-Town Audiences and the Creation of Movie Fan Culture* (1996). *The Autobiography of Joseph Jefferson* (first published in 1897; 1964 reprint edited by Alan S. Downer), still makes for lively reading.

For more on flappers, sexual norms, social habits, and changing expectations of personality and beauty in the 1920s, see Paula S. Fass, *The Damned and the Beautiful: American Youth in the 1920's* (1977); *An Emotional History of the United States* (1998), edited by Peter N. Stearns and Jan Lewis (especially "The Problem of Modern Married Love for Middle-Class Women," by John G. Spurlock); Kathy Peiss, *Hope in a Jar: The Making of America's Beauty Culture* (1998); David E. Kyvig, *Daily Life in the United States 1920–1940: How Americans Lived Through the Roaring Twenties and the Great Depression* (2002); Frederick Lewis Allen, *Only Yesterday: An Informal History of the 1920s* (1931); Kathleen Drowner and Patrick Huber, *The 1920s* (2004); Joshua Zeitz, *Flapper: A Madcap Story of Sex, Style, Celebrity, and the Women Who Made America Modern* (2006); *Children and the Movies: Media Influence and the Payne Fund Controversy* (2007), edited by Garth S. Jowett, Ian C. Jarvis, and Kathryn H. Fuller; and Beatrice Burton's novel *The Flapper Wife* (1925).

Chapter 4. Hooray for Hollywood

For eyewitness impressions of Los Angeles, see *Early Hollywood: Images of America* (2007), edited by Marc Wannaker and Robert W. Nudelman; Carey McWilliams, *Southern California: An Island on the Land* (1946; a terrific book); *Los Angeles: A Guide to the City and Its Environs* (1941; WPA American Guide Series); Aldous Huxley, *After Many a Summer Dies the Swan* (1939); Edmund Wilson, *The Twenties: From Notebooks and Diaries of the Period* (1975) and *The Thirties: From Notebooks and Diaries of the Period* (1980); *The Grove Book of Hollywood* (1998), edited by Christopher Silvester; Marilynn Conners, *What Chance Have I in Hollywood?* (1924); *The WPA Guide to California* (1934; new ed. 1984) by the Federal Writers' Project, with a new introduction by Gwendolyn Wright; *The Movies in Our Midst: Documents in the Cultural History of Film in America* (1981), edited by Gerald Mast; Morrow Mayo, *Los Angeles* (1933); and Basil Woon, *Incredible Land: A Jaunty Baedeker to Hollywood and the Great Southwest* (1933).

For the atmosphere and history of Warner Brothers, see Rudy Behlmer, *Inside Warner Bros. 1935–1951* (1985); Robert Sklar, *City Boys: Cagney, Bogart, Garfield* (1992); Neal Gabler's fascinating *An Empire of Their Own: How the Jews Invented Hollywood* (1989); and Andrew Sarris, *"You Ain't Heard Nothin' Yet": The American Talking Film, History and Memory, 1927–1949* (1998).

For more on the backgrounds of Warner Brothers screenwriters mentioned in this chapter, see Alvah Johnston, *The Legendary Mizners* (1953); John Bright's memoir *Worms in the Winecup* (2002), written with Patrick McGilligan; and the chapter on Bright in Sylvia Shorris and Marion Abbott Bundy, *Talking Pictures: With the People Who Made Them* (1994).

For more on William Wellman, see the interview with him by Richard Schickel in *The Men Who Made the Movies* (1975), and the documentaries *Wild Bill: Hollywood Maverick* and *The Men Who Made the Movies: William A. Wellman*, both included in the DVD collection *Forbidden Hollywood*, volume 3, from TCM. For Lyle's screen test story, I relied on his tellings (and retellings) of it, but am also quoting from a Q&A with him that appeared in *American Classic Screen*, volume 8, number 2 (April 1984).

Chapter 5. Gangsters, Grifters, and Gold Diggers

A great deal of interesting scholarship has been published in recent years about the politics and history of the Code and about pre-Code films. See, for instance, *Headline Hollywood: A Century of Film Scandal* (2001), edited by Adrienne L. McLean and David A. Cook (especially Sam Stoloff, "Fatty Arbuckle and the Black Sox: The Paranoid Style of American Popular Culture, 1919–1922"); Tino Balio, *Grand Design: Hollywood as a Modern Business Enterprise 1930–1939* (1996); Thomas Doherty, *Pre-Code Hollywood: Sex, Immorality, and Insurrection in American Cinema, 1930–1934* (1999); Mark A. Vieira, *Sin in Soft Focus: Pre-Code Hollywood* (1999); Lea Jacobs, *The Wages of Sin: Censorship and the Fallen Woman Film, 1928–1942* (1995); Leonard J. Leff and Jerold L. Simmons, *The Dame in the Kimono: Hollywood, Censorship, and the Production Code* (1990); Gregory D. Black, *Hollywood Censored: Morality Codes, Catholics, and the Movies* (1994); Mick LaSalle, *Complicated Women: Sex and Power in Pre-Code Hollywood* (2000); and Geoffrey O'Brien, "When Hollywood Dared," *The New York Review of Books*, July 2, 2009.

For more general treatments of 1930s film, and especially films from Warner Brothers, see Tino Balio, *Grand Design*; Andrew Bergman, *We're in the Money: Depression America and Its Films* (1992); Jeanine Basinger, *A Woman's View: How Hollywood Spoke to Women, 1930–1960* (1993); Robert Sklar, *Movie-Made America: A Cultural History of American Movies* (1975); Peter Roffman and Jim Purdy, *The Hollywood Social Problem Film: Madness, Despair, and Politics from the Depression to the Fifties* (1981); Nick Roddick, *A New Deal in Entertainment: Warner Brothers in the 1930s* (1983); and Kristine Brunovska Karnick, "Community of Unruly Women: Female Comedy Teams in the Early Sound Era," *Continuum: Journal of Media and Cultural Studies*, vol. 13, no. 1 (1999).

Among books and essays about individual actors of the 1930s whom I write about, the following were helpful: "Cowboys: William J. Hart and Tom Mix" in Jeanine Basinger, *Silent Stars* (1999); Al DiOrio, *Barbara Stanwyck* (1983); Dan Callahan, *Barbara Stanwyck: The Miracle Woman* (2012); Wendy Lesser, "Stanwyck," in *His Other Half: Men Looking at Women Through Art* (1981); Bette Davis, *The Lonely Life* (1962); Ed Sikov, *Dark Victory: The Life of Bette Davis* (2008); Lynn Kear and John Rossman, *Kay Francis: A Passionate Life and Career* (2006); Scott O'Brien, *Kay Francis: I Can't Wait to Be Forgotten* (2007); and Daniel Bubbeo, *The Women of Warner Brothers: The Lives and Careers of 15 Leading Ladies* (2002).

For more on Warden Lawes, see Ralph Blumenthal, *Miracle at Sing Sing: How One Man Transformed the Lives of America's Most Dangerous Prisoners* (2004).

On the 42nd Street Special, and the Warner Brothers–Roosevelt connection, see Neal Gabler, *An Empire of Their Own*; Lary May, *The Big Tomorrow: Hollywood and the Politics of the American Way* (2000); Jack L. Warner, *My First Hundred Years in Hollywood* (1965); Charles Eckert, "The Carole Lombard in the Macy's Window," in *Stardom: Industry of Desire* (1991), edited by Christine Gledhill; and Rian James, *42nd Street* (screenplay; 1980 ed.), edited and with an introduction by Rocco Fumento.

Chapter 6. Man About Town

For interesting treatments of how stars were found and groomed, see Jeanine Basinger, *The Star Machine* (2007); Alexander Walker, *Stardom: The Hollywood Phenomenon* (1970); and Christopher Finch and Linda Rosenkrantz, *Gone Hollywood: The Movie Colony in the Golden Age* (1979).

Details about the Westmore dynasty can be found in Frank Westmore and Muriel Davidson, *The Westmores of Hollywood* (1976).

For a nice essay about Whitley Heights, see David Wallace, *Lost Hollywood* (2001).

On Estelle Taylor, see Roger Kahn, *A Flame of Pure Fire: Jack Dempsey and the Roaring '20s* (2002). On Lina Basquette: Lina Basquette, *Lina: DeMille's Godless Girl* (1990); Barry Paris, "The Godless Girl," *The New Yorker*, February 13, 1989; and *The Brothers Warner: The Intimate Story of a Hollywood Studio Dynasty* (1998), as told by Cass Warner Sperling and Cork Millner with Jack Warner, Jr. On Dorothy di Frasso: Jane Ellen Wayne, *Cooper's Women* (1988); and John Buntin, *L.A. Noir: The Struggle for the Soul of America's Most Seductive City* (2009).

Chapter 7. Empty Bottles

For information on Hollywood nightlife, and actors at play, see John Buntin, *L.A. Noir*; Christopher Finch and Linda Rosenkrantz, *Gone Hollywood*; Gregory Paul Williams, *The Story of Hollywood: An Illustrated History* (2005); Betty Goodwin, *Hollywood du Jour: Lost Recipes of Legendary Hollywood Haunts* (1993); Leo Rosten, *Hollywood: The Movie Colony, the Movie Makers* (1942); and Jim Heimann, *Out with the Stars: Hollywood Nightlife in the Golden Era* (1990).

On specific venues and amusements discussed in this chapter, see Carol Martin, *Dance Marathons: Performing American Culture in the 1920s and 1930s* (1994); Horace McCoy, *They Shoot Horses, Don't They?* (1935; 1995 ed.); John Chilton, *Louis: The Louis Armstrong Story* (1971); Warren G. Harris, *Gable and Lombard* (1974); Marion Davies, *The Times We Had* (1975); and David Nasaw, *The Chief: The Life of William Randolph Hearst* (2000).

Chapter 8. Unionizing Actors, Uniting Fans

For the opening observations about life in L.A., see Matt Weinstock, *My L.A.* (1947). On gangsters in Hollywood, see John Buntin, *L.A. Noir*, and Christopher Finch and Linda Rosenkrantz, *Gone Hollywood*.

On the history of the Screen Actors Guild, including working conditions and the Guild's struggles with the mob, see Tino Balio, *Grand Design*; Paul Henreid, *Ladies' Man* (1984); James Cagney, *Cagney* (1976); David F. Prindle, *The Politics of Glamour: Ideology and Democracy in the Screen Actors Guild* (1988); Murray Ross, *Stars and Strikes: Unionization of Hollywood* (1941); David Witwer, *Shadow of the Racketeer: Scandal in Organized Labor*; Florabel Muir, *Headline Happy* (1950); Neal Gabler, "When the Mob Ruled Hollywood," *Playboy*, June 2011; Mike Nielsen and Gene Mailes, *Hollywood's Other Blacklist: Union Struggles in the Studio System* (1995); Kerry Seagrave, *Actors Organize: A History of Union Formation Efforts in the United States, 1880–1919* (2007); Otto Friedrich, *City of Nets: A Portrait of Hollywood in the 1940s* (1986); Scott Allen Nollen, *Boris Karloff: A Gentleman's Life* (1999); George Murphy, "*Say . . . Didn't You Use to Be George Murphy?*" (1970); and the profiles of and interviews with early SAG members assembled by the Screen Actors Guild Foundation and available at www.sag.org.

On Mae West, see Marybeth Hamilton, "*When I'm Bad, I'm Better*": *Mae West, Sex, and American Entertainment* (1995); and Emily Wortis Leider, *Becoming Mae West* (1997).

On moviegoing and fandom in the 1930s, see Lary May, *The Big Tomorrow: Moviegoing in America: A Sourcebook in the History of Film Exhibition* (2002), edited by Gregory Waller; Douglas Gomery, *Shared Pleasures: A History of Movie Presentation in the United States* (1992); Kathryn H. Fuller-Seeley, *Hollywood in the Neighborhood: Historical Case Studies of Local Moviegoing* (2008); Anthony Slide, *Inside the Hollywood Fan Magazine: A History of Starmakers, Fabricators, and Gossip Mongers* (2010); Margaret Thorp, *America at the Movies* (1939); and Samantha Barbas, *Movie Crazy: Fans, Stars, and the Cult of Celebrity* (2002).

Chapter 9. Broadway and B Movies

For more on the Broadway theater and other entertainment during World War II, see *At This Theatre: 100 Years of Broadway Shows, Stories, and Stars* (2002), edited by Louis Botto and Robert Viagas; Richard Lingeman, *Don't You Know There's a War On? The American Home Front, 1941–1945* (1970); and Allan M. Winkler, *Home Front U.S.A.: America During World War II* (1986).

For more on the 1939–1940 World's Fair, see E. L. Doctorow, *World's Fair* (1985); Bill Cotter, *The 1939–40 New York World's Fair* (Images of America; 2001); and the DVD *The 1939 World's Fair* (PRS Studio, 2010).

The New York night life is described in Arnold Shaw, *52nd Street: The Street of*

Jazz (1971); Rachel Shteir, *Striptease: The Untold History of the Girlie Show* (2004); and Robert Klara, "The Riviera of Dreams," *New Jersey Life*, May 1995.

On Hollywood at war, see Otto Friedrich, *City of Nets*; Richard Lingeman, *Don't You Know There's a War On?*; Allan M. Winkler, *Home Front U.S.A.*; Thomas Schatz, *Boom and Bust: American Cinema in the 1940s* (1999); John E. Moser, "'Gigantic Engines of Propaganda': The 1941 Senate Investigation of Hollywood," *The Historian*, Summer 2001.

On movie serials, see Jim Harmon and Donald F. Glut, *The Great Movie Serials: Their Sound and Fury* (1972); Ken Weiss and Ed Goodgold, *To Be Continued . . . : A Complete Guide to Motion Picture Serials* (1972); Les Daniels, *Batman: The Complete History* (2004) and *Superman: The Complete History* (2004); and William C. Cline, *In the Nick of Time* (1984).

A definitive scholarly treatment of exploitation films is Eric Schaefer, *"Bold! Daring! Shocking! True!" A History of Exploitation Films* (1999). For the stories of Lila Leeds and of Robert Mitchum's arrest, see the Schaefer book, as well as Lee Server, *Robert Mitchum: "Baby, I Don't Care"* (2001).

On the marriages of Henry Miller, and on Eve McClure specifically, see Robert Ferguson, *Henry Miller: A Life* (1991); Mary V. Dearborn, *The Happiest Man Alive: A Biography of Henry Miller* (1993); and *Big Sur Women* (1985), edited by Judith Goodman.

Chapter 10. From Ed Wood to Ozzie and Harriet

A good source on Ed Wood, featuring memorable interviews with people who knew him and worked with him, including Lyle, is the documentary *The Haunted World of Ed Wood* (2002), directed by Brett Thompson. I also appreciated "I Was a Movie Star for Ed Wood," an article based on an interview with Lyle, which ran in the *San Francisco Examiner* in October 1994.

For more on TV representations of American families and on American families themselves in the 1950s, see Lynn Spigel, *Make Room for TV: Television and the Family Ideal in Postwar America* (1992); Elaine Tyler May, *Homeward Bound: American Families in the Cold War Era* (1988); and Stephanie Coontz, *The Way We Never Were: American Families and the Nostalgia Trap* (1992).